GOD AND CULTURE

CARL F. H. HENRY

God and Culture

ESSAYS IN HONOR OF

Carl F. H. Henry

edited by

D. A. Carson and John D. Woodbridge

WILLIAM B. EERDMANS PUBLISHING COMPANY
GRAND RAPIDS, MICHIGAN

THE PATERNOSTER PRESS
CARLISLE

Copyright © 1993 by Wm. B. Eerdmans Publishing Co.
255 Jefferson Ave. S.E., Grand Rapids, Michigan 49503
All rights reserved

Published 1993 jointly by Wm. B. Eerdmans Publishing Co. and
The Paternoster Press Ltd.
P.O. Box 300, Carlisle, Cumbria CA3 0QS England

Printed in the United States of America

Library of Congress Cataloging-in-Publication Data

God and culture: essays in honor of Carl F. H. Henry /
edited by D. A. Carson and John D. Woodbridge.
p.   cm.
Includes bibliographical references.
ISBN 0-8028-3709-3
1. Christianity and culture. 2. Christianity — 20th century.
I. Henry, Carl Ferdinand Howard, 1913- . II. Carson, D. A., 1946- .
III. Woodbridge, John D., 1941- .
BR115.C8G63   1993

261 — dc20   92-38839
                                                        CIP

Paternoster ISBN 0 85364 553 1

Contents

Contents

Preface

EVER SINCE the publication of his classic book *Christ and Culture*,[1] it has been common to adopt H. Richard Niebuhr's typology of possible Christian responses to culture: (1) Christ against culture; (2) the Christ of culture; (3) Christ above culture; (4) Christ and culture in paradox; and (5) Christ the transformer of culture. The questions raised by this typology are particularly challenging to contemporary evangelicals who are struggling to understand and articulate just how they should relate to the broader, swirling currents around them.

When we decided that we would like to organize a book of essays in honor of Carl F. H. Henry, the topic and title almost suggested themselves. For more than half a century, Carl Henry has been one of a handful of American evangelical leaders who have sought to reestablish the primacy of the Bible and of the Bible's gospel in American life and thought, in the wake of the disastrous losses occasioned by the rise of modernism and postmodernism. When Henry began writing and teaching, evangelicals had been squeezed out of most of the institutions of influence and leadership. In consequence, many evangelicals thought of "Christ against culture." Henry was one of the first to call evangelicals back to their broader heritage, the Augustinian vision of what Niebuhr called "Christ transforming culture." Henry's 1947 book *The Uneasy Conscience of Modern Fundamentalism* was a watershed.

Now, decades later, the dynamics are greatly different. Evangelicalism has grown, but against the backdrop of a culture that not only is

1. Niebuhr, *Christ and Culture* (New York: Harper Colophon Books, 1951).

fragmenting but has largely lost touch with the Judeo-Christian heritage that so greatly nourished it for three centuries and more. And evangelicalism itself has changed: it too has fragmented, and, more importantly, it now fosters many mutually exclusive visions of what relations it should sustain with the surrounding culture. The sobering, tantalizing question to be asked is this: To what extent has evangelicalism, in its attempt to influence the surrounding culture, been so drastically shaped by that culture that it is in danger of selling its biblical and theological heritage for a mess of the pottage of perceived cultural relevance?

Certainly such questions have long exercised Carl Henry. In the pages that follow, we do not directly aim to provide a general critique of culture, like Paul Tillich's *Theology of Culture*.[2] Nor do we seek to establish the nature of the relationship between Christianity and culture, using anthropological categories, as Charles Kraft does in his *Christianity and Culture*.[3] Nor is it our primary aim to probe the interplay among theology, anthropology, and missions, as Harvie Conn does in *Eternal Word and Changing Worlds*,[4] or to explore the interaction between the modern missionary movement and concurrent developments in the social sciences, as Charles Taber undertakes in *The World Is Too Much with Us*.[5] Still less do we examine, from an evangelical framework, exactly the same sort of ground covered by several recent Roman Catholic studies, such as Louis Luzbetak's *The Church and Cultures*[6] or Aylward Shorter's *Toward a Theology of Inculturation*.[7] And finally, we do not attempt to address the breadth of religious thought reflected in *Religion and Culture: Essays in Honor of Paul Tillich*.[8]

Although we do a little of all of the things just mentioned, our focus is different. We have selected a number of distinct elements in American (and more broadly Western) culture and have invited Christian thinkers to articulate how in their view Christians should think about those areas. We might have adopted a different approach. For example, underlying so many of these

---

2. Tillich, *Theology of Culture,* ed. Robert C. Kimball (New York: Oxford University Press, 1959).

3. Kraft, *Christianity and Culture* (Maryknoll, NY: Orbis Books, 1979).

4. Conn, *Eternal Word and Changing Worlds* (Grand Rapids: Zondervan, 1984).

5. Taber, *The World Is Too Much With Us: "Culture" in Modern Protestant Missions* (Macon, GA: Mercer University Press, 1991).

6. Luzbetak, *The Church and Cultures: New Perspectives in Missiological Anthropology* (Maryknoll, NY: Orbis Books, 1988).

7. Shorter, *Toward a Theology of Inculturation* (Maryknoll, NY: Orbis Books, 1988).

8. *Religion and Culture: Essays in Honor of Paul Tillich,* ed. Walter Leibrecht (New York: Harper and Brothers, 1959).

questions is how the Christian should view the relationship between the church and the world. And that question in turn depends in no small part on how Christians put their Bible together — that is, on their understanding of the relationship between the covenants and of the hermeneutical keys that hold the Bible together as one unified revelation. But such analysis, though it might usefully be undertaken elsewhere, could easily devote so much attention to theological questions that it would finally say very little about the culture in which we live. We therefore chose the approach adopted here, understanding that whatever their theological synthesis believers have to come to grips with these practical realities. This is not to say that these essays shun theology. Far from it — most of them are, at least in part, explicitly theological. But their immediate concern is to help Christians think their way through huge swaths of contemporary culture.

Some of the essays in this book will provide a useful guide for all Christians; others adopt stances with which some might wish to disagree. But all reflect an attempt to think "Christianly" about the culture in which we live and witness. Certainly there are many more topics on which we could have commissioned essays, but we had to draw the line somewhere.

We count it a privilege to offer our deep thanks to the contributors, who generously supported this project with their knowledge and enthusiasm. The essays themselves are an expression of thanks to God for Carl F. H. Henry on the occasion of his eightieth birthday, especially for his steadfast articulation of Christian truth for more than half a century. And we would be remiss if we did not simultaneously express gratitude to God for his wife Helga, who has participated in Carl's work to a much greater degree than many appreciate.

Soli Deo gloria.

D. A. CARSON
JOHN D. WOODBRIDGE

Contributors

GEOFFREY W. BROMILEY Senior Professor Emeritus of Church History and Historical Theology, Fuller Theological Seminary

NIGEL M. DE S. CAMERON Associate Dean, Academic Doctoral Programs, and Chairman, Department of Systematic Theology, Trinity Evangelical Divinity School

D. A. CARSON Research Professor of New Testament, Trinity Evangelical Divinity School

SIR FRED CATHERWOOD Member of the European Parliament for Cambridge and North Bedfordshire, and Vice Chairman, Foreign Relations Committee

EDMUND P. CLOWNEY Emeritus Professor of Practical Theology, Westminster Theological Seminary

WARREN J. HEARD, JR. Assistant Professor of Pastoral Counseling and Psychology, Trinity Evangelical Divinity School

PHILLIP E. JOHNSON Jefferson A. Peyser Professor of Law, University of California–Berkeley

KENNETH S. KANTZER Dean Emeritus, Distinguished Professor of Biblical and Systematic Theology, Trinity Evangelical Divinity School

GEORGE I. MAVRODES Professor of Philosophy, University of Michigan

ARMAND M. NICHOLI, JR. Associate Professor of Psychiatry, Harvard

xi

Medical School; Clinical Associate in Psychiatry, Massachusetts General Hospital

J. I. PACKER   Sangwoo Youtong Chee Professor of Systematic Theology, Regent College

LARRY W. POLAND   President and founder of Mastermedia International

ROBERT J. PRIEST   Assistant Professor of Missions and Intercultural Studies, Columbia Bible College and Seminary

LELAND RYKEN   Professor of English, Wheaton College

IAN SMITH   Lecturer in Economics, St. Salvator's College, University of St. Andrews

LEWIS W. SPITZ   William R. Kenan University Professor, Professor of History, Stanford University

CHARLES B. THAXTON   President of Konos Connection; lecturer in origins and history of science with the Slovak Technical University in Bratislava, Czechoslovakia, and the Biomathematical Institute in Craiova, Romania

KEVIN J. VANHOOZER   Lecturer in Theology, New College, University of Edinburgh

LOREN WILKINSON   Professor of Interdisciplinary Studies and Philosophy, Regent College

JOHN D. WOODBRIDGE   Professor of Church History and the History of Christian Thought, Trinity Evangelical Divinity School

The World Well Staged?
Theology, Culture, and Hermeneutics

KEVIN J. VANHOOZER

All the world's a stage,
And all the men and women merely players.
They have their exits and their entrances,
And one man in his time plays many parts.

— William Shakespeare, *As You Like It*

SHAKESPEARE often used the metaphor of the stage to speak of life. Prior to Shakespeare, medieval mystery plays were often three-tiered productions: action on earth was performed on a middle stage (Tolkien's Middle-earth?), stages above and below revealed the attitudes of God and Satan respectively to the unfolding action on the principal stage. "When we are born, we cry that we are come / To this great stage of fools."[1] It is part of theology's task to discover and articulate the way of wisdom through the stage, and the stages, of life with the Word of God — the ultimate set of stage directions. However, no theologian, even one armed with the Word of God, enjoys a God's-eye point of view, for the Word of God must be interpreted. A little lower than the angels, we human players do not have direct access to the things of heaven but must interpret. Those cast as theologians, like those given other parts, play the role of actor and critic simultaneously. Theology is an attempt to evaluate world performance by

1. William Shakespeare, *King Lear,* act 4, scene 6, ll. 182-83.

the criterion of the Word of God. Interpretation is doubly part of theological work: not only the Word but the world itself must be interpreted.

Culture is a "performance" of one's ultimate beliefs and values, a concrete way of "staging" one's religion. Individuals are the actors, but they are culturally and historically costumed and thrown into plots that are culturally and historically conditioned. They may not be given particular lines, but they are given a particular language. Culture is the scenery, the environment, the world into which one is thrown when one appears onstage. The cultural scenery influences and conditions what the actors see, say, and do. If the world is a stage, culture provides the props that fill it.

Carl Henry has rightly grasped the importance of a theological interpretation and analysis of culture and cultural trends. Indeed, Henry opens his magisterial *God, Revelation and Authority* with a perceptive description of "The Crisis of Truth and Word" in our times: "No fact of contemporary Western life is more evident than its growing distrust of final truth and its implacable questioning of any sure word."[2] This crisis — which at its root is a crisis of epistemology and theology — may well be the dusk before the "night of nihilism" and a new Dark Ages.

In an analysis that bears some interesting similarities with that of Jean Baudrillard (see below), Henry suggests that the modern mass media have provided humans, who are by nature idolatrous, with a fantastic myth-making machinery that is virtually able to shape a new reality (and newly able to create a virtual reality) at will. Nietzsche's belief that humans must be their own gods, creating reality by their will to power, seems to have received a technological verification. For Henry, the situation is dire: "Not alone human culture, but human destiny as well, depend on whether sight and sound are reserved only for human speculation and transitory happenings, or are lent equally to the Word and truth of God" (23). There is at present a growing distrust of the Word, and of words in general. The cult of nonverbal experience threatens the whole cultural inheritance of Western civilization. "To deverbalize an already depersonalized society is all the more to dehumanize it" (26).

According to Henry, every culture has "a certain convictional glue, an undergirding outlook on life and reality that preserves its cohesiveness" (44). Some convictional frameworks, such as that of the ancient Greeks, were able to produce an impressive culture apart from a Judeo-Christian foundation. But the ancient Greeks did believe in an invisible, eternal,

---

2. Henry, *God, Revelation and Authority,* vol. 1: *God Who Speaks and Shows, Preliminary Considerations* (Waco, TX: Word Books, 1976), p. 1. Subsequent citations will be made parenthetically in the text.

spiritual, and rational reality that served as a foundation for their attempts to impose this invisible rational order onto the visible worldly order. However, they lacked the spiritual resources to make their vision visible; they lacked the necessary means of grace that would have enabled them to embody the spirituality they discerned. But twentieth-century cultures are in even worse straits. In the West, industrial and postindustrial societies find it difficult to believe in an ultimate otherworldly order after which earthly life should be patterned.

Where then do the values that shape contemporary cultures come from? People today must either believe their own myths or else view them as convenient and necessary fictions that have pragmatic worth. Either we must think that our values and beliefs about the ultimate are true, or else we must recognize them for the useful fictions they are. Many contemporary Western thinkers are declaring all convictional frameworks to be the fruit of myth-making and are celebrating them as such. Henry's assessment of the present is a sobering one: "Pragmatism is the last stand for a culture that has lost a true center" (41). In an age without absolutes, humankind's problem is that of "freely fashioning . . . life, history and nature through self-creativity" (139). Ironically, such sheer creativity will ultimately consume humanity. Like sharks that sense the ebbing of life, modern men and women will feed upon themselves in a kind of "freedom frenzy," desperately trying to stave off nihilism by investing life with values that the underfunded convictional frameworks cannot support. Is there an alternative, a way to life and truth? For Henry, this is perhaps the most pressing question that confronts human being: "The most critical question in the history of thought is whether all the convictional frameworks through which different peoples arrive at the meaning and worth of human life are by nature mythical" (44).

Henry's work provides an excellent introduction to our topic: the relation of theology, culture, and hermeneutics. If the theologian is to minister the Word of God to today's world, both the Word and the world must be understood. Theology must engage in both biblical and cultural hermeneutics. Interpretation is one of the fundamental categories of theological thinking.[3] Theology should be in the business (at least part-time) of cultural interpretation. Of course, we must quickly acknowledge that theology itself is culturally conditioned. The theologian thinks from a particular point in place and time with a language and set of categories that reflect the time and culture in which he or she lives. It is therefore as

---

3. See Werner H. Jeanrond, *Text and Interpretation as Categories of Theological Thinking* (New York: Crossroad, 1988).

legitimate to speak of the culture of theology as it is to speak of the theology of culture. Moreover, because of the present loss of faith in absolutes and in an absolute (God's-eye) point of view, thinkers are happy to speak of interpretation but not of knowledge, particularly the absolute variety. Perhaps more than any previous age, ours is the age of interpretation. That we are not in a position to know things is widely accepted as a given. Absolute knowledge — of good and evil or anything else — unlike the paradisaic Tree, is always out of human reach. For this reason we will have to examine the culture of interpretation as well as the interpretation of culture.

In this essay I examine the role of theology in the interpretation of culture and in our present culture of interpretation. I first define culture and hermeneutics, and then argue that culture is an appropriate object of interpretation. Next I review some ways in which culture has been interpreted by historians, sociologists, philosophers, and theologians. I suggest that contemporary culture in the West is one in which hermeneutics itself is now considered one of the ultimate values. I speak here of the culture of hermeneutics rather than the hermeneutics of culture, for in the postmodern situation creative interpretation is taken to be one of the prime virtues of human being. In the final section I argue that there is more need than ever for the theologian to be interpreter and critic of contemporary culture, as well as champion of a counterculture that should be embodied in ecclesial existence — that is, in the church. It is only as we interpret Scripture that we will be able to establish an effective counterculture, which itself will be the most effective critique of the dominant culture. Ultimately, the interpretation that counts most is one's "performance" of the biblical text. The theologian as interpreter-critic is thus a player on the stage of world history. Theology's "staging" of the world displayed in the Christian Scriptures should constitute a crucial voice, or chorus of voices, in contemporary debates about cultural values and institutions. As players and interpreters of culture, both theologians and believers act as social theorists and social activists alike. This, at least, is the demanding role thrust upon Christian disciples, upon the community of those who assemble together to "do" the Word.

OF NATURE AND NURTURE, COSMOS AND CULTURE

The distinction between the natural and the human sciences exposes both the nature of culture as a social phenomenon and the corresponding need for hermeneutical understanding as opposed to causal explanations of culture and society. The natural sciences study, as their name implies, nature.

Since Kant, it has been fashionable to distinguish the realm of nature from freedom. Nature is ruled by laws, laws that causally determine what happens in space and time. Nature is marked by a certain necessity: force will always equal mass multiplied by acceleration, no matter what the climate or country. The goal of natural science is thus a catalogue of those causal laws that explain what invariably happens in nature. Scientists can "read" the book of nature intelligently when they have adduced the mathematical causal laws that govern the workings of the "mechanical" universe.

Human beings, on the other hand, are only partially determined by natural laws. Human bodies may be subject to causal laws, but not so the human spirit. Whereas tennis balls have no choice in the way they fulfill their vocation, human beings enjoy a measure of freedom. Human beings have futures — genuine possibilities — in ways that machines, molecules, and marbles do not. Human beings also have pasts. Indeed, history is the page upon which freedom writes. And one does not understand the book of history, the record of human freedom, by causal explanation. The historian is a human scientist — that is, one who studies humans — and history, along with the other human sciences, searches for understanding rather than explanation.[4]

Now from the point of view of, say, the biologist who studies human being as a phenomenon of nature, humanity is one. The biologist classifies all human beings as belonging to the same species. But for the historian (as well as for the cultural anthropologist or sociologist), humanity is multiple. No single set of laws, no matter how complex, can explain human beings and what they have done. No unified field theory charts the flow of human freedom. Yet one need not conclude from this that human being and human history are unintelligible. It was Wilhelm Dilthey who argued for a methodology that would study human being scientifically while at the same time respecting human individuality, freedom, and uniqueness.[5] Dilthey aimed at understanding rather than explanation, an understanding that meant reliving the experience and thought processes of individuals who have lived and thought before us. According to Dilthey, the study of history is possible because humans "objectify" or express their thoughts and values (their "spirit") through what they do, through their respective "works." History, which is about the actions of persons in the past, thus

4. The search is for understanding because the subject matter of history is the individual particular, not the individual as an instance of a universal and necessary law. In history, one is always conscious that it all might have happened otherwise.

5. See Raymond Williams, *Culture* (London: Fontana, 1981), pp. 15-16, and Paul Ricoeur, *Hermeneutics and the Human Sciences* (Cambridge: Cambridge University Press, 1981), chaps. 1-2.

becomes the study of signs and the interpretation of traces. Paul Ricoeur's verdict on Dilthey is telling: "history thus becomes the field of hermeneutics."[6] History is the stage for the appearances — the entries and the exits — of the human spirit.

A culture is the objectification, the expression in words and works, of the "spirit" of a particular people who inhabit a particular time and place. The spirit of the age (the *Zeitgeist*) is far from being invisible; on the contrary, it is constantly expressed in concrete forms. Culture is the effort of the human spirit to express itself by building and embodying values and beliefs into concrete forms (e.g., cathedrals, colosseums, cemeteries, cinemas, colleges, cash stations, car washes, etc.). Culture is the process (and result) whereby form and meaning are given to material through freedom.[7] A spider's web is not a cultural product because it is not a work of freedom. The spider's web, despite its intricacy, is neither a message nor an expression of a set of values and beliefs. There are no arachnid equivalents of our Gothic, Enlightenment, or Romantic — not to mention Cubist — cultural styles. The spider's web has no meaning; rather, it serves an instrumental purpose. The weaving of the web may be admired; it cannot be interpreted.

Culture refers to the expressive work of human freedom in and on nature. Unlike any other species, human being inscribes itself into nature by making meaningful marks — everything from small scratches of black ink on white paper to the scratches of a skyscraper on a sunlit sky. Culture, in its broadest sense, refers to the "world of human meaning."[8] The point about culture is that its "marks," its benchmarks and its landmarks, have meaning. They are to be understood rather than explained. But how? "The Greek culture has left its mark on Western civilization" — well and good, but how are we to understand the "mark" that is Greek culture? The grandeur that was Rome?

Ricoeur defines hermeneutics as "the theory of the operations of understanding in their relation to the interpretation of texts."[9] Hermeneutics, the art and science of interpretation, pertains primarily to the principles and procedures for making sense of and appropriating the meaning of texts. As we shall see, several recent thinkers have extended the notion of the

6. Ricoeur, *Hermeneutics and the Human Sciences*, p. 52.

7. As Herman Dooyeweerd puts it, "Cultural activity always consists in giving form to material in free control over the material" (*Roots of Western Culture: Pagan, Secular, and Christian Options* [Toronto: Wedge, 1979], p. 64).

8. Julian Hartt, *A Christian Critique of American Culture* (New York: Harper & Row, 1967), p. 49.

9. Ricoeur, *Hermeneutics and the Human Sciences*, p. 43.

"text" to include dreams (Freud), film, fashion (Roland Barthes), and culture as a whole (Raymond Williams). And natural scientists have, of course, long referred to the cosmos as the "book" of nature.

Ricoeur argues that the human sciences are hermeneutical insofar as their object displays "textual" features, and inasmuch as the method of the human sciences develops the same kind of procedures used to interpret texts. But how are cultures and cultural works like texts? A text is a set of marks (words) that fixes the meaning of the author. The saying of the author may disappear in time, but the marks, and the meaning, remain. Similarly, an action may "leave its mark." Human words and works alike can convey meaning. Max Weber defined the object of the human sciences as "meaningfully oriented behaviour." Studying meaningful human action, therefore, is like reading a text.[10] Unlike events, which are susceptible of causal explanation, human actions must be understood. Actions are meaningful works inscribed on the fabric of history or nature.

Culture refers to the meaningful actions of an individual, group, or whole society. Culture pertains to those human works that express in objective form some value for or shape of human freedom, some meaning or orientation for the wandering human spirit. Culture is not an impersonal cosmos but a meaningful world. As opposed to nature, which is indifferent to human being and human concerns, culture nurtures — cultivates — the human. If meaningful action can be likened to a text, then culture is the library in which these texts are classified by value and shelved in corporate memory.

A culture expresses the totality of what a group of humans value. Like a book, culture has a certain unity of plot or thesis. For Raymond Williams, culture is a signifying system that communicates and reproduces a social order through its various signifying practices, practices that include the arts, philosophy, journalism, advertising, fashion, and so on.[11] We try to express who we are and why we are valuable through our works (our "texts"): through paintings, monuments, symphonies. Such cultural anthologies may be the best means of pursuing cultural anthropology. Cultural hermeneutics is the study of how and what these multifarious signifying expressions really mean. By interpreting culture, we try to find the spirit in what has been bodied forth. Cultural hermeneutics is the study of people's beliefs about the meaning of life and about what it means to be human.

10. See Ricoeur, "The Model of the Text: Meaningful Action Considered as a Text," chap. 8 in *Hermeneutics and the Human Sciences*.

11. Williams, *Culture*, p. 13.

Culture is a signifying system that expresses in objective forms what a people take to be the values that guide and sustain human freedom. What aspect of culture is most significant? Kenneth Clark claims that architecture is the best index of the character of a civilization. Hans Rookmaaker says that painting is the most revelatory of a culture's mood. Nathan Scott says that it is literature; T. S. Eliot, that it is poetry. One is hard pressed to decide among these options. For Ricoeur, it suffices to say that culture, unlike economics (having) or politics (power), is established at the level of the imaginary. A culture is a cohesive social group because the individuals in the group share the same imaginative world, the same vision about what is most important and about how the social world should be ordered. At the heart of a society or civilization is a narrative, some story or history or drama, which accounts for its origin and destiny and which enshrines and grounds its system of values. Every culture tells its story — its past and future — in a particular way that gives it a sense of direction and a means of understanding itself. Some call this foundational narrative a "metanarrative"; others call it "myth." Whatever one calls it, I believe that theology should be allowed to tell, and argue for, its metanarrative version of the world too. It is theology's privilege and responsibility to join the conflict of interpretations about the meaning of the human condition and about the best means to achieve its fulfillment.[12]

Culture is an ongoing historical drama. The world stage embraces many cultures, many metanarratives, many stories and works that embody various visions and prescriptions for ordering life together. Traditionally, culture has been cherished as an indispensable instrument of nurture for the human spirit. In the preface to the 1873 edition of *Literature and Dogma,* Matthew Arnold defined culture as "the acquainting ourselves with the best that has been known and said in the world, and thus with the history of the human spirit." Arnold was concerned with the perfection of the individual. But as T. S. Eliot observed, "culture" may be used with reference to individuals, to a group or class, or to society as a whole. It is on this latter level that the study of culture and social theory intersect and that the presence of theology is most needed. For there is a growing chorus of naysayers who deny that there is anything in culture that is worth preserving. Against Arnold's quest for the best, many today argue that what earlier cultures took for the "best" was really a function of male domination, or political imperialism, or even racism. What does it mean to be human? What means should we take to attain genuine freedom?

12. Abraham Kuyper did this when he suggested that "Calvinism," alongside paganism, Islam, Roman Catholicism, and modernism, is one of five main systems of thought in the history of civilization (*Lectures on Calvinism* [Grand Rapids: Eerdmans, 1931], p. 32).

These are currently disputed questions. Theology, with no other credentials than the Word of God and the cultural mandate, must dare to enter the arena of critical discourse and put forth its prescription for culture beside those of the other social theorists.

THE HERMENEUTICS OF CULTURE

Culture is the world of human meaning, the sum total of a people's works that express in objective form their highest beliefs, values, and hopes — in short, their vision of what it is to be fully human. Culture is a text that calls for interpretation. But why should we want to interpret culture, and what are the principles that govern its correct interpretation? With regard to the "why" part of the question, I believe we must interpret culture in order first to understand the "other," the culturally distant, and then to understand ourselves, the culturally near.

Can other cultures, distant from us either geographically, linguistically, or chronologically, speak to us or contribute something to our being? Is it not our belief that we can learn from others that stimulates travel and exploration, not to mention reading? Without this interpretive effort, without this attempt to grasp or comprehend the other, certain values and ways of living would be lost to humanity. Culture, for Matthew Arnold, referred to those works of the human spirit that are worth preserving. In some sense, humanity would be diminished if the contents of the Louvre were suddenly to vanish. We read, we visit museums, and we listen to music in part to understand how others have experienced and understood life. Culture is a way of sharing what other people consider valuable ways of thinking and living. A given set of ideas and values would disappear unless they were culturally transmitted from one people group, from one generation, to another. A tradition is a kind of ongoing cultural interpretation of certain foundation works. If we would benefit from history, we must interpret in order to overcome cultural distance.

We also interpret culture in order to understand ourselves. The world we live in is so immediate and complex that it is difficult, if not impossible, to gain an objective perspective. We find it difficult to detach ourselves from the immediate so as to inquire after its meaning. And yet we can distance ourselves from our way of life. We may not have objectivity, but we can contemplate the "objectifications" of our way of life; for as we have seen, cultures produce works that, like texts, may be interpreted. Similarly, individuals produce works — works of labor, love, and art. These various works are expressions of an individual's spirit, of a person's desire and effort to exist in one way rather than another. By interpreting what we do (by interpreting our "story"), we have a better understanding of who we are. We may learn that we are far different than we had imagined. Ancient Israel's inflated opinion of itself, for instance, was shattered by the prophetic interpretation of its history and culture. Things that the Israelites interpreted as signs of God's favor were for Amos signs of Israel's corruption. We therefore see that a certain amount of "distance" is healthy for a hermeneutics that would preserve a critical moment in its interpretation. Though distance can be a barrier to understanding, a certain distance — namely, the distance afforded by the textual productions of a culture — is the condition for honest self-appraisal.

Bultmann's question about biblical interpretation — is exegesis without presuppositions possible? — may be applied to the hermeneutics of culture as well. It is evident that there can be false interpretations of culture. French scholars are still debating the causes and the meaning of the French Revolution. It is tempting to judge a foreign culture by the standards of one's own. For instance, Enlightenment thinkers cast the medieval era, which relied on divine revelation rather than on autonomous human reason, as the Dark Ages. Bultmann himself judged New Testament culture to be primitive compared to the scientific culture of the modern world. Ironically, some philosophers and social theorists are now arguing that "modernity" has run its course. Just what was (is) modernity and what did (does) it mean? This is an important, though disputed, question. Again, we who are in the thick of things see only darkly.

The conflict of interpretations of culture involves the clash of methods as well as disagreements about a culture's fundamental motifs. We have said that culture is the objectified expression, in works of art and styles of life, of a way of being human in the world. These cultural works manifest not only a particular style but also a particular structure and organization. This cultural structure, like the structure of a text, can be observed and explained. One can point to various aspects of the structure as evidence for one's explanation of it. And once one has analyzed the cultural form, one is then better able to grasp or understand the cultural content that it carries and expresses. Though different analytic techniques may be used for different types of cultural works, it is quite possible that one will discover the same cultural form shaping, say, an architect's cathedral, a musician's concerto, and an artist's canvas. The spirit of an age can be objectified in any number of cultural media. Some cultural interpreters therefore look for the same recurring themes or motifs throughout the various branches of culture. As we shall see, such motif criticism of culture has been especially popular with Christian thinkers.

How does one justify one's interpretation of culture? Take the following perfunctory interpretation of contemporary civilization: the West in the 1990s is a carbohydrate culture. It is fattening, energetic, but ultimately short-lived and unfulfilling. What we need is more protein in our culture, the stuff of life, rather than a carbohydrate diet, which lives on stuff. Is this an insightful interpretation or not? What methods could we use in order to assess and evaluate such an interpretation? Like human being itself, cultures are susceptible to a number of different disciplinary explanations. For Freud, psychology unlocks the mystery that is humankind. For Marx, there is no mystery, only market economies. Does one academic discipline or scientific method explain culture better than the others? "Positivism" is the term for the belief that all phenomena can be explained with the same scientific method. Culture and the human beings who carry and create it constitute too rich a reality to yield up their meaning to a single explanatory framework, no matter how sophisticated.

Raymond Williams's *Culture* is an example, first, of a hermeneutical approach to culture from a nontheological discipline (sociology); second, it represents a hermeneutics of cultural suspicion, as well as a positivist (in this case "materialist") hermeneutics. Williams shares with Karl Marx a certain skepticism with regard to the stories cultures tell about themselves. Marx argued that these stories were actually cleverly devised strategies for legitimating a certain political order and power structure. Even religion, Marx argued, served a political purpose by distracting the masses from social injustices by encouraging them to project their hopes onto an otherworldly future. Religion, along with other cultural institutions, thus served, wittingly or unwittingly, an ideological function. For Marx and Williams, an ideology is the principal set of beliefs and ideas that justify a certain social order. Ideology includes a group's conscious beliefs, as expounded in its philosophy, economics, law, and so forth, as well as its less formulated attitudes and feelings, displayed in its drama, poetry, painting, etc. Williams believes, as did Marx, that ideologies, while making a pretense to the status of objective knowledge, actually mask the real interests of those who wield cultural and political power. For Marx and Williams, one must approach culture with a hermeneutics of suspicion. The supposed values embodied in culture may only be a disguise for economic and political interests.

Williams is a cultural materialist. While acknowledging that culture pertains to the cultivation of a particular way of life, his real interest is in the (material) means and processes by which culture, and even ideology, develop. Whereas the cultural idealist lays emphasis on the "spirit" that informs cultural practices, Williams reverses the order and focuses on the cultural practices that constitute a culture's "spirit." For Marx, as for Williams, a society or culture could only be explained in historical and empirical terms. In other words, culture should be studied as a concrete form of life, in relation to rather than abstracted from the economic, technological, and political forces of the day. Williams's focus on cultural practices leads naturally to his adopting sociology as his method of choice. Sociology yields a method of observational analysis: "A *sociology* of culture must concern itself with the institutions and formations of cultural production."[13] As a sociologist of culture, Williams is more interested in explaining how cultural institutions such as universities and churches work to produce ideas and practices than he is in the truth or the rightness of these ideas and practices themselves. By explaining how cultural conditions change, Williams believes he can better account for a culture's *Zeitgeist.* This is a hermeneutics of suspicion. Williams believes he can unmask the lies cultures tell about themselves by discovering the material laws that govern their social conditions and relations. For instance, he believes that both the form and the content of the eighteenth-century realist novel can be "explained" in terms of certain social facts, such as the increasing importance of the bourgeoisie.

If Williams's sociological interpretation tends toward a materialist explanation of culture, speculative philosophers of history and philosophically oriented historians have traditionally fallen into the camp of the cultural idealists. Philosophical historians have tended to see ideas as the generative forces behind cultural practices rather than the converse. Cultures are deemed to be understood if one can uncover the ideological basis or the root ideas that undergird and fund cultural production and social practice. The structure of cultural works reveals a more basic intellectual ground. A Mozart symphony, for instance, displays the "classical" mind, marked by a love of order, symmetry, and balance — values that informed the politics and religion of the eighteenth century as well as its art. Speculative philosophers of history claim to have discovered overall patterns in the history of culture and civilization. Some believe the history of civilization to be progressive and linear; others believe it to be cyclical. In any case, these are further attempts to offer full-blown interpretations of world history. Interestingly enough, most speculative philosophers of history have tried to discover the purpose or meaning behind the pattern. Does the ebb and flow of culture and civilization have some ultimate purpose? With this question, the philosophy of history becomes positively religious in its hermeneutics of culture.

Enlightenment philosophers of history were generally not only cultural

---

13. Williams, *Culture,* p. 30.

idealists but optimists as well. As cultural idealists, they believed that ideas tell the main story about culture. As cultural optimists, they believed that the march of ideas that informed culture was onward and upward. G. W. F. Hegel represents perhaps the clearest illustration of an idealist philosophical reading of the history of human culture. For Hegel, the history of culture is simply the story of the outworking of philosophical ideas. Hegel viewed human history as the progressive development of Mind or Spirit *(Geist)*. The "spirit" of an age is only one stage in the unfolding of Spirit, which is for Hegel the rational idea of freedom. For Hegel, the Spirit that animates human beings, the Spirit of reason, is moving inevitably toward absolute truth and freedom. Hegel believed that world history manifests this development of human freedom through successive types of social organizations, from the earlier master-slave organization through stoicism and Christianity to, at last, Enlightenment rationality. Hegel immodestly viewed his own philosophy as the culmination of the whole process. He believed that his philosophy had absorbed whatever was of value in previous manifestations of Spirit, and that the history of ideas and culture alike had reached its peak around the year 1821, when he published his *Philosophy of Right.* Hegel's philosophy is generally considered the last, and the greatest, attempt to gain a God's-eye point of view on human history. For Hegel, there is only one way to view the world — namely, with the mind's eye. Hegel believed that he had not merely offered an interpretation of human history but had actually attained absolute knowledge about it. Hegel's example is instructive: human beings cannot adopt a perspective outside history from which to observe and interpret it. It was Hegel's obliviousness to the interpretive problem that led him to make such pretentious claims to have discerned the one true "Spirit" that progressively informs every human culture.

After the First World War, philosophers of history were less willing to speak of the "development" of ideas or culture. There was also an attempt to make the study of history more scientific and less speculative. Oswald Spengler represents both trends. Spengler believed that an inductive study of history would lead to the discovery of the laws that govern cultural development. These laws could then be used to predict what would happen in one's own culture. Spengler considered explanation by laws to be constitutive of science in general, including the human sciences. His was an attempt to overcome the dichotomy between the natural and human sciences in order to give his historical interpretation the prestige of the "hard" sciences such as physics. Accordingly, in his *Decline of the West* (1918-22), Spengler argued that culture invariably passes through four stages (birth, maturity, old age, and death) and that his own culture was no exception.

Several recent examples of historical and philosophical interpretations of society well demonstrate that the debate between cultural idealists and materialists is far from over. Again, the question concerns the relative priority of idea over the material conditions of social existence. As we try to make sense of a culture and its development, which do we say comes first, the principle or the practice? For Arthur Toynbee, the proper object of historical study is neither great individuals nor cultures, but civilizations. Unlike Hegel, Toynbee viewed history as a series of back and forth movements in which civilizations rise and fall. Their fall is as much from internal failures as from external attacks. Toynbee's major project, his twelve-volume work entitled *A Study of History* (1934-61), began when, at the beginning of the First World War, he noted some striking similarities between ancient Greco-Roman and modern European civilizations. Toynbee found that civilizations, like texts, have certain structural similarities, certain recurring themes. He tended to portray his study of history as scientific and inductive. He looked at twenty-one civilizations, from Sumerian and Egyptian to the present, and discovered the same ebb and flow pattern. His critics have accused him of cultural eisegesis, of reading a pattern derived from ancient Hellenic culture into other, very different, civilizations. Again, the conflict of interpretations over civilizations is very much like debates between literary critics over texts. Disputes over how to identify a civilization are similar to debates over identifying a literary genre. Such identification is crucial to Toynbee's task, since the twenty-one civilizations he examined are species of the same genus.

Arthur Lovejoy, the first editor of the *Journal of the History of Ideas*, believed, as Francis Schaeffer did after him, in the efficacy of ideas. For Lovejoy, we understand a culture when we grasp its leading ideas. He was particularly intrigued when certain ideas, such as romanticism or evolution, migrated into fields with which they had no logical connection. An idea that began its life in biology (e.g., evolution) might turn up in art, logic, or even religion. In the nineteenth century, for example, not only nature but also religion was thought to be subject to evolutionary development. Ideas inform many aspects of a culture. In a similar vein, Franklin Baumer has written a history of ideas from the seventeenth to the twentieth centuries that tells the story of the gradual victory of the category of "becoming" over the category of "being." Baumer explains a wide number of cultural phenomena — including art, literature, and theology — in terms of this ideological drama. What's in an idea? For Baumer, if "becoming" or flux is king, then all fixities and absolutes are banished: "it is hard to see how a civilization can long endure on becoming alone."[14]

14. Baumer, *Modern European Thought: Continuity and Change in Ideas, 1600-1950* (New York: Macmillan, 1977), p. 23.

By contrast with philosophers who believe that ideas are the hermeneutic key for unlocking the meaning of culture and its development, Fernand Braudel, the founder of the *Annales* school of French historiography, maintained that history is better understood by attending to the works of "Everyman" rather than "the Great Man." Instead of focusing on the acts and documents of kings and philosophers, Braudel investigates the documents of ordinary life: laundry lists, church registers, etc. Members of the *Annales* school believe that the history of culture must be written "horizontally" — that is, with reference to the broad social setting — not "vertically," with reference only to the ideas of great thinkers (mostly philosophers) who somehow transcend their times. The cultural historian should be just as interested in the opinions of the peasant as in the arguments of the philosopher. The "texts" that convey the meaning of culture are not only the great books but also the artifacts of day-to-day existence.

THEOLOGICAL INTERPRETATIONS OF CULTURE

Cornelius Van Til never tired of telling his theology students that created reality does not exist as brute, uninterpreted fact. It is always already meaningful because it is interpreted by God. The theologian's task is thus to "think God's thoughts after him." The contrast between a secular and a theological hermeneutics of cultural history may be illustrated by comparing Edward Gibbon's and Augustine's respective interpretations of the fall of ancient Rome. Gibbon's *History of the Decline and Fall of the Roman Empire* (1776) is one of the greatest histories ever written in English. Gibbon's thesis is that Christianity was the central destructive force in the Empire's collapse, a collapse that meant the triumph of barbarism and religion. Christianity, in Gibbon's view, far from leading to a Protestant work ethic (Max Weber's idea to explain the culture of European capitalism), led instead to the undermining of the Roman ethical system — that is, their rational pursuit of virtue and rewards. Gibbon thus offers a naturalistic explanation of the fall of Rome that casts the Christian faith as the villain.

Augustine's interpretation, on the other hand, is supernaturalistic. His *City of God* (412-26) is not simply a history of Rome; it is a Christian philosophy of world history in general as well as a penetrating theological analysis of human culture and its religious roots. Augustine envisaged the course of human history as a struggle between two communities: the earthly city of Man and the heavenly city of God. Through divine revelation we know that the city of God (i.e., the church, which has better claim to the epithet "the eternal city" than Rome) will ultimately triumph. Augustine's interpretive framework, with divine providence as its essential feature, is theological and supernaturalistic. History includes the marks of *God* in the past, and all human culture is to be interpreted as either aiding or hindering the progress of the city of God.

Augustine's *City of God* is often treated as a speculative philosophy of history because it applies a conceptual framework to experience. For Augustine, it is the mind's eye, illumined by faith, that perceives the meaning and significance of the historical process. Where empirical observation might perceive historical cycles, it could not explain the reasons behind these cycles. The goal that gives meaning to history is itself outside history. It is an eschatological work of God in the future. Here we may indeed speak of the world as "well staged," for Augustine presents world history as a drama that has a divinely appointed beginning, climax, and conclusion. History is not cyclical; rather, it is a progressive linear sequence, with humankind as a "subplot" in the divine comedy.

A large part of the *City of God* consists in debunking pagan myths and earthly values, which for Augustine are only temporary and therefore of only relative worth. The fall of Rome is the indictment not of Christianity but of sin, for the city of Man is characterized by self-love rather than by love of God. True freedom and goodness can never be attained on the basis of self-love, for human fulfillment ultimately depends on something greater than humanity. Human being is fulfilled only by the love of God. This is the meaning of pagan culture for Augustine: self-centered humanism is ultimately self-defeating.

In the twentieth century, Augustinian interpretation of culture is perhaps best represented by Dutch-American Reformed theology. To be Reformed in the Dutch-American tradition means taking Calvin's principle of the sovereignty of God and applying it to all areas and aspects of life. Christ is Lord of culture. Evangelicals such as Carl Henry have agreed with Abraham Kuyper and Herman Dooyeweerd that the Christian world and life view must be related to all areas of culture.[15] For Kuyper, Calvinism means recognizing the Lordship of Christ over all areas of life. This recognition led him in 1880 to found the Free University of Amsterdam as a place where the Bible may be applied to all aspects of life and thought. Culture is not some neutral, nontheological activity but an activity that is inherently religious. Every sculpture, every film, every novel, every building, every expression of human freedom in some concrete form presupposes

15. See George M. Marsden, "Reformed and American," in *Reformed Theology in America,* ed. David F. Wells (Grand Rapids: Eerdmans, 1985), pp. 1-12, for the "culturalist" tradition in Reformed theology.

some worldview, a set of beliefs and ideas about the nature of ultimate reality and the good.

For Kuyper, the dichotomy between sacred and secular is misbegotten if the earth, and all that is in it, is indeed the Lord's. No human activity is religiously neutral: "I maintain that it is the interpretation of our relation to God which dominates every general life system."[16] Kuyper pictures not two cities but two world and life views engaged in mortal combat: modernism, which builds its worldview on naturalistic principles, and Calvinism, which constructs its worldview from Christian principles.[17] Kuyper argues, for example, that though Calvin himself was not artistically inclined, his theological principle of the Lordship of Christ allowed him to view art as a divine gift. Art for Calvin was not simply an imitation of nature but a means of disclosing a higher reality than our present fallen world. Art gives us a taste of creation and restoration, of the beauty that was God's original intent for the world. Art that points back to creation and forward to redemption is thus truer than art that merely imitates our fallen present. The values embodied by art are inescapably religious; art makes theological statements.

Herman Dooyeweerd, another Dutch Calvinist, similarly argues that the roots of culture are always religious. Dooyeweerd claims that every culture is animated by a religious "ground motive."[18] This ground motive refers to the basic direction of an individual's or society's life, the source of its energy and direction — its "heart." On the deepest level, every culture is driven by either a God-affirming or a God-denying ground motive. These ground motives are not only the forces that shape cultures and communities; they are also the "hermeneutic keys for understanding and interpreting periods and patterns of history and culture."[19] Dooyeweerd thus interprets the history of Western civilization in terms of the religious ground motive that shapes a given culture. If cultures are texts, then Dooyeweerd's ambition is to uncover their "deep grammar."

What other thinkers have called the "spirit" of the age is for Dooyeweerd a religious spirit, one that either accepts or denies God's Lordship over culture and creation. For Dooyeweerd, the Christian's ground motive is that of creation-fall-redemption. Fallenness means that human culture

---

16. Kuyper, *Lectures on Calvinism,* p. 24.

17. Kuyper believed that Calvinism embodies the Christian principle — the Lordship of Christ — more purely and consistently than other Christian movements (*Lectures on Calvinism,* p. 17).

18. See C. T. McIntyre's chapter on Dooyeweerd in Wells, ed., *Reformed Theology in America,* pp. 172-85.

19. Dooyeweerd, *Roots of Western Culture,* p. x.

will always be, at best, "on the way." Redemption means that human culture should actively affirm, in the power of the Spirit, God's rule over all creation. In Dooyeweerd's scheme, modern culture stems from Kant's "nature and freedom" ground motive, a motive that denies the religious character of life and thought. Instead of recognizing the authority of God over all areas of life and thought, modern culture, animated by the religious ground motive of freedom and nature, has declared its autonomy. The world stage includes only nature and natural facts on the one hand, and free human beings with their self-made values on the other. Modern human beings are, therefore, a law unto themselves. Modern culture is simply an expression of this ground motive.

Two other thinkers, from different theological traditions, largely agree with Augustine and Kuyper with regard to the essentially religious nature of culture. T. S. Eliot, in his *Notes Towards the Definition of Culture,* suggests that culture and religion are roughly synonymous: "We may ask . . . whether what we call the culture, and what we call the religion, of a people are not different aspects of the same thing: the culture being, essentially, the incarnation (so to speak) of the religion of a people."[20] For Eliot this implies two things: (1) that culture cannot be preserved in the absence of religion, and (2) that religion cannot be preserved in the absence of culture. What then is culture? Eliot suggests that it refers to that which makes life worth living, to that which creates a meaningful home out of an otherwise impersonal cosmos. Culture refers to the characteristic interests and activities of a people; for Eliot, an Englishman, these included the annual Henley Regatta (a boat race), the dart board, Wensleydale cheese, nineteenth-century Gothic churches, and the music of Elgar.

According to Eliot, culture is lived religion: "behaviour is also belief" (32). Where does one learn patterns of behavior? For Eliot, the primary channel of transmission of culture is the family. It is in the life of the family that religion is "interpreted" in terms of daily life. Can there be a family of nations united by Christian faith? Some forty-five years before the founding of the European Economic Community, Eliot raised the question of the unity of European culture. The problem he correctly foresaw was this: true religious reunion involves a commonality of culture, not simply a common profession of faith. Without a common faith, "all efforts towards drawing nations closer together in culture can produce only an illusion of unity" (82). Cultures themselves are mired in a conflict of interpretations about the way to the good life. The only common point is the common

---

20. Eliot, *Notes Towards the Definition of Culture* (London: Faber & Faber, 1948), p. 28. Subsequent citations will be made parenthetically in the text.

spiritual heritage of Europe — the Christian Scriptures and the Christian faith: "I do not believe that the culture of Europe could survive the complete disappearance of the Christian faith" (122). The greatest task at hand, according to Eliot, is that of preserving our common culture and our spiritual heritage. The very survival of Europe depends on its continual mining of culture for the religious roots that sustain it.

Yet another Protestant theologian, Paul Tillich, also believes that culture is essentially religious. Tillich has produced what is perhaps the most comprehensive theology of culture in the twentieth century. In his view, simply being human is a fundamentally religious enterprise. To be or not to be, to exist as finite, raises ultimate questions for any human being who pauses to consider his or her situation. What is our situation? Danger lurks just offstage; our being is threatened in many ways. First of all, there is the threat of nonbeing — that is, death. Second, we find ourselves morally responsible for our being, and this leads to the threat of guilt and condemnation. And finally, there is the threat that we will find no meaning to our lives. Tillich calls these the anxieties of death, guilt, and meaninglessness, respectively.[21] Furthermore, Tillich interprets the history of Western civilization in terms of a progression through these three anxieties. Ancient civilizations were preoccupied with death and immortality; medieval cultures centered their reflection and activity on the problem of sin and salvation; and the modern age desperately seeks alternatives to the despair of spiritual emptiness.

Tillich believes that the human condition as such, whatever the age or culture, provokes religious questions. Ordinary human experience is anxious; human being is always a question, and a religious question at that. This is so because for Tillich, religion has to do with an individual's or a people's ultimate concern. Religion has to do with the "depth dimension" of all human experience. What does Tillich mean by "depth"? "It means that the religious aspect points to that which is ultimate, infinite, unconditional in man's spiritual life."[22] Religion is the name for that which concerns us ultimately. Tillich's interpretation of the human condition and human culture is ontological or existential. An analysis of the human situation inevitably leads to the question of how we can overcome the anxieties that are part and parcel of our being human. This is a religious question, a question about something that concerns us ultimately. Religion is the state of being grasped by an ultimate concern. In Tillich's concise but important

21. See Tillich, *The Courage to Be* (New Haven: Yale University Press, 1952), pp. 40-63.

22. Tillich, *Theology of Culture* (London: Oxford University Press, 1959), p. 7.

formula, "religion is the substance of culture, culture is the form of religion. . . . He who can read the style of a culture can discover its ultimate concern, its religious substance."[23]

Each of the theologians we have surveyed shares the conviction that culture is a form of lived religion. We learn what a people really believes and values by interpreting that people's works, art, and forms of life. However, the principles of cultural hermeneutics differ from theologian to theologian. Augustine, Kuyper, and Dooyeweerd are tied to biblical motifs in a way that Tillich is not. But common to all of them is the belief that there is no such thing as a purely secular culture; the way people live and express themselves in their works has religious meaning. "By their fruits ye shall know them" (Matt. 7:20, KJV). Culture is thus the fruit of a theology or a worldview. After noting the Thomism of Dante, the Calvinism of Rembrandt, the Lutheranism of Bach, and the Puritanism of Milton, Denis de Rougement remarked that neither nineteenth- nor twentieth-century liberalism had similarly inspired any great artist or poet.[24] If culture is the fruit of theology, what happens to culture when God is not merely debilitated but dead? Nietzsche announced God's demise in the late nineteenth century, and the message was repeated in the 1960s. If culture is a form of lived religion, what might a post-theistic culture look like? I believe it looks something like our present culture of radical hermeneutics. After all, if there is no God, as Dostoyevski said, everything is permitted . . .

THE CULTURE OF HERMENEUTICS

To this point we have been considering culture as a hermeneutical phenomenon. Culture, that shared set of meaningful human activities and works that express ultimate beliefs and values, is a "religious" text that calls for theological interpretation. We have seen how theology functions in the hermeneutics of culture, but what of theology's role in the present culture of hermeneutics? By speaking of the "culture of hermeneutics" I mean to call attention to the fact that more and more academic disciplines (including theology) have become increasingly aware of their own hermeneutic status. Epistemology, the study of the nature and means of knowledge, has taken on a hermeneutical hue. *Homo sapiens* has given way to *Homo interpretans*. We humans see very little of reality directly; we see

---

23. Tillich, *Theology of Culture*, pp. 42-43.

24. Recounted in Bernard Ramm, *After Fundamentalism* (San Francisco: Harper & Row, 1983), p. 175.

neither its ultimate subatomic components, nor its past, nor its meaning. What knowledge we have is not direct but indirect — that is, the world comes to us mediated through language. Hermeneutics is an interdisciplinary phenomenon because all disciplines meet on the common ground of language.

The extension of hermeneutics beyond its original home in literary criticism reaches even into the natural sciences.[25] Thomas Kuhn has argued that even the scientist's eye is not innocent: all observations are theory-laden. The scientist comes to "objective data" with some kind of interpretive framework already in place (Kuhn calls it a "paradigm"): "An apparently arbitrary element, compounded of personal and historical accident, is always a formative ingredient of the beliefs espoused by a given scientific community at a given time."[26] In other words, scientists are caught up in the hermeneutical circle with the rest of us. Recent philosophers of science acknowledge the hermeneutical dimension of the natural sciences by speaking of theories as "models." Ian Barbour defines a model as "an imaginative tool for ordering experience, rather than a description of the world."[27] Barbour says that scientists take their models seriously but not literally. They are heuristic devices — "useful fictions." Max Black has compared scientific models to poetic metaphors: both the scientist and the poet explore various aspects of reality by using language in a creative way.[28] Science involves inventing and interpreting metaphorical models of the real. Mary Hesse is quite explicit about the hermeneutical dimension of the natural sciences: "My thesis is that there is . . . a linear continuum between the empirical and the hermeneutic. . . . At each stage of the continuum, appropriate interpretive conditions enter the process of theorizing."[29] Truly, the book of nature has become a text.

"Textuality" is indeed one of the leading notions that distinguishes the contemporary "postmodern" situation from the "modern" era. Everything from dreams to denim is today regarded as text. Not only words but the clothes we wear and the cars we drive are "signs" in a system of signs. The study of sign systems, or "semiotics," derives from a series of lectures

25. See Vern S. Poythress, *Science and Hermeneutics* (Grand Rapids: Zondervan, 1988).

26. Kuhn, *The Structure of Scientific Revolutions* (Chicago: University of Chicago Press, 1970), p. 4.

27. Barbour, *Myths, Models, and Paradigms: A Comparative Study in Science and Religion* (San Francisco: Harper & Row, 1974), p. 6.

28. See Black, *Models and Metaphors* (Ithaca: Cornell University Press, 1962).

29. Hesse, *Revolutions and Reconstructions in the Philosophy of Science* (Bloomington: Indiana University Press, 1980), p. 225.

on linguistics delivered by Ferdinand de Saussure at the University of Geneva between 1906 and 1911. Saussure argued that the relation of signs (signifiers) to things or concepts (signified) is a matter of arbitrary social convention. It just so happens that the sign GOD signifies a supreme being and DOG a canine being. More recently, Roland Barthes and Umberto Eco, among others, have argued that the theory of semiotics may be applied beyond words to a whole range of cultural phenomena. Everything in culture is a signifier in some system of signs. A Ford Escort sends one signal about one's social status, a Porsche quite another. Perfumes, hairstyles, movies, toys, margarine, shoes — all signify.

Augustine and other Christian theologians would be happy to accept, I think, this "textuality" of culture. The dividing of the ways only appears when one asks whether such and such a text has a determinate meaning.[30] A number of French thinkers in the 1960s applied Saussure's insights into the arbitrariness of language to texts in general. Every text is an indeterminate signifying system, a network of signs that refer to one another. Furthermore, it is impossible to stop the "play" of signs and say decisively what a text means. Why? Because the signs do not refer to reality but to one another; they gain their meaning precisely through their opposition to other signs (e.g., "hot"/"cold," "blue"/"red," etc.). A text has a "texture" but no substance. Its meaning is indeterminate. To define "the" meaning of a text would be considered the height of hermeneutic pontification; there is simply no one correct order of an arbitrary sign system. For Roland Barthes, this is a liberating discovery because the reader is freed to be creative. Like Nietzsche, Barthes believes we are never more human than when we are creating our own meaning and values. The alternative is to endure the hermeneutic bondage of having to discover the "correct" interpretation of a text. Barthes maintains that sign systems are open, susceptible to many combinations. The point, after all, is to play with the text as one would with a Rubik's cube that had no one solution. In order to achieve total interpretive freedom, however, Barthes has to get rid of the idea of an "author." Barthes says that the author must die so that the reader may live. But this is simply a repetition on the textual level of the death of God (the Author of all) on the metaphysical level. What is the meaning of life? If there is no Author, no authority, who can say? Once one abandons the idea of determinate textual meaning and correct textual interpretation, everything in interpretation is permitted. The death of God thus leads to the cult of Hermes.

---

30. See my book *Is There a Meaning in This Text? The Bible, the Reader, and the Morality of Literary Knowledge* (Grand Rapids: Zondervan, forthcoming).

"Postmodern" is the name many give to the present culture of hermeneutics.[31] John Caputo believes that the postmodern world has abandoned modernism's metaphysical quest and embraced a radical hermeneutics. Metaphysics is the attempt to answer rationally the ultimate questions concerning life and reality. The modern world believed that rcason in its metaphysical mood could reach and formulate these universal truths. Hermeneutics, on the other hand, restores life to its "original difficulty," to use Caputo's phrase. Radical hermeneutics "exposes us to the ruptures and gaps, let us say, the textuality and difference, which inhabits everything we think, and do, and hope for."[32] To have answers for the ultimate questions of life is to have the "one true perspective," the one true interpretation of the book of life. But this is precisely what postmodernist thinkers deny to human beings. Human being is irremediably perspectival: the way we think, talk, perceive, communicate, act, marry, play — all these activities, including knowing, are conditioned by our "place." One's outlook on God, self, and world is affected by the time and place in which one lives, one's upbringing, one's social class, one's sex, one's biochemistry, and so on. Metaphysics is a hopeless quest for an epistemological grail. The most a thinker can hope for is not knowledge, but an interesting interpretation.

The postmodern mind-set and culture alike are characterized by self-consciousness: postmodern authors and artists are all too aware of the fact that they are writing, that they are painting — so much so that their writing and painting represent not reality but rather writing and painting! Postmodern writing, art, and television call attention to their artificial, man-made nature. For Jean-François Lyotard, the postmodern condition is one that is suspicious of all "metanarratives," those stories that pretend to explain everyone else's story and tell it the way it is.[33] Postmodern culture no longer believes in such metanarratives, be they Marxist, rationalist, or Christian. What this means is that there is no overarching story that will inform culture. Instead, Lyotard looks forward to a way of life that would celebrate "tribal" diversity. For Lyotard,

31. Scott Lash believes that postmodernism is a kind of culture and thus is open to sociological description. He believes that whereas modern culture differentiated between the theoretical, ethical, and aesthetic realms, postmodern culture is characterized by "de-differentiation." In postmodernism, the lines between the theoretical, moral, and aesthetic begin to blur, as does the line between reality and its representation. See his *Sociology of Postmodernism* (London: Routledge, 1990), pp. 9-13.

32. Caputo, *Radical Hermeneutics: Repetition, Deconstruction, and the Hermeneutic Project* (Bloomington: Indiana University Press, 1987), p. 6.

33. See Lyotard, *The Postmodern Condition: A Report on Knowledge* (Manchester: Manchester University Press, 1984).

freedom means that everyone can tell, and enact, his or her own story or
narrative. In the postmodern world, reality disintegrates into myriad stories and systems of signs. Jean Baudrillard believes that the television
screen is the most appropriate metaphor for postmodern culture. Instead
of the permanence of a painting, television is an electronic field of
flickering images. Television is, as Steven Connor puts it, "a world of
simulations detached from reference to the real, which circulate and
exchange in ceaseless, centreless flow."[34] One clear instance of this is the
rock video, where images of past and present, dreams and waking cease-
lessly intermingle, thus short-circuiting any attempt to privilege one image
and use it as an interpretive key of the whole.

Theology is not immune from the influence of its surrounding culture.
A number of theologians are already hard at work on a hermeneutical or
postmodern theology. David Tracy understands "modern" as referring to
the conviction that the human subject is rational and can attain knowledge
and truth. But this Enlightenment "faith" is now at an end. Tracy acknowl-
edges, with other postmodern thinkers, the finite and perspectival nature
of all human knowing. We must interpret because of the plurality and
ambiguity of language and history. Though all cognition is interpretation,
Tracy believes that a more modest form of rationality survives the passing
of modernity: conversation. In conversation, one respects the other's interpretation as much as one's own. Rationality is the art of conversing about
texts; rationality is hermeneutical. Religion here performs an invaluable
service according to Tracy: its object — the Transcendent — serves as a
permanent reminder that our attempts at knowing will always be incomplete. Religion reminds us that no one is in a position to dominate or
end the conversation. For Tracy this means that the Christian theologian
cannot assume that the Christian metanarrative — the gospel — is superior
to the stories of other religions. There is no room for absolutes in the
hermeneutic inn.[35]

Don Cupitt welcomes the end of modernity and its myth of a transcendent rational order. For Cupitt, postmodernism means ceasing to
believe in any absolute Beginning or End, Ground or Presence. Augustine's
world, where everything is a sign for something eternal, has been stood on
its head. Or better, his world has been declared flat. Cupitt writes: "The
interpretive movement is not from sign directly on to thing signified, but

---

34. Baudrillard, cited in Steven Connor, *Postmodernist Culture: An Introduction to
Theories of the Contemporary* (Oxford: Basil Blackwell, 1989), p. 168.

35. See Tracy, *Plurality and Ambiguity: Hermeneutics, Religion, Hope* (San Francisco:
Harper & Row, 1987).

sideways from sign to sign."[36] The end of fixed views and the reign of flux means that humans are free to be creative: "It is up to *us* to reimagine Christianity, to re-invent faith for our time" (2). Theology, like poetry, must conjure up a meaningful world out of nothing. Creation *ex nihilo* characterizes the theologian's work, not God's. Worldviews are imaginative creations. Modern metaphysics was just pretentious poetry. But if we are honest about the fictions we fabricate, can we really believe and respect them? Imaginative visions can, after all, be generated from reason as well as madness, and indeed, who is to say which is which?

One of the aims of culture is the preservation of knowledge, creative achievements, and values. Those who contribute to culture believe that there is a meaning that is worth transmitting to others. But Cupitt questions whether culture really expresses timeless truths. Both philosophy and theology have claimed to teach truth, and in the case of Christianity the church has often exercised a cultural hegemony: "God was the absolute Memory, the guarantor of lasting knowledge and value and the refuge from the mere contingency that people need if life is to have worth" (84). But for Cupitt, an apostle of postmodernism, the use of God to validate cultural norms is illegitimate. "Language and interpretation are beginningless and endless in a way that rules out ideas of indisputable first principles and final truths" (88). Cupitt's cult and culture of Hermes lead, ironically, to the annihilation of the very idea of culture. In the end, he must conclude that nothing is worth preserving. Anything permanent would be a burdensome restriction on his freedom to create endlessly his sideways world. The culture of hermeneutics is one of free play, where everything is turned sideways, upside down, and inside out. Devotees of the cult of Hermes thus lead lives of riotous interpretive play; their worship is neither in spirit nor in truth, but in the carelessness of carnival.[37]

THEOLOGY AND THE CRITICAL RECONSTRUCTION OF CULTURE: THE HERMENEUTICS OF FAITH

A critical hermeneutics of culture is committed, first, to discovering what a civilization is up to. Theological criticism of contemporary culture dis-

---

36. Cupitt, *The Long-Legged Fly: A Theology of Language and Desire* (London: SCM, 1987), p. 21. Subsequent citations will be made parenthetically in the text.

37. For an explication of the suitability of this metaphor, see Nathan Scott, "The House of Intellect in an Age of Carnival: Some Hermeneutical Reflections," in *The Whirlwind in Culture: Frontiers in Theology,* ed. Donald W. Musser and Joseph L. Price (New York: Meyer-Stone Books, 1988), pp. 39-54, esp. p. 42.

covers that the "lived religion" behind postmodern culture is the religion of Hermes, the winged messenger, god of mystical doctrines and patron of thieves. It celebrates rather than confesses its article of faith — namely, that there is no authorized version of reality, only interpretation. Postmodernism means the priesthood of all believers minus a text in which to believe. If the Author is dead, does all authority disappear too? Not necessarily. In the postmodern world, the priesthood of all believers leads to mass culture. In mass culture authority becomes a function of popular opinion. Indeed, Julian Hartt defines mass culture as "the elevation of popular taste and conviction to an effectively unchallenged supremacy over all the principal modes of action and thought in our civilization."[38] How can such a culture be criticized or reformed? Hartt laments the church's loss of prophetic voice: "Popular Christianity is rapidly approaching the state of perfect homogenization. It is religiousness rather than faith; it is geniality rather than love; it is wish rather than hope; it is opinion rather than truth."[39] The Christian criticism of mass culture must begin with the church, with those in the household of faith.

In a culture of hermeneutics, there is more need than ever for theology — even in the church. But what can theology offer? What should be its reaction to the deconstruction of stories, texts, and whole cultures? Theology must become involved in the reconstruction of culture. Theology must lay the intellectual foundations for lived biblical religion. It must serve that community of interpreters who believe that the Bible witnesses to God's acts in the world and in his Word, Jesus Christ. Amid the ruins of our age, biblical interpretation is the best means of rebuilding the walls of a culture originally built upon the Book. The community of biblical interpreters is, of course, the church. The church is a hermeneutical community, a community of interpreters constituted by the Word and enlivened by the Spirit. Indeed, the Spirit is the enabling power that ministers the Word and renders it effective. Hermeneutics, we may recall, involves not only the explanation of textual meaning but also its appropriation. It is not enough to explain what a text meant; one must decide what it means today. Meaning must be *applied* — to the church, to the world, to oneself. Hermeneutics, in the broadest sense of the term, pertains not only to "hearing" but also to "doing" the word. The most important interpretation of the Bible is the way we live our lives. We appropriate the meaning of a text when we let its world into ours, when we put its pages into our practice. We apply a text's meaning to our lives when we perform the text. Our response to a text constitutes its "lived meaning."

38. Hartt, *A Christian Critique of American Culture*, p. 391.
39. Hartt, *A Christian Critique of American Culture*, p. 394.

We have examined the hermeneutics of culture and the culture of hermeneutics. What I am now proposing to consider is hermeneutics itself as a means of constructing culture. A community's performance of a text gives rise to a particular way of life and thus to a particular culture. Augustine's rules for biblical interpretation, for example, yielded a Christian culture that lasted almost a thousand years.[40] Hermeneutics — the art and science of applying as well as interpreting texts — is thus an important aspect of creating cultures. Ricoeur speaks of living in the "world" of the text. If we dwell in a text's world long enough, it will begin to shape our vision and our values. This is the function of culture — the world of meaning — too. It is by faith that the community of biblical interpreters believingly enters the text; it is the Spirit who enables the Word's world to cultivate the image of God that we bear and that we are. The church's aim should be to render a faithful interpretation of Scripture. Augustine's rule for biblical interpretation can be neatly extended to the church's interpretive performance: when faced with a plethora of possible meanings, choose the interpretation that fosters love of God and love of neighbor. "Correct" interpretation of Scripture means living a life of love and service to God, to the church as the people of God, and to the world. We only really understand the story of Jesus when we perform it.

Performing the story of Jesus leads to an interpretive practice that challenges the predominant cultural trend. The story of Jesus is one of humiliation and exaltation, in that order. Hearing and doing the story of Jesus produces a style of life characterized by humility, service, and love. But these theological virtues must characterize our hermeneutic practice too. The church should strive to exemplify what for lack of a better term we might call the "hermeneutics of faith," a hermeneutic not of irresponsible iconoclasm nor of prideful play, but of charity and humility. A theological hermeneutics of faith will resist both dogmatism (interpretive pride) and skepticism (interpretive sloth). On the one hand, it will not claim too much for itself; its commentary must never presume to usurp the primary text. On the other hand, a hermeneutics of faith respects the text as a given. A hermeneutics of faith will work to seek textual understanding. This means attending to and respecting the text's voice rather than one's own.

This last point is important. The church is not immune to the conflict of interpretations. Are there any norms that may help us decide which community's reading or performance of Scripture is the most adequate?

40. See Augustine's *On Christian Doctrine,* trans. D. W. Robertson, Jr. (Indianapolis: Bobbs-Merrill, 1958).

There are, I believe, two such criteria. The first is the text itself, the fixed point from which various interpretations may be challenged. As Martin Luther successfully demonstrated during the Reformation, the text can be used *against* the community of its interpreters. Second, some interpretations or performances of a text may be more "fruitful" than others. But what does "fruitful" mean in the context of biblical hermeneutics? It means, first, a reading that explains more of the text and displays more of its rich internal coherence. But second, an interpretation may be judged to be fruitful if it disperses the riches of the text among its readers. Augustine pointed to charity as a kind of criterion for a good reading of the Bible. Jesus said we would recognize his disciples by their love. Should we not, therefore, prefer the reading that gives rise to a way of living that most approximates the life of Jesus himself, the harbinger of the kingdom of God? Orthopraxis — right living — is a sign of the Spirit's enlivening presence with the Word. Christian culture is not just a means to preach the gospel; it is rather the means for us to come to know the gospel and to know what it means. Christ must be not only the eternal Word but also the church's "living idiom."[41]

Culture and readers alike are restored only by God's grace. The story of Jesus Christ — his "lived meaning" — has been staged in our world through the centuries by his body, the church. Again, it is the Spirit who animates this life. We can only perform the gospel because the gospel has been lived by Christ and then enabled by his Spirit. It is for these reasons that Donald Bloesch can speak of "God the Civilizer."[42] Culture, according to Bloesch, "is the divinely appointed means for men and women to realize their humanity."[43] As such, culture is both human achievement and divine gift. It is the church's role to be a light to the nations. The church should be the model for the right use of human freedom; the church should be the civilized society par excellence. The community of believers represents a prophetic counterculture that challenges the gods and myths of the day with regard to which world and life view best fulfills humanity. The church's challenge will only be as strong as its expression of the biblical world and life view. Again, this is not only a matter of correct doctrine but also a matter of faithful biblical performance. The church must be the cultural incarnation of the story of God in Christ. Bloesch is careful to note that the church is in no position to lord it over secular culture; her performance of Scripture will also be reviewed. Karl Barth viewed the world as

41. Hartt, *A Christian Critique of American Culture*, p. 353.
42. Bloesch, "God the Civilizer," in *Christian Faith and Practice in the Modern World: Theology from an Evangelical Point of View*, ed. Mark A. Noll and David F. Wells (Grand Rapids: Eerdmans, 1988), pp. 176-98.
43. Bloesch, "God the Civilizer," p. 177.

the field, but not the source, of the redemptive activity of God. Though human culture can be influenced by the divine command and the divine promise, the kingdom of God will always "outrun" human achievements.[44] The church is to be a humble witness to the kingdom of God, not its political administrator.

The believing community "reads" the world in light of the Word of God. In other words, the church interprets the world and the surrounding culture through the lens of the biblical text. But just as importantly, its hermeneutics of faith issues in a community performance of the biblical texts. To repeat: it is not enough to hear and understand; one must also appropriate the meaning of a text and "do" the words. To understand the Bible properly is to "follow" it, and this in two senses: first, we follow a text when we understand it, when we grasp its meaning. But "follow" also means going along a particular path or way. To follow the word in this sense is to put it into practice, to perform it. The hermeneutics of faith demands nothing less than discipleship. Faith comes from hearing and reading the Word of God. To have Christian faith means having your thinking, imagining, language, and life shaped by the biblical texts — by biblical law, wisdom, songs, apocalyptic, prophecy, gospel, and doctrine. These literary forms of Scripture are constitutive of Christian identity and practice alike. The literary critic William Beardslee wrote: "A particular literary style is not only appropriate to, but generative of, a life style."[45] An "evangelical" is one whose life and thought conform to the gospel of Jesus Christ. The believer performs the gospel *(euangelion)* when he or she puts it into practice, following the Word to grace and freedom in Christ, and then showing and telling others the way to follow.

The way of life generated by the biblical texts is not, ultimately, the way of this world. Insofar as the church successfully performs Scripture, it will produce a culture that, far from being in easy complicity with the world, will rather be a permanent revolution. The world is the theater of action for the people of God, not their final home. It is at best a staging area for a group of wandering pilgrims and minstrels who perform parables of the kingdom of God. Culture that is genuinely evangelical accepts the gospel as the given from which it first derived its life and upon which it continues to draw for its intellectual, imaginative, and practical resources. Culture is evangelical if it accepts the revelation of God in Christ and the salvation of God in Christ. Its response to God's grace *(charis)* should be

---

44. See Barth, "Church and Culture," in his *Theology and Church: Shorter Writings, 1920-1928* (New York: Harper & Row, 1962).

45. Beardslee, *Literary Criticism of the New Testament,* p. 76.

one of *eucharist* —thanksgiving and gratitude. *Evangelical culture is the eucharistic response to the gift of Christian freedom.* Culture is, as we have seen, the sphere in which freedom manifests itself. Cultivating Spirit-given freedom is perhaps our greatest privilege; it is certainly our greatest responsibility. The most important interpretive task of the church is to create an evangelical, eucharistic culture in which Christian freedom would be expressed in obedience to God and oriented to God's glory. It is neither trivial nor irrelevant that Johann Sebastian Bach concluded each of his musical compositions with the dedication *"sola Dei Gloria."*

A hermeneutics of faith concerns itself with the interpretation of texts that purport to engender and give shape to human freedom. After all, culture is about shaping human freedom into social practices that express ultimate values and that fulfill human beings. A hermeneutics of Christian faith interprets the world in terms of the literary framework of the Word. In light of this Word, we must conclude that the so-called freedom of our contemporary culture of hermeneutics is illusory. Freedom that leads to the frustration rather than the fulfillment of human being is no true freedom at all. But this is only the negative, critical side of a hermeneutics of faith. Its positive agenda is expressed by two phrases: "faith seeking understanding" and "understanding seeking faithful performance." To be an interpreter means to be an incessant seeker. If we no longer needed to search for meanings, we would have absolute knowledge, and interpretation would no longer be needed. If we no longer needed to criticize our performances, we would have absolute goodness. We who live on Middle-earth, however, have neither absolute knowledge nor absolute goodness; hermeneutics is thus our common human lot — our privilege and our responsibility. Saints and sinners, our interpretations and performances will always fall short. But through Christ, a new "culture" has entered the world and is growing at a fabulous rate, a benign bacterium with the power to heal humanity. I refer, of course, to the culture engendered by the Word of God and sustained by the Spirit. At first no louder than a whisper, the Christian story quickly toppled empires and gave birth to civilizations. Our Christian performances are not in vain because of the living Word's performance in the first act. The community of faith continues the story, sustained by memory and hope. It lives in the second act — commemorating the first, and holding its breath for the last. Christian interpreters perform not gospel but apocalyptic when they contemplate that glorious Finale, when the world will indeed be well staged and all manner of things shall be well.

Christian Witness in an Age of Pluralism

D. A. CARSON

ONE OF THE compelling features of contemporary Western culture is the increasingly pervasive influence of pluralism. That *pluralism* is difficult to define cannot discount its power. It has an immediate bearing on how Christians think of themselves; it penetrates to the core of what we mean by "mission"; it offers opportunities and casts up dangers as it contributes to the globalization of theology.

The subject has become extraordinarily complex, the books and articles legion. In what follows I shall not provide an overview of the debate or an exhaustive catalogue of the major players. Rather, I shall attempt to outline some of the salient features of contemporary culture that Christians need to think through, and then I shall sketch in some areas of Christian teaching that speak directly to these features.

THE NATURE OF THE CHALLENGE

(1) *On most definitions, there is much more pluralism than ever before in the United States and in Western nations generally.*

Because this point turns in part on the way *pluralism* is popularly used, it is important to distinguish the following three tendencies:[1]

1. Among the more important treatments are these: Thomas Robbins and Dick An-

I would like to thank Kenneth Kantzer, John Woodbridge, Paul Hiebert, Harold O. J. Brown, and Mark Krause for reading an earlier draft of this paper and offering helpful suggestions.

(a) *Pluralism* may refer to the growing diversity in Western culture.[2] In the United States, to go no further, there is a diversity of race, heritage, religion, and value systems far beyond anything the nation has experienced before. The United States is the largest Jewish, Irish, and Swedish nation in the world; it is the second largest black nation, and soon it will become the third largest Hispanic nation. Moreover, these large proportions reveal nothing about the enormous diversity generated by countless smaller ethnic and racial communities. Many of these are growing, owing in part to contemporary patterns of immigration and to a fresh emphasis on the preservation of ethnic and cultural distinctions.

Religiously, Roman Catholicism is slightly increasing its numbers, owing primarily to the influx of Hispanics. Even so, the most rapidly growing religious movement at the moment is Islam. The most careful estimates place the number of Muslims in this country somewhere around 1.4 million. Numerous studies document the rise of new age religion and the revival of paganism. Most projections foresee that by A.D. 2000, WASPs (White, Anglo-Saxon Protestants) will be in a minority.[3] None of this was foreseen by the Founding Fathers; little of it was foreseen even forty years ago.

(b) *Pluralism* may refer, somewhat vaguely, to the value of toleration for this diversity. In this usage, when people speak of our "pluralistic society" they mean not only that our society is extraordinarily diverse but that by and large it is tolerant of the diversity, or should be.

This respect — even appeal — for pluralism crops up within many substructures of our society, not least where some would not apply it to the culture at large. For example, in a recent lecture at a meeting of the Association of Theological Schools (A.T.S.), the academic dean of a major evangelical seminary defended the virtues of pluralism in theological education. The kind of pluralism the dean had in mind dealt with the stratification of the age of faculty members in each department, the breadth of their methodologies, the virtue of complementary skills, and "cross-

---

thony, eds., *In Gods We Trust: New Patterns of Religious Pluralism in America* (New Brunswick: Transaction, 1981); Ted Peters, "Pluralism as a Theological Problem," *The Christian Century* 100 (28 Sept. 1983): 843-45.

2. David Tracy would prefer to use *plurality* for the phenomenon and *pluralism* for the perspective. He writes: "Plurality is a fact. Pluralism is one of the many possible evaluations of that fact" ("Christianity in the Wider Context: Demands and Transformations," in *Worldviews and Warrants: Plurality and Authority in Theology,* ed. William Schweiker and Per M. Anderson [New York: University Press of America, 1987], p. 2). But although a few have joined him in this usage, it is still far more common to find authors using *pluralism* in the first sense described above.

3. For some basic statistical data, see George Gallup, Jr., and Jim Castelli, *The People's Religion: American Faith in the 90s* (New York: Macmillan, 1989).

pollination of schools, mentors, theologies and ethnic/cultural/or gender perspectives."[4] But had he been pressed, this dean would also have insisted on the *limits* of the virtues of *theological* pluralism. That he could cast his paper in this way suggests his sensitivity to the buzzwords of our age; that he did not feel obliged to articulate limits may suggest the same thing.

At a different level, many voices now appeal for a kind of ecumenicity of supernaturalist "Christians" — that is, a coalition of those who believe the ancient Christian creeds, against the prevailing naturalism of modernity.[5] At many levels, such a course may prove salutary. On the other hand, to submerge centuries of faithfulness to an evangelical understanding of the gospel into an ecumenicity of Christian supernaturalism, all in the name of confronting the single specter of "modernism," may prove short-sighted. It presupposes that there is only one condition to be confronted, while both Scripture and history warn us that the gospel must often be defended on more than one front.

As a movement, evangelicalism itself is now divided over the complex questions of pluralism and tolerance. As Douglas Sweeney astutely observes:

> The strange schizophrenia of modern evangelicalism owes [much] to the increasing tension between historic evangelical ecumenism [i.e., evangelicals cooperating across denominational lines] and historic evangelical thought. Because theological modernism divided evangelicalism's ecumenical heritage, the neo-evangelicals were forced to decide between an exclusive fellowship within the harbor of historic evangelical doctrine, and historic evangelical piety on the sea of American pluralism. While the founders opted for the former, the story of the unraveling of neo-evangelical identity is the story of their scions setting out to sea.[6]

(*c*) But *pluralism* in many circles refers to a philosophical stance. This stance insists that tolerance is mandated on the ground that no current in the sea of diversity has the right to take precedence over other currents. In the religious sphere, no religion has the right to pronounce itself true and the others false. The only absolute creed is the creed of pluralism (in this third sense) itself.

4. Walter C. Kaiser, Jr., " 'Pluralism' as a Criterion for Excellence in Faculty Development," paper presented at an A.T.S. meeting on "Building Theological Faculties," 2 March 1991, p. 3.

5. See, e.g., Andrew Walker, "We Believe," *Christianity Today* 35 (29 April 1991): 25-27.

6. Sweeney, "The Essential Evangelicalism Dialectic: The Historiography of the Early Neo-Evangelical Movement and the Observer-Participant Dilemma," *Church History* 60 (1991): 84.

I am referring now not only to philosophers and to theologians who offer sophisticated defenses of universalism but to the popular mind. If you ask university students if the person who holds that all ideas are equally valid is more or less open-minded than the person who assigns different values to different ideas, most would instantly respond "More." The more sophisticated might distinguish "ideas of fact" (i.e., stemming from the so-called hard sciences) and "ideas of opinion" (stemming from everything else) — thus preserving a false but popular disjunction about which I shall say more in a moment — but would arrive at the same conclusion with respect to the latter category. The student who believes, for instance, that the Bible tells the truth is automatically considered narrow-minded.[7]

In other words, in the popular mind open-mindedness is no longer connected with a willingness to consider alternative views but with a dogmatic relativizing of all views. It no longer focuses on the virtues of rational discourse among persons of disparate beliefs, as a *means* to pursuing the truth, but on the *conclusions* of the discourse.

At a still more popular level, try to testify to what Christ has done in your life and you are likely to be asked, "What about all the people in the world who have never heard of Christ?" In some instances, of course, the question is only a smoke screen; in others it is a serious inquiry that demands a serious answer. But in every case it reflects massive built-in assumptions about the inadmissibility of any religion claiming a truth status above another religion.

(2) *At the same time, there are several startling limits to the pluralism that is now engulfing Western culture.*

The first limit is imposed by the entailment of the third definition of pluralism that we just examined. Those who are committed to the proposition that all views are equally valid have eliminated the possibility that one or more of those opinions has a special claim to being true or valid. They have foreclosed on open-mindedness in the same breath by which they extol the virtues of open-mindedness; they are dogmatic about pluralism in the third sense, and thereby banish pluralism in the second sense.

This has generated some astonishing anomalies. In the name of openness and pluralism numerous deeds of astonishing intolerance are sometimes perpetrated. Barbara Bush felt the pressure when she was invited to speak at Wellesley College. Substantial numbers of students opposed the

---

7. I use *truth* here in a strong sense, in which anything that unambiguously contradicts it must be false. If all "truth" is relative, believing the Bible speaks the "truth" is not problematic but merely one opinion among many.

invitation extended to her because she had chosen to live and work as a wife and mother rather than pursue a career external to the home and therefore more acceptable to the modern mood. At the University of Connecticut, a student can be expelled for derisive ("inappropriate") laughter. At Stanford University countless students chanted, "Hey, hey, ho, ho, Western culture's got to go." At Duke University, one student displayed political correctness in action by proclaiming in class, "I wouldn't touch Milton. I know what that guy was up to — he was a sexist through and through." One wonders if the same student would refuse to study John F. Kennedy and Martin Luther King, Jr., because they were sexually immoral. Several accrediting associations have recently displayed much more interest in upholding the dogmatisms of political correctness than in maintaining academic integrity.

The same pressures run amok in many scientific institutions. The competent and well-known science writer Forrest Mims was denied a column in *Scientific American* for no other offense than admitting to his prospective editor that he was a "non-believer in evolution." It was not that he was writing in this area, or using his articles to articulate his understanding of biology, that got him fired; it was simply that he held a view the editors judged inadmissible. As Phillip Johnson puts it:

> The Mims episode shows us that science is beset by religious fundamentalism — of two kinds. One group of fundamentalists — the Biblical creation-scientists — has been banished from mainstream science and education and has no significant influence. Another group has enormous clout in science and science education, and is prepared to use it to exclude people they consider unbelievers. The influential fundamentalists are called Darwinists.[8]

There are religious forms of political correctness as well. Four years ago, at a major seminary that often displays evangelical credentials, an acquaintance of mine with a European doctorate in New Testament studies was asked to serve as a visiting professor to lecture on the Pastoral Epistles. Sensitive to the fact that the seminary in question strongly favors the ordination of women while he does not, this young scholar decided, when he reached disputed passages such as 1 Timothy 2:8-15, to lay out as evenhandedly as possible a number of interpretations both within and outside the evangelical camp. When he came to his own view, which he labelled "traditional," such animus erupted against him that some students

8. Johnson, "Unbelievers Unwelcome in the Science Lab," *Los Angeles Times,* 3 Nov. 1990; cf. his book *Darwin on Trial* (Washington: Regnery Gateway, 1991).

complained to the administration. Some students not in his class threatened to withdraw from the seminary and ask for a tuition rebate, whereupon he was called on the carpet and criticized for listing this view as a possible interpretation, and was asked to apologize to the class for offending them. Posters started to appear around the campus announcing that he thought with his genitals. The administration then put a packet of about one hundred pages of information into every student's mailbox that defended the politically correct line.

Both the irony and the tragedy of this fierce intolerance stem from the fact that it is done in the name of tolerance. It is not "liberal education" in the best sense; it is not pluralism in the best sense. It is fundamentalistic dogmatism in the worst sense.

The second limit on pluralism is that in many ways America does not represent a lively pluralism where perspectives compete for credibility in the national discourse — a kind of tasty stew with some large lumps of meat and vegetables; rather, it represents a thin gruel with some indigestible gristle and bones. For instance, increasingly in education we aim for the lowest possible common denominator, the thin gruel. As Jewish talk-show host Dennis Prager puts it:

> Liberals are always talking about pluralism, but that is not what they mean. . . . In public school, Jews don't meet Christians. Christians don't meet Hindus. Everybody meets nothing. That is, as I explain to Jews all the time, why their children so easily inter-marry. Jews don't marry Christians. Non-Jewish Jews marry non-Christian Christians. Jews for nothing marry Christians for nothing. They get along great because they both affirm nothing. They have everything in common — nothing. That's not pluralism.[9]

Then, almost by way of reaction, various groups compensate by becoming defensive. They circle the wagons and damn the outsiders. The thin gruel becomes laced with gristle. Small wonder, then, that Stanley S. Harakas can affirm that the prevailing worldview in America is not pluralistic (at least, not in the second sense I have identified) but atomistic and anti-religious.[10]

Third, a number of recent studies have shown that, on every front, media people are on the whole farther "left"[11] in their opinions than is the

9. Cited in *Christianity Today* 35 (27 May 1991): 40.

10. Harakas, "Educating for Moral Values in a Pluralistic Society," *Greek Orthodox Review* 29 (1984): 393-99.

11. Of course, the word *left* is slippery. I use it here as a catch-all for many spheres

population at large, and this can generate an impression of a greater degree of pluralism (in all three senses!) than is in fact the case. Indeed, Peter Berger identifies an entire "new class" — namely, the "knowledge industry." This new class is "devoted to the production and distribution of what may be called symbolic knowledge," and consists of "educators (from preschool to university), the 'communicators' (in the media, in public relations, and in a miscellany of propagandistic lobbies), the therapists of all descriptions (from child analysts to geriatric sex counselors), and, last but not least, substantial elements of the bureaucracy (those elements concerned with what may be called 'lifestyle engineering') and the legal profession."[12] This new knowledge class is "generally left of center" and "stands to gain from a shift of power from business to government."[13] Religious leaders of the mainline denominations, Berger insists, have largely identified themselves with this class.

Whether or not this analysis is entirely correct, it is surely fair to conclude that the constant projection of one form or another of pluralism through the channels of education, media, entertainment, and many "people helper" groups contributes to an impression of advancing pluralism that may be slightly overrated. On the other hand, the same bombardment ensures that resistance in the populace at large is gradually eroded.

Fourth, assumptions about what "the good life" consists in have become more and more narcissistic and materialistic. In the depth of the Great Depression, President Roosevelt could say in a radio address, "Our difficulties, thank God, concern only material things."[14] It is impossible to imagine a president in the 1990s speaking the same way. Despite the continuation of some forms of civil religion, no president would publicly articulate the view that spiritual values are more important to the nation than material ones — especially when the nation is gripped by ugly depression.

On other fronts, judicial decisions have all too frequently interpreted the "wall of separation" between church and state to enforce a "hands off" policy with respect to the establishment of religion, but not with respect to its free exercise. The nation as a whole is feeling the pressure of secularization, which signals not the abolition of religion but the squeezing of

---

of discourse — e.g., politics, religion, educational theory, ethical theory — and not simply economics.

12. Berger, "Different Gospels: The Social Sources of Apostasy," in *American Apostasy: The Triumph of "Other" Gospels*, ed. Richard John Neuhaus (Grand Rapids: Eerdmans, 1989), p. 4.

13. Berger, "Different Gospels," p. 5.

14. Quoted by Senator Dan Coats in *Imprimus* 20, 9 (Sept. 1991): 1.

religion to the periphery of life and thought. As a nation we have become so individualistically self-centered[15] that even during the "conservative" eighties we did not, as in the fifties, strive to build something better for our children's tomorrow. Far from it: we borrowed from their future, demanding more security and benefits and refusing to countenance the taxes to support such demands. Belatedly, children were born into baby-boomer families that had discovered their biological clocks were ticking; but that did not mean they were more cherished. Careers and double incomes were far more important than family life. Children were parked in front of televisions for seven hours and thirty-six minutes a day; families that spent fifteen minutes talking or playing together were remarkable aberrations.

Increasingly, Christianity itself has been packaged as an agent that meets our needs, makes us feel fulfilled, and contributes to family stability. Only rarely is it presented as God's gracious self-disclosure to reconcile rebels to himself; only rarely is God's glory at the very center of the Western church's thought. While evangelicals may be encouraged by the resurgence in numbers and institutions and seminaries across the last half-century, with only rare exceptions this resurgence has played itself out against the back-drop of a national decline in spiritual values. Words and concepts precious to the Founding Fathers, and still important fifty years ago — words such as *duty, honor, valor, courage, integrity, civility* — now sound almost corny. Narcissism and materialism have very largely triumphed, even among evangelicals. And insofar as this has occurred, so far also has there been a flattening of important distinctions and a decline in the best kinds of pluralism.

(3) *The focus of tolerance has changed.*

In a relatively free and open society, the best forms of tolerance are those that are open to and tolerant of people, even when there are strong disagreements with their ideas. This toleration for people, if not always for their ideas, engenders a measure of civility in national discourse while still fostering spirited debate over the relative merits of this or that opinion. Because of the rise of the third kind of pluralism, however, tolerance in many Western societies increasingly focuses on ideas, not people.

The result of adopting this new brand of tolerance is less discussion of the merits of competing ideas — and less civility. There is less discussion

15. See Robert Bellah et al., *Habits of the Heart: Individualism and Commitment in American Life* (New York: Harper & Row, 1985). And see esp. Francis Canavan, "Pluralism and the Limits of Neutrality," in *Whose Values? The Battle for Morality in Pluralistic America*, ed. Carl Horn (Ann Arbor: Servant, 1985), pp. 153-65, who probes the point at which "pluralism" degenerates into "individualism."

because toleration of diverse ideas demands that we avoid criticizing the opinions of others; there is less civility because there is no inherent demand, in this new practice of tolerance, to be tolerant of people.

In the religious field, this means that few people will be offended by the multiplying new religions. No matter how wacky, no matter how flimsy their intellectual credentials, no matter how subjective and uncontrolled, no matter how blatantly self-centered, no matter how obviously their gods have been manufactured to foster human self-promotion, the media will treat them with fascination and even a degree of respect. But if any religion claims that in some measure other religions are wrong, a line has been crossed and resentment is immediately stirred up: pluralism (in the third sense) has been challenged. Exclusiveness is the one religious idea that cannot be tolerated. Correspondingly, *proselytism* is a dirty word.

What is sometimes forgotten is that this vision of tolerance is, at one level, akin to the view of religious tolerance in some remarkably intolerant countries. In some Muslim countries, for example, it is perfectly acceptable to *be* a Christian; but it may be illegal and is certainly dangerous to *become* a Christian.[16] What is overlooked is that genuine religious freedom necessarily includes the right to convert and to encourage others to convert. At the heart of such freedom is the assumption that ideas matter and that they must be argued out in the marketplace, and that individuals have the right to change their minds and adopt new positions even if everyone around them is convinced that their ideas are preposterous. Of course, these rights are still maintained in the United States. By and large, however, they are not cherished, for the focus of tolerance has changed. Pluralism has managed to set in place certain "rules" for playing the game of religion — rules that transcend any single religion. These rules are judged to be axiomatic. They include the following: religiously based exclusive claims must be false; what is old or traditional in religion is suspect and should probably be superseded; "sin" is a concept steeped in intolerance. The list could easily be expanded.

(4) *The constitutional separation of church and state is changing its focus.*

Most historians affirm that the United States was considerably more homogeneous, religiously speaking, in its first decades than it is now. This is not to deny that the point has been overstated by some popular conservatives. After all, in many intellectual circles in the early years of the nation, Deism was more highly prized than orthodox Christianity. And conflicts

---

16. Of course, in such countries there are no corresponding penalties for conversion the other way. The same is true, of course, in Israel.

between denominations were more intense than they are today. Even so, the Federalist Papers show that limited government was widely understood to be possible only where society was largely constrained by a moral consensus. John Adams went so far as to say that the system of government being adopted was "wholly inadequate" if that consensus did not exist. Even James Madison's remonstrance that religion flourishes best where there is no government interference did not take issue with this judgment. Madison, a Virginian, was referring to the Massachusetts Bay Colony, which until that time had operated in large measure as a theocracy; he was opposed to the intertwining of some denomination(s) with government, very much the sort of thing that characterized not only the Bay Colony but also England. He was not wrestling with the degree of religious diversity we face today. Moreover, despite occasional statements to the contrary, the virtues of a system of checks and balances were extolled, not on the grounds that unrestrained pluralism is an inherently good thing, but on the grounds that human nature is corrupt and that bad people must not be given too much power. Since we cannot be sure of thwarting bad people with good people, it is far better to introduce a structure of checks and balances so that unfettered power never falls into the hands of one person or group without the possibility of nonviolent redress.

But none of the Founding Fathers envisaged a land where various forms of Christianity coexist with Mormonism, atheism, Buddhism, Islam, and much more — a total of about 1200 separate religious bodies. Almost inevitably, the growth in religious diversity has brought with it some restrictions on free exercise. For instance, in 1878 the Supreme Court, in *Reynolds v. United States,* upheld a federal law prohibiting polygamy against a Mormon challenge, on the ground that although the right to hold religious beliefs is absolute, the state has the right to limit the practice of religion in the interest of the public good. Probably few Christians would want to see that judgment overturned on the particular issue then being examined, even though casual extension of the principle would prove extremely troubling. Moreover, the remarkable growth of government, with its intrusion into more and more spheres of a citizen's life, has contributed in no small way to the growing clash between church and state. The 1947 Supreme Court decision, written by Justice Hugo Black, that neither federal nor state governments can "pass laws which aid one religion, aid all religions or prefer one religion over another" becomes a powerful separatist tool in a society where state funds and state laws touch almost everything we do.[17]

17. Mr. Justice Black asserted (in *Everson v. Board of Education,* 1947) that the "First Amendment has erected a wall between church and state. That wall must be kept high and

Although the Court has often upheld free exercise, the challenges it faces today are extraordinarily complex. When Muslim, Buddhist, Jewish, Orthodox, Roman Catholic, liberal Protestant, evangelical, agnostic, Satanist, and atheistic children all meet together in the same classroom, it seems slightly simplistic to appeal to the intentions of the Founding Fathers to support judicial restraint. I do not want my children inculcated with the doctrines of the Qur'an; I understand why Muslim parents may not want their children taught Christian doctrines. What is perhaps more disturbing is that many schools therefore say nothing whatever about religion. Such silence is a totally irresponsible approach to the teaching of history, in which religion has often determined the shape of what took place. Worse, it establishes by default a kind of secular religion in which pluralism in the third sense is taught as a public virtue when in fact it is intellectual nihilism. The result, however unwitting, is a double standard by which an essentially secular "faith" is subsidized by the state, but no others are tolerated.[18] Though one can readily appreciate the pressures that have brought this about, surely there is something scandalous, not to say odious, about legislative and judicial decisions that make it lawful to support with government funds "art" that submerges a cross in urine, but makes it unlawful to recite the Lord's Prayer in a state-supported school.

It is not easy to see a way out of this dilemma. Nor is this essay the place to discuss, for instance, the advantages and the dangers of a voucher system in education, or, still less, the merits of the thesis that minimalist government and relative freedom cannot be sustained when moral consensus in the populace is lost. Certainly Christians need to give more thought to the shape of a desirable public policy in this complex, pluralistic society.[19] Certainly we must vigorously expose the intellectual nihilism

---

impregnable. We could not approve the slightest breach." This "impregnable wall" Black justified not on the intent of the framers of the Constitution as expressed in the Constitutional Conventions or in the state ratifying conventions, but on the experiment with religious liberty in the State of Virginia. See Daniel P. Larsen, "Justice Hugh L. Black and the 'Wall' Between Church and State: Reasons Behind the *Everson* v. *Board of Education* (1947) Decision" (M.A. thesis, Trinity Evangelical Divinity School, 1984).

18. These and related matters are ably discussed in James Davison Hunter and Os Guinness, eds., *Articles of Faith, Articles of Peace: The Religious Liberty Clauses and the American Public Philosophy* (Washington: Brookings Institute, 1991).

19. One of the few noteworthy efforts along these lines is Os Guinness's essay, "Tribespeople, Idiots or Citizens? Evangelicals, Religious Liberty and a Public Philosophy for the Public Square," in *Evangelical Affirmations*, ed. Carl F. H. Henry and Kenneth S. Kantzer (Grand Rapids: Zondervan, 1990), pp. 457-97; and the work on which it is partly based, *The Williamsburg Charter Survey on Religion and Public Life* (Washington, DC: The Williamsburg Charter Foundation, 1988).

inherent in all attempts to create a legal system with a meaningful distinction between good and evil, once God has been eliminated from the intellectual horizon.[20] Perhaps judicial decisions will be handed down that will reevaluate precisely what coercive force is in play when citizens articulate their religious convictions, whether in contexts that are touched by the almost ubiquitous hand of government or not.

One wonders at times exactly what factors unify the United States. Is it a commonly accepted scientific worldview? Is it blind faith in technology? Is it the shared vision of reality pumped out by television? Is it sports, comment on which occupies about twenty-five percent of most newspapers? Is it some combination of these? The point is that the nature of the nation's unity, or lack of it, decisively shapes the character of the espoused pluralism.

But the horizons of this essay are more limited. So far I have been concerned primarily to expose the nature of the challenges of contemporary pluralism. Since in the United States (though not in other Western nations) the evolving shape of judicial decisions compounds these challenges, they cannot be ignored. My purpose here, however, having surveyed the terrain, is not to discuss every aspect of pluralism but to reflect on a selection of Christian teachings that bear on the relations between pluralism and mission.

SOME CHRISTIAN PERSPECTIVES ON THE CHALLENGE

Each of the points in what follows could usefully be expanded into a chapter or a book. But while there would be virtue in detailed exposition of these points, there may be some value in providing a brief statement of some historical and biblical realities that Christians must recognize and even cherish as they seek to make their way through the thicket of complexities.

(1) *It is vital to remember that the challenges of pluralism are not new.* This historical reality is especially important in the light of assumptions that contemporary pluralism is so startlingly new that fair and honest treatment of it demands that we reshape traditional Christian theology.[21] But pluralism (in all three senses) is not all that new.

However much ancient Israel or even the patriarchs took over com-

20. See esp. Phillip E. Johnson, "The Modernist Impasse in Law," pp. 180-94 in this volume.

21. See, e.g., many of the essays in John Hick and Paul F. Knitter, eds., *The Myth of Christian Uniqueness: Toward a Pluralistic Theology of Religions* (Maryknoll, NY: Orbis Books, 1987).

mon religious rites and structures from the surrounding nations (circumcision, for instance, did not begin with Abraham), Yahweh's gracious self-disclosure tied those elements to his own exclusivistic claims and covenant. In pre-exilic times, Israel not only confronted the diversity of deities in the nations that surrounded her but also repeatedly wrestled with the same phenomena within her own ranks.[22] Yahweh's predictable response to religious pluralism lay behind the advice of Balaam to Balak (Rev. 2:14; cf. Num. 25). The pathetic decline during the period of the judges testified not only to the lengthening spread of time from the original redemption from Egypt but also to the attractiveness of the surrounding religious claims. During the monarchy, the ups and downs of both the southern and the northern kingdoms turned in no small part on the response of the rulers to the blandishments of pluralism. Sometimes this pluralism was akin to the second variety defined above: it was an appeal for limitless tolerance. Sometimes (if for different reasons) it promoted the crude intolerance of the third variety: Elijah's dramatic challenge at Mount Carmel was itself a response to the imperialistic claims of Baal worship increasingly imposed by royal sanction (cf. 1 Kings 18).

Of course, it might be objected that the parallels are poor, not only because the philosophical underpinnings of contemporary pluralism are far removed from that found in ancient Israel, but even more because under the old covenant the locus of the covenant people of God was a nation, and that locus had to be distinguished from the locus of the remnant. But pluralism is no less a feature with which new covenant believers must contend. The precise shape of the pluralism the church confronted doubtless varied from place to place throughout the Roman Empire, but enough is known about particular sites to give us some idea of what early Christians faced.[23] The imperial cult became increasingly important, with cities vying for the privilege of becoming *neokoros* — that is, being granted permission to build a temple to honor and worship a particular Caesar. A city like

---

22. See esp. Richard S. Hess, "Yahweh and His Asherah? Epigraphic Evidence for Religious Pluralism in Old Testament Times," in *One God One Lord in a World of Religious Pluralism*, ed. Andrew D. Clarke and Bruce W. Winter (Cambridge: Tyndale House, 1991), pp. 5-33.

23. See, among others, Bruce W. Winter, "Theological and Ethical Responses to Religious Pluralism — 1 Corinthians 8–10," *Tyndale Bulletin* 41 (1990): 210-15; David W. J. Gill, "Behind the Classical Façade: Local Religions of the Roman Empire," in *One God One Lord*, pp. 72-87; Clinton Arnold, *Ephesians: Powers and Magic* (Cambridge: Cambridge University Press, 1989); Thorsten Moritz, " 'Summing-up All Things': Religious Pluralism and Universalism in Ephesians," in *One God One Lord*, pp. 88-111; and Colin J. Hemer, *The Letters to the Seven Churches of Asia in Their Local Setting*, Journal for the Study of the New Testament — Supplement Series 11 (Sheffield: JSOT Press, 1986).

Corinth not only had temples in honor of traditional Greek deities such as Apollo and Neptune; it also boasted a sanctuary of the Egyptian gods Isis and Serapis.[24] The many mystery cults entered their own mystical appeals. The goddess Artemis, cherished not only at Ephesus but in other parts as well (e.g., in Patras in northern Peloponnesus), demanded sacrifices in which large numbers of birds and animals were burned to death, the people enraptured by the spectacle and excited by the shrieks. Such sacrifices provided large quantities of meat. The healing gods, the fertility cults, the forms of religion bordering on pantheism — all made their appeals. Despite the fact that some classicists tend to purge the Greco-Roman tradition of all that might be judged ignoble, David Gill and others have graphically shown that at the popular level the "early church was addressing people who worshipped rocks, believed plants could be deities, had sacred animals, accepted ritual castration and prostitution. In addition there were the cults that we normally associate with the Roman empire: Jupiter and the other Capitoline deities, as well as the cult of the Emperor himself."[25]

This enormous religious potpourri was pluralistic — that is, it was not a conglomeration of mutually exclusive religious groups, each damning all the others. Rather, the opinion of the overwhelming majority was that the competing religions had more or less merit to them. True, many religious adherents judged that their favored brand was best; but probably most saw no problem in participating in many religions. Indeed, the cultural and religious diversity within the Empire, enhanced by the imperial decisions to arrange "god-swaps" between the Roman pantheon and the gods favored by newly subjugated peoples, ensured that most religions made few exclusive claims. Jews were viewed as an intransigent exception. Not only could they not show what their God was like, but they were prepared to die to defend their peculiar views. The Empire therefore made a grudging exception in their case, and it extended that exception to Christians as well, at least for as long as the imperial powers thought of Christianity as a sect within Judaism. Certainly the pluralism of the Roman Empire was not driven by the engines of naturalism (though some thinkers, such as Lucretius, were philosophical naturalists). Even so, the religious world that nascent Christianity confronted was profoundly pluralistic, and from this fact two observations must be made.

First, the responses of the New Testament writers to the pluralism of their day can be applied with relative directness to the analogous pluralism of our day. Thus, against the claims of other intermediaries, Colossians

---

24. According to Pausanias 2.4.7.
25. Gill, "Behind the Classical Façade," p. 87.

insists not only on the supremacy of Christ but also on the exclusiveness of his sufficiency. While others recognize many "lords," many (pagan) baptisms, a wide variety of "hopes" (i.e., diverse visions of the *summum bonum*), Christians recognize one Lord, one faith, one baptism, one hope, and one God (Eph. 4:4-6). While some Greek philosophers opined that there was "one god," this projected deity was almost always portrayed in pantheistic terms (which is one of the prime reasons why many Greek writers could alternate between "god" and "gods" without any apparent difference in meaning). They could speak of "one god" but could not confess that "God is One." Paul insists that the one God is the God and Father of our Lord Jesus Christ, the God of creation and of the old covenant, who has supremely disclosed himself in his Son (Rom. 1; 1 Cor. 8). One cannot read Revelation 2–3 without discerning the titanic struggle the early church faced from the multifaceted pressures of pluralism. Indeed, it is surely safe to conclude that, by and large, the New Testament writers did not readily distinguish the pluralism of the day from the idolatry of the day: the destruction of the one was the destruction of the other.[26]

For the moment it is enough to recognize that in the current unraveling of Western culture we find two opposing hermeneutical effects. At one level our culture is departing from the heritage of Judeo-Christian values that so long sustained it, and so we are removing ourselves from the worldview of New Testament writers. At another level we are returning, through no virtue of our own, to something analogous to the pluralistic world the earliest Christians had to confront, and so in this sense the New Testament can be applied to us and our culture more directly than was possible fifty years ago. The fundamental difference, of course, is that the modern rush toward pluralism owes a great deal to the church's weaknesses and compromises during the past century and a half, while the church in the first century carried no such burden. Even so, we shall be less morbid and despairing if we read the Scriptures today and recognize that the challenges of pluralism are not new.

Second, the locus of the new covenant community was no longer a nation (as in the old covenant community) but a trans-national fellowship seeking to live out the new life imparted by the Spirit in a world that could not be expected to share its values. Moreover, this world, politically speaking, was not a democracy in which ordinary citizens could have much direct say in the organization and direction of the Empire. The question to

---

26. Many texts cry out for detailed exegesis, some of which I hope to undertake in a later publication, and a little of which is summarized below. Some texts that are often cited in support of a less exclusivistic stance are also briefly mentioned.

be asked, then, is this: How did the early church conceive of itself and of the outcome of the mission it undertook? In other words, what were its ecclesiology and eschatology?

Contemporary answers to this question are complex and hotly contested. I should like to address them in another venue; I shall venture a few words about them later in this essay.

(2) *Recognized or not, the doctrine of God lies at the heart of contemporary debates over pluralism.* If God is a certain kind of being, then religious pluralism in the third sense is possible, perhaps even necessary; if God is another kind of being, then religious pluralism in the third sense is not only impossible but deeply rebellious, sinful. And between these two poles one can imagine many other theologies.

Suppose God is an undefinable being who has not particularly disclosed himself (herself? itself? themselves?) in any religion, but rather is such that all religions reflect him (her? it? them?) equally and imperfectly. In this view, one cannot even say that one religion preserves more truth about God than another. Each religion is no more than one appropriate response to this undefinable God. One ends up with the thoroughgoing pluralism of, say, John Hick.[27] Never mind that it is extremely difficult to believe that every religion is equally valid and valuable,[28] from animism to Satanism to Zen Buddhism to Shi'ite Islam to the eclecticism of the Rev. Moon to medieval Roman Catholicism to the evangelicalism of the Great Awakening. On the face of things it appears as if Hick and his colleagues have adopted thoroughgoing pluralism as the ultimate good, the one non-negotiable, and have then written up a view of God that might be compatible with such a vision. From any Christian perspective, of course, such a procedure is normally called idolatry.

Suppose God is a being whose sole focus is justice. This God, we might say, is the hypostasis of justice. Then those who pursue justice are his servants, and those who are unjust are his enemies. We end up with a God who is particularly congenial to the various liberation theologies. Never mind that we have not asked whether our notions of justice have defined and domesticated this God, or whether this God in his very character, ways, and laws forms and reforms all human concepts of justice; never mind that justice in the public arena cannot easily be separated from righteousness in the private world, even though not all of those who are

27. Of Hick's many works, see esp. *God and the Universe of Faiths* (London: Macmillan, 1973); *God Has Many Names* (Philadelphia: Westminster, 1982); and *Problems of Religious Pluralism* (New York: St. Martin's Press, 1985). See also Hick, ed., *The Myth of God Incarnate* (London: SCM, 1977); and Hick and Knitter, eds., *The Myth of Christian Uniqueness.*

28. Hick does allow certain pragmatic criteria to operate (briefly mentioned below) — but not so as to vitiate his thoroughgoing pluralism.

passionate about the former are equally concerned for the latter. On the face of it, this God is concerned only with horizontal relationships; or, better expressed, horizontal relationships constitute the only valid demonstration of real connection with this God. The cross, the resurrection, and the *parousia* become appendages to our thought about this Deity, optional extras that need taming so that they will support the central vision.

Suppose God cannot be differentiated from what we commonly think of as the created order. Suppose pantheism is right: God is not a personal, transcendent being but is somehow coextensive with the universe or is its animating principle. If such pantheism is shaped one way, Buddhism becomes a live option; if shaped another way, the same could be said for some branches of Hinduism. At the popular level, Shirley Maclaine's exuberant "I am God!" becomes vaguely coherent, even if not very precise. Historic Christianity must simply be dismissed, as must all forms of monotheism that postulate the existence of a personal/transcendent Creator who existed before the universe began and who will one day judge us all. Never mind that the pantheist's God encourages — indeed, mandates — self-focus and self-fulfillment (whether of an ascetic or a hedonistic variety) at utter variance with the gospel (cf. Mark 8:34-35). Never mind that pantheism is intrinsically incapable of supporting a stable moral structure with roots beyond ourselves. On the face of it, this pantheistic brand of monotheism repeats the ancient temptation to confuse the Creator and the creation (Gen. 3:5; Rom. 1:18-25) — the foundation of all idolatry.

Suppose God is personal and in certain respects finite. Suppose that, though he may antedate time, he cannot now invariably see his way clearly through it, let alone control events in it. Whether because of some intrinsic necessity or because he has granted absolute freedom to human beings, he can neither ensure nor infallibly predict the outcome of human contingent decisions. This is the current God of Clark Pinnock;[29] it is also a God, it seems fair to say, who bears a troubling resemblance to the God of the process theologians (which is not to say, of course, that Pinnock agrees with the process theologians in every particular: for instance, unlike them, he holds to an *ex nihilo* creation by God).[30] Never mind that this God's sovereignty is so severely

29. See esp. Pinnock's essay in *Predestination and Free Will: Four Views of Divine Sovereignty,* ed. David Basinger and Randall Basinger (Downers Grove, IL: InterVarsity, 1986), pp. 141ff. It must not be thought that Pinnock's position reflects an Arminian position. Neither Arminius nor Wesley would recognize Pinnock's God.

30. One thinks of such seminal works as Alfred N. Whitehead, *Religion in the Making* (New York: Macmillan, 1926); Alfred N. Whitehead, *Process and Reality* (New York: Macmillan, 1929); Charles Hartshorne, *The Divine Relativity* (New Haven: Yale University Press, 1948); Schubert Ogden, *The Reality of God and Other Essays* (New York: Harper & Row, 1963); Ewer H. Cousins, *Process Theology* (New York: Newman, 1971); and David R. Griffin, *God,*

limited that any traditional understanding of his providence must also be jettisoned. Never mind that, while this understanding of God can be squared with many biblical texts depicting God as a personal, interrelating being, it cannot be squared with countless other biblical texts that do not hesitate to ascribe to God the most unqualified and unrelenting sovereignty.[31] On the face of it, this God squares nicely with only part of the biblical evidence, evidence that is then constructed into a grid to eliminate other biblical evidence. The cost is not only a substantial amount of evidence but also biblically mandated mystery: this God has been domesticated.

From a Christian perspective, many of these and other disparate views of God preserve some important elements of the truth. It is important, for example, to insist that God is not entirely definable; that he is passionately concerned for justice; that he is personal and interacts with his creatures in time. What is most deeply objectionable about so many of these visions of God is that they are reductionistic. Their defenders fasten on some corner of the truth and turn it into the whole, or at the very least use their corner to establish a grid that eliminates other equally important elements.

I think it can be shown that the God who has disclosed himself in the Bible is transcendent, immanent, triune, utterly sovereign, personal, holy, loving, just, and gracious. It is possible to set up a polarization such that his stern justice swamps his love and his forbearance, or the reverse; it is possible so to stress his sovereignty that we fall into mechanistic fatalism, or so to emphasize his personal relationships that we sacrifice his sovereignty. A substantial part of responsible biblical theology is learning how to tie complementary truths together. Indeed, it is arguable that compatibilism (the view that God's sovereignty and human responsibility are compatible, even if we cannot exhaustively show how this is the case) is simply an assumption of many biblical writers, an assumption that surfaces in countless texts (e.g., Gen. 50:19-20; Isa. 10:5-11; Acts 4:27-28; Rom. 9–11). Indeed, it is the post-Enlightenment drive toward human autonomy, and its elevation of reason to the level of utterly independent arbiter, that has implicitly denied biblical compatibilism and consequently constructed visions of God that progressively diminish him.

Power and Evil: A Process Theodicy (Philadelphia: Westminster, 1976). Among the more useful responses are Royce Gordon Gruenler, *The Inexhaustible God: Biblical Faith and the Challenge of Process Theism* (Grand Rapids: Baker, 1983); Ronald Nash, ed., *Process Theology* (Grand Rapids: Baker, 1987); John S. Feinberg, "Process Theology," *Evangelical Review of Theology* 14 (1990): 291-334; and the response by Rodrigo D. Tano in the same issue (pp. 335-40).

31. I have discussed some of the more important passages in my book *Divine Sovereignty and Human Responsibility* (London: Marshall, Morgan & Scott, 1981), and in *How Long, O Lord?* (Grand Rapids: Baker, 1990), chaps. 11 and 12.

But the general point to be made here is that the doctrine of God one espouses largely controls countless other areas of life and thought. It will exercise a profound impact on one's view of people and their powers, the nature of sin, the nature of the gospel, and the nature of spirituality.

How then shall we know what God is like?

(3) *Responsible discussion of pluralism cannot avoid the question of revelation.* At least some of the disparity among the visions of God just listed turns on mutually exclusive views of revelation. For example, Hick's thoroughgoing pluralism must insist that God has not revealed himself more completely in one religion than in another. Hick will not allow, for instance, the modified pluralism that insists that God has revealed himself in some measure in all religions, but most completely in Jesus Christ and the Christian Scriptures. Such modified pluralism, he argues, is finally nothing more than a sophisticated exclusivism. And of course he is correct! Inevitably that means that he must handle many Christian truth-claims, not to mention claims to exclusivism (e.g., Acts 4:12), as expendable items. The resulting Christianity is a far cry from the kind of Christianity reflected in the Bible. At what point has Christianity sacrificed its own internal integrity on the altar of Hick's pluralism?

Of course, my second and third points belong together. The kind of God Hick envisages largely governs what status Hick assigns to anything that claims to be revelation from God. Conversely, Hick's understanding of revelation, applied to the Bible, means that he cannot correct his vision of God by the revelation that God has in fact provided. What Hick does not anywhere address (so far as I know) is how he knows that God is the sort of being he postulates. Apart from the felt need to meet the demands of thoroughgoing pluralism — a criterion arbitrarily adopted because it is on the contemporary agenda — how does Hick know that God, if he exists, is of a nature to meet this felt need? He cannot claim revelation of a sort different from the revelation-claims in other religions, for to do so would destroy the pluralism he espouses. And if, *mirabile dictu,* he were to claim some sort of revelation, how could he, on his premises, establish any sort of criteria by which to assess the value of these revelation-claims over against the revelation-claims of other religions? But if he neither claims revelation nor offers criteria to validate such revelation, on what basis does he advance his position? So far as I can see, he does so only on the basis of what seems to him most reasonable *once he has already committed himself without reserve to pluralism as the* summum bonum.

The Christian's vision of God, of course, is similarly tied to his or her understanding of revelation. We might begin with the revelatory events to which the Bible bears witness: the burning bush, Sinai, the resurrection of Jesus, and much more. We might think of Jesus, the ultimate revelation (Heb. 1:1-4), the Word of God incarnate; we might think of the Scriptures themselves. Two of these forms of revelation, of course, are mediated through the third, the Scriptures. In each case, if we have high regard for the value of the revelatory claim, our picture of God is built up. For instance, if we begin with Scripture and start reading the opening lines of the Bible, we start to think of God as Creator; we learn that he is a talking God, a God who speaks; we learn that human beings are made in continuity with the rest of creation, yet distinct from the creation in that we alone are made in God's image. We learn of our accountability to God, of God's displeasure at our rebellion, of his forbearance despite our rebellion. And so we could go on, constructing our vision of God from Scripture.

Alternatively, if a believer begins with a more or less traditional Christian understanding of God, then, just as Hick's view of God shapes what he will allow in revelation, so the believer's vision of God will shape what he or she will allow in revelation. If God is a personal yet transcendent being who governs all things yet can break into his regular pattern of upholding all things to perform what we call a "miracle," we can find nothing intrinsically irrational in belief in miracles. If God has made human beings in his image (however disputed the precise meaning of this term may be), both to know God and to be known by him, there is nothing intrinsically strange in the notion of such a God accommodating himself to human speech in order to communicate with the people he has made. In other words, for both Hick and the believer, one's vision of God and one's understanding of revelation are deeply intertwined.

There is not space here to discuss the many proposals that have been put forward for evaluating such mutually exclusive visions of God, reality, and revelation — that is, for deciding which vision, if any, is superior, or is the truth by which competing visions must be judged. One can adopt, for instance, the straightforward fideism of Lesslie Newbigin,[32] the modified fideism of Paul Helm,[33] an assortment of functionalist criteria,[34] or the modified coherence theory of Harold Netland[35] — to name just a few

32. See Newbigin, *The Open Secret* (Grand Rapids: Eerdmans, 1978) and *Truth to Tell: The Gospel as Public Truth* (Grand Rapids: Eerdmans, 1991).

33. See Helm, "Faith, Evidence, and the Scriptures," in *Scripture and Truth,* ed. D. A. Carson and John D. Woodbridge (Grand Rapids: Zondervan, 1983), pp. 303-20, 411.

34. See, e.g., John Hick, "On Grading Religions," *Religious Studies* 17 (1982), reprinted in Hick, *Problems of Religious Pluralism,* pp. 67-87; and Paul F. Knitter, "Toward a Liberation Theology of Religions," in *The Myth of Christian Uniqueness,* pp. 181ff.

35. See Netland, *Dissonant Voices: Religious Pluralism and the Question of Truth* (Grand Rapids: Eerdmans, 1991), esp. pp. 180-95.

of the options. But if these extraordinarily difficult epistemological arguments cannot be probed here, at least two things must be said.

First, to allow for the existence of revelation from a personal/transcendent God, revelation that can be variously located in events, words, and even in the person of the incarnate Son, is to open up space for some important advantages. However difficult it may be to construct a religious epistemology that will prove universally satisfying in order to defend such a stance, one must not overlook the fact that once the stance is adopted (on whatever grounds) it provides some sort of ground on which to stand, various kinds of criteria by which to evaluate. Those who adopt thoroughgoing pluralism must finally insist that there are no criteria: there is no place on which to stand. Gordon Kaufman insists that "there really is no such universally human position available to us."[36] The most insightful exponents of this position understand the entailments. Thus Langdon Gilkey writes, "But [this position] has its own deep risks, and one of them is this specter of relativity, this loss of any place to stand, this elimination of the very heart of the religious as ultimate concern."[37] D. Z. Phillips is simply being consistent, then, when on these premises he is not prepared to condemn child sacrifice in some remote tribe, simply because he does not properly appreciate what such a practice might mean to that tribe.[38] Indeed, to be perfectly consistent, such a stance does not even have the right to condemn those who reject pluralism and espouse exclusivism, for to do so implies that there is a sure standard of evaluation after all. If there is no place on which to stand, we must finally abolish all distinctions between good and evil that are more than pragmatic or utilitarian. One gradually sinks either into the slough of intellectual nihilism or, more likely, into the entanglements of massive intellectual inconsistency. By contrast, the Christian, however much he or she may quarrel with others over the precise meaning and application of the revelation, cannot reasonably doubt the validity of the opposition between truth and error, between right and wrong, between good and evil — and that insight accords much better with the way people actually live their lives than with the alternatives presented by thoroughgoing pluralism.

Second, Christians foreclose on one important element in the revelation they have received when they reduce the epistemological problem to

36. Kaufman, "Religious Diversity, Historical Consciousness, and Christian Theology," in *The Myth of Christian Uniqueness,* p. 5.

37. Gilkey, "Plurality and Its Theological Implications," in *The Myth of Christian Uniqueness,* p. 44.

38. Phillips, *Faith and Philosophical Enquiry* (New York: Schocken Books, 1970), p. 237.

exclusively intellectual dimensions. That these intellectual dimensions are extremely important no one should deny; that the problem of religious epistemology has exclusively intellectual dimensions the Christian *must* deny. The alternative is to play the game only by the rules of those who deny the Christian revelation in the first place; it is to buy into the world-view that predominates in the West, the worldview that presupposes that human beings are autonomous, that human reasoning processes (as opposed to the purely mechanical relations of logic) are both reliable and morally neutral, that God, if he exists, must present his credentials to us in such a fashion that we remain the arbiters.

Christians insist that God cannot be captured, measured, weighed, manipulated, or domesticated. He transcends space and time; we are locked in space and time. We have no vantage point from which to take our determining measurements. That is one of two primary reasons why revelation is necessary. But it is the second reason that is almost never acknowledged in the wider discussion, and that is nevertheless more important. The Bible insists that we are hopelessly self-centered. In God's universe, where he alone ought to be acknowledged as both the source and the end of all his creatures, not least those made in his image, our deep self-centeredness is rebellion; it is sin. This sinfulness has so deeply warped our personalities that, although none of us is as evil as we might be, there is no part of our personality that is unaffected. Our choices, our judgments, our reasoning, our hopes, our affections — all are warped by this corrosive rebellion.

From a biblical perspective, that is why God's gracious revelation, whether general or specific,[39] is so often not seen for what it is. The light comes into the world, but people prefer the darkness to light, because their deeds are evil (John 3:19-20). According to Paul in Romans 1, God's existence and power are disclosed even in the creation, but we are so twisted that we evaluate the evidence differently and end up worshiping created things rather than the Creator. When God speaks, there will always be some who say it thundered (John 12:28-29). If we understand the message of the cross, it is because "God has revealed it to us by his Spirit" (1 Cor. 2:10) — which suggests that although God reveals himself on the stage of history in the cross and in other redemptive events, he must also reveal himself by his Spirit to individuals or they will still not take in what he has done. Thus "the spiritual man" — that is, the person who has the Spirit of God — "makes judgments about all things, but he himself is not subject to any

39. There is not space here to discuss the relevance of the distinction to the subject of pluralism. For a brief treatment, see Bruce A. Demarest, "General and Specific Revelation: Epistemological Foundations of Religious Pluralism," in *One God One Lord,* pp. 135-52.

man's judgment" (1 Cor. 2:15). The idea is not that the person with the Spirit enjoys a perfect grasp of quarks, fusion, and molecular biology, but that his or her understanding covers the sweep of human experience, including both the knowledge of the profane person and the knowledge of God. By contrast, profane persons are not in a position to stand in judgment of the person with the Spirit (however much they may protest to the contrary), since the dimension given by the Spirit of God is a closed book as far as they are concerned (1 Cor. 2:14).

This description of what takes place must not be confused with those forms of mysticism that encourage human beings to try to merge with Deity, or experience the Deity directly, with little or no consideration given to the larger questions of sin, guilt, accountability toward God, judgment, and forgiveness. The Spirit in the new covenant is tied to the cross of Jesus. Nor does this description of Christian conversion and experience provide any reasonable warrant for arrogance toward those who have not similarly known the enlightening work of the Spirit, for in the final analysis there is nothing in the believer that has attracted this work of grace. The Christian is never more than one poor beggar telling other poor beggars where there is bread. What is clear, I think, is that this account of what makes a Christian a Christian turns on an adequate understanding of the work of the Spirit and, antecedently, of the moral corruptions that ensure that human beings will simply not find God on their own.

In other words, one element of the Christian vision openly insists that part of what we claim as the basis for our knowledge of God is *not* in the public domain. We acknowledge that God has disclosed himself in powerful ways in the universe he has created and *in history* (and thus in the public domain), and supremely in his Son Jesus Christ, whom he raised from the dead — an act that takes place *in history,* the results of which were attested by hundreds of witnesses. But all human beings are so self-centered — that is, on this issue so profoundly tied to the rightness of their own opinions, to the sanctity of their right to judge, to their insistence that even religion, even God himself, be made to conform to their preferences and expectations — that apart from the work of the Spirit we will prove so blind that we will not see what God has graciously disclosed. We are, in short, dead in transgressions and sins. We are like arrogant amateurs staring at the paintings in the Louvre and offering cheap and scathing criticism of the talent that surrounds us: in this museum it is not the paintings that are being judged. So also with respect to all our learned evaluations of God, our reconstructions of his nature, our refusal to accept what he has disclosed of himself, our insistence that he meet the high standards established by our moral sensibilities (not least if they are shaped by the great god Pluralism): in reality, in this universe it is not God who is being judged. We simply condemn ourselves, for our odious self-centeredness and therefore our deep unbelief are culpable stances, however sophisticated they may be.

This, or something like it, is an essential component in any biblically faithful Christian vision. What we proclaim as God's truth is in one sense in the public domain: God has graciously disclosed himself in words and deeds, and supremely in his Son. But that very revelation leads us to believe that a further self-disclosure of God by his Spirit is necessary if our culpable blindness is to be overcome. Doubtless the Spirit often uses means, not least the means of well-argued, well-presented gospel truth. But it is not the naked truth itself, conceived exclusively in propositions and their relationships, that suffices: in that case becoming a Christian would depend more on one's I.Q. than on faith. The reality is more humbling. By God's grace we begin to see how alienated from him we are. We ask for mercy, we learn to trust him, and that very trust entails a turning aside from the self-confidence and self-centeredness that marked our lives before; in short, it entails repentance. In other words, we are saved by grace, through faith — and even that faith is finally not of ourselves; it is the gift of God.

Many Christians have engaged with unbelievers in protracted debates over the ways in which truth, not least religious truth, can be known. Some of these debates have been fruitful. For pedagogical and other reasons it may sometimes be wise to address some of the questions of religious epistemology from the perspectives of those who deny the Christian givens. But it is unwise to remain there too long; it may become a surreptitious denial of the Christian revelation, an implicit claim that we can simply argue people into the kingdom. In fact, one wonders if the classic debates between, say, evidential and presuppositional apologetics, between empiricism and fideism, would look vastly different if they were forced to butt up against a well-articulated analysis of the entailments of the fall and of biblical presentations of God's rich bounty in providing general, specific, and *personal* revelation to meet our moral and spiritual blindness.

(4) *In recent discussion, questions of revelation and truth have been sidestepped by appealing to hermeneutical realities, and this practice has become one of the most difficult features in the challenge of pluralism.*

So great has been the change in our understanding of what "hermeneutics" treats that it is sometimes hard to believe that a bare generation ago all conservative seminaries understood the subject to be the art and science by which people (the "knowers") could accurately interpret the Bible (the "known"). Indeed, two or three generations ago all Western seminaries and theological colleges adopted a similar stance.

Today almost no one does. Contemporary hermeneutics begins with the finiteness, the limited perspective, of the reader. What we ask of the text and what we are prepared to accept from the text are bound up less with the text than with us. The text does not so much speak objective things as things some particular reader perceives — things that are quite different from what some other reader perceives, and possibly quite different from what the same reader perceives on another occasion or in a few months' time. In some versions of this new hermeneutic, no meaning resides in the text; all meaning resides in the reader/interpreter of the text. Perhaps more commonly, all "interpretations" or "readings" of a text are understood to be a set of culturally conditioned projections, a coherent symbol-system that is only one of many possible symbol-systems.[40]

The older questions about the truthfulness of the text are thus neatly avoided. In postmodernism, pluralism in any case sees truth as systematic rather than absolute, but the new hermeneutic ensures that the "system" is infinitely flexible. Because of the difficulty inherent in any finite creature or culture knowing anything truly, questions about the truthfulness of the text (in an objective or absolute sense) are simply dismissed as irrelevant, out of date, and incredibly naive. Paul Griffiths and Delmas Lewis are correct when they charge that Hick believes that "religious belief . . . is . . . determined exclusively by large-scale cultural variables or small-scale psychological ones, and in any event by historical accident and not by a conscious attempt to apprehend and incarnate a true world-view. . . . [T]he apparently conflicting truth-claims which form an important part of the major religious world-views are not really in conflict because they are not really truth-claims."[41]

From this perspective one may meaningfully speak of a liberation theology hermeneutic, or a feminist hermeneutic, or a sub-Saharan black African hermeneutic, or a North Atlantic WASP hermeneutic. At no point, however, does this perspective afford us any vantage point from which to assess these diverse hermeneutical stances and their results. The only useful criteria are purely pragmatic.

It is important to recognize that this approach to interpretation dominates not only biblical study but almost all of the humanities. Law, economics, literature, history, sociology, political science, anthropology, and much more — all are struggling with the uncontrolled relativism that invades each discipline where this new hermeneutic has intruded.

40. Consider the title of a recent and important book by Charles Mabee, *Reading Sacred Texts through American Eyes: Biblical Interpretation and Cultural Critique,* Studies in American Biblical Hermeneutics, 7 (Macon: Mercer University Press, 1991).

41. Griffiths and Lewis, "On Grading Religions, Seeking Truth, and Being Nice to People — A Reply to Professor Hick," *Religious Studies* 19 (1983): 76, 78.

The problem is compounded by the dichotomy still commonly drawn by the lowly undergraduate and by the person on the street — the dichotomy between the "facts" of science and the "opinions" of all other disciplines. This dichotomy has seemed so absolute and so unfair to many Christian observers that they have invested not a little energy in breaking it down. Science itself, they say, depends on paradigms, models, inferences — and exactly the same thing is true of biblical religion. Their aim in arguing this way is to bolster the credibility of Christianity's truth-claims, or at least get them onto the agenda for discussion, by showing that in many ways religion and science deploy similar techniques in the formation and modification of "doctrine."[42]

But the thoroughgoing pluralists are unmoved. If the work of the "hard" sciences is parasitic on paradigms that can shift with time,[43] however complex those shifts might be,[44] then the degree of subjectivity inherent in these phenomena only confirms the pluralists' point. Thus Paul Knitter insists that today "truth is no longer defined according to the Aristotelian notion of science: 'certain knowledge through causes.' Rather, 'modern science is not true; it is only on the way towards truth.' . . . On the personal level, truth is no longer seen as the pursuit of certainty but as the pursuit of understanding — ever greater understanding. This means that all 'true understanding' will be open to change and revision."[45] It comes as no surprise that he criticizes the law of noncontradiction. Truth should be seen as relational: "what is true will reveal itself mainly by its ability to relate to other expressions of truth and to grow through these relationships."[46]

We must not delude ourselves into thinking that this outlook on the world belongs exclusively to the intelligentsia. When presented with the statement "There is no such thing as absolute truth; different people can define truth in conflicting ways and still be correct," twenty-eight percent

42. So, e.g., several chapters of Lesslie Newbigin's thoughtful book *The Gospel in a Pluralist Society* (Grand Rapids: Eerdmans, 1989). See also the generally excellent work of Earl R. MacCormac, *Metaphor and Myth in Science and Religion* (Durham, NC: Duke University Press, 1976).

43. The idea became much more widely spread with the publication of Thomas Kuhn, *The Structure of Scientific Revolutions*, 2d ed. (Chicago: University of Chicago Press, 1970).

44. See the important qualifications introduced in Frederick Suppe, ed., *The Structure of Scientific Theories*, 2d ed. (Urbana: University of Illinois Press, 1977); and Gary Gutting, ed., *Paradigms and Revolutions: Applications and Appraisals of Thomas Kuhn's Philosophy of Science* (Notre Dame: University of Notre Dame Press, 1980).

45. Knitter, *No Other Name? A Critical Survey of Christian Attitudes toward the World Religions* (Maryknoll, NY: Orbis Books, 1985), p. 32.

46. Knitter, *No Other Name?* p. 219.

of the American populace agree strongly, while a further thirty-nine percent agree somewhat — a total of sixty-seven percent, over against only twenty-nine percent who disagree somewhat or disagree strongly (five percent indicated "don't know").[47] Even if we allow that the test statement is a bit loose (the second half might be thought by some to allow for discrepancy at the merely linguistic level), the results demonstrate the scale of the problem that Christian witness must confront.

How are we to think our way through the new hermeneutic? At the risk of oversimplification, one can discern two positions at opposite ends of the spectrum of hermeneutical options.

At one end of the hermeneutical spectrum stands the position ably represented by David Tracy.[48] To the pluralism of the present religious context, he responds with a *hermeneutical* pluralism. The truth-claims of various religions, and of various traditions within each religion, do not drive him to radical deconstructionism. He argues that one of the faults of post-Kantian modernity is precisely the drive to elevate human reason above the entangling constraints of tradition. This, he says, cannot be done: *every* act of understanding is *necessarily* an interpretation. There are no "brute" facts. Even the language we use is colored by culture; it is part of our culture and therefore part of our tradition. Tracy's advocacy of hermeneutical pluralism thus makes a virtue of what he perceives to be a necessity. Multiple interpretations of even the Christian heritage, let alone of world religions, are inevitable; Tracy declares them desirable, and he attempts to delineate what responsible, moral, and authentic hermeneutical options should look like.

The work of Tracy and his followers is in some respects a welcome relief from modernism, with its perpetual assumption of the independence and reliability of human reasoning. What is disappointing is that Tracy's focus is so constantly and narrowly hermeneutical that he never deeply addresses the possibility of revelation that is simultaneously true and culturally encoded. He has not, so far as I am aware, wrestled with a traditional

---

47. George Barna, *The Barna Report: What Americans Believe* (Ventura: Regal, 1991), pp. 83-85.

48. Since 1968 Tracy has written eight books and many articles. For the purposes of this article, his most important books are these: *Blessed Rage for Order: The New Pluralism in Theology* (New York: Seabury, 1975); *The Analogical Imagination: Christian Theology and the Culture of Pluralism* (New York: Crossroad, 1981); (with John Cobb) *Talking About God: Doing Theology in the Context of Modern Pluralism* (New York: Seabury, 1983); *Plurality and Ambiguity* (San Francisco: Harper & Row, 1987); and *Dialogue with the Other: The Inter-Religious Dialogue* (Louvain: Peeters/Grand Rapids: Eerdmans, 1990). The most important (sympathetic) evaluation of Tracy's work is found in Werner G. Jeanrond and Jennifer L. Rike, eds., *Radical Pluralism and Truth: David Tracy and the Hermeneutics of Religion* (New York: Crossroad, 1991).

(and biblical) presentation of revelation articulated to meet postcritical and postmodern objections. No less seriously, although he thinks he has avoided the pitfalls of deconstructionism by advocating hermeneutical pluralism, it is difficult to see how he can avoid an equivalent intellectual nihilism. To talk about responsible, moral, and authentic hermeneutical options sounds reassuring, but in Tracy's thought all three adjectives are necessarily tied exclusively to individual or cultural subjectivity. His concern that we intelligently practice a "hermeneutics of suspicion and retrieval" so that we learn to criticize our own tradition, and thus avoid merely being locked in it, presupposes a set of criteria by which we pick and choose. But by his own thesis, the choice of such criteria cannot be other than interpretive acts, reflecting a different set of human, cultural pressures and traditions (including reactions against them). Despite the high-flown language of Tracy's moral concerns, I do not see how he avoids the radically arbitrary.[49]

The other end of the hermeneutical spectrum might be represented by William J. Larkin.[50] Larkin ably chronicles the change from modernism to postmodernism and powerfully depicts the epistemological quagmire into which we have flung ourselves. He argues that Christians must recognize that we possess in Scripture a transcendent stance that is *above* or *outside* culture, and we must use that stance to shape our questions, to form our perceptions of reality, and to establish our methods.

Before attempting to evaluate Larkin's work, it will be useful to reflect on another point along the spectrum. This stance has few theoretical proponents but many practitioners. It is perhaps best represented by Charles H. Kraft.[51] Despite many anthropological insights of great value in his work, his approach to Scripture is perhaps what is most startling in his work. He treats the Bible as a casebook, in which different narratives or passages might reasonably be applied to one particular culture but not to another. Thus if Christianity begins to exert influence in a polygamous African culture, the appropriate "case" might be Abraham or David (his example). When pressed to ask if there is anything at all in the Bible that is normative and unyielding and applicable in every culture, Kraft responds that there are some basic Christian nonnegotiables that transcend culture: "Jesus is Lord," for instance, and a number of other foundational confessions.

---

49. In fairness to Tracy, he tries to avoid this pitfall by deemphasizing the individual and by stressing the importance of the community and its traditions. But this decision itself, it appears, is arbitrary. Communities and traditions can embrace barbaric cruelty.

50. See esp. Larkin's book *Culture and Biblical Hermeneutics: Interpreting and Applying the Authoritative Word in a Relativistic Age* (Grand Rapids: Baker, 1988).

51. See Kraft, *Christianity in Culture: A Study in Dynamic Biblical Theologizing in Cross-Cultural Perspective* (Maryknoll, NY: Orbis Books, 1980).

As I have discussed Kraft's work at length elsewhere,[52] I shall not repeat myself here. In brief, however, it appears as if Kraft's reliance on contemporary hermeneutics has simultaneously gone too far and not far enough. It has gone too far in that by treating the Bible as a casebook he does not ask how the pieces fit together. Indeed, he necessarily assumes that they do not. Basic questions must then be asked about what the Bible is and how we are to read it (see below). But he does not go far enough in that he fails to recognize that even basic statements such as "Jesus is Lord" are in certain respects culturally conditioned. The statement, for a start, is in English, and all language is culturally constrained. "Jesus" is not an entirely unambiguous proper noun: are we referring to the Jesus of the Mormons, the Jesus of the Jehovah's Witnesses, the Jesus of liberal Protestantism, the Jesus of orthodox Christianity? One could raise similar questions about "is" and "Lord." Translate the expression into Thai and utter it in a Buddhist temple in Thailand, and it will be taken to mean that this Jesus, whoever he is, is inferior to Gautama the Buddha, of whom nothing can be predicated — the highest state of exaltation.

I am not saying that the truth of what orthodox Christians mean when they confess "Jesus is Lord" cannot be expressed in Thai. Rather, I am saying that not only because of differing linguistic conventions but even more because of divergent worldviews the expression of this truth to a Thai-speaking Buddhist requires some care, and it may demand the construction of a biblical worldview to ensure that the confession is rightly understood.[53]

But this example enables us to see that even on an orthodox under-standing of the Bible as divine, authoritative revelation, it is not for that reason entirely outside culture. The Bible was written in human languages. Frequently it specifically adopts or presupposes the human conventions of some society. It customarily addresses concrete historical situations about which our knowledge is fragmentary. But it will not do to conclude that the authority of the Bible is thereby hopelessly compromised. In historic Protestantism it was common to speak of the doctrine of accommodation — the manner in which God accommodated himself to human language and culture in order to communicate with human beings in categories they could take in. In one sense, the ultimate "accommodation" is the incarna-tion: that is one reason why theologians have often drawn attention to the parallels between the Word written and the Word incarnate (though there

---

52. See my essay "Church and Mission: Reflections on Contextualization and the Third Horizon," in *The Church in the Bible and the World*, ed. D. A. Carson (Exeter: Paternoster/Grand Rapids: Baker, 1987), pp. 213-57, esp. 242ff.

53. Kraft himself would deny that there is such a thing as a "biblical worldview."

are also profound differences). What is needed today is an updating of the doctrine of accommodation to address contemporary problems without jettisoning the revelation that God has graciously given.

It is perhaps at this point that Larkin has opened himself up to some criticism. I am not saying that he would necessarily disagree with the points just articulated. Rather, it is his lack of discussion of such matters that will draw fire and perhaps lead, in some circles, to an unnecessarily hostile readership. Of course, many reject his work entirely, since they have long since abandoned any place in their thought for authoritative revelation, especially propositional revelation. But some find fault with Larkin for not exploring in greater detail the manner in which the Bible is simultaneously authoritative — God's Word written (and thus in certain respects beyond or outside any one cultural framework) — and a word accommodated to several concrete historical cultures.

Once again, it is impossible to plow new furrows here. But Christians will want to argue, surely, that it is the transcendent/personal God who guarantees the truthfulness of what he says, even if he casts what he says in human speech; that all of his revelation coheres, precisely because it is his; that human attempts to read and understand that revelation, though they are doomed to fall short of perfect understanding, are not doomed to utter subjectivity or even solipsism. Various hermeneutical models have been put forth: instead of a hermeneutical circle, one may conjure up a hermeneutical spiral in which readers cycle closer and closer into the meaning of the text. Or one may approach such meaning asymptotically (a useful mathematical model), fuse the horizon of one's understanding with the horizon of understanding presupposed by the author (as revealed in the text), or, less technically, admit that while we might not understand perfectly there is no necessary impediment to understanding truly. After all, unless contemporary pluralists think they are merely playing cynical word games, they expect to be (more or less) understood by their readers when they argue for their positions. Cannot they allot the same courtesy to, say, Paul, while recognizing that the task of understanding what he has written must cross additional barriers of time, language, and culture?

There are one or two benefits that have come from this revolution in hermeneutics, but I shall reserve them for my concluding reflections.

(5) *An adequate response to pluralism (in the third sense) must work outward from a profound and deepening grasp of the Bible's entire story line.*[54]

---

54. I use the term *story line* not to cast doubt on the truthfulness of the Bible's witness as to what took place in history, but because alternative expressions — *plot, salvation-history, history, narrative* — cast up their own connotations of doubtful usefulness for my purposes.

There was a time when Christian witness in this country rested primarily on calling people back to what they already knew and on living a life in conformity with that call. Even where the basics of the gospel had to be rearticulated, such proclamation took place against the backdrop of a populace that was basically familiar with the Bible's story and theology.

No longer. Even Christian witness to the churched can no longer assume very much. How much less may we legitimately assume when we announce the good news to the unchurched?

What this means is that we must begin farther back. Christian witness becomes more and more a matter of confronting a bewildering variety of worldviews with the Bible's story and with the gospel as its crowning point. We cannot afford to advance piecemeal. If we try, we shall lose ground piecemeal. Worse, we shall not even be understood.

There is not space here to sketch in the Bible's story and show the importance of each turning point to the challenge of pluralism. One or two points were suggested above when we reflected on disparate visions of God and on the nature of human evil. But there are many other points.

We may begin with the creation and fall. The Bible insists that human beings are important (because they were made in God's image) but rebellious. The contemporary mood declares that we are unimportant but not evil; we are the chance conglomerations of atoms and molecules, the statistically unlikely product of the primordial ooze. These competing visions cannot be assigned to debates over origins and left there as if they are irrelevant to other subjects. Unless the biblical perspective on this matter of origins is accepted, the nature of our dilemma will not be perceived, and therefore the gospel that purports to address the human dilemma will not be understood. Our fundamental problem is not loneliness, alienation from other human beings, lack of fulfillment, materialism, poverty, corrupt government, or ecological malfeasance. All of these things are deep problems; they constitute part of the human dilemma; they must be addressed. Thank God, Christians are among many others who seek to address them. But the root problem behind all problems is rebellion against God. The most desperately needed solution is reconciliation to God.

Suppose someone were to say that this is nothing but privatized religion — that the Bible itself preserves the gospel according to Amos, a message of social reform. How should we evaluate this counterclaim? It is of course far too easy to assume a veneer of religious respectability. But reconciliation to God, according to the Scriptures, is never so glib. Whether according to Amos or Paul, the concern to do what is right is motivated and empowered by a right relation with the personal/transcendent God who is passionately concerned about justice. But both Amos and Paul are part of the Bible's story line. One cannot take a bit of Amos and eschew Paul because we find the former a little more congenial to our current tastes. And when we ask how Amos, say, is treated in later revelation (see, e.g., Acts 15), we find links to the righteous kingdom that the resurrected Jesus was inaugurating. The prophets as a whole treat social injustice as part and parcel of the rebellion against God. They are not so foolish as to think that social justice can be achieved apart from reconciliation to God. In other words, an appropriate evaluation of the counterclaim is possible only by reexamining Amos and related themes within the Bible's story line.

We might turn to the giving of the law. God discloses himself as the God who makes demands, who defines what is right and wrong for his people. But because we are reading each part of the Bible in the light of the whole, we cannot help but reflect on how Leviticus is related to the Epistle to the Hebrews. We think through what was being taught by the various sacrificial systems mandated under the old covenant, and we think through their fulfillment in the sacrifice of Christ Jesus himself. We learn what the conditions of reconciliation to God entail. We begin to understand the place of Christ Jesus within God's redemptive purposes and plan.

So far I have said nothing about the Abrahamic covenant, the Wisdom literature, or the Gospels. I have not here reflected very much on the nature of the church: her responsibility to live in this world, but not be of it; her mandates, responsibilities, and privileges; and her relations with the wider world. Moreover, we might follow the Bible's story line to its end and reflect on biblical eschatology. There we learn of God's great forbearance now and of the certainty of the judgment to come. We must face death and afterlife, and we must live in the prospect of a complete accounting before a sovereign and infallible God. We learn to live in the light of a new heaven and a new earth to which some are admitted and from which some are shut out. We discover the ways in which the church is to serve even now as an outpost of the new heaven and the new earth.

All of these elements, and more besides, constitute the Bible's story line. Together they establish what the gospel is, that from which we are saved, the nature of the One to whom we must give an account, the relative importance of this world and the next so far as the focus of our hopes and investments is concerned, the desperate plight in which we find ourselves as we reject the grace of God, the wonders of God's grace along with the ineffable brilliance of his holiness, and much more.

Now if this entire vision is set over against the competing visions of the pluralists (in the third sense), we immediately discover that the issues dividing Christian from pluralist are not merely epistemological, or christological, or reducible to any simple set of points. An entire vision of reality is at stake. Moreover, the pluralist, seeking to give an account of the world, must explain the Christian, and will doubtless conclude that the Christian is too tightly bound by tradition, naive in the area of epistemology, intolerant of other views, and so forth. The Christian response, while striving to address the pluralist's agenda in a responsible fashion, must also articulate how the pluralist will be perceived in the Christian's worldview. The pluralist is an idolator, worshiping the created world more than the Creator. He or she so relativizes God's truth that God's own Son becomes an incidental on the religious landscape, and his sacrificial death and miraculous resurrection become insignificant and unbelievable respectively. Pluralists are inconsistent in that they want to be understood univocally while insisting that ancient authors, let alone God himself, cannot be. They may have many religious experiences, but none of them deals with the heart of the human problem, the sin that is so deeply a part of our nature. In short, we must deal with massively clashing worldviews, and part of our responsibility is to explain competing worldviews from our vantage point. We cannot possibly engage at that level unless we ourselves have thoroughly grasped the biblical story line and its entailed theology.

In exactly the same way, the various forms of universalism cannot be responsibly addressed from a Christian perspective unless they are placed within the context of the Bible's story line. One thinks of the absolute universalism of Hans Urs von Balthasar[55] or of Peggy Starkey,[56] in which expressions such as "all things are yours" (1 Cor. 3:21) or "reconcile to himself all things" (Col. 1:20) or "new humanity" (Eph. 2:15, NRSV) are lifted out of their contexts and given enormous and independent weight, while exclusivistic texts are whittled away. One also thinks of the qualified universalism of Neal Punt,[57] of the post–Vatican II strugglings with pluralism and the theory of the anonymous Christian,[58] of assorted evangelical attempts to assign saving virtue to what is traditionally called "general revelation."[59] One also thinks of recent attempts to treat the old covenant

---

55. See, e.g., Balthasar's *Truth Is Symphonic: Aspects of Christian Pluralism* (San Francisco: Ignatius, 1987).

56. Starkey, "Biblical Faith and the Challenge of Religious Pluralism," *International Review of Mission* 71 (1982).

57. Punt, *Unconditional Good News* (Grand Rapids: Eerdmans, 1980).

58. Perhaps the best recent treatment of this difficult subject is that of David Wright, "The Watershed of Vatican II: Catholic Attitudes Towards Other Religions," in *One God One Lord*, pp. 153-71.

59. One thinks, for instance, of the quite different attempts of Peter Cotterell, *Mission*

and the new covenant as alternative routes to salvation[60] (even though Paul is reported to have said, "I have declared to both Jews and Greeks that they must turn to God in repentance and have faith in our Lord Jesus" [Acts 20:21]). In each case, the issue is the same: the nature of the "good news," and its relation to the Bible's story line.

Christian efforts to expound that story line, that biblical theology, and apply it to modern settings must be undertaken with both humility and boldness: with humility because an essential part of our beliefs is that we too were "dead in [our] transgressions and sins" and "like the rest . . . objects of wrath" (Eph. 2:1, 3), and if we have been reconciled to God, it says much about his great grace, and nothing about our wisdom or goodness; and with boldness because, with Paul, we hold that we are debtors to all, and we cannot envisage that that truth which has been graciously given, both in the public arena of history and in the private watch of transformed experience — truth given by the self-disclosing, personal/transcendent, Trinitarian God of Christian monotheism — is of merely idiosyncratic relevance.

CONCLUDING REFLECTIONS

Although much of this essay has focused on the challenges cast up by pluralism (in the third sense), I have hinted now and then that there are also some advantages. In a few concluding lines I would like briefly to highlight some of them.

First, even though many of the reasons why we have fallen into this state are bad, if we listen attentively to the New Testament we will discover that thoughtful application of the gospel to us and to our society now becomes more immediate and powerful, precisely because our society is

---

and Meaninglessness (London: SPCK, 1990), and of Clark H. Pinnock, "Toward an Evangelical Theology of Religions," *Journal of the Evangelical Theological Society* 33 (1990). A preliminary response is found in Demarest, "General and Specific Revelations." See also Ajith Fernando, *The Christian's Attitude Toward World Religions* (Wheaton: Tyndale, 1987).

60. See, e.g., Norbert Lohfink, *The Covenant Never Revoked: Biblical Reflections on Christian-Jewish Dialogue* (New York: Paulist, 1991); Michael Shermis and Arthur E. Zannoni, eds., *Introduction to Jewish-Christian Relations* (New York: Paulist, 1991); and Michael Goldberg, *Jews and Christians: Getting our Stories Straight* (Nashville: Abingdon Press, 1985). For an evangelical variation on Jewish-Christian dialogue, see esp. Marc H. Tannenbaum, Marvin R. Wilson, and A. James Rudin, eds., *Evangelicals and Jews in Conversation on Scripture, Theology, and History* (Grand Rapids: Baker, 1978); A. James Rudin and Marvin R. Wilson, *A Time to Speak: The Evangelical-Jewish Encounter* (Grand Rapids: Eerdmans, 1987); and Marvin R. Wilson, *Our Father Abraham: Jewish Roots of the Christian Faith* (Grand Rapids: Eerdmans, 1989).

approaching the pluralism of the Roman Empire in the first century. This point has already been made.

Second, another face of pluralism (in all three senses) is "globalization." The phenomenal communications abilities we possess today, and the increasingly complex ways in which nations and peoples make an impact on other nations and peoples, ensure that more and more people think of the world as a "global village." Recognition of this reality can help the church to think globally — as in any case we ought to. We have moved, in missionary circles, from colonialism to anti-colonialism to globalization.[61] To take but one example: we can no longer think of the Western nations as missionary-sending nations and of all other nations as missionary-receiving nations. As more and more so-called Third-World nations send out missionaries, missiologists estimate that the number of such people will exceed 162,000 by the year 2000 — far more than all those sent out by churches in the West. Christian outreach is becoming a truly international enterprise, and that is for the good. Among the desirable effects will be the reduction of the triumphalism and condescension that has often crippled Western Christianity.

Third, in the light of the forces of globalization, there is at least some prospect of a cross-fertilization of biblical theology from culture to culture. There are substantial lessons to be learned from the new hermeneutic. This is not to allow the absolute relativizing of all of the Bible's truth-claims. Rather, as, for example, the sub-Saharan black African church develops leaders, so also will it produce people who articulate biblical theology within an African context. If the Bible is the "given," such theologies will overlap at countless points with the theologies of the West where the Bible is held in similar reverence — theologies with which we are more familiar. But they are also likely to diverge at some points. For instance, they will be far more sensitive to corporate metaphors and realities, since as a culture (or group of cultures) they are far less prone to raw individualism. They are also likely to be more sensitive to the biblical descriptions of the spirit world. Genuine exchanges and mutual correction among leaders who hold a high view of Scripture but who work and labor in highly diverse contexts should prove enriching to the entire church of God.

Finally, if we keep our heads and do not capsize the bark in the churning sea of pluralism, the experience may actually help us to understand the truth of the gospel more clearly. It is a commonplace of historical theology that sophisticated denial of some area of Christian truth is often

---

61. See Paul Hiebert, "Beyond Anti-Colonialism to Globalism," *Missiology* 19 (1991): 263-81.

the means by which the church achieves greater precision and understanding in that area of truth. Precisely because pluralism has generated so many forms of rejection of the gospel, there is at least the opportunity to think through many basic issues with a degree of clarity that might not otherwise be possible. This is especially true in the areas of evangelism and mission.

Whether we actually move in this direction, of course, or sell our biblical heritage for a mess of pluralist pottage, is something that remains to be seen. May God have mercy on us.

Eschatology: The Meaning of the End

GEOFFREY W. BROMILEY

I. COMMON THEMES

THE THEMES of eschatology all have direct cultural relevance. No culture, for example, can evade death (cf. Gen. 3:3; Ps. 90; Rom. 5:12) or attempts to explain and handle it. Even highly secularized societies necessarily retain rites of burial and forms of commemoration. Even the most this-worldly philosophies wrestle unavoidably with the fact that sooner or later we no longer have life in this world. Even the least religiously oriented culture must face the hard question: Why does human life have to end in death? What then, if any, is the meaning of all our striving, struggling, and suffering? Is there perhaps some form of immortality, if only in the memory of others or in the contribution we make to the ongoing (but hardly permanent) existence of the race?

The Christian hope of Christ's return (Mark 13:26; 1 Thess. 1:10; etc.), remote and fanciful as it might appear to non-Christians, also has direct cultural pertinence. Societies and cultures run up against the problem of destiny that is also the problem of destination. What is the goal of humanity, or of our specific portion of it? Where are we finally heading even here on earth? Does the race have a goal? Individuals might live for purely selfish ends, for self-aggrandizement or self-gratification. But cultures also take into account the larger question of orientation, direction, and purpose to which Christianity supplies the answer of the coming and the kingdom.

The ultimate answer of Christian eschatology — the new heaven and the new earth (Isa. 65:17; Rev. 21:10) — reaches beyond the present order.

At this point, too, a certain link exists with many cultures. Certainly secularized cultures show little concern for transcendent goals. Even they, however, cannot wholly eliminate the question whether a final goal might not lie beyond the horizon of earth or the present cosmos. A culture suffers terrible poverty in its thinking, art, music, literature, religion, practice, and mores if it does not at least grope after the concept or hope of a transcendent consummation.

The conviction that such a consummation also means judgment (Acts 17:31, etc.) touches again on something basic to almost every culture. Opinions of right and wrong may vary. They may be viewed as relative. Nevertheless a moral sense, however diffuse, forms an integral part of human life in society. The moral sense cries out for justice. Law and legal systems of various kinds have a necessary place in culture. Insofar as human justice functions only imperfectly and impermanently, however, the demand arises for a more equitable and definitive judgment. In this regard some might look to legal progress, perhaps at the international level. Others might set their hopes on the immanent judgment of history: "Die Weltgeschichte ist das Weltgericht" (Schiller). Christians proclaim the last judgment. The answers differ, but they are answers to a similar question.

Separating good and evil (cf. Matt. 25:31-46; 1 Thess. 1:9; etc.) constitutes, perhaps, a more disputed issue. Secular cultures today presuppose the final annihilation of both the good and the bad. Sentimentalists presuppose the one destiny of reconciliation. Yet societies and cultures of all kinds show no hesitation in making temporal separation. Wrongdoers run the risk of incarceration, banishment, social exclusion, economic ostracism, even execution. If the final separation of heaven and hell sounds a harsher note, cultures can understand the rationale. A primary human aim is a society free from crime, violence, oppression, and fear. It cannot achieve this goal so long as it permits some to terrorize others by crime, violence, or oppression. If it cannot restrain such people, it has to separate them. By a final separation God himself achieves the goal that human cultures set themselves and in their own ways seek to attain. At this point again culture and eschatology share a common theme.

The ultimate consummation in Christian eschatology involves the kingdom of God, the definitive establishment of the divine reign of peace and righteousness (cf. 1 Cor. 15:24-28; Rev. 11:15). At this point, too, the connection with human culture is plain. In the broad sense culture involves attempts at an ordering of human affairs that brings tranquility and prosperity. In the political sphere various systems ranging from anarchy at the one pole to dictatorship at the other have found supporters in both academic writing and practical action. Even theocracy, an attempted human actualization of divine government, has put its stamp on human society, often with less than happy results. Eschatology offers the divine answer to the question that cultures also seek to answer, whether at the political level of government or at the more general level of standardized forms of conduct.

The element of realized eschatology (cf. Luke 17:21; John 3:18-21) might seem to confront us with a more specifically Christian concept, for the claim that God's kingdom has come proleptically in Jesus Christ is a unique claim. Yet here again, if relatively rather than absolutely, human cultures do in fact posit more or less definitive turning points or achievements in human history, and in many cases they even associate them with specific individuals. Until the eighteenth century, did not classical antiquity serve as an artistic norm for western Europe? Do not revolutions try to introduce new datings to stress their decisive role in initiating a new order? Did not Hegel see in the Prussian state an attainment of the goal of history? Part of the cultural enterprise, it would seem, is to achieve or discern a supreme turning point when the old passes away and things are made new. Thus far there is affinity between realized eschatology and culture.

II. TENSIONS

Christian eschatology and culture deal with common themes, but their different approaches and answers quickly bring them into tension and even open opposition. Either explicitly or implicitly, eschatology confronts every culture with new thinking, and the culture responds either by resisting the thinking, by developing its own variations upon it, or by offering alternatives.

Tension emerged at once as Christian eschatology, rooted in the Old Testament and Judaism, invaded the Hellenistic world of the far-flung Roman Empire. For instance, the idea of moving toward the goal of divine consummation clashed with the cyclical view of eternal return or recurrence that prevailed in many quarters.[1] Christianity recognizes that there may be nothing new under the sun (Eccl. 1:9), for human nature changes little, but it does not see an endless repetition of events or patterns or cycles. It posits a history that begins in creation, has its center in Jesus Christ, and reaches its goal in the kingdom of God. It proclaims the history of God's dealings with humanity and the world. Acceptance of Christianity meant abandonment of a basic cultural presupposition with all its implications for art and thought and conduct.

1. See Mircea Eliade, *The Myth of the Eternal Return* (New York: Pantheon Books, 1954).

Tension took an even sharper form as the eschatological hope of the resurrection of the body came into contact with the Hellenistic distinction or separation of body and soul. A common Hellenistic metaphor described the body as the prison of the soul.[2] Immortality, then, could include only the survival of the soul apart from the body. The intensity of the conflict may be seen from the attempts of Gnostics and Marcionites to bring this line of thinking into Christian circles with their urging that matter is bad, that the true God cannot have created it, that Jesus came from the true God, that he took only the appearance of a body, and that his saving work was to liberate the exiled soul from the body and to restore it to its true home.[3] An ascetic life-style — or in some cases a licentious life-style[4] — corresponded to these notions. Against them the church clung to its doctrine of creation — "I believe in God the Father Almighty, Maker of heaven and earth" — and also to its eschatology: "In the resurrection of the body, and the life everlasting."[5] Not always with equal success, it resisted the implied asceticism. A whole new perspective on bodily life and its significance came into the cultural world of Hellenism with Christian eschatology, though Christians themselves would often fail to give this full or fitting cultural expression.

Along similar lines tension arose regarding the future of the created earth. Early Christian premillennialism, which looked ahead to a reign of peace that would also give the earth its originally intended beauty and fruitfulness,[6] was plainly incompatible with the doctrine that a bungling demiurge created this world and that God has no purpose for it. Later postmillennialism would not, perhaps, bring out the contrast so sharply, yet here again the earth comes within the purview of the divine purpose. Even amillennialism includes a new earth as well as the resurrection of the body in its final scenario. Cultures that involve an attempted spiritualizing of human life and destiny to the exclusion of the earth quickly collide with gospel eschatology, both at the theoretical level and in their practical ramifications.

Eschatology naturally cuts across the concept of the transmigration of souls, which had an appeal in the Greek and Hellenistic world[7] as it did,

---

2. See Eduard Schweizer, "σῶμα . . . ," in *Theological Dictionary of the New Testament*, 9 vols., ed. Gerhard Kittel and Gerhard Friedrich, trans. Geoffrey W. Bromiley (Grand Rapids: Eerdmans, 1964-74), 7:1025ff.

3. Irenaeus *Adv. Haer.* 1.1ff.; Tertullian *Against Marcion.*

4. Irenaeus *Adv. Haer.* 1.1.11-12.

5. Irenaeus *Adv. Haer.* 5.2.1-2.

6. See Eusebius *H.E.* 3.39 on Papias.

7. See Mircea Eliade, citing Empedocles in *Death, Afterlife and Eschatology* (New York: Harper & Row, 1967), p. 57.

and still does, over a broader religious spectrum, and which can have considerable cultural impact. On the Christian view, God gives only the one life on earth. After this life he judges (Heb. 9:27). The time for repentance and faith is now (2 Cor. 6:2). Cycles of life no more exist for individuals than they do for the race and its history as a whole. Life ends in death, and after that the resurrection, the judgment, and either eternal life with God or separation from him. Christian eschatology invalidates both transmigration itself and its cultural implications.

At the same time eschatology has its own implications for life and conduct. In the first Christian centuries of the church these gradually changed the cultural face of the Roman Empire. Orientation to a positive goal dispelled the pessimistic fatalism that affected much of the pagan world and the hedonism that it engendered in wide circles. A higher estimation of the body ran counter to both excessive asceticism and bodily abuse. Awareness of approaching judgment curbed to some degree both materialistic indulgence on the one hand and irresponsible cruelty on the other. The promise of eternal life prevented shortsighted concentration on the achievements, pleasures, and rewards of this life and cast a new light on death — a light that found expression in the art of the catacombs and new interment practices, and even more vividly in the otherwise unintelligible readiness for martyrdom.[8] The belief that with Christ a new era had come gave to Christianity a historical basis on which it could celebrate each Sunday as the day of the Lord,[9] with a backward look to Easter and a forward look to the new creation.

If tensions marked the relation between eschatology and Hellenistic culture, they unavoidably arise wherever the gospel goes and substitutes the Christian message of the last things for non-Christian ideas and their associated rituals, practices, and artistic manifestations. To be sure, parallels to Christian teaching exist in many cultures: concepts of an afterlife and resurrection, of the end of the world, of judgment, of a coming Messiah (sometimes in assimilation to the Christian hope), of a future paradise and perdition.[10] Nevertheless, the essential incompatibility of the relevant ideas and expressions with Christianity needs little demonstration, being no less evident even where some intermingling with Christian doctrine has taken place. In virtue of this incompatibility the acculturation of the gospel can be successfully achieved only with great discernment and delicacy. Cul-

8. Tertullian *To Scapula* 5.
9. *Didache* 14.1.
10. For examples see J. A. MacCulloch's article "Eschatology," in the *Encyclopedia of Religion and Ethics*, ed. J. Hastings (Edinburgh, 1908-26), 5:373-91.

tures, of course, contain large areas of adiaphora, so that the introduction of biblical eschatology does not have to involve a total cultural revolution and reconstruction. Nevertheless, where divergent or even partly parallel ideas, rituals, and practices exist, along with their broader implications for life and conduct, tensions unavoidably arise.

Nor are such tensions restricted to lands into which the gospel penetrates from outside. They arise no less sharply in christianized countries that have undergone a process of secularization. We see this only too plainly when we consider the conflicts between eschatology and parallel notions that impregnate and characterize the cultures of the industrialized West, notwithstanding the powerful impact that Christianity still has on Western literature, music, institutions, practices, and mores.

For example, Christian eschatology necessarily involves a certain otherworldliness. At times believers have carried this to extremes, but in proper proportion (as, for example, in Calvin's meditation on the future life)[11] it does not have to exclude this-worldly concerns. A secularized culture, however, puts the emphasis strongly or even totally on the this-worldly aspect. In so doing it complains of an eschatological distortion of perspective. Concentration on the future, it argues, crowds out concern for the present. Study of heavenly things leaves little time for earthly pursuits, including those in art and letters. Concern for the final judgment quenches zeal for the attainment of individual, social, economic, legal, and international justice. Last things alone count. The complaint may be exaggerated, but it bears witness to the tension. Eschatology will not permit a thoroughgoing secularization or secular orientation. The things that are not seen are of ultimate importance, for they alone are eternal (2 Cor. 4:18). Earthly attainments may be important, but they are no more than penultimate. If this life is to be lived to the full, it is with a view to the new and true life with God. Eschatology runs against the grain of a secularized culture, for although much in conduct and practice may remain the same, it proclaims the folly of a hope only for this life, and it raises sharply the issue of meaninglessness or meaning.

Similar tensions exist, of course, regarding the expectation of a final deliverance by divine intervention. Eschatology of almost every type maintains that God will come at last to establish or consummate the kingdom. What human striving can accomplish only partially and temporarily, God will achieve totally and definitively, first perhaps by his divine rule on this earth (Rev. 20:4), but indubitably in the new heaven and the new earth (21:1). This eschatological hope of an act of God inevitably offends the

---

11. Calvin, *Institutes of the Christian Religion*, 3.9.

secular mind in a secularized culture. It postulates a divine action for which scientific rationalism finds no place. It characterizes human aspirations as ultimately illusory and ascribes to human attainments at most a restricted value. To secularists, indeed, it seems to make unnecessary and even presumptuous all efforts at human betterment, so that inaction and acceptance of the status quo are the logical implications.

The tension here perhaps comes to clearest expression in the hackneyed Marxist description of religion as the opium of the people (Marx) or as spiritual alcohol (Lenin).[12] Eschatology with its hope of an eternal reward lies behind the accusation. At a practical level Marxists have opposed Christianity because it seemed to lull people into acquiescence in present misery and injustice on the promise that, if docile and obedient, they would enjoy a future reversal of their circumstances. To those who wished to correct the situation now, having no trust in future expectations, eschatology seemed to be cruel and cynical manipulation. Yet the charge itself gives evidence of a cruel distortion that Marxists themselves — or the peoples in Marxist lands — have come to realize as their systems have proved unworkable, as they have had to experience an inertia that does not derive from "pie in the sky when you die," as they have had to contend with real alcohol (vodka!) among the many other intractable ills that disrupt human life and society, as Marxism engaged in its own cultural manipulation. It may well be that some preachers did to some extent fall victim to manipulative authorities and use eschatological themes to induce submission to wrongs and injustices. If they did, however, they neglected the basic fact that the message of the day of the Lord carries a threat to oppression (Amos 5:18; Joel 1:15) and a summons to righteousness (Amos 5:24). Eschatology itself, then, involves an indictment of unjust societies and accuses cultures of perversions that promote social evils and thrive upon them.

The resurrection, of course, constitutes an obvious point of tension with a secular culture. Idealists might still postulate an immortality of the soul, but they would agree with materialists in accepting no equivalent destiny for the body. For materialists indeed — and a secularized culture includes many such — death presents a particularly terrible and enigmatic face. In confrontation with it, present fulfillment becomes an urgent requirement, even if it takes the form of sensual indulgence or is at the expense of others. Frustration of this-worldly hopes makes of life a pointless enterprise. If bodily resurrection in particular seems to defy all scientific knowledge or probability, its

---

12. See the article "Marxismus," in *Evangelisches Kirchenlexikon,* 2d ed. (Göttingen: Vandenhoek & Ruprecht, 1992), 3:302ff.; see also "Marxismus und Christentum," 3:320ff.

denial leaves only a nebulous immortality at best, or at worst a futility that the consolation of living on in achievement or memory can never dispel. This futility finds bleak expression in the art and letters and mores of a materialistic age,[13] not least in burial rituals, which, even when conventional, offer the secularist no real message of comfort.

A culture that enshrines a concept of progress can hardly fail to clash with Christian eschatology, which proclaims final human declension rather than advance. Progress may take the evolutionary form whereby history will bring either a higher form of humanity or a form or forms beyond it. The incompatibility of this idea with the eschatological reading of the situation and its reliance upon divine intervention stares us in the face. Evolving accords with neither the biblical beginning nor the biblical end. It necessarily regards the eschatological scenario as a figment of the religious imagination. It has cultural ramifications that at least in part press eschatologists into their own subculture. In return, of course, eschatology finds in the hope of evolutionary advance an illusion that history itself refutes, and in its cultural manifestations — at any rate at some levels — a testimony to human degeneration.

Progress may also take a technological form. In what Jacques Ellul describes and deplores as a technological society and culture,[14] the tension is perhaps at its strongest today. Technology has obviously made astonishing advances in recent decades. Achievements have become possible that a few generations ago would have seemed to be impossible or miraculous. The potential for future progress appears to be unlimited. Technology undoubtedly has to reckon with darker possibilities as well — ozone depletion, global warming, nuclear disaster, toxification. It may itself bring catastrophe on an eschatological scale. Nevertheless, confidence exists that technology can overcome every problem, even the problems of its own creating. It can do what it will not allow that God can do: it can do what it will. It also has its own implications for culture, which it imposes to some extent willy-nilly on all those who come within its range. Many of these are neutral, of course, but for all the wonders of the new technology they represent no true or lasting betterment of humans and their situation. Technology has no real solution to the human plight. History has as its goal, not a perfected technology, but an eschatological consummation when God will put his own transcendent technology to work and the culture will be that of his kingdom.

13. See, e.g., the works of Jacques Monod.
14. Ellul, *What I Believe* (Grand Rapids: Eerdmans, 1989), pp. 133ff.; *The Technological Bluff* (Grand Rapids: Eerdmans, 1990).

Ecology joins forces with eschatology in its reservations about technological progress. Yet tension also arises between the allies. The main charge of ecologists, of course, focuses on the Genesis direction to humanity to have dominion over the earth (Gen. 1:26, 28). They see this as an invitation to environmental exploitation and spoliation of which the Christian West has taken full advantage with its advancing industrialization, not to mention its treatment of hunting and fishing as sources of pleasure rather than survival. Blame can also attach to the eschatological hope, however, if it leads to the conclusion that since the earth is either to be destroyed or to be rehabilitated at Christ's coming, it matters little if we make the fullest use of its resources and do damage in the process.

Eschatology as such can have little real quarrel with ecology. It envisions perfect ecological balance in the restored earth or in the new heaven and the new earth. It might complain that ecologists paint too idyllic a picture of the harmony that can now be achieved and that they seek to impose too excessively restrictive a life-style on both individuals and society. It realizes that nature itself in its present state can cause disruption. It also regrets the tendency of some ecologists to deify nature instead of nature's God, or even to slip themselves into the role of God. It contends for the truth that the God who created the world has a plan for it that he will unquestionably bring to fulfillment. The divine action certainly does not absolve us from the duty of conservatorship, but it prohibits us either from looking to nature alone for environmental solutions or from pessimistically concluding that no solutions are possible.

Tension can hardly be avoided between the thesis of eschatological judgment and the various relativisms that characterize much of society today. Whether social or subjective, utilitarian or hedonistic, relativism excludes the norms that the divine judgment presupposes and that God has either built into his world or revealed in his Scriptures. Relativism can acknowledge no suprahuman authority. It can allow relative judgments but no "last judgment." It finds in the invoking of divine judgment merely a means of imposing one's will on others, of thwarting their true development, of frightening them into submission to what are after all, it thinks, no more than relative human opinions. Against this moral relativism and its expression in literature, art, and life-style, eschatology proclaims the norms that God has set and the account that all must one day give to him. Relativism involves a false autonomy; the last judgment involves a heteronomy that, being a theonomy, guarantees authentic autonomy!

The tension perhaps finds clearest illustration of all when eschatology declares its message to debased or disintegrating cultures of violence, self-seeking, greed, cruelty, licentiousness, and lawlessness. It has done this across the centuries through periods of decay, disruption, and disaster. The eschaton means ultimate accountability, which is prefigured in the historical judgments that sooner or later overtake all human cultures. For all their vaunted achievements, cultures constantly have to face the immanent eschatons of history. They are tried and found wanting. They will always be found wanting. Christians admire and applaud genuine cultural attainments in the various spheres of human life. They appreciate their worth. But they have no confidence in cultures as such. Cultures come and go. They blossom, but even as they do so they carry the seeds of their own decline. For each of them the historical eschaton arrives. Cultural relativism itself may accept this. What it fails to allow is that there is an ultimate as well as a historical eschaton. The historical eschaton is penultimate. At the true end, cultures will have to face the divine Judge who sets the standards that all of them fail to meet and many of them foolishly ignore and shamelessly violate. The greater the deviation from the divine norm, the sharper the tension.

The tension behind all tensions, of course, is the one between God himself and cultures that do not truly know him or even perhaps want him. Christian eschatology points to him who is the end as well as the beginning (Isa. 41:4; Rev. 21:6). Cultures substitute their own concepts of God and shape their scenarios accordingly. In many cases, indeed, they leave no place for transcendence and have only immanent scenarios, with death not as the last enemy (cf. 1 Cor. 15:26) but as itself the eschaton, at least for individuals. Cultures set other gods in consort or competition with God. Or they dismiss God as merely a human concept of deity, himself a cultural product. Even cultures of Christian derivation easily tend to put distorted or manufactured ideas of God in the place of God himself. The resultant tension comes out at many points — creation, providence, redemption. It unavoidably finds expression in eschatology. Deep down, however, it is the tension between God and culture as such — or rather, between God and the humanity that has gone so far from God that its cultures necessarily bear the marks of this alienation.

III. INTERACTIONS

Eschatology and culture inevitably collide. Nevertheless, they deal with common themes and belong to the same human story. Hence they no less inevitably affect one another. We must speak of interactions, then, as well as tensions, of interactions in tension even though there are also tensions in interaction.

Biblical eschatology itself offers an illustration. It clearly reflects the Hebrew and Judaic milieu in which it arose. It employs the imagery of the time, depicting God's rule as monarchy (Ps. 47:7; Rev. 19:16), calling for a trumpet blast in intimation of Christ's coming (1 Thess. 4:16; 1 Cor. 15:52), or adducing themes from paradise to describe the new creation (Rev. 22:1-2, 14).

When eschatology entered more fully into the Hellenistic world, a premillennial option seemed most appropriate for Christ's reign, since the church had the status of a minority and there was apparently no chance whatever of replacing on earth the dominant political, social, economic, and cultural power of Rome. Even so, however, contemporary images of superabundant fertility gave the depiction a materialistic thrust that would eventually discredit it.[15] Montanist prophesyings that apparently rested on Phrygian models[16] served the more effectively to undermine the primitive premillennialism.

In the same early period Hellenistic notions of psychosomatic disjunction seduced some believers or fringe adherents into an eschatology that left no place for the risen body. Gnostics, Marcionites, and later Manicheans all in different ways advocated a dualism of body and soul that postulated the soul's alienation in the body and redemption from it. They thus engaged in a total reconstruction of eschatology (as well as creation and soteriology) that mainline Christianity wisely resisted and rejected. An Augustine, however, still had to fight hard to preserve his belief in bodily resurrection in view of his Platonic heritage and Manichean detour.[17] Associated concepts such as the soul's preexistence and transmigration had no little appeal to the more speculative Origen.[18] Transmigration in particular made possible a universalist alternative to definitive judgment.[19] Dualistic disparagement of the body also promoted a more rigorous asceticism, though not to the abandonment of a final hope for the body in resurrection and new creation.

The changed situation after Constantine's accession brought with it the new prospect of a Christian empire and society that not only gave believers new cultural possibilities, though with strong resistance from the Hellenistic schools, but also hastened the transfer from a premillennial to

---

15. Eusebius *H.E.* 3.39.12.

16. Eusebius *H.E.* 5.16.6ff.

17. See Paula Fredriksen, "Vile Bodies: Paul and Augustine on the Resurrection of the Flesh," in *Biblical Hermeneutics in Historical Perspective,* ed. Mark S. Burrows and Paul Rorem (Grand Rapids: Eerdmans, 1991), pp. 75-87.

18. Origen *De Principiis* 2.8.3.

19. Origen *De Principiis* 1.6.3.

a virtual postmillennial understanding of Christ's reign. As some now saw it, the "millennial" age was coming with the church age. Church and kingdom may not be coextensive, but the city of God was present in history. The "millennium" was running its course within secular events. Cultural change thus involved eschatological change. Yet the eschatological change had its own cultural implications. If the millennial age was coming, the church had a wider task than mission. It had to bring all facets of life under the impact of the gospel and faith. It had a civilizing ministry that would become all the more urgent as the Empire in the West crumbled under "barbarian" attack. The goal could be no less than that of a Christian culture. The millennial fulfillment must find expression in every sphere of life — politics, economics, society, art, architecture, letters, music, law, philosophy, and scholarship.

In the attempted achievement of this goal even otherworldly devotion made a substantial contribution. Monks and nuns had seemingly renounced human society and culture in despair over the world and out of the desire to live a more consistent Christian life free from secular entanglements. Nevertheless, their very focus on eternal realities helped them to play a notable part in the preserving of ancient culture and the forging of a new Christian culture as the Empire collapsed and unevangelized peoples swept across the North and West and even into Italy itself. The monastic communities that ultimately arose not only undertook most of the work of evangelism but in addition to their liturgical exercises did much to hand down literature, to foster art, to develop music, to patronize architecture, to nurture learning, and to promote economic growth. They thus gave the lie to the thesis that concentration on the next world necessarily excludes the exerting of any powerful influence on the present world.

The Middle Ages, of course, failed by a long way to conform to the millennial model. In the process of this failure they added their own distortions to the eschatological picture. The medieval imagination ran riot in inventing torments for the damned, aided by — and also aiding, perhaps — the tortures at which authorities both political and ecclesiastical proved to be so adept. Often depicted no less graphically than hell itself, purgatory took up a harmfully dominant position in medieval thinking and practice. Purgatory, indeed, had considerable cultural impact when we consider not only the attempts to describe it but also the means devised either to reduce or to nullify it: pilgrimages and the associated shrines, relics manufactured and collected, masses endowed and celebrated, alms more generously distributed, churches and colleges endowed, dedications to the monastic life, penitential exercises, and indulgences and their peddling. Purgatory may even have helped to keep alive beliefs in ghosts and hauntings and the practices relating to the All Saints and All Souls period. Its addition to earth, heaven, and hell also contributed to the demand for a more accurate eschatological cartography with a special limbo for unbaptized infants. Medieval burials in some sense symbolized the eschatology with a special unconsecrated part of the churchyard for unbaptized infants, and with interment outside the churchyard for any who died in mortal sin — for example, suicides.

Now that the millennium had supposedly begun, expectation of the final consummation caused recurrent crises, especially with the approach of the year A.D. 1000. Miserable conditions of war, famine, poverty, disease, and tyranny brought their own crises as well. Popular discontent produced explosions that could take on an apocalyptic character. Eventually the Peasants' War of the 1520s, the Münster episode in the 1530s, and the Fifth Monarchy Movement in the mid-seventeenth century entailed either a revision of postmillennialism or a revival of premillennialism involving the use of violence for millennial ends and the hope of divine intervention to ensure success. The eschatological thinking of the Reformation — for example, the equation of Rome with Babylon, the Turk with Antichrist, and Reformation teaching with the everlasting gospel (Rev. 14:6) — provided a favorable climate in which eschatological expectations might flourish. More traditionally the theme of the last judgment, which the proximity of death made it hard to ignore, offered itself as a suitable subject for art as well as exerting an ongoing influence on religious and moral practice.

The rise of humanism incontestably increased the tension between eschatology and culture, but it also initiated new forms of interaction. At one level the impact of humanism was merely technical. Thus the invention of movable-type printing increased the circulation of eschatological as well as other writings and therefore resulted in the enhanced interest, knowledge, and expectation that we see, for example, in the Puritan movements associated with Brightman and Mede. Indeed, the wider dissemination of knowledge in general could have an eschatological thrust as a sign intimating the end of the age (cf. Dan. 12:4). So could the global missionary work (cf. Matt. 24:14) made possible by the oceanic explorations that opened up Asia, Africa, and the Americas.

Humanism had its anti-religious and anti-clericalist side as well. We see this especially among the French Encyclopedists, in the German Enlightenment, and among the English Deists. Rationalism could find room for some type of immortality, but it tended to deride traditional eschatology. Nevertheless, even in the midst of eighteenth-century rationalism culture could not escape the eschatological impact of ongoing Roman Catholicism and upsurging Pietism and Evangelicalism. Thus the solemnity of the last day found impressive expression in the *Requiem* of the irrepressible Mozart, and the hope of the resurrection has seldom been given a more beautiful statement than in Handel's *Messiah*. Eschatology had by no means abdicated its role as a cultural determinant.

More broadly humanism sponsored the belief in progress that has had such a powerful impact on Western culture.[20] Regard for the past had proved an obstacle to this belief. In the arts at least, it was thought, antiquity had achieved an excellence to which moderns could only aspire. A turning point came in eighteenth-century France with the famous *Querelle des anciens et des modernes* and the gradual emergence of the view that the life of humanity or of a civilization resembles that of an organism with progressive stages from infancy to maturity — old age and decay being ignored for the moment as remote. By the late eighteenth century Condorcet's plea for perfectibility[21] had helped the idea of progress to take firm root, aided by the impressive discoveries now being made in the natural sciences. Increasing scientific and technological advance joined forces with evolutionism to confirm the doctrine. The horrors of two world wars and environmental problems have shaken but not destroyed it.

What has this belief to do with eschatology? Do not the two collide? Indeed they do, as noted already. Yet they also interact. For human progress may be set in the context of the kingdom of God, whether in a postmillennial or a premillennial form.

For the clearest illustrations of the interaction we may turn to the more liberal theologies of the nineteenth and twentieth centuries. Stressing the upbuilding of the kingdom of God by the expansion of Christian ideals and the pressing of political, social, and economic reforms, these theologies make common cause with the doctrine of progress from which they draw much of their thinking. Ostensibly progressive themselves, they engage in a reciprocating process of secularizing eschatology and of eschatologizing secularism. A heavily contextualized version of eschatology approximating the dream of progress replaces biblical and traditional eschatology, with a consequent commitment at many points to the parallel secular aims and models. Unhappily this version of eschatology is no less exposed than secular belief to the disillusionment caused by twentieth-century catastrophes, and not least by the failure of Marxist socialism, to which many have pinned their millennial hopes. The inability of the churches to move substantially toward fuller unity has also been a disappointment in view of the efforts invested in the ecumenical venture and the quasi-millennial expec-

20. See J. B. Bury, *The Idea of Progress* (New York: Dover Publications, 1960).
21. In his *Esquisse d'un tableau historique des progrès de l'esprit humain* (1793).

tations associated with it. Nevertheless, secularized eschatology has not yet become an outdated phenomenon. It affects not merely the thinking but the lives and activities of vast numbers of people worldwide, Christians and non-Christians alike.

Even a more biblical eschatology could still be caught up in interaction with the prevailing belief in progress. Already in the seventeenth century many Christians were anticipating a global turning to the gospel prior to Christ's return. With the rapid nineteenth-century development of missions this hope seemed at last to be capable of fulfillment.[22] For postmillennialists the expansion of the gospel might well be the final expression of the kingdom before the end, while for premillennialists it would be the worldwide proclamation that precedes the millennial kingdom. In any case, however, a hope of almost unbounded progress held sway.[23] Nor was this merely the progress of the gospel, for mission included the exporting of elements of supposedly superior Western culture. Eschatology, then, fell fairly smoothly into step with Western hopes of human progress. The end time might be different, but before that time, before the eschatological close of the age, unparalleled advance might be expected, aided, and even in part initiated by Christian mission, and it would involve a global communication of Western culture.

The culture of scientific and technological progress has also had eschatological implications. Thus the more ample provision of luxuries as well as necessities, along with the medical extension of life expectancy, could hardly fail to affect adversely the focus on heavenly things that has always been an eschatological component. One way of dealing with this situation is that of an eschatological adjustment that gives relatively higher value to the penultimate. A second way is that of an eschatological counterculture in either a secular or a biblical form. Not a few have moved in this direction, resisting the blandishments of advertising, rejecting the affluence that technological progress offers, and devoting themselves either to ultimate earthly ends or to those that are authentically ultimate in the service of God and neighbor. Unwittingly, however, even Christians who profess solid eschatological convictions find themselves entangled in not very conspicuously eschatological life-styles and a loss of eschatological sensitivity.

The accelerating awareness of ecological problems has aroused concern about technological progress. Ecology and eschatology come into constructive interaction in this regard. Ecology has awakened the churches

22. See James H. Moorhead, "Prophecy, Millennialism, and Biblical Interpretation in Nineteenth-Century America," in *Biblical Hermeneutics in Historical Perspective*, pp. 291-302.

23. See Charles Hodge, *Systematic Theology*, 3 vols. (New York: Charles Scribner, 1872-75), 3:790ff.

to the human responsibility of stewardship in and for God's creation. The primary relation here is to creation and its preservation. Nevertheless, the New Testament tells us that stewardship is an occupying until the Lord comes (cf. Matt. 24:45-51). This stewardship refers first, of course, to the dispensing of the mysteries of God (1 Cor. 4:1-2). Lesser concerns should not deflect Christians from this compelling duty. Yet surely one may also see a valid reference to the stewardship vested in the human race at creation (Gen. 1:26). For this stewardship, too, the eschaton will be a time of accounting. The Lord himself will undoubtedly set things right at his coming, whether by redress of the old creation first, or directly by the new creation. But he will have words of commendation for those who work for the integrity of creation and words of rebuke for those who abuse his handiwork to selfish or wicked ends. The eschatological requirement of faithfulness in stewardship of the earth's resources reinforces the cultural shift from environmental exploitation to environmental conservation, slow though the process may be in both secular and eschatological circles.

The concept of progress has taken a dialectical as well as a linear form. Hegel followed this line idealistically, Marx materialistically. It posits advance by thesis and antithesis leading to the synthesis that becomes the new thesis until final synthesis is reached. The concept has considerable cultural implications in both forms, but most extensively through Marxism, in which it could produce both the excesses of the Chinese cultural revolution and the sterility of the party-dictated art and literature. Some nineteenth-century historians tried to impose the process on Christianity and its history, but does it bear any possible relation to eschatology?

An answer lies, perhaps, in the earlier stages of dialectical theory. This thinking derived to some extent from the epistemological upheaval occasioned by Kant. Culturally, as Friedrich Schlegel saw it, Kant's linking of knowledge to the subjective categories meant that artists and writers can no longer claim to be giving objective depictions of life. Subjective art has replaced objective art. People and things are now portrayed as they appear to artists or authors. The depiction stands in a dialectical relation to what it depicts, though perhaps with hope of a final synthesis.[24]

This Romantic theory, which had momentous cultural repercussions, had little immediate relevance to eschatology. Nevertheless, the Schlegel circle quickly saw a Christian application of the triadic principle. Novalis found a

---

24. See Schlegel's essays "Vom Wert des Studiums der Griechen und Römer" and "Über das Studium der griechischen Poesie," *Auswahl*, ed. O. Walzel (Stuttgart, n.d.), pp. 255ff. Schlegel, of course, saw a conflict between nature and freedom throughout history, and a thrust toward freedom in Christianity.

thesis in medieval Christianity, an antithesis in Protestantism, and a movement toward a future synthesis.[25] Schelling saw a similar pattern in human history as a whole — the thesis in original innocence, the antithesis in the fall, and the synthesis in reconciliation.[26] Hegel could postulate a trinitarian triad of Father (idea), Son (matter), and Spirit (resolution).[27] Schleiermacher perceived in the triadic principle the basic Christian insight, with God as thesis, man as antithesis, and the God-man (Christ) as synthesis.[28]

The dialectic has a progressive character when there is movement to a final synthesis. Bringing the process into Christian history might thus supply an eschatological version, though the main impact has been in the form of a secularizing of eschatology. At the same time Schleiermacher's finding of an absolute synthesis already in Christ suggests a dialectical form of realized eschatology. With reconciliation, the eschaton has already come in some sense in Christ. The great turning point of history is now behind us. This bold use of the triad accords less well, of course, with the dialectic of modern culture. Nevertheless, it has a message for Christians that modern theology has developed on a more solid biblical basis — namely, that Christians should now be in their lives what they are already in Christ, that they should live in the light of the Already of eschatological fulfillment, yet aim steadfastly toward the Not Yet of the final eschatological consummation.

IV. CONCLUSION

The relation between eschatology and culture carries a constant reminder of Paul's admonition that God's people are to be in the world but not of it (cf. 1 Cor. 5:9-13). The tensions and interactions arise as we walk the narrow ridge of the "in" but "not of." As Barth perspicaciously observed of the church in general, the abyss of secularization awaits us if we fail to observe the "not of," but the abyss of sacralization gapes before us if we try to avoid the "in."[29] Contextualizing the gospel and the Christian life is a requirement if Christians are not to be permanently marginalized as a subculture, but contextualizing must not mean absorption into a prevailing non-Christian culture, whether religious or secular. The solution of a Chris-

25. Novalis also postulated an innocence, fall, redemption triad; see *Hymnen an die Nacht*, in *Schriften*, vol. 1, ed. J. Minor (Jena, 1907), p. 32.

26. In some works Schelling found the first step into freedom after the flood, but genuine freedom came with Christianity. Schelling also postulated a trinitarian triad.

27. Hegel, of course, also saw triads within history.

28. Schleiermacher, *On Religion* (New York: Harper, 1958), p. 241.

29. Barth, *Church Dogmatics,* IV/2:667ff.

tian culture — which the Middle Ages ardently but far from successfully sought — remains, of course, the ideal. As eschatology teaches us, however, it is an ideal to which we can only approximate as we move toward the eschatological consummation. In this life even our eschatology, like all else, lies exposed to constant vicissitudes, temptations, dangers, and possibilities as cultural change occurs and as the gospel moves into new and often uncharted cultures. Our eschatology, too, must be in the world, expressed in its terms, exerting its own influence upon it. Yet it must be careful not to be of the world, neither resolving the unavoidable tensions, nor allowing itself to be submerged in worldly cultures.

By its very nature eschatology deals with last things. Fittingly, then, it must have a last word. This last word is not about either eschatology in culture or culture in eschatology. It is about culture in the eschaton. The eschaton will bring with it the cultural fulfillment that attempted Christian cultures fall so far short of achieving. But this fulfillment, as Ellul has so constructively and provocatively reminded us,[30] includes the bringing of all the riches of the kingdoms into the kingdom of God and his Christ (Rev. 21:24, 26). Expositors, Ellul thinks, too readily assume that the reference here is simply to material wealth or political power or terrestrial glory. But why should we not also think of a recapitulation of all the great and worthy artistic, literary, technical, political, and legal achievements of the whole race, which Calvin had already attributed to the general working of the Holy Spirit?[31]

Ellul makes this suggestion only tentatively, for we have no detailed biblical information on such matters. But the suggestion has obvious merit. God's love extends to all the life that he has given. He will hardly let the good results of so much time and labor go for nothing. After all, the kingdom has the form of a city,[32] and if the earthly city is the site of much evil, it is also the cultural center. Human culture has done much good as well as harm. The good has served its turn, but why should God allow it to perish? Purged of all that is base, culture, too, can have the more glorious fulfillment of its own eschaton when acculturation can be no threat because culture, like all else, has undergone the divine renewing and sanctifying. Today, in the tangle of history short of the eschaton, eschatology and culture remain in the tense interrelation in which neither can overwhelm or fulfill the other. Tomorrow, in the eschaton that eschatology awaits, culture will certainly have an end, but an end that is perhaps, by the involved incorporation into the kingdom of God, its true and definitive beginning.

30. Ellul, *What I Believe*, pp. 217ff.
31. Calvin, *Institutes of the Christian Religion*, 2.2.12-17.
32. Ellul, *What I Believe*, pp. 219-20; cf. Rev. 21:10-27.

Cultural Anthropology, Sin, and the Missionary

ROBERT J. PRIEST

AS A CHRISTIAN anthropologist my commitments lie within the discipline of anthropology. I find in anthropology wonderful possibilities. Yet my relationship to the discipline is characterized by cognitive tension — tension stemming from my relations to two different social communities and to two different conceptual worlds.

I was socialized into the evangelical thought world of a missions center, a Bible college, and an evangelical seminary. I learned concepts, not just about God, but about human beings. Pivotal to my learned understanding of the human condition were concepts implying human sinfulness — pride, envy, lust, covetousness, guilt, etc. In my subsequent teaching and preaching I used these biblical concepts to interpret people to themselves. The success of my message was directly dependent on the extent to which listeners were enabled to make sense of themselves in terms of such biblical categories.

But then at the University of Chicago and later at the University of California at Berkeley I was socialized into a different community, that of cultural anthropologists, and was introduced to a different set of conceptual tools — culture, social structure, function, adaptation, taboo, etc. As I did research and wrote papers these were the concepts I was expected to use in making sense of the human condition.

How then was I as a Christian anthropologist to relate these two thought worlds, one grounded in the sacred text and in the discourse of theologians and biblical scholars, and the other grounded in the empirical scientific study of human realities and in the rational discourse of the university community of scholars? One appealing solution would be to emphasize that the two

85

discourses concern incommensurable realities. The independent authority of each could be assumed and the possibility of substantive overlap or conflict between them denied. Yet both deal with the subject of humankind. Anthropology does not limit its subject matter to a narrow slice of life but aspires to an all-encompassing look at humanity in its diversity and complexity. I argue in this essay that the apparent incommensurability of the two discourses is not exclusively or primarily the result of a differing anthropological subject or method; rather, it is a consequence of an active anthropological enterprise that developed its ideas in part in opposition to, and as replacement of, Christian views of humankind — most notably views of human beings as sinners. Any effort to chart a course for Christians in anthropology must explore this opposition.

In his presidential address to the 1975 American Anthropology Association, Walter Goldschmidt stated, "Missionaries are in many ways our opposites; they believe in original sin."[1] Goldschmidt was correct, first, in implying that the concept of human sin lies at the heart of the evangelical missionary enterprise. Evangelical theology, missions appeals, and evangelism courses all stress that human sin is central to the meaning of the cross and foundational to the need for evangelism and missions. Second, Goldschmidt was correct in positing a fundamental opposition between anthropologists and missionaries.[2] And third, as I try to document in this essay, he was correct in locating the source of that opposition in a disagreement by anthropologists with the notion of sin and all that it implies.

The roots of anthropology go back to the encounter of the West with social others. At the time of the discovery of the New World, the concept of sin was at the heart of Western reflection on the human condition. Christian theology (then queen of the sciences) emphasized the centrality of sin. The Catholic practices of penance and, following the Fourth Lateran Council (1215), of annual obligatory confession required and generated enormous and complex discourses (theological treatises, confession manuals, confessors' handbooks, sermons) on human sin.[3] The literature of Dante, Chaucer, Milton, Spenser, and countless others made abundant use of sin concepts — lust, anger, pride, envy, covetousness, gluttony, and sloth — in their reflections on human nature and behavior.[4] Murals, sculptures,

1. Goldschmidt, "Anthropology and the Coming Crisis: An Autoethnographic Appraisal," *American Anthropologist* 79 (1979): 296.

2. For a review of writings that explore this opposition see Sajaak Van der Geest, "Anthropologists and Missionaries: Brothers under the Skin," *Man* 25 N.S. (1990): 580-601.

3. Cf. Jean Delumeau, *Sin and Fear: The Emergence of a Western Guilt Culture 13th-18th Centuries* (New York: St. Martin's Press, 1990), pp. 189ff.

4. Morton W. Bloomfield, *The Seven Deadly Sins: An Introduction to the History of*

and paintings featured personifications of the seven deadly sins, occasionally locked in combat with seven virtues. Thus, in this pre-psychological society, theology, sermons, the confessional, art, literature — in short, the whole culture — united in instructing people to reflect on and to interpret themselves and their every act and motive in the light of sin concepts. This is the context in which Western reflection and discourse on non-Western men and women was born. This cultural context predetermined what types of issues were to be raised in such discourse, and it accounts for the impulse and dynamic of two competing strands of thought — still with us today — incarnated in the opposition between missionary and anthropologist.

One strand of thought, when faced with those who seemed unaware of their own sin and accountability to God or of Christ's salvation from sin, insisted that since God is creator of all, his standards should be normative for all. This approach denied innocence to anyone, pointing to such things as head-hunting, cannibalism, or infanticide as evidence of universal human depravity and need of salvation. The missionary became the concrete embodiment of this way of understanding and relating to social others.

A second strand of thought, which eventually was to find its consistent incarnation in the cultural anthropologist, involved not a reaffirmation of Christian verities in the face of social disagreement but the creation of a discourse on social others designed to undercut such received verities. For many a Westerner raised in a culture that emphasized sin and guilt, the notion that there were people without such a consciousness of sin and guilt was electrifying. When in 1555 Villegaignon led six hundred Huguenot colonists to Brazil to civilize and Christianize the natives, Pierre de Ronsard reproached him for trying to influence in this way a people so

> innocently and completely untamed and nude, as naked in dress as they are stripped of malice, who know neither the names of virtue nor vice.... Live happy, you people without pain, without cares. Live joyously: I myself would wish to live so.[5]

In this brief comment, several important themes in the exploding discourse on social others are alluded to. Nudity and innocence are linked. Here are people who are naked and not ashamed! Like Adam and Eve prior to eating of the tree of the knowledge of good and evil, but very unlike sixteenth-century Europeans, they "know neither the names of virtue nor vice." From Tahiti came reports of people who conducted extramarital sexual relations,

---

a Religious Concept, With Special Reference to Medieval English Literature (East Lansing: Michigan State University Press, 1967).

5. Ronsard, cited in Delumeau, *Sin and Fear,* p. 127.

not secretly and furtively in awareness of shameful transgression, but openly and exuberantly with play and laughter, condemned by none. Lack-.ing the European's sense of sin, such people were thought to enjoy a happiness that escaped the guilt-ridden European. Thus Ronsard opposed the missionary as bringer of sin and guilt, destroyer of joyful innocence. For a guilty people, the image of people without guilt was a powerful and moving symbol to be continuously exploited in discourses designed to remove guilt and sin.

In his first two books on Tahiti, *Typee* and *Omoo,* Herman Melville skillfully exploited such themes, focusing on the triad of social others, sin, and the missionary. Having been raised in a Dutch Reformed Church, Melville spent a lifetime struggling against Calvinist views of humankind.[6] In *Typee* he argues that, cannibalism aside, Tahitians are "more kindly" and "more humane than many who study essays on virtue and benevolence." Having lived with them, he declared, "I formed a higher estimate of human nature than I had ever before entertained."[7] Such people live in a land close to Eden: "The penalty of the Fall presses very lightly upon the Valley of Typee" (249). Rather than needing missionaries, such people should send missionaries to America (159).

Because of public outcry over *Typee,* Melville was temporarily convinced to allow anti-missionary rhetoric to be expunged from the second edition. Quickly regretting his weakness, he renewed his attack in *Omoo* (meaning "sacred wanderer"), which parodied the missionary in a deliberate act of (in the words of one Melville scholar) "profaning the sacred."[8]

Somerset Maugham was another who exploited such themes in his short story "Miss Thompson" (later called "Rain"). This brief story of a prostitute and a missionary couple in the Pacific Islands was made into a Broadway play in 1922 that was sold out for eighteen months, running for 648 consecutive performances. Three Hollywood movies have come out based on this short story. Pivotal to the extraordinary grip of this play on American viewers was the theme of the repressed missionary bringing sin to an exuberant, life-filled people. Maugham has the missionary say:

> When we went there, they had no sense of sin at all. They broke the commandments one after the other and never knew they were doing

6. T. Walker Herbert, *"Moby-Dick" and Calvinism: A World Dismantled* (New Brunswick: Rutgers University Press, 1977).

7. Melville, *Typee* (New York: Wiley and Putnam, 1846), pp. 258-59. Subsequent citations will be made parenthetically in the text.

8. John Samson, "Profaning the Sacred: Melville's *Omoo* and Missionary Narratives," *American Literature* 56 (1984): 496-509.

wrong. And I think that was the most difficult part of my work, to instill in the natives the sense of sin. . . . We had to make sins out of what they thought were natural actions. We had to make it a sin, not only to commit adultery and to lie and thieve, but to expose their bodies, and to dance and not to come to church. I made it a sin for a girl to show her bosom and a sin for a man not to wear trousers.[9]

His wife said the natives had formerly been "crazy about dancing," but she noted with pride that after the missionaries had done their work, "no one has danced in our district for eight years."[10] The story concludes with the missionary's life-denying ethic exposed as unhealthy and false when he commits suicide after committing adultery with the prostitute he had so publicly condemned.

So impressed was James Michener by Maugham's short story that he "admits" that he usually rereads at least the first few paragraphs of "Rain" before doing any writing on this part of the world.[11] Eventually Michener picked up the same themes in his "historical novel" *Hawaii*, contrasting beautiful Hawaiian women, who "don't know right from wrong"[12] and who splash naked and unashamed through the waves for a joyous time with sailors, to the missionary Abner Hale, whose God "never smiles,"[13] who feels guilt even for marital pleasures, and whose missionary goal and joy is to instill in the natives a sense of sin. Suspecting Michener of caricaturing the missionary, ethnohistorian Alan Tippett conducted an extensive study of the missionary archives and wrote a devastating critique of the book's distortions. He concluded that "Abner Hale is the most unreal and phony thing in the whole book"[14] and suggested we look for the meaning of Abner Hale not in past history but in the present psyche of Michener and contemporary readers who embrace the book.

A final influential novel, virtually unknown in evangelical circles but widely read by anthropologists, is Peter Matthiessen's *At Play in the Fields of the Lord,* in which missionary graduates of Moody Bible Institute attempt to contact and evangelize the wild Niaruna Indians of the Amazon. While

---

9. W. Somerset Maugham, "Rain," reprinted in *The Maugham Reader* (Garden City, NY: Doubleday, 1950), pp. 279, 281.

10. Maugham, "Rain," pp. 272-73.

11. Michener, cited in Ted Morgan, *Maugham* (New York: Simon and Schuster, 1980), pp. 257-58.

12. Michener, *Hawaii* (New York: Random House, 1959), p. 140.

13. Michener, *Hawaii*, p. 125.

14. Tippett, "Skeletons in the Literary Closet," in *Aspects of Pacific Ethnohistory* (Pasadena: William Carey Library, 1973), p. 171.

the Niaruna went nude and "indulged publicly and with much laughter and enthusiasm in erotic games," the missionaries reacted with horrified condemnation of their "sinful" and "dirty" practices.[15] Yet the missionaries themselves were consumed with lust for each other and for others. Then a split developed among the missionaries. One of them, Martin Quarrier, began to conclude that Indian nudity and sexual play were "natural," not "sinful" or "filthy." After his son died of fever and his wife went insane, and shortly before he himself was killed by the sole mission "convert," Quarrier lost his faith and made plans to become an anthropologist who would study Niaruna culture and help them with medicine and food. Another missionary, the beautiful Andy Huben, demeaned as "dirty" by her missionary husband, looked up when bathing nude at a secluded pool to see a nude "Indian" facing her. As she later recalled the event,

> I *was* naked, and I wasn't ashamed. Am I a sinner . . . ? . . . For the first time the jungle seemed like paradise . . . he was beautiful. And *I* was beautiful. . . . He wanted me, really *wanted* me. . . . I wanted *him* . . . but I pushed him away. . . . And my immortal soul was saved. (259-61)

Matthiessen skillfully weaves a narrative in which the missionaries "were pinned like butterflies to the frame of their own morality" (312), a life-denying morality. Leslie Huben threatened to withhold medicine from dying Indians unless they would submit to his direction. "Better dead than to live in sin," he cried (291). His wife Andy lost her faith, rejected her husband, and offered herself to a soldier of fortune. "Maybe everybody has to sin once," she said. "I don't even know what sin is anymore" (357). By the end of the novel, sin has been deconstructed and the sacred profaned. Never is a prayer recorded in this novel unaccompanied by a lustful thought, by an overheard profanity, by someone scratching their crotch, or by some other desanctifying accompaniment to the prayer. Small wonder that when anthropology professors assign or recommend this novel, as they not infrequently do, their evangelical students commonly find themselves, upon reading it, virtually shaking with anger.

Clearly evident in the above novels is a value-laden symbolic manipulation of images of sin, the missionary, and social others. What is perhaps more surprising is that the "scientific" community of anthropologists would rely on, share, and propagate the same value-laden discourses; but it does. Frank Salamone writes: "The ideal culture of anthropological students codes missionaries as 'enemies.' There is no really conscious teaching of

---

15. Matthiessen, *At Play in the Fields of the Lord* (New York: Random House, 1965), p. 148. Subsequent citations will be made parenthetically in the text.

that datum; it simply seems to be learned unconsciously as part of the general enculturation process of becoming an anthropologist."[16] Gold-schmidt has suggested that the notion of sin is key to the opposition between missionary and anthropologist.

In his important anthropology textbook, Roger Keesing writes about missionaries, sin, and social others: "A pall of Protestant gloom hangs over many a community in the Pacific and tropical South America that once throbbed with life, laughter and song. The concept of sin must rank with smallpox among our most damaging exports."[17] In Brian Moser's film about missionaries in South America, *War of the Gods,* anthropologist Peter Silverwood-Cope comments, "About the only two Indo-European concepts that have come through are sin and laziness." In his review of the book *Is God an American? An Anthropological Perspective on the Missionary Work of the Summer Institute of Linguistics,* anthropologist Enrique Mayer emphasizes that missionaries have been bringers of "cosmic guilt." He summarizes the import of the book thus:

> The [Summer Institute of Linguistics'] claim that they respect the cultures of the groups with which they are involved is also refuted in this work as being a philosophical impossibility. Either one believes that the natives live in sin and thus is motivated to save them from their culture, or one respects other people's culture and thus has no motive to convert anyone.[18]

Similar statements occur repeatedly in anthropological discourses on missionaries. Rather than multiply examples, I conclude with a single incident close to home. Allyn Maclean Stearman, an anthropologist who studied the tribe to which my parents, Perry and Anne Priest, were missionaries, wrote:

> Raul had been drinking steadily for months, depriving his family of necessities, abusing his wife, and generally making a nuisance of himself. He spent several afternoons with Perry on the porch, huddled over in earnest conversation. I could only guess at the content of these discussions; but the following Sunday, Raul got up in church and with eyes brimming over, begged forgiveness of everyone for his past behavior, promising to reform his ways. I thought the entire episode humiliating.

16. Salamone, "Epistemological Implications of Fieldwork and Their Consequences," *American Anthropologist* 81 (1979): 54.

17. Keesing, *Cultural Anthropology* (New York: Rinehart and Winston, 1981), p. 40.

18. Mayer, review of *Is God an American? An Anthropological Perspective on the Work of the Summer Institute of Linguistics,* ed. Peter Aaby and Soren Hvalkof, in *American Ethnologist* 10 (1983): 618.

When I looked around, however, I realized I was the only one in the congregation with any misgivings. Raul had slowly been alienating himself from the community. . . . When it was over there was thunderous applause.[19]

"Since Stearman obviously knew of Raul's wife-beating and other abuses, why," my mother asked me in sheer baffled incomprehension, "did she instinctively respond to Raul's public confession and repentance with such distaste?" The answer, of course, is that the anthropologist's response tells us less about the objective properties of the situation than about the anthropologist herself. This appears to me to be true in the majority of cases where anthropologists refer to missionaries.

What then is a cultural anthropologist? A cultural anthropologist is one who studies social others. To what end? The anthropological project is not primarily directed toward changing or "helping" social others.[20] Nor is it motivated by simple curiosity about the idiosyncratic and different. Rather, anthropologists study other cultures and generate discourses about them designed to change understandings in their own society, understandings about what it means to be human. Clifford Geertz writes:

At the moment when [anthropology] seems most deliberately removed from our own lives, it is most immediate, when it seems most insistently to be talking about the distant, the strange, the long ago, or the idiosyncratic, it is in fact talking also about the close, the familiar, the contemporary, and the generic. From one point of view, the whole history of the comparative study of religion . . . can be looked at as but a circuitous, even devious, approach to a rational analysis of our own situation, an evaluation of our own religious traditions while seeming to evaluate only those of exotic others.[21]

In her pivotal book *Patterns of Culture,* Ruth Benedict gives a rational disquisition on cultural differences. She notes, for example, that while homosexuality is stigmatized in some cultures, in others it is not and may even be the object of ritual respect. What Geertz alerts us to is that Benedict is not exclusively concerned about social others, but is in fact implicitly concerned about realities in her own society. But while Geertz suggests that such a

19. Stearman, *No Longer Nomads: The Siriono Revisited* (New York: Hamilton Press, 1987), p. 118.
20. See my essay "Anthropologists and Missionaries: Moral Roots of Conflict," in *Current Concerns of Anthropologists and Missionaries,* ed. Karl Franklin (Dallas: The International Museum of Cultures, 1987), pp. 18ff.
21. Geertz, *Islam Observed* (Chicago: University of Chicago Press, 1968), p. 2.

"circuitous" means of writing has the goal of truth, it is more accurate to say that the goal is to construct a truth. The anthropologist is not neutral. Benedict dispassionately notes that the homosexual's "guilt, his sense of inadequacy, his failures, are consequences of the disrepute which social tradition visits upon him, and few people can achieve a satisfactory life unsupported by the standards of their society."[22] What her biographers now make clear is that behind her outwardly calm, mild demeanor and rational discourse was a woman of private torments and desires, a woman who, among other things, had homosexual relations with the bisexual Margaret Mead and with others.[23] My point, I hasten to emphasize, is not that this fact discredits her or Mead as profoundly insightful scholars. But it does alert us to the fact that the rational discourses of Benedict and Mead on sexual morality were not the product of dispassionate, uninterested examination. When Benedict attempts to account for the homosexual's guilt, inadequacy, and sense of failure, her version of an "other" is also implicitly a construction of a "self." Geertz writes, "All ethnography is part philosophy, and a good deal of the rest is confession."[24] He means that since the anthropological object of study is closely related to the self, efforts to understand others are inextricably intertwined with personal concerns and values and that thus, unwittingly, ethnography tellingly reveals as much of the author as of the object of study. When Benedict writes that Puritan divines spread "suffering and frustration" through their notions of sin and guilt,[25] she is not offering a dispassionate analysis unrelated to the self.

In her celebrated work, Benedict articulates the anthropological doctrine of cultural relativism:

> We recognize that morality differs in every society and is a convenient term for socially approved habits. Mankind has always preferred to say "It is morally good," rather than "It is habitual" . . . but historically the two phrases are synonymous.[26]

She argues that norms are learned, that they differ from society to society, and thus that they are merely conventional. We should respect other cultures

---

22. Benedict, *Patterns of Culture* (Boston: Houghton Mifflin, 1934), p. 100.

23. See especially Mary Catherine Bateson, *With a Daughter's Eye: A Memoir of Margaret Mead and Gregory Bateson* (New York: William Morrow, 1984), pp. 115-27; and Margaret M. Caffrey, *Ruth Benedict: Stranger in this Land* (Austin: University of Texas Press, 1989), pp. 188-205.

24. Geertz, *The Interpretation of Cultures* (Chicago: University of Chicago Press, 1973), p. 346.

25. Benedict, *Patterns of Culture*, pp. 276-77.

26. Benedict, *Patterns of Culture*, p. 195.

with their different moralities as valid for them. But while she phrases
cultural relativism in positive terms as respect for social others, this assertion carries with it an implicit denial, the denial that our own norms, or
any norms at all, are really binding or God-given. Rather than affirming
our own norms as valid for us, she juxtaposes them to other cultural norms
so as to show the arbitrary and prejudiced nature of our own. What appears
to be positive affirmation of the worth of other moralities is really a
disguised attack on our own morality, a morality that, because of its Christian base, carries with it notions of sin and guilt. She repeatedly calls for
a "rational social order" based on a "realistic social faith" to replace the
present order. Her doctrine of cultural relativism is more a rhetorical tool
than a systematic philosophical position consistently maintained — not
simply an inference the facts force her to accept, something she discovers
in her data, but something she intentionally constructs out of her cultural
materials. She invokes the scientific will to truth in order to suppress her
equally present will to discredit another truth.

Evangelical theologian Carl F. H. Henry tells us that fallen
humankind "devotes human reasoning to the cause of spiritual rebellion."[27]
From different commitments, psychological anthropologist Weston La
Barre makes a similar point, arguing that the anthropologist conducts "his
private rebellion in the arcane language of academic books — strong medicine for those who would understand him, for he casts up relativities fully
as threatening as those of Freud, Einstein, and Marx."[28] I think it is fair to
say that Benedict was in rebellion against the traditional view of sinful
men and women before a righteous God, a private rebellion that she
conducted in the "arcane language of academic books."

Benedict is not unique. Rather, she is characteristic of the dominant
trend in anthropology. When the "father" of modern anthropology, E. B.
Tylor, penned the phrase "theologians all to expose, 'tis the mission of
primitive man,"[29] he was indicating one attraction the study of primitive
human beings has for the anthropologist: the utility of using the study of
social others to undercut and discredit the worldview of theologians — that
is, Christian theologians. In his article "Religion and the Anthropologists,"
E. E. Evans-Pritchard says that anthropologists are for the most part
"bleakly hostile" toward the Christian faith. Few British anthropologists

27. Henry, *God, Revelation and Authority,* 6 vols. (Waco, TX: Word Books, 1976-83),
2:135.

28. La Barre, *The Ghost Dance: Origins of Religion* (Garden City, NY: Doubleday,
1970), p. 4.

29. Tylor, cited in Mark Kline Taylor, *Beyond Explanation: Religious Dimensions in
Cultural Anthropology* (Macon, GA: Mercer University Press, 1986), p. 17.

are Christians, and as for America, "I do not know of a single person among the prominent . . . anthropologists of America at the present time who adheres to any faith."[30] His observations are still largely true today.

What anthropologists do generally adhere to is the ethic of cultural relativism. Sol Tax writes:

> Whatever propensities and values may unite and distinguish anthropologists, first among them is a view of life that is relativistic and pluralistic. . . . We are the only profession, or even community, for which this view of life is definitive. . . . It must be kept in mind that anthropology is a free association. Nobody has to stick with it, or with us. Hence the self-selection for propensities and values becomes confirmed by association, . . . books, . . . contacts with fellow students (etc).[31]

Tax is suggesting that what the anthropological community shares is not just a scientific method or a specific subject matter but a set of value orientations best summarized as a commitment to relativism. He suggests the existence of a self-selection process whereby those most attracted to relativism are most likely to become anthropologists, but he only hints at mechanisms of social exclusion and control that also operate within the social institutions connected with anthropology, an important topic we unfortunately cannot pursue here.

It follows that if the key anthropological virtue is cultural respect, then the primary sin is to evidence a lack of such respect, that is, to cross cultural boundaries with a message implying moral judgment — in a word, to be ethnocentric. And if, as Clifford Geertz says, "the anthropologists' severest term of moral abuse" is the term "ethnocentric,"[32] then the anthropologist's clearest example of ethnocentrism is the missionary. (We cannot explore here the inherent contradiction of a true relativist morally abusing anyone.)

One anthropologist writes, "As anthropologists, we talk a lot about missionaries, but we seldom write about them. One cannot but wonder why this is true."[33] The answer becomes clear if we examine the contexts in which anthropologists talk about missionaries. For years, I have carefully noted each anthropological reference to missionaries I have heard or read, and it is quite clear that in the vast majority of cases the missionary is

---

30. Evans-Pritchard, "Religion and the Anthropologists," in *Essays in Social Anthropology* (New York: The Free Press of Glencoe, 1963), p. 45.

31. Tax, "A Community of Anthropologists," *Practicing Anthropology* 1 (1978): 8.

32. Geertz, *The Interpretation of Cultures*, p. 24.

33. David Spain, review of *Colonial Evangelism*, by T. O. Beidelman, in *American Anthropologist* 86 (1984): 205.

referred to as an exemplar or symbol of ethnocentrism, a symbol invoked when socializing others to relativistic values or when warning that such values are threatened. The following quote from an anthropology textbook is a typical instance of the pattern:

> The premises of missionary work are directly opposite to those of anthropology. As cultural relativists, anthropologists begin with the assumption that any cultural system is as good or bad as any other system. Missionaries begin with the ethnocentric view that their religion is the true path to salvation. . . . Conversion to Christianity was the major objective of missionary work. Conversion often involved the destruction of native beliefs and rituals. One of the crudest, but most effective techniques for proving the inferiority of native deities was the desecration of native shrines, temples, and holy places. Missionaries in the Pacific are known to have urinated and defecated on native shrines to demonstrate graphically that their god was superior to native deities.[34]

The student, of course, is not in a position to challenge the veracity of such undocumented claims. (The authors' use of the phrase "are known" suggests that they are repeating hearsay rather than giving firsthand knowledge.) But in a real sense, from the authors' standpoint, careful documentation is beside the point. It is the allegorical and symbolic meanings that are key. Even if it turned out that missionaries never defecated on others' shrines or that it was an unusual exception, the authors are not quibbling about whether or not certain things happened historically. They are making the symbolic claim that the essence of ethnocentrism is to defecate on the gods and sacred values of other people and that this is what all missionaries, in essence, do. I suggest that most anthropologists are less interested in understanding the missionary than in using the missionary as a symbol. This, in part, explains why they do not often make the missionary the object of careful documented study but, while socializing students to relativistic values, do refer frequently to the missionary in oral contexts where they cannot be held accountable for accuracy or neutrality. Where they do try to merge symbol and allegory with sustained written analysis of actual missionary situations — as in the book *Is God an American?* — they commonly end up damaging their own credibility and cognitive authority.

Evangelical anthropologists regularly testify to the value conflicts they face in a consistently relativistic community. Missionary anthropologist Wayne Dye gives an example of the pressure he felt:

---

34. Eugene N. Cohen and Edwin Eames, *Cultural Anthropology* (Boston: Little, Brown, 1982), pp. 376-77.

I still have painful memories of walking across the University of Michigan campus one beautiful spring day with my closest friend among my fellow graduate students. Suddenly, out of the blue he said, "If I were in your shoes and were planning to go to New Guinea and make Christians of them, I couldn't sleep nights." I had been committed to missionary work for years, but his words, and the knowledge that he expressed the sentiments of all my colleagues brought much inner conflict.[35]

But while value pressures on evangelicals entering anthropology are potentially dangerous, a far more subtle danger is embedded in the cognitive concepts, categories, and understandings the anthropologist is expected to learn and employ. This is because the history of the discipline, with its development of research agendas, processes of concept formation, theoretical development, and so forth, is embedded in a specific context and shaped by shared assumptions and value commitments. In a classic article on the history of anthropology, Irving Hallowell notes that anthropology addresses the same subject matter that religion has traditionally addressed and that the secular anthropologist replaces priests and theologians as the "class of persons to whom one could turn for authoritative answers to anthropological questions."[36] He continues:

> All cultures provide answers to some anthropological questions which are considered to be authoritative and final. Traditional knowledge of this kind may be characterized as folk anthropology, i.e., a body of observations, beliefs, and socially sanctioned dogmas which parallel folk knowledge about other aspects of the phenomenal world. . . . In early western culture, the level of knowledge represented in the traditional Christian world view is equivalent to folk anthropology. . . . This traditional world view of the West is the historical backdrop against which changes in the answers to anthropological questions may be plotted.[37]

Earlier in this essay, I pointed out one aspect of Christian "folk anthropology," one aspect of "the historical backdrop against which changes in the answers to anthropological questions may be plotted." That is, I pointed out the extent to which sin concepts were once pivotal to all sorts of Western cultural discourses reflecting on the human condition.

35. Dye, "On the Ethics of Evangelism," in Franklin, ed., *Current Concerns of Anthropologists and Missionaries,* p. 88.

36. Hallowell, "The History of Anthropology as an Anthropological Problem," in *Contributions to Anthropology: Selected Papers of Irving Hallowell,* ed. Raymond Fogelson et al. (Chicago: University of Chicago Press, 1976), p. 22.

37. Hallowell, "The History of Anthropology," p. 24.

Following Hallowell, I suggest that anthropological concepts and categories are intended as replacements of, and not simply as compatible with, such prior concepts. Furthermore, I suggest that anthropologists are generally hostile to concepts implying ethical choice, moral accountability, conscience, human evil, and the like, and therefore that changes in concepts reflect changes in value positions and philosophical assumptions as much as they do refinements in scientificity.

When anthropologists do fieldwork with flesh-and-blood people around the world, they listen as people talk about moral rights and duties of husband and wife, father and son, mother's brother and sister's son. They listen to the gossip about the moral failings of others, about those who are stingy with food when they ought to be generous, of those who are lazy and do not contribute their share. They overhear parental admonitions, warnings, and moral harangues at youth whose moral delicts threaten to dishonor their family's reputation. Sentiments of gratitude, of disapproval, of resentment, of love, of feeling hurt, and of obligation or responsibility are the stuff of day-to-day interaction and discourse. Interpersonal conflicts with their accusations, expressions of indignation, jealous defense of marital rights, and expressions of guilt, remorse, and shame are universally present.

Yet anthropologists have fairly consistently refused to utilize an analytical vocabulary appropriate to the sociocultural interpersonal order as a moral order. Instead, they have borrowed from mathematics the concepts of structure and function; from physics they have borrowed terms such as *equilibrium, statics, dynamics,* and *friction;* from biological evolutionary theory have come terms such as *adaptation, carrying capacity,* and *evolution;* and from other societies have come terms such as *taboo, mana,* and *gens* — all of which were adopted as analytical concepts to be applied in contexts far removed from where they originated. My point is not to deny the utility of such concepts but to note that they were developed to the exclusion and neglect of other equally viable concepts, concepts that, if used, would call our attention to the moral dimensions of life.

In his book *The Seven Deadly Sins: Society and Evil,* sociologist Stanford Lyman writes that the "rise and proliferation of the sciences of man since the 1850's have been attended by the fall and contraction of the idea of sin."[38] He argues that the contemporary "sciences of man" have ceased to view people as active moral agents who are responsible for the evil they choose and are characterized by, and that as a result, such sciences have ended up with one-sided and distorted understandings of human

---

38. Lyman, *The Seven Deadly Sins: Society and Evil* (New York: General Hall, 1989), p. 119.

realities. He endeavors to show the ongoing utility and relevance of sin concepts for understanding human empirical realities. But his is an isolated voice. As Karl Menninger documented in his book *Whatever Became of Sin?*

> [sin] increasingly disappeared from public view. . . . Sin was no longer a topic of conversation, debate, argument, accusation, and public remorse — as it had long been. . . . It became a word of mild disapproval, less and less frequently applied — or a jocular word.[39]

Assumptions and beliefs about human nature continue to exist only as long as cultural discourses sustain them. And as Menninger points out, sin is now absent from the major discourses of our society. Television, newspapers, magazines, university professors (psychologists, sociologists, and anthropologists), textbooks, and books of pop psychology invite us daily to reflect on every aspect of the human condition using concepts that were developed independently from an organic unity with a biblical world-view. But while one would expect the clergy to continue to utilize a sin discourse, Menninger notes that even they increasingly borrow their concepts from psychology and seem uncomfortable talking about sin. While sin does appear in occasional sermons in church as the pastor expounds an ancient text, sin is likely to disappear when the pastor actually gets into the business of counseling someone, and other conceptual tools are introduced to interpret people to themselves and to direct them toward hope. Furthermore, as church members leave the brief Sunday morning exposition, they return to normal life, where in all other institutional settings the discourses to which they are exposed use other concepts, categories, and interpretations to help them think about themselves — concepts and interpretations that frequently bear the cognitive authority of science and the university.

In one northern California survey, one hundred percent of Southern Baptists, ninety-three percent of Presbyterians, and ninety-six percent of Catholics affirmed the divinity of Jesus Christ — a relatively high degree of orthodoxy. But when asked about the traditional orthodox concept of original sin, fifty-five percent of Southern Baptists and sixty-eight percent of Presbyterians denied it. Among Catholics only nineteen percent denied the doctrine of original sin.[40] Apparently people's capacity to think in terms of sin is affected less by the formal orthodoxies of their church than by the

---

39. Menninger, *Whatever Became of Sin?* (New York: Hawthorne Books, 1973), p. 46.
40. R. Stephen Warner, *New Wine in Old Wineskins: Evangelicals and Liberals in a Small Town Church* (Berkeley: University of California Press, 1988), p. 55.

extent to which their church maintains a strong sin discourse, something the Catholic church maintains because of its practice of confession and penance.

Were Jonathan Edwards to preach his famous sermon "Sinners in the Hands of an Angry God" in most contemporary churches, it would not generate revival but would make people uncomfortable and ill-at-ease, not with guilt at the horror of their own sin, but with the bald assumption of radical human wickedness — something we affirm in principle but have a hard time linking conceptually to the surface of human life as actually lived. Evangelicals are weak not in formal orthodoxy but in developing deep and profound understandings of the human person based on biblical assumptions and in generating sophisticated, empirically based discourses resting on such assumptions.

Evangelicals respond to a secular culture with apologetics, philosophy, and a defense of the historicity of the faith, while that culture with its discourses quietly chips away at biblical foundational assumptions of who we are as humans — giving new categories to think with and grounding its assumptions in sophisticated empirical studies. The result is that we defend, philosophically and historically, a faith that ceases to make sense of our condition, a faith that in terms of our subjective perceptions ceases to have face validity or subjective plausibility. With the demise of sin, hell becomes indefensible, grace loses its appeal, missions faces a crisis of legitimacy, and the cross of Christ has no meaning.

As I have shown, cultural anthropology, through its particular approach to understanding people of other cultures, has contributed to this demise of sin, a contribution evidenced both in the United States and in missions contexts. Anthropology's damaging effects in this area are aided by the fact that culture does pose difficult issues for biblical understandings of humankind, issues that secular anthropologists have skillfully exploited but that evangelical scholars have largely failed to address. Missionaries to Tahiti, for example, found people whose consciences were apparently unbothered by open extramarital affairs, but who reacted with horror to the idea of men and women eating together. A veteran missionary recently said to me, "The [X——] just don't feel sin like we do. They have no feeling of guilt if they lie to you, only embarrassment if they're caught." Another missionary to a tribal society told me that their response to the gospel message made him feel like he'd been trying for thirty years to sell them a white elephant. The gospel, he felt, simply held no appeal for them. He concluded that in most missions contexts when people "become Christians" they do so for motives other than recognition of sin, repentance, and desire for the forgiving work of Christ — motives such as desire for material benefits, physical healing, or social status. Again and again missionaries have expressed puzzlement when their message of sin, judgment, mercy, justification, and salvation so evidently elicited no inner assent, no spontaneous response of the soul. On the other hand, missionary successes frequently raise equally intriguing issues, though these are largely unexplored — successes resting, for example, on a symbolism found both in Scripture and in cultures until now unaffected by Scripture, such as the symbolism of sin as a defiling filth from which we need cleansing, or the symbolism of guilt as a debt that must be either paid or forgiven.

Since missiology looks to evangelical anthropologists for help in understanding native peoples, there is a practical need for evangelical anthropologists to try to shed light on such topics as moral sentiments and judgments, defilement and debt, sin and taboo, shame and guilt. But even apart from practical applications, intellectual fidelity to biblical assumptions requires that we make such understandings central to our knowledge of humankind. Yet, for reasons alluded to earlier, the discipline of anthropology as a whole has not encouraged pursuit of such understandings and emphases.

A diagnostic question assessing how we as evangelical anthropologists are doing is this: Does the work and teaching of evangelical anthropologists tend to enhance missionary ability to employ biblical concepts in other cultures, or to make their use more problematic? I believe that, unfortunately, the answer is largely the latter. Evangelical anthropologists have made many good contributions to missiology, but, with minor exceptions,[41] not in this area. Their main contribution here has been to call on missionaries to respect cultural differences and to warn them that the impulse to condemn is ethnocentric. This is an important contribution, a needed first step. We are culturally ethnocentric. We do judge in terms of our own cultural norms. Crossing cultural lines with a gospel implying judgment and condemnation makes it all too easy for the missionary to confuse his or her own culture with the gospel. As a result of anthropological warnings about ethnocentrism, the missionary now feels nervous, and rightly so, when using sin language to speak to people of another culture. The problem comes when the evangelical anthropologist stops here and does not go on in a second stage to help the missionary develop conceptual tools that are appropriate for speaking to sin and conscience in other cultural contexts, a prerequisite to speaking of grace and forgiveness.

The result of our failure here is that there tend to be two kinds of

---

41. For a brief but important exception, see Wayne Dye, "Towards a Cross-Cultural Definition of Sin," *Missiology* 4 (1976): 27-41.

missionary. One kind has learned the anthropological lesson well, that we must respect culture and try to understand it, but feels uneasy using the biblical language of condemnation and a call for repentance from sin. Those with the most anthropological training are frequently least comfortable using the biblical concepts. And then there are those who reject the anthropological lesson, who unflinchingly speak with the concepts of Scripture, but whose insensitivity and refusal to seek cultural understanding are destructive of genuine moral and spiritual change. Missionaries are pulled in two opposing directions because of the fact that missionary anthropology has not yet carved out a middle way that allows for a balanced integration. Evangelical anthropologists must not just challenge inappropriate uses of the concept of sin in the cross-cultural context but must also, in a second stage, give the concept of sin back to the missionary, refitted for the task of gospel witness in a cross-cultural context and appropriate for speaking to people of other cultures and engaging an affirmation in their consciences of the goodness and truth of God's righteous judgments, before which all of us stand condemned and thus in need of grace.

An anthropological understanding that is faithful both to empirical realities and to the biblical view of human beings as active moral agents is extremely difficult to attain. It requires a mastery of two intellectual traditions (mastering even one is a monumental task) and a capacity to work through contradictory values and assumptions in order to create a fruitful integration that recaptures biblical concepts, not just in relation to an expounded biblical text, but as analytical tools capable of being used to interpret real people in the real world, in cultural worlds, to themselves and to others. Evangelical anthropologists will not drift into correct understandings through a passively submissive relation to the discipline and its paradigms, values, and relevance structures. Instead, there must be active recognition and documentation of ways in which bias distorts the discipline, and active, intentional intellectual activity that seeks to generate new empirically based discourses on subjects that the discipline has heretofore ignored or distorted, but that biblical assumptions would suggest should receive attention.

For this to happen requires that we give attention to the institutional supports needed for such understanding to be generated. Clearly the university is strategic as the institutional setting most supportive of academic research. Yet if the evangelical anthropologist receives intellectual stimulation exclusively in such a setting, the institutional context overwhelmingly militates against the likelihood of the individual ending up with genuinely biblical anthropological understandings. Only if institutional settings are created where university-based evangelical anthropologists are able to interact with each other and with other evangelical scholars about the implications of biblical teaching on human nature will such anthropologists be able consistently to resist being co-opted and to move toward biblical understandings.

The anthropologist who makes his or her home in an evangelical seminary has less institutional support for intellectual activity but benefits by being in perhaps the only institution of higher learning today that unashamedly uses biblical concepts with which to think about human beings. The drawback is that such concepts in seminary are used with reference to the text and to theology, while the relation of evangelicals' understanding to empirical human realities is problematic. Ground-breaking work in generating new understandings must be field-based. The seminary is too far from the field to be the best or only setting in which anthropological theoretical understanding is pursued by evangelicals.

Evangelical missionaries have the advantage of being field-based, of spending years or even decades with people of another society, an advantage even anthropologists can't begin to match. But while the task of the cross-cultural missionary is one of the most difficult on earth, raising complex issues that cry out with the need for an understanding that only systematic study and analysis can give, evangelical mission agencies have consistently sought candidates with zeal and passion while downplaying the need for context-specific intellectual work. Such missionaries generate popular discourses about the situations they face that are designed to inspire the hearts of home supporters with the needs and successes of missions, but they generate no regular intellectual discourses about the people to whom they are ministering designed to inform, instruct, and stimulate the minds of colleagues or others.

The Summer Institute of Linguistics, or SIL (better known to evangelicals by its sister organization, Wycliffe Bible Translators), is unusual in that this large organization of evangelical missionaries combines lengthy commitments to minority societies with strong academic values (it includes over 225 members with Ph.D. degrees). SIL has powerful field-based institutions for intellectual development, theoretical stimulation, and guidance, and it gives support to advanced studies in linguistics. Theory merges with local realities for a sophisticated understanding of minority languages, an understanding that forms the basis of Bible translation. But when it comes to an intellectual understanding of the native conscience, of sin, and of how best to communicate the gospel, these missionaries become intellectual isolates operating on an ad hoc basis and relying on understandings gleaned from personal Bible study and devotional life or on past biblical training in formal settings far removed from the realities of tribal life. Missionary after missionary may be frustrated by a lack of response or may be puzzled by questionable response, by confusions over sin and how to address the conscience such that grace makes sense. As a religious community, SIL will acknowledge such concerns in its prayer meetings; but as an intellectual community, it gives institutional support only to solving problems of language. How to understand the native conscience is something each missionary must do privately, using intuitive guesswork. Each will be encouraged, even required, to write a linguistic grammar, dictionary, and so forth, but I know of no SIL person who has been encouraged to write a moral grammar, to explore academically the moral code of a people.

In Latin America, there are hundreds of evangelical missionaries with decades of experience working in tribal societies. Each of these missionaries faces very similar sets of issues, issues posed by shamanism, by traditional interpretations of suffering and death, by taboo-based moral orders, by the pervasiveness of envy and envy-avoidance behavior, by the centrality of shame and the question of whether guilt is felt, etc. Yet such missionaries operate as intellectual isolates fumbling through these issues on their own. What knowledge and insight is attained remains with the individual and does not become shared knowledge from which others may benefit. There is little institutional or value support for generating an intellectual discourse for missionary colleagues. If missionaries turn to anthropological writings on these societies, they will find a lot on ecological adaptation in the rain forest, on social structure, on the economic and political aspects of Native Americans' current situation, on gender relations, on binary oppositions in native mythic thought, and on native cognitive classification of plants, animals, or colors. While they may learn some things deemed relevant, they will rightly be frustrated by an inability to relate such topics to their own concerns.

The point is that if missionaries, in conjunction with evangelical anthropologists, do not pursue such concerns, non-Christian anthropologists will not do it for them. Missionaries have pioneered in developing conceptual tools for analyzing unwritten languages, and SIL has developed academic value commitments and an institutional superstructure highly supportive of missionary intellectual analysis of language. There is no reason, given the right support structure, why missionaries could not play an equally pivotal role in analyzing the moral dimensions of life in non-Western societies. Given the relatively small number of evangelical anthropologists and the large number of evangelical missionaries strategically positioned in other cultures, it is in the best interests of all concerned to develop stronger ties between the two. If evangelical anthropologists can research issues highlighted in this essay, they will both expand and correct anthropological knowledge, and they will do so in an area most likely to convince missionaries that anthropological study can strategically aid their understanding. It is not inconceivable in such a case that many missionaries would be inspired to anthropological study and, in collaboration with professional evangelical anthropologists, would make substantial contributions to a knowledge of humankind that at one and the same time rests on biblical assumptions, is grounded in empirical realities, and strategically informs missionary practice.

Evangelical anthropologists must necessarily be dependent on the discipline and its institutions, but if they are not to be co-opted by it they must actively construct interactional ties with an intellectual community of those committed to Scripture, and they must self-consciously stand in tension with many of the assumptions, paradigms, and values of the discipline. Concepts, ideas, and insights given by the Ancient Text must somehow inform and inspire the development of research agendas and analytical tools. Fidelity to God's revelation requires it.

Eschatologically Oriented Psychology:
A New Paradigm for the Integration
of Psychology and Christianity

WARREN J. HEARD, JR.

INTRODUCTION

IT HAS BEEN forty years since H. Richard Niebuhr published his important work *Christ and Culture*.[1] Since that time his analysis, which outlines the possibilities describing the relationship between Christianity and culture, has given rise to much fertile discussion. Niebuhr's analysis has been applied by J. D. Carter and B. Narramore to explore the relationship between psychology and Christianity.[2] These authors suggest that a person can adopt one of four positions with regard to the Christian's position toward psychology. First, the Christian can be against the integration of psychology and Christianity. Certainly there are many representatives who advocate this position.[3] A second approach assumes that psychology and Christianity have a good deal of common ground and that the Christian can benefit greatly by exploring this common material.[4] Yet another formu-

---

1. Niebuhr, *Christ and Culture* (New York: Harper & Row, 1951).

2. Carter and Narramore, *The Integration of Psychology and Theology* (Grand Rapids: Zondervan, 1979).

3. For example, J. Adams, *Competent To Counsel* (Grand Rapids: Baker, 1970); C. R. Solomon, *Handbook to Happiness* (Wheaton: Tyndale, 1975); W. K. Kirkpatrick, *Psychological Seduction: The Failure of Modern Psychology* (New York: Thomas Nelson, 1983); M. Bobgan and D. Bobgan, *The Psychological Way/The Spiritual Way: Are Christianity and Psychotherapy Compatible?* (Minneapolis: Bethany House, 1979); et al.

4. M. James and L. Savary, *The Power at the Bottom of the Well: T. A. and Religious Experience* (New York: Harper & Row, 1974); S. Hiltner, *Theological Dynamics* (Nashville: Abingdon Press, 1972); J. Sanford, *Dreams: God's Forgotten Language* (Philadelphia: Lip-

lation suggests that the two disciplines, psychology and Christianity, are separate disciplines and that the integrity of each is threatened if the theorist attempts to integrate them. Nevertheless, there are "parallels" between them. Thus the "superego" may merely be another word for the "conscience," and the "id" may be roughly equivalent to Paul's notion of the "sin nature" or John's "lust of the flesh." But these are correlations only, the lining up of parallel concepts from two disciplines.[5] These three options are rejected by Carter and Narramore in favor of a final option in which psychology and Christianity are thoroughly integrated.[6]

Carter and Narramore's model of the integration of psychology and Christianity is grounded in their belief that God is the author of all truth.

> Reason, revelation, and the scientific method all are seen as playing a valid role in the search for truth. Since the human being is created in the image of God and since God has revealed Himself in a special way throughout Scripture and in a general way through creation, we expect to find congruence between Scripture and the findings of psychology. . . . The Integrates approach emphasizes both psychology and the Scriptures because they are allies. . . . Believing in the unity of truth, proponents of the Integrates model . . . assume that since God is the Author of all truth . . . there is only one set of explanatory hypotheses.[7]

The model of integration suggested by Carter and Narramore is helpful, but it does not satisfactorily address a central issue — namely, conflicting conclusions from the disciplines of psychology and Christian theology. They do admit this possibility and therefore enjoin their readers to remain humble in their truth statements because of human limitations and fallibility;

---

pincott, 1968); C. Jung, *Psychology and Religion* (New Haven: Yale University Press, 1962); P. Meehl, *What Then Is Man?* (St. Louis: Concordia Publishing House, 1958).

5. Cf. P. Clement, "Behavior Modification of the Spirit," in *Psychology and Christianity,* ed. J. R. Fleck and J. D. Carter (Nashville: Abingdon Press, 1981), pp. 112-20; C. Narramore, *The Psychology of Counseling* (Grand Rapids: Zondervan, 1960); P. Barkman, *Man in Conflict* (Grand Rapids: Zondervan, 1965); M. Sall, *Faith, Psychology and Christian Maturity* (Grand Rapids: Zondervan, 1975); J. Drakeford, *Integrity Therapy* (Nashville: Broadman, 1967).

6. Besides Carter and Narramore, some proponents of this position include W. Hulme, *Counseling and Theology* (Philadelphia: Fortress, 1956); P. Tournier, *Guilt and Grace* (New York: Harper & Row, 1962); K. Farnsworth, *Whole-Hearted Integration* (Grand Rapids: Baker Book House, 1985); M. Wagner, *Put It All Together* (Grand Rapids: Zondervan, 1974); G. Collins, *The Rebuilding of Psychology* (Wheaton: Tyndale, 1977); A. van Kamm, *Religion and Personality* (Garden City, NY: Doubleday, 1968). Cf. L. Crabb, *Effective Biblical Counseling* (Grand Rapids: Zondervan, 1977), for yet another analysis of possible integration models, but since his work is on a more popular level it will not be considered in detail here.

7. Carter and Narramore, *Integration,* pp. 103-4.

moreover, they extol as a primary virtue the ability to tolerate ambiguity. But they do not decisively address the problem of conflicting results.[8] Furthermore, they do not address the issue of the fall recorded in Genesis 3. Because of Adam's sin, God's creation was marred. God does continue to reveal himself through his created order (cf. Ps. 19:1-6; Rom. 1:18-32; etc.), but the study of natural revelation by the sciences is *not* the study of God's *perfect* creation; rather, it is the study of God's creation marred by sin. Therefore, when conclusions are drawn in psychology (or, for that matter, in any of the sciences), care must be exercised because the effects of the fall remain and may well distort the observer's conclusions.

A final drawback regarding the suggestion of Carter and Narramore is that they have not constructed a model that yields a truly *Christian* psychology. Rather, while the model that they have produced justifies the rigorous study of both psychology and Christianity and suggests a way to integrate material common to both, the results of integration using their model do not produce that which is uniquely Christian. Moreover, Carter and Narramore do not provide us with a theory or methodology by which Christian faith has functional control over the discipline of psychology.

In his book *Whole-Hearted Integration,* Kirk Farnsworth advances the discussion begun by Carter and Narramore with his inclusion of epistemology and his emphasis on life application. Farnsworth uses similar categories and is obviously indebted to Carter and Narramore, who in turn are indebted to Niebuhr. Like Carter and Narramore, Farnsworth emphasizes the unity of truth; consequently he places an equal emphasis upon natural and special revelation. Neither category of revelation is elevated over the other; thus Scripture cannot be used as the final arbiter if a conflict arises between psychology (the product of studying natural revelation) and Christianity (the product of studying special revelation). Rather, according to Farnsworth, if a conflict does arise the true integrationist re-studies the empirical data, being careful that the scientific method has been meticulously followed, and also does his or her exegetical work again to attempt to arrive at sound theological conclusions. If the conclusions reached in both spheres are still in conflict, the integrationist puts the issue into abeyance because a final arbiter between them apparently does not presently exist; more research in both areas is needed to resolve the issue in an unbiased way.

Farnsworth is particularly critical of what he terms "theological imperialism." To decide an issue merely on the basis of whether the conclusion is derived from natural or special revelation is, for Farnsworth, an unjustified imperialism.

---

8. Carter and Narramore, *Integration,* pp. 117-18.

The larger problem . . . concerns theological imperialism. In other words, theology has assumed functional control over psychology. . . . [C]laiming that theological findings are superior to, or automatically "truer" than psychological findings makes a mockery of the additional claim that all truth is God's truth and he is Creator and Sustainer of all creation. When trying to relate into a single idea a psychological finding and a theological finding that . . . look as though they are in conflict, there are two choices: one or the other is true, or they are both false. They cannot both be true if they disagree with each other. Nor is the theological finding automatically the true one. What one must do is go back and reverify the methodological/hermeneutical procedures that were involved in arriving at each conclusion. If this does not resolve the issue, then integration cannot proceed. . . . The problem is dogmatism: an unqualified certainty that the two disciplines are in hierarchical relationship, with theology automatically at the top.[9]

It is this issue of "theological imperialism" that needs to be addressed. The remainder of this essay will attempt to justify an approach that places the careful results of biblical exegesis in the superior position, not only to adjudicate conflicting conclusions between psychology and Christianity, but also to exercise *functional control* over the development of psychological theory as well as therapeutic interventions.

THE PROBLEM OF EPISTEMOLOGY

Part of the problem is related to epistemology. Empiricism, the method of psychology as well as of the rest of the sciences, is generally regarded as a methodology that, if responsibly and consistently applied, produces objective results. Thus when a conclusion is reached in the branch of science known as psychology, this conclusion is regarded as true because it has been proven empirically. Christianity, on the other hand, is regarded by empiricists as a faith system, which by definition is subjective. It is therefore inconsequential whether the interpreter's exegetical method is responsible or not: the results remain subjective. This kind of scientific imperialism is common, and it has caused a number of Christian writers to overreact and condemn all psychology (along with many of the other sciences) as an inappropriate means to determine truth.

The way the above argument is framed misunderstands the relation between "objectivity" and "subjectivity." Many scientists have urged that

9. Farnsworth, *Whole-Hearted Integration*, pp. 97-98.

to be "objective" entails assuming a methodology that will provide the inquirer with some sort of Archimedean point from which one can escape the shackles of one's worldview and observe without bias, "objectively." In other words, that which is "out there" (object) is assumed to be independent of its observer (subject), and true knowledge occurs when the observer correctly describes or represents the object being studied. "Subjectivity," on the other hand, merely notes that the subject is always involved with that which is being observed (the object). The subject's culture, biases, personal experiences, worldview, and so forth will, to some extent, shape how the object being observed is perceived. Though there is an object that exists independently, and theoretically could be known "objectively," the lens through which the subject views the object may prevent the subject from perceiving the object without bias. Arthur Holmes notes that important distinction:

> What is fact? Metaphysically, a fact is an objective state of affairs that pertains at a given time and place and in a given set of relationships, independently of whether any of us know it at all. Epistemologically, a fact is a "fact of experience," related to the whole complex flux of inner and outer experience of which it is a part. Subjectivity has intruded and shaped it. The facts we know, then, are not bare facts clothed only in a birthday suit of metaphysical objectivity, but "interprefacts" perceived and understood by a human person who clothes them in the habits of his human experience and perspective.
>
> Both our interprefacts and our larger and more deliberate interpretations of things, being shaped in measure by what we are, are shaped as well by world-view perspectives and what we consider to be objectively real.[10]

Most of the founders of the social sciences, including psychology, did not view reality in the way it is described above by Holmes. Being influenced by the scientific method, most early social scientists believed that social facts are "things" — that is, that they exist independently as real entities apart from the realm of human experience. Moreover, they concluded that the researcher can study social reality without concern for the process of social production, and, even more importantly, that whoever engages in the study of this social reality, given the use of the proper method, will arrive at the same conclusions. The study of the social sciences was modeled after this particular approach to the study of the natural sciences.

Wilhelm Dilthey, who followed Schleiermacher, the father of modern

10. Holmes, *Contours of a World View* (Grand Rapids: Eerdmans, 1983), pp. 150-51.

hermeneutics, attempted to forge a methodological basis for the *Geistes-wissenschaften* to parallel that which Kant had erected for the *Naturwis-senschaften*. Dilthey reasoned that each human's existence is, above all, historical, and therefore that a *Critique of Historical Reason* could be produced to complement Kant's *Critique of Pure Reason*. In Dilthey's mind, one's existence and personal history are grounded not in transcen- dental reality but in the reality of lived experience. Lived experience is therefore the *bruta facta* for the *Geisteswissenschaften*. Dilthey also argued that in the human sciences objective interpretations are possible. Indeed, expressions of a person's inner life, the imprint of a human on phenomena, can be the object of study. This is true whether these expressions are historical acts, gestures, law codes, art, literature, etc. Moreover, these objectifications have a fixed nature that makes objectivity possible.[11]

This belief in the objectivity of the sciences, whether human or natural, has largely been accepted in the Western world. In recent decades, however, confidence in the scientific method has been eroding. At one time it was believed that the methods of inquiry established by science could produce objective knowledge. The researcher could, through the rigorous use of the scientific method, reach some Archimedean point outside the system and actually make objective observations. This belief has now been seriously questioned. Philosophers of science,[12] sociologists of science,[13] historians of science,[14] natural scientists,[15] critical theorists,[16] and social

11. Dilthey, *Gesammelte Schriften,* 14 vols. (Göttingen: Vanderhoeck & Ruprecht, 1913-67).

12. R. Bernstein, *Beyond Objectivism and Relativism* (Philadelphia: University of Penn-sylvania Press, 1983); R. Rorty, "Solidarity or Objectivity?" in *Post-Analytic Philosophy,* ed. J. Rajchman and C. West (New York: Columbia University Press, 1985); R. Rorty, "Science and Solidarity," in *The Rhetoric of the Human Sciences,* ed. J. Nelson, A. Megill, and D. McCloskey (Madison: University of Wisconsin Press, 1987); R. Rorty, *Objectivity, Relativism, and Truth.* Philosophical Papers, vol. 1 (New York: Cambridge University Press, 1990).

13. K. Knorr-Cetina, *The Manufacture of Knowledge: An Essay on the Constructivist and Contextual Nature of Science* (New York: Pergamon Press, 1981); K. Knorr-Cetina and M. Mulkay, *Science Observed* (London, 1983).

14. T. S. Kuhn, *The Structure of Scientific Revolutions,* 2d ed. (Chicago: University of Chicago Press, 1970); T. S. Kuhn, *The Essential Tension* (Chicago: University of Chicago Press, 1977).

15. J. Hayward, *Perceiving Ordinary Magic: Science and Intuitive Wisdom* (Boston: New Science Library, 1984); H. Maturana and F. Varela, *The Tree of Knowledge: The Biological Roots of Understanding* (Boston: New Science Library, 1987).

16. J. Habermas, *Knowledge and Human Interests* (London: Heinemann, 1968; Boston: Beacon Press, 1971); T. Popkewitz, *Paradigm and Ideology in Educational Research* (New York: Falmer Press, 1984); T. Popkewitz, "Whose Future? Whose Past? Notes on Critical Science and Methodology," in *The Paradigm Dialogue,* ed. E. Guba (Beverly Hills: Sage, 1990).

scientists[17] have all argued that the scientific method does not guarantee objective results. These scholars have despaired of science ever producing a general methodology that, when consistently applied, would yield the kind of certainty that the positivist or empiricist approach to science had claimed just a few short decades ago. They persuasively argue that every discipline and every method of inquiry has its own biases and limitations. Moreover, "facts" cannot be totally separated from values, and the scientific enterprise, along with each discipline (including psychology), has agendas of its own.

SCIENCE AND HERMENEUTICS

It seems better to understand the method of the sciences as *hermeneutical.* Generally the field of hermeneutics covers three distinct but related enterprises. The first enterprise is biblical interpretation, or, more generally, the interpretation of religious traditions and sacred texts. The work of Heidegger, Gadamer, Ricoeur, and Bultmann provides new challenges to those concerned with biblical narrative, the interpretation of religious traditions, and the role that theology might play in the twentieth century. The second enterprise is the understanding and interpretation of legal and literary texts. The Italian scholar Emilio Betti has been an arch rival to Gadamer as the interpreter of this hermeneutical tradition. In his major work, translated into German in 1962, *Die Hermeneutik als allgemeine Methodik der Geisteswissenschaften* (and in Hirsch's *Validity in Interpretation,* published in 1967, which owes a great deal to Betti), it is forcefully argued that Heidegger and Gadamer lead us to a self-defeating historicism and relativism. Against Gadamer, both Betti and Hirsch argue that it is crucial to distinguish and separate the three traditional moments of hermeneutics that Gadamer blends together: understanding, interpretation, and application. The third enterprise, and the one that we intend to explore here in greater detail, is the understanding of the natural and social sciences (including psychology).

In contemporary reexaminations of the sciences there seems to be a growing understanding of the hermeneutical dimension in these disciplines. This same trend can be traced in post-empiricist philosophy and the history of science. Kuhn, for example, remarks in the preface to a collection of his articles:

17. K. Gergen, *Toward Transformation in Social Knowledge* (New York: Springer-Verlag, 1982); D. Polkinghorne, *Methodology for the Human Sciences: Systems of Inquiry* (Albany: State University of New York, 1983).

What I as a physicist had to discover for myself, most historians learn by example in the course of professional training. Consciously or not, they are all practitioners of the hermeneutic method. In my case, however, the discovery of hermeneutics did more than make history seem consequential. Its most immediate and decisive effect was instead on my view of science.[18]

Kuhn also suggests that

The early models of the sort of history that has so influenced me and my *historical* colleagues is the product of a post-Kantian European tradition which I and my *philosophical* colleagues continue to find opaque. In my own case, for example, even the term "hermeneutic" . . . was no part of my vocabulary as recently as five years ago. Increasingly, I suspect that anyone who believes that history may have deep philosophical import will have to learn to bridge the longstanding divide between the Continental and English-language philosophical traditions.[19]

Specifically, this hermeneutical dimension of science has begun to emerge in the critiques of logical positivism and empiricism, in the questioning of the claims of the primacy of the hypo-deductive models of explanation, in questioning the sharp dichotomy made between observation and theory, and in the exploration of the ways in which all description and observation are theory-impregnated.

Mary Hesse has articulated similar concerns and has summarized the new, post-empiricist account of natural science in the following five points:

1. In natural science data [are] not detachable from theory, for what count as data are determined in the light of some theoretical interpretation, and the facts themselves have to be reconstructed in the light of interpretation.
2. In natural science theories are not models externally compared to nature in a hypothetico-deductive schema, they are the way the facts themselves are seen.
3. In natural science the lawlike relations asserted of experience are internal, because what count as facts are constituted by what the theory says about their inter-relations with one another.
4. The language of natural science is irreducibly metaphorical and inexact, and formalizable only at the cost of distortion of the historical

18. Kuhn, *The Essential Tension*, p. xiii.
19. Kuhn, *The Essential Tension*, p. xv.

dynamics of scientific development and of the imaginative construc-
tions in terms of which nature is interpreted by science.
5. Meanings in natural science are determined by theory; they are understood by theoretical coherence rather than by correspondence with
   facts.[20]

These five incisive points criticizing the natural sciences are also applied
by Hesse to the human sciences. Furthermore, Hesse notes the hermeneutical nature of the entire scientific enterprise. The methodology of the
sciences is irreducibly circular: the part cannot be understood without the
whole, which itself depends on the relation of its parts; data and concepts
cannot be understood without theory and context, which themselves depend
on relations of data and concepts. Hesse notes that these contrasts have not
always been clearly formulated, particularly in relation to meaning and
interpretation. Hesse's critique reveals that it can be persuasively argued
that the sciences' methodology is hermeneutical.

It would be a mistake to conclude that post-empiricist philosophers
of science have been directly influenced by hermeneutics. By and large
they have been virtually ignorant of the hermeneutical tradition. It is primarily because of the internal debates among contemporary philosophers
of science and by reflection on, and argumentation about, a correct understanding of scientific inquiry that they have come to stress those features
of science that are hermeneutical. But this coincidence and convergence
should open the way to a serious consideration of hermeneutics in the
sciences and especially in psychology.

THE HERMENEUTICAL CIRCLE

The term *hermeneutical circle* is a venerable one in traditional hermeneutics.[21] The hermeneutical circle refers to the dialectical relation between a
whole and its parts during the process of interpretation.[22] There are different

---

20. Hesse, "In Defense of Objectivity," in her book *Revolutions and Reconstructions
in the Philosophy of Science* (Brighton, England: Harvester Press, 1980), pp. 171-72.
21. Bultmann adopted this term for Heidegger. On Heidegger's view of the hermeneutical
circle, see Anthony C. Thiselton, *The Two Horizons: New Testament Hermeneutics and Philosophical Description with Special Reference to Heidegger, Bultmann, Gadamer, and Wittgenstein*
(Grand Rapids: Eerdmans, 1980), pp. 104-5, 166, 196-97. For Bultmann's view, see
W. Schmithals, *An Introduction to the Theology of Rudolf Bultmann* (Minneapolis: Augsburg,
1968), pp. 243-48, and Bultmann's own article, "Is Presuppositionless Exegesis Possible?" in
Existence and Faith, ed. Schubert M. Ogden (London: Hodder and Stoughton, 1961).
22. A "dialectical" relation juxtaposes different or contradictory ideas and seeks to

versions, varieties, and occasions of the hermeneutical circle, depending upon the extent and nature of what is being interpreted. For example, the hermeneutical circle may operate with respect to a sentence: the whole of the sentence is understood only in light of the parts of the sentence, and the parts of the sentence are understood only in light of the whole sentence. Or it may operate with respect to a whole book: the whole of Ecclesiastes (or some other literary composition) is understood only in light of the parts of the book, and the parts of the book are understood only in light of the whole book. Moreover, it may be possible for one hermeneutical circle relation to operate with another hermeneutical circle relation in a dialectic in which both relations are parts of one larger relation or whole. To illustrate this point, note first that the hermeneutical circle, operating within each sentence, paragraph, and chapter, up to the whole book, enables an interpreter to understand a literary text. This text, in turn, may be one of the sources or "parts," along with other texts, artifacts, reports, and events, used by a historian to interpret a period of history.

It is interesting to witness how thinkers working in different contexts have discovered for themselves the centrality of hermeneutics. Thomas Kuhn records a "decisive episode" when he made this discovery in his struggle to make sense out of Aristotle's physics:

> When reading the works of an important thinker, look first for the apparent absurdities in the text and ask yourself how a sensible person could have written them. When you find an answer . . . when those passages make sense, then you may find that more central passages, ones you previously thought you understood, have changed their meaning.[23]

In order to make sense of "apparent absurdities," the reader needs to experiment with alternative readings that themselves can only be tested by seeing whether or not they make sense with other parts of the text the reader is seeking to understand. Whatever "subjective processes" take place in an interpreter — whether this happens in a flash on a hot summer day or is the result of a laborious struggle — the essential question is the adequacy of the interpretation, which can be judged only by returning to the texts themselves.

---

resolve their conflict by passing the opposing entities over into one another. Doubtless there are dialectical relations that are not of the hermeneutical circle variety. However, all hermeneutical circles are dialectics between a whole and its parts. Moreover, Wolfhart Pannenberg, *Theology and the Philosophy of Science* (Philadelphia: Westminster Press, 1976), flatly states that "dialectic and hermeneutic share the fundamental feature of being concerned with the analysis of the interrelation of wholes and parts" (p. 189).

23. Kuhn, *The Essential Tension*, pp. xi-xii.

But it is not just in Kuhn that we detect the importance of the hermeneutical circle. This is the very process that Clifford Geertz so eloquently characterizes (and explicitly relates to the hermeneutical circle), "namely, a continuous dialectical tacking between the most local of local detail and the most global of global structure in such a way as to bring both into view simultaneously."[24] The hermeneutical circle is also critical for Peter Winch. Although he does not explicitly mention it, the tracing of the circle is the procedure that he follows in seeking to understand Zande witchcraft.[25]

Charles Taylor also defends the importance of the hermeneutical circle when he argues that there is an unavoidably hermeneutical component to the sciences. Taylor is acutely aware that the appeal to the hermeneutical circle challenges the biases of those schooled in empiricism who demand some method of definitive empirical verification in testing hypotheses. Moreover, Taylor identifies the most frequent objection to the hermeneutical circle — namely, that it is really a *vicious* circle. For if we "validate" our global interpretations by appealing to the interpretations of the "parts," then we fail to break out of the circle of interpretations. When Taylor responds to this objection, he introduces a suggestion that is crucial in Gadamer's own understanding and transformation of the hermeneutical circle. According to Taylor, a hermeneutical science of humanity

> would not be founded on brute data; its most primitive data would be readings of meanings, and its object would have the [following] three properties . . . : the meanings are for a subject in the field or fields; they are, moreover, meanings which are partially constituted by self-definitions, which are in this sense already interpretations, and which can thus be re-expressed or made explicit by a science of politics. In our case, the subject may be a society or community; but the intersubjective meanings . . . embody a certain self-definition, a vision of the agent and his society, which is that of the society or community.

Such a science

> cannot but move in a hermeneutical circle. A given reading of the intersubjective meanings of a society, or of given institutions or practices, may seem well founded, because it makes sense of these practices or the

24. Geertz, "From the Native's Point of View: On the Nature of Anthropological Understanding," in *Interpretative Social Science: A Reader,* ed. P. Rabinow and W. M. Sullivan (Berkeley: University of California Press, 1979), p. 239.

25. Winch, *The Idea of a Social Science and Its Relation to Philosophy* (London: Routledge & Kegan Paul, 1958).

development of that society. But the conviction that it does make sense of this history itself is founded on further related readings.[26]

It is at this point that the empiricist or positivist objects. For the empiricist demands some clear procedure, some method that can break out of the circle of interpretations and serve as a touchstone for determining which interpretations are correct and which are not. Edward Schillebeeckx says it well:

> All understanding takes place in a circular movement — the answer is to some extent determined by the question, which is in turn confirmed, extended or corrected by the answer. A new question then grows out of this understanding, so that *the hermeneutical circle continues to develop in a never-ending spiral.*[27]

Or as D. A. Carson notes, the "hermeneutical circle . . . has no necessary terminus."[28] Hirsch makes this a major point in his attack upon Heideggerian forms of hermeneutics. In his view, the "hermeneutical circle model of hermeneutics" leads to relativism. It is difficult to argue with him on this point. The methodical level of hermeneutics — elementary "principle of interpretation" — provides a kind of objectivity, but when this level is taken into the hermeneutical circle, a type of "relativism"[29] occurs that seems to be more fundamental than the methodical level itself.

The hermeneutical circle is, in all its occurrences, an operation of preunderstandings-of-a-whole guiding an interpretation of parts so that the resulting interpretation experiences a gain in understanding. The previous conception of the "whole" and the "parts" is qualified and corrected, and a new preunderstanding-of-the-whole is the result. But all these preunderstandings-of-the-whole are conceptions or horizons that continuously need further expansion and seemingly lack any terminus. Unless the whole can be at least provisionally projected, the hermeneutical circle lacks an anchor.

26. Taylor, "Interpretation and the Sciences of Man," in Rabinow and Sullivan, *Interpretative Social Science: A Reader,* pp. 65-66.

27. Schillebeeckx, *God the Future of Man* (New York: Sheed and Ward, 1968), pp. 7-8; italics added.

28. Carson, "Hermeneutics: A Brief Assessment of Some Recent Trends," *Themelios* 5 (1980): 15.

29. The term *relativism* here can be misleading. It can connote either (1) that we can have no real, intersubjective, public knowledge because knowledge depends upon the perspective of the knower and one person's perspective is no better than another's, or (2) that our knowledge, while it may be real and intersubjective, is probable rather than certain and is limited by our human condition. It is this latter connotation that I have employed here.

What is necessary is to be able to project the whole of reality; without this projection the parts remain unclear.[30]

ESCHATOLOGICALLY ORIENTED ONTOLOGY

To project, at least provisionally, the whole of reality, we must first describe what is meant by "the whole of reality." Wolfhart Pannenberg says that the best single word to express the biblical view of reality is *history*.[31] Generally, the sciences have followed one of the early Greek philosophical traditions, which conceived of reality as atemporal, eternal, unchanging, and static. This Greek philosophical tradition asserted that the temporary, dynamic conditions of everyday life do not constitute reality but are rather a pale reflection of the eternal world of ideas. The Hebrews, on the other hand, understood history to be moving toward a goal. Hendrikus Berkhof rightly notes that "we must thank not Greece nor Persia, but Israel for our sense that history is goal-directed, and that as such it has meaning."[32] The Hebrews conceived of reality not as a static entity opposed to change, but as that which occurs and can be perceived; its final and decisive character will only be disclosed in the future. For the Hebrews, total reality and ultimate truth come fully into being and become totally manifest only in the eschaton. As Pannenberg notes,

> All constancy, whether it be in the orders of nature, in the life of nations, or in the individual, is embraced by the truth of God and is grounded in it. . . . The decisive point in this connection is the circumstance that the Greek dualism between true being and changing sense-appearances is superseded in the biblical understanding of truth. Here, true being is

30. The projection of the "whole of reality" is the projection of a "third horizon," the future, which will provide an anchor for the hermeneutical circle. This idea, explicated later in this essay, is heavily dependent upon J. C. McHann, *The Three Horizons* (Oxford: Oxford University Press, 1992, forthcoming). It is in this work that Pannenberg's notion of eschatologically oriented ontology is wed with Thiselton's two horizons, resulting in a third horizon that grounds the hermeneutical circle. See also T. Peters, "Method and Truth: An Inquiry into the Philosophical Hermeneutics of Hans-Georg Gadamer and the Theology of History of Wolfhart Pannenberg" (Ph.D. diss., University of Chicago, 1973).

31. Pannenberg, *Faith and Reality* (Philadelphia: Westminster Press, 1977), p. 10. See also J. V. L. Casserly, *Toward a Theology of History* (London: A. R. Mowbray, 1965).

32. Berkhof, *Christ the Meaning of History* (London: SCM, 1966), p. 21. See also A. D. Galloway, *Wolfhart Pannenberg* (London: George Allen and Unwin, 1973): "alone among the nations, Israel was enabled to see history neither as sheer caprice of the gods nor as nature" (p. 57).

thought of not as timeless but instead as historical, and it proves its stability through a history whose future is always open.[33]

Thus reality does not exist presently in its final form but is disclosed in ever new ways throughout history. Our trust in God therefore is based upon God's faithfulness in the past and his promises regarding the future. The ancient Hebrew view of history had two poles. On the one hand, God revealed himself in those events that were unpredictable, unforeseen, and novel; on the other hand, he revealed himself by fulfilling expectations precipitated by Israel's previous history. This polarity gave rise to a unique view of God, nature, and history. A. D. Galloway insightfully observes:

> It is the novel, the contingent, the unforeseeable which distinguishes history from nature. This novelty raises the question of the creative source of the 'new thing' that has come to pass. When again and again the people of Israel found themselves led into new and unforeseeable circumstances, again and again unpredictably delivered from their enemies or the improbable victors in a struggle, they felt impelled to say, "This is the Lord's doing and it is marvellous in our eyes."[34]

Conversely, Israel's neighbors related to their gods through natural processes — movements of the stars, seasons, agricultural cycles, etc. Their emphasis was upon the regularity of nature, the predictable — not the novel or contingent. These gods manifested themselves by a direct incursion into human affairs independent of the course of history. It is true that within

33. Pannenberg, "What Is Truth?" in his *Basic Questions in Theology,* 3 vols. (London: SCM, 1970-73), 3:9. Galloway provides a proper qualification to the generalizations being used by Pannenberg when he says: "[Pannenberg's] account of the contrast between the Greek and Hebrew traditions is broadly true. But it involves some rather sweeping generalizations. Pannenberg frequently uses the Hebrews and the Greeks as representative types rather than with reference to the complex variety of their cultural traditions" (*Wolfhart Pannenberg,* p. 23n.7). Cf. J. Barr, *Semantics of Biblical Language* (Oxford: Oxford University Press, 1961), whose work remains as a corrective for these types of overgeneralizations. Nevertheless, as long as the great variety in both cultural traditions is acknowledged, it does not seem inappropriate for Pannenberg to make some historical generalizations for the purpose of philosophical analysis if the generalizations are broadly true.

34. Galloway, *Wolfhart Pannenberg,* p. 54. Unfortunately, until the present this Hebrew notion has not been the dominant voice in Western philosophy and Western approaches to science, including psychology (cf. Pannenberg, "What Is Truth?" p. 10). But as our discussion above has implied, "It is generally conceded by philosophers, physicists, biologists and social scientists that reality is fundamentally temporal and historical in character. The ancient and medieval conception of our universe as a static eternal substructure with an ephemeral changing superstructure is no longer held in any modern scientific or scholarly discipline" (Peters, "Method and Truth").

Israel God did act directly, even including epiphanies. However, the stress is certainly upon the indirect revelation of God in the course of human history, and even when God did act in novel ways, these events were not radically contingent or arbitrary. Rather, they were always linked to God's acts in the past and his promises for the future.[35]

Thus a tension exists between the promises with their expected fulfillments and the novel, unexpected, contingent events. It is this tension, however, that provided the soil from which the Hebrew notion of history grew. If only novelty and contingency frame one's view of history, then events are random — sheer whim and caprice. Conversely, if unambiguous fulfillments of expectations based upon past events frame one's view of history, then history is indistinguishable from the laws of nature; God would be bound to nature like the *Baalim* of the Canaanites. Only if "novelty and contingency are significantly and positively related to predictability and expectation can the idea of history as we know it arise."[36] The Exodus illustrates this point. Though it was related to Israel's past, the Exodus was new and totally unexpected; it was not simply the outworking of Israel's historical antecedents. The Exodus was a fulfillment of God's promises to Abraham, Isaac, and Jacob, but not in a way any of them would ever have expected. In fact, after the Exodus, the promises to the patriarchs had to be interpreted differently, and Israel's expectations for the future had to be revised. Pannenberg summarizes this idea:

> The God of the Bible is shown to act in each new event in the light of what he has done before in history and in most cases the earlier happening is seen in a fresh light, the light thrown on it by the later event. In this way, there is in the Bible an underlying historical continuity within the series of new and extraordinary events. *This continuity should not, however, be thought of as a process of evolution in which certain tendencies from the past have an effect in the present and on the future.* On the contrary, it can best be seen as a kind of bridge leading, not from the past to the present or the future, but rather in the opposite direction, that is from the historical present at any given time back into the past.[37]

When the "present," finally, is the end of history, the ontological continuity of historical reality will be effected from that moment, too, all the way back to the beginning of history. Since the end of history is still future, in the present moment Pannenberg speaks of the totality of (historical) reality as an "eschatologically oriented ontology."

---

35. Galloway, *Wolfhart Pannenberg*, pp. 54-55.
36. Galloway, *Wolfhart Pannenberg*, p. 56.
37. Pannenberg, *Faith and Reality*, pp. 11-12; italics added.

The difference between eschatologically oriented ontology and static ontology is noteworthy. Within a static ontology the universe is regulated by laws that are manifestations of the unchanging, foundational structure of the universe. Pannenberg, however, reasons that reality is essentially a succession of new events (history), and "laws" are merely patterns that recur with some degree of regularity. Since "laws" demand replication, while reality (history) is a series of unrepeatable events, reality cannot be completely subsumed under general "laws."[38] Rather, the patterns in history ("laws" of nature) are "the free ordinances of the faithfulness of God, who keeps the world in being through them."[39] These "laws" are no less than the manifestations of God's faithfulness based upon his past historical acts, which engenders trust in his present and future promises.

> The Almighty God does not abandon "the work of his hands." He is faithful, holding fast to what he once did and willed. But this very holding fast takes place in continually new and surprising ways. It is impossible ever to say positively from the standpoint of the present what the enduring things are — what will last and remain. Only the future will decide what is the enduring essence of things. Thus the God of the Bible initiates the continuity and unity of the whole context of events, by returning to the past in the light of the future, holding fast to these events in his own way. By still reverting again and again . . . to his initial will in every unexpected turn of events . . . the God of Israel gave the unity of history to the riot of events. This unity only becomes visible at the end of a whole complex of happenings. . . . God creates the world in the light of its latter end, because it is only the end which decides the meaning of the things and beings with which we have to do in the present.[40]

Contrary to modern thinking in the Western tradition (and especially in psychological theory), instead of viewing history (reality) in a teleological or evolutionary manner in which the continuity runs from the past through the present to the future, Pannenberg reverses the direction: the continuity of reality begins in the future and extends back into the past. God builds bridges back into the past to save it from getting lost.[41] E. F. Tupper writes:

38. Pannenberg, *The Apostles' Creed in Light of Today's Questions* (London: SCM, 1972), p. 41.

39. Pannenberg, *Faith and Reality*, p. 19.

40. Pannenberg, *The Apostles' Creed*, pp. 38-39.

41. Pannenberg, *Theology and the Kingdom of God* (Philadelphia: Westminster Press, 1969), p. 67.

Every event casts light back upon earlier occurrences, which then appeared in a new relationship to the sequence of events itself. Thus Israel's
historical thinking implied an eschatological ontology., i.e. the true essence of a specific occurrence eventuates only in the end. Since Israel's
logic implied a final future, creation itself must be understood from the
End. The continuity of history, therefore, does not exist primarily as
evolution but must be established retroactively.[42]

Pannenberg agrees:

Creation is not to be understood as an act that happened one time, ages
ago, the results of which involve us in the present. Rather, the creation
of all things, even including things that belong to the past, takes place
out of the ultimate future, from the eschaton, insofar as only from the
perspective of the end are all things what they truly are.[43]

For Pannenberg, reality as history is not only open to the future, *but is
determined by the future.*

THE ANCHOR FOR THE HERMENEUTICAL CIRCLE

The problem as outlined above is clearly hermeneutical. The past and
present (the parts) can only be understood in light of the future (the whole).
But the future is not yet, so the hermeneutical circle (spiral) continues
without any terminus, without any anchor, leaving the interpreter afloat on
the sea of relativism until the eschaton appears. Since history (reality) is
not yet complete, the person within history has no Archimedean point from
which the whole of reality can be objectively viewed. In the present,
projections of the whole of reality can be made, the future can be anticipated; but it is only when the End arrives that the constancy and identity
of meaning and truth through time will be decisively demonstrated. In
Dilthey's words,

One would have to wait for the end of a life and, in the hour of death,
survey the whole and ascertain the relation between the whole and its
parts. One would have to wait until the end of history to have all the
material necessary to determine its meaning.[44]

42. Tupper, *The Theology of Wolfhart Pannenberg* (Philadelphia: Westminster Press,
1973), p. 221.
43. Pannenberg, *Theology and the Kingdom of God,* p. 136.
44. Dilthey, cited by Pannenberg, *Basic Questions in Theology,* 1:163.

However, in the Christ-event a proleptic view of the End, the whole, has been graciously provided. Pannenberg aptly describes it:

> Jesus of Nazareth is the final revelation of God because the End of history appeared in him. It did so both in his eschatological message and in his resurrection from the dead. However, he can be understood to be God's final revelation only in connection with the whole of history as mediated by the history of Israel. He is God's revelation in the fact that all history receives its due light from him.[45]

When we affirm that the Christ-event is the hermeneutical principle through which all of history is to be interpreted, we are not closing off the future; rather, the future remains open because it has not yet come in all its fullness, it has only come as prolepsis. This partial nature of our knowledge does not indicate an inadequacy in the Christ-event; it only underlines the proleptic structure of knowledge itself.[46] The Christ-event provides an accurate anticipation in the present of that which is not yet. Jesus Christ is therefore both part of history and part of the future. As Pannenberg says,

> it is just this, at first sight so seemingly alien, basically apocalyptic characteristic of the ministry and destiny of Jesus that, by means *of its anticipatory structure,* can become the key to solving a fundamental question facing philosophical reflection in the problematic post-Hegelian situation in which we still seem to be involved. It is possible to find in the *history of Jesus* an answer to the question of how 'the whole' of reality and its meaning can be conceived without compromising the provisional and historical relativity of all thought, as well as openness to the future on the part of the thinker who knows himself to be only on the way and not yet at the goal.[47]

Whenever we seek to understand the significance of a past event, whether consciously or unconsciously, we project a third horizon comprehensive enough that the past can be mediated to the present. As humans we are finite, history-bound, and unable to project this third horizon with any degree of veracity. However, through the Christ-event we can create *informed* projections of this third horizon because Jesus, though in history and therefore accessible to us, is not himself bound by history. Indeed, the

---

45. Pannenberg, *Revelation as History* (London: Sheed and Ward, 1969), p. 125.
46. Tupper, *The Theology of Wolfhart Pannenberg,* p. 84.
47. Pannenberg, *Basic Questions in Theology,* 1:164.

Christ-event provides an informed projection of this third horizon by which every event both past and present eventually will be judged. As Jesus came preaching the eschatological reality of the kingdom of God, his message had an imperatival claim upon the present because the present is determined by the future.

Our interpretations will still be culturally conditioned, at least to some degree, and we will remain in a type of hermeneutical circle. However, using the Christ-event as a prism, our interpretations can have a focus, and the hermeneutical circle will actually be a spiral toward that future horizon which has not yet arrived but can be anticipated because the End has arrived proleptically. This eschatological schema then provides an ontological anchor for the hermeneutical circle (spiral). Indeed, Jesus is the rock in which the anchor holds.

The hermeneutical process described above is discernible in Jesus' own approach to understanding. The pericope in Luke 24:13-35 describes Jesus' appearance to the two disciples on the road to Emmaus. Unable to recognize Jesus and confused about Jesus' death and apparent failure, these disciples listened as Jesus began with Moses and the prophets and "explained to them what was said in all the Scriptures concerning himself" (v. 27). The problem with these two disciples' understanding was not that they needed more information about the Old Testament or about the ministry of Jesus, but that they were not able to fuse the two horizons together and make sense out of them. Jesus provided them with a third horizon, a future event brought into the present (his resurrection), and with this *eschatological* perspective they were then able to unite all of the data into a coherent whole. R. Palmer explicates this dynamic well:

> [This passage] is clearly an example of explanation, for Jesus was doing more than merely repeating or reasserting the older texts; he *explained* them and himself in terms of them. Here interpretation involves the bringing in of an *outside factor*, the Christ, to point up the "meaning" of the older texts. Only in the presence of this factor do the texts become meaningful. . . . What does this suggest hermeneutically? It suggests that meaning is a matter of context; the explanatory procedure (principle) provides the arena for understanding. Only within a specific context is an event meaningful. . . . Explanatory interpretation makes us aware that explanation is contextual, is "horizontal." It must be made within a horizon of already granted meanings and intentions. In hermeneutics, this area of assumed understanding is called preunderstanding. One may fruitfully ask what preunderstanding is necessary in order to understand the (given) text. Jesus supplied his listeners with the element necessary

to understand the prophetic texts; this was part of the necessary explanation.[48]

In other words, Jesus identified himself as the context-event by which the Scriptures are to be explained. The Christ-event supplied these disciples with the contextual, horizontal preunderstanding through which the Scriptures could be properly understood. This process is of course true for all of human history, as has already been suggested.

ESCHATOLOGICALLY ORIENTED PSYCHOLOGY

I have argued thus far that the scientific and theological enterprises are basically hermeneutical. The difficulty with hermeneutics is epistemological; there is no necessary terminus to the hermeneutical circle. However, reality (as history), when complete, would provide the necessary terminus to the hermeneutical circle so that interpretation could be objectively grounded. The Christ-event, an end-time event brought into the present, provides a proleptic view, a tentative conception of the terminus for the hermeneutical circle. Indeed, ontology must be eschatologically oriented.

If ontology is eschatologically oriented, then psychology must be as well. Eschatology has traditionally been overlooked in discussions on integrating psychology and theology, but it seems to me to be a key in developing a truly Christian psychology. So often psychotherapy has taken on the dimensions of an archeological expedition into the client's past in order to determine the cause of a present problem. This etiology presupposes that a conflict from the past remains unresolved in the client's psyche; this conflict, then, needs to be brought to resolution. Once this tension is resolved, it is believed, the problem behavior will spontaneously move to solution. This approach to human problems assumes that the individual's behavior is pushed from the past in deterministic fashion. Problem behavior exists because of the particular combination of influential variables arising from previous events in the client's life.

In light of our earlier discussion it seems that a better approach would involve a third horizon, the future. The client would project a third horizon that would include a resolution to the problem behavior. Rather than being pushed from the past in a deterministic way, the client would be pulled

48. Palmer, *Hermeneutics: Interpretation Theory in Schleiermacher, Dilthey, Heidegger and Gadamer* (Evanston: Northwestern University Press, 1969), pp. 24-25.

into the future by the projection of this new horizon. Moreover, it is the future that holds the key to unlock a solution to the present problem; for we have seen that meaning in the present is determined by the future, not the past. Most importantly, each person has a responsibility to construct this future horizon, which then functions heuristically to give meaning to the present and to guide into the future.

This interplay between the horizon of the future and the horizon of the present seems to underlie a familiar dynamic in Paul: the indicative-imperative. Paul likes to move from the indicative to the imperative, from the descriptive to the prescriptive. For example, in Romans Paul lays out his first eleven chapters with very dense theological material. Then in chapters twelve through sixteen Paul brings out the life implications of this theological material; he calls for behavior based upon the reality that he has just articulated. This same pattern appears in Ephesians: the descriptive chapters, one through three, give way to the prescriptive chapters, four through six. This pattern appears not only in Paul's structure on the macro level, but also in his content, on the micro level. For example, in Romans 6:2-11 Paul declares that all of those who are in Christ have died to sin. This is a clear example of the indicative. Paul then goes on to command, "Therefore do not let sin reign in your mortal body. . . . Do not offer the parts of your body to sin, as instruments of wickedness" (6:1-13); this is the imperative. Clearly the new life in its moral manifestation is the re-demptive work of God — the indicative; yet it is also a categorical demand — the imperative. Since both the indicative and the imperative show up with such force and consistency, this dynamic may well be best termed a "dialectical paradox."[49]

In this discussion it must be mentioned that the imperative rests upon the indicative and not vice versa. The imperative follows the indicative by way of conclusion, often with "thus" or "therefore" (e.g., Rom. 6:12-14; 12:1; 2 Cor. 5:11, 20; Col. 3:5; et al.). To reverse these two and place the imperative first is to degenerate into legalism. Rather, the imperative is grounded on the reality that has been established with the indicative, and the implementation of the imperative will bring that reality into its full development. Paul's use of the indicative seems to be eschatologically oriented. The indicative states what will be true in the future, what is so certain that often it can be described as if it has already occurred. The indicative then grounds the imperative. Eschatology gives meaning and direction to the present.

Take, for example, Colossians 3:1: "Since [lit. 'if'], then, you have

49. E. Stauffer, *New Testament Theology* (London: SCM, 1955), p. 157.

been raised with Christ, set your hearts on things above." In the protasis the "if" is certainly not hypothetical; rather, the protasis is an accepted presupposition from which the imperative logically follows.[50] The protasis, therefore, is a view from the End; it is eschatologically oriented. If we accept this Pauline construct, then the new life consists of decisions made in faith, and a sharp distinction should not be drawn between "life imparted by the Spirit" (denoted by the indicative) and "walking by the Spirit" (demanded by the imperative).

Our discussion suggests that the imperative is grounded in the indicative (eschatologically oriented ontology). It is to be accepted once for all (it is the view from the End) *and* existentially (it is how the believer behaves now). When the imperatives are followed, the potential (the eschatological) becomes actual. Every act that realizes the imperative actualizes the indicative and is directed toward a greater actualization, toward growth and progress in the new life. When we compare the reality that stands behind Paul's treatment of the indicative and the imperative, we find a reality that is congruent with our notion of eschatologically oriented psychology.

It seems important at this point to distinguish between content and process. The psychological *process* that produces growth is eschatologically oriented. The person projects a future construction of reality and it then functions heuristically to focus the person's attention and to guide into the future. Eschatologically oriented psychology also offers content, a descriptive model that the person can imitate; it provides an answer to the question "What does mental health look like?" Of course, the model for the Christian is the example of Christ. Both the content (what) and the process (how) of Christian maturity are addressed by the paradigm of eschatologically oriented psychology.[51]

The emphasis upon creating a new Christ-centered horizon that pulls one into the future, rather than focusing upon the pain in one's past, seems to be supported in Paul's exhortation to the Philippians:

> Brothers, I do not consider myself to have taken hold of it. But one thing I do: Forgetting what is behind and straining toward what is ahead, I press on toward the goal to win the prize for which God has called me heavenward in Christ Jesus. (3:13-14)

50. The form of this conditional is first class and in this instance is a condition of fact.

51. Recent trends in family therapy have emphasized the notion of "process." Traditional psychotherapies have emphasized "content." The approach that flows out of our "eschatologically oriented psychology" incorporates both content and process.

Here Paul advocates "forgetting" the past. Obviously Paul is not suggesting that the Philippians "forget" everything in their past because Paul constantly mentions material worthy of remembrance (e.g., 2 Cor. 7:15; Gal. 2:10; Eph. 2:11; Col. 4:18; 1 Thess. 1:3; 2:9; 2 Thess. 2:5; 2 Tim. 2:8). Rather, Paul is advocating a selective "forgetting" and a selective "remembering." Hawthorne surmises that this selective "forgetting" included forgetting wrongs done — for example, Paul's persecution of the church, which could paralyze him with guilt and despair — as well as attainments achieved as a Christian, which could cause him to assume that he had already "arrived."[52] Instead, Paul advocates focusing completely upon what lies ahead. These verses remind the believer of the dialectic between the "already" and the "not yet."[53] Notice, however, that Paul's movement into the future is not aimless; it is fixed upon a goal (κατὰ σκοπός). This noun (σκοπός) frequently refers to the marker at the finish line upon which the sprinters fix their gaze. It is often used metaphorically for the goal that controls a person's life.[54] For Paul, this "straining toward what is ahead" is purposeful and is constructed from his projection of the future. In J. H. Michael's words: "It is the vision of the end of the race that ever directs and speeds his hastening feet."[55] In these verses in Philippians, Paul outlines an eschatological orientation that facilitates growth into maturity in Christ.

Perhaps an example at this point might be helpful. Consider a woman in her thirties who was repeatedly sexually abused by her stepfather as a child. This woman has recently become a Christian and has heard a number of sermons about forgiveness. She knows that she is being challenged to forgive, but her recollections maintain their power and immediacy as her mind relives the past events. Each time she thinks about these terrible incidents she is gripped afresh by the intense emotions attached to the memories. To control her cognitions and simply not to think about these events risks repressing the emotions, which then may well work themselves out in other unhealthy ways. Thus it is important deliberately to access this material cognitively *and* emotionally. However, going over this highly

---

52. Hawthorne, *Philippians* (Waco, TX: Word Books, 1983), p. 153.

53. Hawthorne, *Philippians*, p. 154.

54. Plato, *Gorgias* 507D. For references see Ernst Fuchs' article in *Theological Dictionary of the New Testament*, ed. Gerhard Kittel and Gerhard Friedrich, trans. Geoffrey W. Bromiley (Grand Rapids: Eerdmans, 1964-74), 7:413-14; and Walter Bauer, William F. Arndt, F. Wilbur Gingrich, and Frederick Danker, *A Greek-English Lexicon of the New Testament and Other Early Christian Literature* (Chicago: University of Chicago Press, 1979), pp. 756-57.

55. Michael, cited in Peter O'Brien, *The Epistle to the Philippians,* New International Greek Testament Commentary (Grand Rapids: Eerdmans, 1991), p. 430.

emotive material again and again in psychotherapy to gain insight and process some of the residual emotion can only help so much. Instead, this client needs to be guided through these painful events from a new perspective: the perspective of the future. She must project herself into the future, appropriate her identity and position in Christ, see herself as one who is whole, and then, *from the perspective of the future,* be guided back through those old memories.

It must also be emphasized that the achieving of this eschatological perspective is a *process* and takes place over a period of time. To be able to view events, past and present, from the standpoint of the future is not a product of repeated assertions, either by the therapist or by the client; it is a work of the Spirit, as the Spirit renews the client's mind. Psychotherapy (which includes listening, support, prayer, insight, admonition, Scripture, meditation, encouragement, reading, reflection, advice, confrontation, confession, questioning, interpretation, evaluation, explanation, informing, teaching, empathy, verbalizing feelings, unconditional love, authenticity, trust, wholesome relational experiences, etc.) is a powerful instrument that the Spirit is able to utilize. The therapeutic process can best facilitate the Spirit's work by having an eschatological orientation. Once this eschatological orientation is achieved, the client is able to pass through those past painful events (as well as present ones), not as one whose identity is that of an abused child, as one who conceives of herself as damaged goods, but as one who is healed and whole in Christ (the indicative). From an eschatological perspective this woman is not captive to her emotions and only able to return abuse for abuse in a retaliatory way, but she can now forgive (the imperative) because she is able to envision her stepfather as God does and see herself as whole in Christ.

RELATING COMMON MATERIAL FROM THEOLOGY AND PSYCHOLOGY

We must be careful, however, not to be reductionistic. In addition to eschatology, there are other large branches of theology that bear on psychology and require careful integration. J. Carter and R. Mohline have made some important initial suggestions along these lines by relating the subdisciplines of psychology and theology.[56] Examples of subdisciplines of theology and psychology that might bear upon each other include these categories: theology proper (prolegomena, theism, bibliology, theology)

---

56. Carter and Mohline, "The Nature and Scope of Integration," in *Psychology and Christianity,* ed. R. Fleck and J. Carter (Nashville: Abingdon Press, 1981), pp. 97-111.

and the science of psychology (presuppositions, foundations of psychology, definitions, philosophic roots); biblical anthropology and personality theory; hamartiology and psychopathology; soteriology and human development; ecclesiology and social psychology; Christology and counselor education; angelology-demonology and psychic phenomena; pneumatology and theory of change; discipleship and psychotherapy; and so forth. Some brief explication of a few of these areas might be helpful. But our earlier discussion outlining an eschatologically oriented ontology (and therefore psychology) must be borne in mind as we integrate these subdisciples because Christian theology must have functional control over the final product. The conclusions from these psychological subdisciplines must be subordinate to the conclusions of Christian theology.

Biblical anthropology and personality theory serve as good initial examples of subdisciplines that provide promising material for integration. Biblical anthropology includes a study of the creation of the human race and an examination of the nature of the human person. Exactly what it means to be created in God's image has long been a subject of discussion.[57] But regardless of the interpreter's final conclusions concerning the implications of humanity as God's image-bearer, it is clear that God's image is a fundamental structural concept with significant implications concerning the nature of human persons. Furthermore, certain biblical terms, including *heart, soul, mind, spirit, body,* and *flesh* are important contributions to help us understand what it means to be human. In psychology, personality theory also addresses some of the issues covered by biblical anthropology. Personality theory includes learning, perception, memory, and motivation — all of which will make at least implicit statements concerning human nature. It becomes clear that the *imago Dei* and other anthropological categories mentioned in Scripture are needed to drive a truly Christian theory of personality.

Two other subdisciplines with common material are hamartiology (the study of the doctrine of sin) and psychopathology. Both areas study the lower functioning, loss of potential, and inappropriate behavior related to human activity. Carter and Mohline have suggested that a theological description of humanity's fallen condition falls into four complementary categories: total depravity, condemnation, alienation, and guilt. They sug-

---

57. Augustine suggested that the dimensions of being God's image-bearer include understanding, memory, and will; Luther focused upon innocence and original righteousness. In this century Brunner has argued that it is the ability to engage in interpersonal relationships, while Berkouwer has emphasized humanity's dominion over the earth and the abilities necessary to carry it out.

gest further that these theological categories are also experienced psychologically: total depravity often gives rise to experiences of worthlessness, inferiority, and low self-esteem; condemnation gives rise to experiences of fear and anxiety; alienation gives rise to experiences of guilt. Carter and Mohline go on to suggest that the psychodynamic, behavioral, and phenomenological schools of psychology all emphasize different psychological consequences of the fall.[58]

The integration of personality theory and biblical anthropology and of psychopathology and hamartiology leads naturally to a discussion of how soteriology bears upon developmental theory. Both of these subdisciplines focus upon the issues of health, wholeness, and fully actualizing the human potential for growth. Most of psychology is concerned with the horizontal plane and examines interpersonal and intrapersonal issues; theology includes another dimension — one's relationship with God. At this point no thoughtful Christian would overlook the centrality of the cross in reconciling us to God, or the power and presence of the Holy Spirit in regeneration and sanctification. Nevertheless, the concern for wholeness is shared by both Christianity and psychology, however different their respective visions may be. An appropriate integration promises to bear much fruit in further defining those ingredients of life that give rise to pathology and those that promote health, growth, wholeness, fulfillment, and actualization.

The functional control of Christology over the therapeutic process would show itself in several ways. First, the incarnation provides a paradigm by which the counselor can relate redemptively to a lost and broken world. This connection has often been noted in monographs discussing Christian counseling and provides a rich model with many dimensions to explore. Second, the image of Christ into which all believers strive to be transformed becomes a goal for Christian growth (Col. 1:28-29; Eph. 4:11-16); the mature believer's behavior will resemble that of Jesus Christ. Indeed, the character of the person is to grow and become more and more conformed to that character displayed by Christ in his earthly ministry. Within the Scriptures this goal for our growth has been carefully outlined. Moreover, Jesus' multivariate roles (e.g., lamb, servant, high priest, prophet, shepherd) provide numerous models for the Christian counselor to explore.[59]

58. Carter and Mohline, "The Nature and Scope of Integration," pp. 103-4.

59. See D. Carlson, "Jesus' Style of Relating: The Search for a Biblical View of Counseling," *Journal of Psychology and Theology* 4 (1976): 181-92, for an excellent introduction into the various ways Jesus responded to people in order to help them change. It becomes clear that Jesus used a number of models (not a single model that could then be called "the biblical model") to facilitate growth and change.

Ecclesiology has implications concerning the construction of social psychology. Some of the more important aspects of healthy groups embodying good social psychology include mutuality, acceptance, belonging, security, responsibility, fellowship, and unconditional love. These qualities help define a healthy functioning church that experiences a sense of community around the common bond of faith in Christ. Social psychology can also inform us concerning the dynamics of a healthy group. For example, M. M. Ohlsen and C. Rogers isolate a number of necessary conditions a group must meet in order for a member of that group to experience a measure of actualization — unconditional acceptance, an empathic environment, authentic relationships, and so forth.[60] All of these characteristics can be substantiated with statements from Scripture that describe a healthy Christian community. The goals of the church as described by Paul in Ephesians 4:1-16, for example, demonstrate a decided emphasis upon group unity, individuation, maturity, and acceptance in the context of love. Social psychologists agree that these are among the necessary conditions for a group to function therapeutically.

This brief sketch of possible integration points between theology and psychology and their subdisciplines only scratches the surface, but it does point us in a direction with a plethora of possibilities. The key aspect, which has been developed in some detail but of course still needs more fleshing out, is *eschatologically oriented psychology*. For too long, Christian psychology has been overly dependent upon the theories of secular psychologists, especially those from a psychodynamic orientation that emphasize the past. The paradigm being suggested here can be used as a corrective for this overdependence as well as a source of new therapeutic models and techniques.

CONCLUSION

We began with a summary of the recent applications of Niebuhr's categories to the integration of psychology and Christianity. The attempts by Carter and Narramore and the more recent attempt by Farnsworth, though helpful, do not provide the basis for a truly Christian psychology. We therefore turned to the field of hermeneutics to provide us with an epistemological method in order to accomplish the task of integrating psychology and Christianity. We found that the method of the sciences as well as the method

---

60. Ohlsen, *Group Counseling* (New York: Holt, Rinehart and Winston, 1970); C. Rogers, *On Encounter Groups* (New York: Harper & Row, 1970).

of theology is hermeneutical. The problem with hermeneutics, however, is that the hermeneutical circle has no necessary terminus. The eschatologically oriented ontology of Pannenberg provides this terminus because it is a view from the End, which, consistent with the hermeneutical method, is (at least a proleptic view of) the "whole" that unites the parts.

If all of reality is eschatologically oriented, then this must also include psychology. In relating this notion to psychology, it is clear that eschatologically oriented psychology includes both content and process. In terms of content, the terminus is Christian maturity or Christ-likeness; in terms of the psychological process, the individual constructs a future horizon that is then fused with the present (and past) horizon. Rather than being pushed from the past in deterministic style (as is assumed in most psychological theory), the individual is pulled into the future by this projected future horizon. This process is best exemplified in the writings of Paul, especially in his dynamic construction of the indicative-imperative.

Thus we have argued for a new paradigm in psychology and psychotherapy, a paradigm that recognizes the hermeneutical dimension of both Christian theology and the sciences and that looks to the future to give meaning to the present (and past) — in other words, an eschatologically oriented ontology built upon the Christ-event, which is a proleptic view of the End through which we can view the part in the context of the whole. If all of reality is eschatologically oriented, then psychology must also be eschatologically oriented. This new paradigm justifies us in giving priority to our Christian faith as we develop theories of counseling and psychotherapeutic techniques. May the Christian community value its unique position and, instead of being followers in developing psychological theory and effective therapies, be the leaders in the discipline as we move forward with a biblically informed, eschatologically oriented psychology.

What Is Christian Philosophy?

GEORGE I. MAVRODES

As THE TITLE indicates, this essay is about Christian philosophy. I will assume that my readers will already have some familiarity with philosophical topics, styles, and methods. Most of what I have to say here, therefore, will focus on the ways in which philosophical work might be distinctively *Christian*.

For an initial working definition, I propose that we understand the idea of *Christian philosophy* to be that of philosophy that is "done" — that is, thought out, formulated, and expressed — by Christian men and women who are trying to be true to the Christian faith in their intellectual lives (as well as in other aspects of life). Such philosophy, therefore, will be done by people who, in doing it, hold themselves responsible to a certain religious commitment, that of the worship and service and enjoyment of God as revealed in the incarnation of Jesus Christ.

An important element in this working definition is that it does not identify Christian philosophy merely with philosophy that happens to be done by Christians. It includes the requirement that, in doing the philosophical work, these people are deliberately attempting to be true to their Christian commitments. What I think about how that might be done, and how it might not, is a major theme in the remainder of this discussion.

I must also emphasize, however, that I will be trying to think about how philosophy might be done by actual Christians, living in this world, right now. I will not be talking about how philosophy might be done by an angel (or by a devil, for that matter), nor about how it might be done by a Christian who is living in glory in the new heaven and the new earth of the Book of Revelation. Those restrictions will, I think, be important to some of the things I say below.

Well then, what sorts of things can Christian philosophers expect to do, and what can readers of philosophy reasonably expect to find in the work of Christian philosophers? The remainder of this essay revolves around several foci, each of which expresses something that is, in my judgment, an important determining feature of the general shape of philosophy that is done in a Christian way. The interaction of these several "gravitational centers" determines the complex curve of the philosophical work that we are here trying to understand.

CHRISTIAN PHILOSOPHY HAS MANY FACES

Many people — indeed, many philosophers — when they hear of "Christian philosophy" will think first of Christians engaging in the philosophy of religion. This is a special area of philosophical interest that deals primarily with religious ideas and claims, topics such as the existence and attributes of God, the problem of evil, the significance of religious experience, the resurrection of the body and/or the immortality of the soul, and so on. This area of philosophy is, of course, a sort of "natural" for Christians. Many of them (like me) came into philosophy in the first place because they were interested in problems of philosophical theology, or in apologetics, ways of replying to attacks on the faith, etc. And this is, in fact, an area (perhaps *the* area) in which Christians are currently doing a large amount of original and significant philosophical work.

But philosophy of religion is not the whole of philosophy. There is general metaphysics, for example, and logic, and the philosophy of language, and general epistemology, and aesthetics, and the philosophy of science, and on and on. Now, there are Christian architects who specialize in the design of churches, and there are Christian publishers who major in the publication of Bibles, books of theology, and hymnbooks. But there are also Christian architects who design houses and hospitals, and Christian publishers whose lists consist mainly of books on engineering or pharmacology. While it is natural, and perhaps it will always be common, that Christian philosophers should be disproportionately attracted to the philosophy of religion, there is no reason to suppose that there will not be some who will find their own center of interest in some other field of philosophy.

Someone might suggest that we should think of Christian philosophy as philosophy whose Christian orientation is readily apparent in its content. That idea would work at least moderately well in the philosophy of religion. All the topics there are openly religious. Christians who deal with them are likely to find many connections, both positive and negative, with their own religious commitments and convictions. And readers of their work will probably find traces and expressions of those commitments integrally embedded throughout. But in some of these other fields of philosophy that will not be the case. In them there is nothing like the close relation to Christian doctrines, creedal statements, the biblical material, etc., that obtains in the philosophy of religion. If there is to be Christian philosophy in these other fields, then, it probably cannot be identified by content nearly as readily as in the philosophy of religion. And that fact brings us to the second focal thesis.

NOT EVERY PHILOSOPHICAL FISH IS HOOKED ON A THEOLOGICAL ＬINE (BUT SOME ARE)

Some years ago I heard a Christian man — he was a biological chemist — say, "When I go into the lab I leave Jesus outside." Maybe he exaggerated a little for the sake of a striking statement, but I think I have an idea of what he meant, and some substantial sympathy with it. I think he left Jesus outside the lab because he believed that, by and large, there is nothing for Jesus to do inside the lab. Jesus is not a bottle washer, nor an experimental technician, nor a chemical theoretician, nor anything in between. So he might as well stay outside.

Of course, some moral crisis might arise in the lab, and then this chemist would probably (I hope) pray for Jesus to stand with him in the hour of temptation. Or perhaps some colleague might tell him that her husband has just been diagnosed as having an untreatable cancer, and then the two of them may set aside the work of the lab for a little while to think together about pain, and mortality, and hope, and the gift that is given in the gospel of Christ. There would indeed be something for Jesus to do there, and I suppose again that this man would pray for him to come to them in that hour.

Those things, however, are not the work of the lab, the project that the lab is set to accomplish. The moral temptation and the spiritual turning point do not explain why it was appropriate to appoint a biological chemist, rather than a pastor or a theologian, to direct this lab. But the *work* of the lab, perhaps identifying the DNA code that is crucial to cystic fibrosis, or whatever, does account for the relevance of that appointment. And it is *that* work, the project in biological chemistry, in which there is nothing for Jesus to do.

Of course, Jesus might make what we could call a "cameo appearance" even in the work of biological chemistry. If this chemist, for example, were to write a book about his work, he might well include in it (because he is a Christian) some reference to Jesus. He might acknowledge, probably in a preface, that "by him all things were created: things in heaven and on earth," as we can read in Colossians 1:16. And this man, because he is a Christian, will recognize that in working on DNA he is working on a part of those "all things" that have been created through the Son and for the Son. If he were to say something like that in the preface to his book, then (in my opinion, at least) he would be saying a truth, an important truth about the world and about the part of the world that he works on in his lab. But when he comes to describe the actual work itself, then probably there will be nothing distinctively Christian about the specification of the problem to be addressed, nor about the techniques used in the investigation, nor about the premises or reasoning in the arguments, nor in the data, nor in the conclusions. If one missed the preface, one might well find no further hint of that scientist's Christian faith.

That is how I, at least, understood that man's saying that he left Jesus outside the lab.

It seems to me that something very much like this happens in philosophy — or, to be more exact, it happens in various degrees in the various fields of philosophy, and in connection with various problems. Take general metaphysics, for example. A Christian metaphysician would presumably have no truck with any metaphysical theory that undertook to account for the whole realm of reality purely in terms of "material atoms, chance, and the void," leaving no room at all for the reality of God. She might well hold that the fact that a certain metaphysical theory has this consequence is itself a conclusive reason for rejecting that theory. In that case, her religious and theological commitments would play a negative role in her metaphysical theorizing, ruling out certain options that might otherwise have seemed credible. And that, it seems to me, is an entirely proper way in which she can try to be true to her Christian faith in the doing of her philosophical thinking.

Suppose, however, that she comes to consider a different metaphysical question, that of the nature of the physical world and its mode of reality. And she thinks of the Berkeleyan view that the being of physical objects consists in their being perceived, and that therefore we should construe them as congeries of ideas or sensations. And now she wants to know whether this metaphysical theory of the physical world is true. I suspect that she will very probably find nothing at all in the Christian faith that bears decisively on this question. She may know that George Berkeley was a Christian himself and that he developed arguments designed to prove the existence of God. But she may know, too, that René Descartes, also a

Christian and an inventor of arguments for God's existence, seems to have had a rather different idea about physical objects, saying that their essence consists of extension. Descartes and Berkeley both professed that God is the Creator and Sustainer of the world, but they appear to disagree on just what kind of thing it is that God is there creating and sustaining. And if our contemporary Christian metaphysician is to decide between these two views, or to adopt any other theory on this topic, it will probably have to be on the basis of arguments that do not make much appeal to central elements in the Christian faith.

This sort of situation seems to recur over and over again in philosophy, just as it does in the other intellectual disciplines. Repeatedly we find that the questions we are engaged in discussing and investigating simply are not closely enough related to the cognitive elements in our Christian faith to be decisively settled, or even substantially illuminated, by appeals to that faith. And so we must tackle them in some other way.

Indeed, that happens even in the philosophy of religion, the area in which the idea of a distinctively Christian position would seem to be most plausible. Let me give you briefly just two examples, drawn from debates that are going on right now. One concerns the relation of God to time. One thesis here is that God is an everlasting being — that is, a being without any beginning or end, but otherwise passing through time more or less as we do, with a future, a present, and a past. The contrasting thesis is that God is an eternal being, not in time at all, and having no future or past but only an eternal and all-encompassing present. The other debate is over the question of whether a divine foreknowledge of future human actions would preclude the possibility that those actions will be done in freedom. These questions are actively debated at the present time in gatherings of Christian philosophers. The arguments are often subtle and hard to follow. And the fact is that it has not been possible to come to a widely accepted resolution of these differences among Christian philosophers on the basis of an appeal to a shared faith.

The multiplicity and intractability of cases of this sort certainly suggest to me that the shared faith simply does not contain the cognitive resources for deciding these questions; that is, there simply are no identifiable positions on these topics that are Christian in the sense of being decisively derived from distinctively Christian premises.

It may be said, however, that this may reflect our failure more than a deficiency in the faith. Perhaps the gospel does after all contain the seeds of a solution to these problems, or to some of them, and we simply have failed so far to develop the consequences that are hidden in the divine revelation. I cannot deny that, nor do I want to. We humans are finite

knowers and finite reasoners. None of us has yet teased out all the ramifications of the fundamental tenets of our faith. And so I suggest that an
important aspect of holding ourselves responsible to our Christian commitment is that of deliberately setting ourselves to remain open and alert
to hitherto unsuspected religious ramifications. Philosophers who are fully
engaged in doing their work in a Christian way, it seems to me, will
regularly be asking themselves whether the problem at hand, no matter
how neutral and secular it may initially seem, may not after all have some
discoverable link to the living word of God. And part of their philosophical
reflection will be devoted to exploring that possibility as best they can.
That will be an important factor in making their philosophy Christian rather
than secular. And sometimes, no doubt, they will discover real and surprising connections, to the enrichment of both philosophy and faith.

But if some of these philosophical fish are indeed hooked to a theological line, then that line must be one that is long and convoluted. Hundreds
of years of reflection by Christian philosophers have failed to trace it. And
so it seems to me that we must frankly accept also the possibility that, even
if there really is such a connection, we too may fail to find it. If there is
such a connection, then perhaps it belongs to philosophy as it will be done
in another world. Or maybe it just belongs to some other philosopher who,
here and now, exceeds me in penetration and insight. In any case, if I am
to do my own work in a Christian way then I must do it, so it seems to
me, in an honest and straightforward way. What I think I discover I can
set forth, and let others judge its worth as best they can. And what I cannot
discover I must simply leave aside, proceeding as far as I can with whatever
other resources I can muster. Many of us, perhaps all of us, will find
ourselves in this sort of situation much of the time. And therefore much of
the philosophy that is done by deeply committed Christian philosophers
will be only partly determined, if at all, by a distinctive and identifiable
Christian content. If it is to be identified as Christian in any important
sense, it seems that such an identification will depend primarily on the
commitment and intent of the men and women who are doing that philosophical work.

CHRISTIAN PHILOSOPHY IS A SHAMELESS
(BUT CAREFUL) BORROWER

Was it William Shakespeare who said, "Neither a borrower nor a lender
be"? There may be some profession for which that is good advice, but that
profession is not philosophy, and especially not Christian philosophy. Of

course, Christians cannot do much about the second half of the advice, since in any case they cannot prevent other thinkers from appropriating their ideas and arguments as soon as they have published them. But the first part of that advice is more or less within our power. And historically at least, Christians have largely rejected it. We have borrowed like mad. Christian philosophy has always linked up with, and built upon, philosophical elements that were developed in non-Christian contexts and by philosophers who were not themselves Christians. The Christian philosophers of the first few centuries after the time of Jesus — people such as Augustine, Boethius, and Bonaventure — have recognizable affinities with Plato. And in the thirteenth century Thomas Aquinas (not without considerable opposition) shifted the emphasis in Christian philosophy toward Aristotle, an Aristotelianism that was delivered to him largely through Arabic-Islamic sources.

The tangled connections between Christian and non-Christian philosophies have continued through Western history, and there is a striking example to be observed in our own time. In the second half of this century there has been a remarkable resurgence and flowering of work in the philosophy of religion, and much of this is being done by philosophers whose commitment to the Christian faith is clearly evident in that work. There have been searching and provocative treatments of the arguments for the existence of God, of the problem of evil, of the epistemic significance of religious experience, of the rationality of theistic belief, and of a variety of problems and topics in philosophical theology. These are live topics right now. And much of the very best work in this field, especially the work being published in English, is being done by philosophers in the "analytic" tradition. In the first half of this century, however, analytic philosophy was largely associated with strongly anti-Christian and, more generally, anti-religious views. At that time, a reference to analytic philosophy would probably have made one think immediately of Bertrand Russell or of the logical positivists. But now, a "style" of philosophical work with strong family ties to theirs is turned powerfully to the defense and explication and elaboration of the faith that those earlier analysts evidently despised.

Philosophy has had a long history in the West, among the very longest of the intellectual disciplines. Its beginnings lie several hundred years, at least, before the time of Jesus. So the origins of Western philosophy were not informed by any distinctively Christian doctrines or ideas. Nor, for that matter, is there any important and clearly discernible Hebraic element in the work of Plato, Aristotle, or the other early and influential philosophical thinkers. This fact was not lost on the early Christian apologists and theologians, and it prompted some of them to ask, derisively and rhetorically, "What has Jerusalem to do with Athens?" But that question, at least in my opinion, has a good and straightforward answer. And that answer (again, as it seems to me) is itself a Christian answer, closely linked to a Christian doctrine about reality. Jerusalem has a lot to do with Athens, intellectually as well as in many other ways, because both of them belong to the one and only world there is, the world that is created and sustained by the one and only God there is.

There is a striking account in the New Testament of Paul's visit to Athens. He went there to preach the gospel of Jesus Christ. But before he got to preaching he realized that his words would not be the very first intimation of God in that pagan city. For he saw the altar with the curious, and somewhat paradoxical, inscription "To the Unknown God." And he understood that God, his God, the God and Father of Jesus Christ, was not wholly a stranger in Athens, and that the divine voice had already sounded in those streets. Paul, it seems to me, recognized that Jerusalem and Athens were deeply linked in the one order of reality within the divine love and power. And so he did not undertake to forge a link there from nothing; rather, he connected up with a link already present in the Athenian streets, and in the Areopagus.

In a somewhat similar way, then, Christian philosophy always has been (and still is) *synergistic*. That is, it has combined the contributions of distinctively Christian philosophers with elements derived from other sources. And that, it seems to me, is as it should be. It is, of course, an important fact about these "outside" philosophers that they do not share the Christian faith. But that is not the only fact about them. It is also a fact that all of them, from Plato and Aristotle to Russell and Ayer and on into the future, are human beings created by God, and that they bear the image of God, and that they have minds designed and sustained by God. Furthermore, they live in a world created by God (there is no other world to live in), and they are reflecting on lives that in fact fall within the divine providence. Of course, they have gotten a lot of things wrong. Or at least, so it would seem, for their various views and claims appear not to be compatible with each other (even before we get to comparing them with Christianity). But it would also seem very likely that they have gotten some things right. After all, they have lived all their lives, as we have also, under the pressure of reality — the divine reality and the reality of the divine creation. Would it not be bizarre to suppose that this pressure has produced no genuine cognitive effect outside the bounds of the Christian faith? It doesn't seem to me that Paul would have supposed that, and I know of no good reason why we should suppose it either.

There is, however, a genuine fear associated with this synergism. It is the fear that a philosophy of that sort will be infected with the errors of alien systems. And that danger certainly seems to be real. I suspect that much of the best work that has ever been done by Christian philosophers is damaged in just that way. But what is the really available alternative to this? (I mean an alternative available to us here and now, not in some future and more ideal state.) Is there some other procedure that Christian philosophers could use that would make them proof against error?

Augustine learned Platonism, I suppose, by reading the works of Plato, or perhaps those of some later Neoplatonists. Thomas found Aristotle's views and arguments in the works of Aristotle and in those of Aristotle's Islamic commentators. And I suppose in that way they learned (or at least they supposed they learned) something that they thought was valuable for their own work. Of course, they did not accept everything they found in these classical mentors. They too believed that Plato and Aristotle had gotten some things wrong. But they thought there was something valuable for them in those classical sources anyway.

Now, let us suppose for the moment that the (very weak) *general* proposition "There is some valuable thesis, argument, insight, etc., to be found in non-Christian philosophy" is true. In that case, it would seem to be possible that some Christian philosopher has found such an insight in a non-Christian source and that it has enriched his or her Christian thought. Perhaps Thomas or Augustine is such a philosopher. But of course in finding that insight they have also exposed themselves to the errors that are no doubt also there in the non-Christian systems. There is the possibility of enrichment and also the danger of infection.

Maybe Augustine and Thomas would have been better off if they had not read these classical philosophers at all. They could have produced a "pure" Christian philosophy by beginning "from scratch" and reflecting on the Christian faith and the divine revelation and the divine creation in the light of the Holy Spirit. And if the insight that we posited above really is one that would enrich a purely Christian philosophy, then they would have discovered that insight independently and without the danger of contamination.

That, it seems to me, represents the ideal of a Christian philosophy that is "free standing" rather than synergistic.

It is also logically possible that this ideal should actually be instantiated. After all, if there really is some valuable insight in Plato, for example, then I suppose it was discovered by Plato or by some of his predecessors. And if it could be discovered by them, then I suppose it is possible that it should be rediscovered, independently, by Augustine. And so a free-standing philosophy is not logically bound to be poorer than one that is synergistic. The ideal of a pure Christian philosophy, therefore, is not logically incoherent.

Is there any reason to think, however, that such a philosophy would be any *better* than the synergistic Christian philosophies that have actually been generated, or those that are being actively thought out today? Unless there is such a reason, I would suppose, the idea of a free-standing Christian philosophy would be no more of an ideal than is the idea of a synergistic Christian philosophy.

This question, it seems to me now, has a significance and application well beyond the academic specialty called "philosophy." It bears on how we Christians are to think of our own epistemic situation and activities *in the present world.* What is the real situation of all of our intellectual and cognitive life, philosophy and everything else, here and now?

Well, what is it? A couple of paragraphs back I argued that if there is some genuine and true insight in Plato, then it is possible that Augustine should discover that valuable insight independently. But if there is an error in Plato, then that error was made either by Plato or by some of his predecessors. And it seems to me that the pattern of the previous argument is just as plausible here. If Plato could make that error, then it is possible that Augustine could also make that error *independently.* Somebody made that error from scratch, and so it is possible that a Christian philosopher could also make it from scratch.

But a Christian philosopher will be doing his thinking in obedience to the divine revelation, will he not, and in the light of the Holy Spirit? Yes, in some sense. But so far as I can see, a Christian philosopher who borrows from Plato or Aristotle (or from Russell, for that matter) does his borrowing also in that obedience and in that light. If the divine revelation does not guarantee that we will unfailingly separate the truth from the error when we borrow from the non-Christian philosophers, then I have no reason to think that it will give us any such guarantee of infallibility merely because we are thinking independently rather than borrowing.

And is it not a fact that, whatever has been the effect of the divine revelation in the world, it has not made Christians generally infallible? Is it not evident that divine grace has not kept us from error, even in theology itself, let alone in philosophy? Earlier I argued that the pagan philosophers must have gotten some things wrong, since their theories are not mutually consistent. But is it not also clear that the theology of Arminius and the animadversions of the Canons of Dort cannot both be correct, since they conflict with one another? Our theologies, even though worked out by Christians, are not infallible, and neither are our philosophies. We will have errors and defects, regardless of whether we borrow from the pagans. But the truth that is in the work of pagans is grounded in the very same divine reality as that which grounds the truth discovered by Christians. There simply is no other reality. Of course, if we borrow from pagans we should borrow carefully and critically. For that matter, if we borrow from other Christians we should borrow carefully and critically. But it would be, in my opinion, a mark of overweening pride if we were to deny that the divine truth makes its impact also on those who are not Christians, and that we may sometimes (perhaps often) learn something from them.

FACE THE FRONT, DEAR, AND SPEAK DIRECTLY TO THE AUDIENCE

There may be a few Christian philosophers, here and there, who think only for themselves and who keep what they think to themselves. For better or worse, most of us do not belong to that category. And so we accept an important feature of human life — both Christian and non-Christian — that of community. In community, work and life and thought are shared with some group of others. We enrich each other (and also, no doubt, to some extent we also damage each other). And so Christian philosophers who publish the results of their reflections in private conversations, in classrooms, or in some wider and more formal theater are associating themselves with a community of intellectual work.

It may be important here, however, for Christian philosophers to remember that they may belong to at least two partially distinct intellectual communities. Many of us, at least, will have some intercourse with the general intellectual community of our time and place — with our colleagues, say, in a university, or in a general professional society. But we also belong to the body of Christ here in the world, to the fellowship of Christians, to the church. And we may from time to time address ourselves primarily to one of those communities and only incidentally to the other. The best Christian philosophy, I suggest, will be specially adapted to the audience for which it is intended.

I do not mean that we should speak insincerely for the sake of an effect, or that we should tailor and shave the truth to make it comfortable and palatable. But there are many truths, and not every truth is the right truth for every time and place. Sometime I may be called to do a piece of public philosophy for the sake of those who are already believers in Christ — to strengthen their faith, perhaps, or to arm them against some specious intellectual attack. If that is my task, then of course I should speak the truth to whatever extent I know it. But I should speak the truth that will be useful to those believers, and in a way that they can apprehend and appropriate. And if I argue, then I can appeal to premises, truths, which that group of believers are likely to share with me.

On other occasions, however, I might address myself to those who are outside the faith, perhaps even in the hope "that by all possible means I might save some," as Paul said (1 Cor. 9:22). Again I should speak the truth, as best I can — but maybe not the same truth that I would speak in the church. If I argue here, for example, it would probably be fruitless to appeal to premises which, though true, are truths that are likely to be accepted only by people who are already believers. That would not be a promising way of making the truth of the gospel available to that audience.

To share a piece of intellectual work with an audience in an effective way requires that we address ourselves to *that* audience, with its own peculiarities and its particular setting in the world. That is often a difficult task, and no doubt we will succeed in it only in part. But the very best Christian philosophy, it seems to me, will be addressed to some actual intended audience, and so it will have some actual human impact.

WHAT'S THE BOTTOM LINE?

I think that philosophy, like many other human enterprises, incorporates some notion of success, of achievement, of "getting the job done," or some such thing. And, of course, along with these notions there goes the idea of failure, and the family of related ideas. Philosophy, then, is something in which we might succeed or we might fail — or, more probably, something in which we can succeed to a greater or lesser degree. I might undertake, for example, to invent some argument for the existence of God. But if I were to make a logical blunder so that the argument I produce is flatly invalid, then that would be a serious defect. I think that such an attempt, at least in most contexts, should be counted as a failure — even if the conclusion of the argument is perfectly true — and probably no beauty of language, etc., can make it much of a philosophical success.

That is an easy example of a failure, but it is not nearly so easy to give a clear example of a success. A valid argument for the existence of God (or for anything else) would, I suppose, be a success *in logic*. If we are writing a logic textbook, then perhaps that is all the success we need for the job at hand. And that's okay. But if the argument for the existence of God is part of a different project, then merely having a success in logic may fall far short of the mark. It is trivially easy to generate perfectly sound arguments for the existence of God, arguments with impeccable logic and in which every proposition — premise and conclusion alike — is true. But the arguments of this sort that can be produced with trivial ease are also very likely to be totally worthless, at least for almost any epistemic purpose that we are going to value. Perhaps they are successes on some scale, but the scale is too easy, because it does not connect with any deep value in human life or in the divine purpose, so far as we can know it.

The best Christian philosophy, it seems to me, will be done after some careful reflection on what the point of that philosophy is, what value is to be achieved in it. If we get some clear notion of that, then we might also be able to formulate some standards for our work. We will perhaps have an idea of what characteristics — virtues — our arguments, analyses, explanations, conjectures, etc., should have in order to achieve that value. And those characteristics, then, would provide a set of standards for the success of our work — standards for evaluating the work, and (perhaps even more important) standards to aim at in doing the work.

It will also be possible, in some cases at least, actually to observe whether the intended value is achieved by our work. We might invent arguments for the existence of God, for example, for the sake of converting atheists. That is a fairly clear goal, and it looks as if it expresses a worth-while value. We can then try our arguments and observe what level of success they actually have. If atheists are converted, fine. But if atheists are not converted, then no amount of theoretical sophistication can make those arguments successful, at least in that project and for that value. In that project, the conversion of atheists is the bottom line, and there is no success without it.

Of course, we might construct theistic arguments in the service of some other project, aiming at some other value. But what project, what value? It seems to me that the best Christian philosophy will be done by people who have some idea of the project they are attempting and of the values at which they are aiming. They will have value-oriented standards by which to evaluate their work and by reference to which they may repeatedly improve it.

"NOW WE SEE IN A MIRROR DIMLY"

So Paul said, in his first letter to the Corinthians. And Christian philosophy, if it is true to this Pauline insight, will have a certain humility about it. We can have high ambitions, and we can be bold in our conjectures. But philosophy, even Christian philosophy, does not carry us fully beyond the bounds and limitations of our lives here. No doubt even the best philosophers among us, and those who are most true to the divine revelation, will find (to paraphrase Hamlet) that there are more things in heaven, and even on earth, than we dreamed of in our philosophizing. And we shall also find that some of the things we dreamed were dreamed badly, dimly, shaded and distorted by the mirror of our philosophical reflection. So if philosophy is a work to which God has called us, let us do it as best we can and with a whole heart. But let us do it with a light heart, too, ready to laugh at ourselves even now, and prepared to join with all the saints (and maybe with our Lord himself) in a gale of holy laughter when we have a better chance to compare the glorious reality with the picture that we have made of it here.

The Historian and the Ancient of Days

Lewis W. Spitz

A MERE historian approaches a subject such as this with fear and trembling, for the ground on which he treads is holy ground. Time is the relationship of things in space, and time like space is therefore a creation of the Eternal One. Eternity does not mean an indefinite and infinite extension of time, but, as St. Augustine made clear, there was a time when there was no time. Eternity is what Aristotle called a *metabasis eis allo genos,* a change into an entirely different category, and what that means all will learn to know, for even earthlings sense that there will be a time when there will be no time. The historian works within the constraints of time and space with what the philosopher Arthur Schopenhauer called "the infinite subject matter of history." Perhaps the historian has a perspective on reality that presentists, no matter how slick and *au courant* their discipline, will always lack. As Cicero rightly said, "Not to know what happened before one was born is to remain a child."[1] But let historians be aware of the hazards of their profession, for they, too, exist by divine indulgence. As Samuel Butler

1. Cicero *De Oratore* 34.

Gratitude is the memory of the heart! I wish to thank the Institut für Europäische Geschichte, Mainz, Germany, for asking me to serve as visiting professor with all the leisure, rights, and privileges thereunto appertaining. I am also grateful to the Fulbright Commission for a professorial fellowship that not only made my research time at the Institute possible, but also provided the intellectual stimulation of a seminar in the newly reunited Berlin.

wrote, "It has been said that though God cannot alter the past, historians can; it is perhaps because they can be useful to Him in this regard that He tolerates their existence."[2]

The renowned Cambridge University historian Herbert Butterfield wrote in his well-known book *The Whig Interpretation of History:* "If history could be told in all its complexity and detail it would provide us with something as chaotic and baffling as life itself; but because it can be condensed there is nothing that cannot be made to seem simple, and the chaos acquires form by virtue of what we choose to omit."[3] This challenge transcends the question that is central to all university historiographical seminars on the objectivity/subjectivity question, thought about at least since Thucydides. As Schopenhauer once asked, "Is it necessary in order to honor the dead to deceive the living?" When Leopold von Ranke set up as an unreachable ideal that the historian should strive to write history "as it actually happened" *(wie es eigentlich gewesen ist),* he was quite right. So many youthful cynics deride him, as though he had said that it was achievable, rather than an objective to be approximated, not perfectly achieved, an ever receding horizon as in Texas or Arizona.

Historians are acutely aware of the complexities of every age, the crosscurrents and new dimensions constantly being discovered and explored, especially in ancient and early medieval history. Yet they need general concepts in order to impose order and to give their version of meaning to their account of past actuality. The extent to which their conceptions correspond to the reality of history as past actuality determines its viability, its correctability, and its utility for teaching history. The extent to which general concepts identify the peculiar or unique characteristic of an age, point to its cultural center of gravity, or assist in mentally regulating its multifaceted aspects and variegated components determines their validity. Hermann Hesse in *Magister Ludi* reflected on the notion that historians must expose themselves to chaos while retaining a basic faith in order and meaning. The historian who describes and analyzes the events of any narrowly defined span of time must remain conscious of the long-term, slowly evolving developments consuming centuries or millennia in their unfolding.

Indisputably the group of historians that has dominated the discussion of such immense problems as periodization is that of the French *Annales*

2. Butler, *Erewhon Revisited Twenty Years Later* (London: A. C. Fifield, 1920), p. 169.
3. Butterfield, *The Whig Interpretation of History* (London: G. Bell and Sons, 1963), p. 97.

school and its American epigoni. The late Fernand Braudel, nestor of the *Annales* school, distinguished between the conspicuous history that holds our attention by its continual and dramatic changes and that other submerged history, almost silent and always discreet, virtually unsuspected by either its observers or its participants, that is almost untouched by the obstinate erosion of time.[4] He described the history dealing with short-term realities as *conjuncture* (ten-, twenty-, or thirty-year periods), and that dealing with long-term realities as *structure*. That wizard of the Sixth Section of Hautes Etudes, Paris, had but a very attenuated regard for the traditional periodization of history and the concepts employed to serve as descriptive devices by historians. As Steve Martin has observed, the French have a different word for everything. Historians, Braudel patiently explained, first create concepts, then glue them as labels on their precious bottles, and finally end up giving the labels authority over their contents. The label, to be sure, in order to be useful, must reflect as accurately as is humanly possible the contents of the age, and that is the point at which the discussion must start rather than end. We must, as we bob along in the stream of history, sometimes ourselves totally submerged by the waves of our own times, strive for an overall perspective. Jacob Burckhardt's chosen *uomo universale*, Leon Battista Alberti, was once asked what his most heartfelt wish would be, if it could be granted. To stand at the end of time, was his reply, so that he could look back over the course of history and understand the total sweep of events in time. Meanwhile, we shall perhaps continue mislabeling our Grecian urns and necessarily adjusting our periodization to more contemporary perspectives, as will those who follow after us. Historians, those masters of the millennia, will have to continue to suffer the barbs of those supercilious skeptics such as Oscar Wilde, who observed in *A Woman of No Importance:* "To give an accurate description of what has never occurred is the inalienable privilege and proper occupation of the historian."

The historian must, of course, remain aware of long-term realities and the glacial pace of some basic developments. In a brief span of time only very little can occur that detectably alters the basic climatic, geographic, and demographic features of a land mass such as Europe and the Americas — to say the usual nothing about Asia and Africa. Economic forces and social institutions are patently less volatile and subject to sudden

---

4. Braudel, "History and the Social Sciences," in *Economy and Society in Early Modern Europe: Essays from Annales,* ed. Peter Burke (New York: Harper, 1972), pp. 12-13; and Braudel, "Qu'est-ce que le XVIe siècle?" *Annales, Économies, Sociétés, Civilisations* 7 (1953): 69-73.

change than are political, religious, and intellectual forces. But social historians, who fancy themselves to be on the cutting edge of nineteenth-century historiography and are disdainful of all but statistical evidence and the condition of the masses are in grave danger of producing hoministic rather than humanistic history. The intellectual and spiritual aspects of life, those that grip the heart and mind, are subject to spectacular change. Some historians who could be named knew in September 1989 of the impending collapse of the Soviet communist system, even though many intelligence agencies fattening on tax monies seem bureaucratically not to have known. Sir Lewis Namier, who once observed that fifty men do not make one centipede, believed that history can never be anything else than the story of people in action. Many of the event-makers in history have been uncommon people, the world's most persistent minority group. History is the story of *Homo sapiens* gifted with a capacity for thought and spiritual aspirations. There is nothing inherently more basically sound or more historical in studying sub-Christian groups than in studying the high theological tradition, or in researching non-thinking crowds rather than the thought of sentient and reflective intellectuals. The nineteenth-century Scottish historian Thomas Carlyle queried quite correctly in his *Essays:* "What is all knowledge, too, but recorded experience, and a product of history; of which, therefore, reasoning and belief, no less than action and passion, are essential materials?" Acknowledgment of this elementary fact is necessary as a first step in weighing the factors that play into the writing of narrative history, and writing narrative history is the supreme test of a good historian. Biography therefore remains a necessary adjunct to history.

The nineteenth-century bourgeois mentality has persisted among Western historians to the end of the twentieth century, preventing some scholars from appreciating the truly revolutionary character of thought. There is a tendency on the part of all too many to reduce even ideas to shades of gray, mostly derivative, incapable of inducing "real" change and impotent in the face of relentless and impersonal social forces. Perhaps historians of thought could learn something special from the historians and analysts of science such as Thomas S. Kuhn, the late Heinz R. Pagels, K. C. Cole, or Christine Sutton.[5] Scientific progress has come about not merely through accretion, like the growth of a coral reef, to the sum of

5. See Kuhn, *The Structure of Scientific Revolutions,* 2d ed. (Chicago: University of Chicago Press, 1970); Pagels, *The Cosmic Code: Quantum Physics as the Language of Nature* (New York: Simon and Schuster, 1982); Sutton, *The Particle Connection — The Most Exciting Chase Since DNA and the Double Helix* (New York: Simon and Schuster, 1984); and esp. Cole, *Sympathetic Vibrations: Reflecting on Physics as a Way of Life* (New York: Morrow, 1985).

cumulative knowledge, but through individuals who broke with the received paradigm, be it in physics or in chemistry, and in biology and
medicine as well. There have been radical breaks in intellectual, religious,
and political tradition that substantively as well as conveniently mark
discontinuities in history and signal the beginnings of a new period. As an
old cliché has it, ideas make for change and institutions for continuity —
that is, until they suddenly collapse, as in eastern Europe today.

All historians — Christian, non-Christian, or anti-Christian — face a
common set of problems: objectivity/subjectivity problems; problems of
evidence; and how to divide up the pie — that is, the problem of periodization, which is in no sense innocent, for it reflects the historian's and
Western person's understanding of the meaning of history.[6] Temporal divisions, even reflecting the substance of the past as factual actuality, remain
artificial to a degree, though useful and necessary devices. The strange poet
E. E. Cummings was impatient with such temporal divisions. "As for a
few trifling delusions like 'past' and 'present' and 'future,' " he exclaimed,
"of quote mankind unquote, they may be big enough for a couple of billion
supermechanized submorons but they're much too small for one human
being." But for all human beings in Western civilization taken collectively,
such temporal categories are unavoidable. It is not true of the major periods
of history that historians have merely arbitrarily concocted labels and
applied them to their story, for the process of interpreting history has been
far more interesting and complicated than that. A certain notion of the
meaning of an age is born — usually in the minds of the intellectual elite
of the time, or during the course of the decades succeeding, by lesser minds.
The meaning is discussed, argued, simplified, reduced to a formula, a
phrase, a term, and is then adopted by historians, canonized in their books,

6. Dietrich Gerhard, "Periodization in European History," *American Historical Review*
61 (1956): 901 n. 3; and Gerhard, *Old Europe: A Study of Continuity, 1000-1800* (New York:
Academic Press, 1981). For further reading relevant to the problem of periodization see
Wallace K. Ferguson, *The Renaissance in Historical Thought: Five Centuries of Interpretation* (Boston: Houghton Mifflin, 1948); William J. Bouwsma, *The Interpretation of Renaissance Humanism* (Washington, DC: Service Center for Teachers of History, 1959); Karl
Heussi, *Altertum, Mittelalter und Neuzeit in der Kirchengeschichte: Ein Beytrag zum Problem
der historischen Periodisierung* (Tübingen: J. C. B. Mohr [Paul Siebeck], 1921); H. Span-
genberg, "Die Perioden der Weltgeschichte," *Historische Zeitschrift* 127 (1923): 1-49; Oscar
Halecki, *The Limits and Divisions of European History* (South Bend, IN: University of Notre
Dame Press, 1962); and Horst Walter Blanke, "Von Chytraeus zu Gatterer. Eine Skizze der
Historik in Deutschland vom Humanismus bis zur Spätaufklärung," in Horst Walter Blanke
and Dirk Fleischer, *Aufklärung und Historik: Aufsätze zur Entwicklung der Geschichtswis-
senschaft, Kirchengeschichte und Geschichtstheorie in der deutschen Aufklärung. Mit
Beilagen* (Waltrop, 1991).

and institutionalized in university curricula and in college courses and degrees catalogs. It becomes part of the minds of teachers and students and is thus perpetuated nearly indefinitely, difficult if not impossible to change.

History can be a real liberating force, freeing us, as Lord Acton once observed, from "the tyranny of the air we breathe." But at times the discouraged intellectual is inclined to agree with the Parisian, Henri Petoit, who sighed: "We are living in Rome in the age of the barbarians." Robert Maynard Hutchins, a former president of the University of Chicago and a heroic battler for the humanities, in later years once wrote plaintively and apprehensively: "I am sorry to repeat that the striking thing about young people today is that they are frightfully ignorant of the past. I don't see how this can ever be an advantage. I understand the advantages of innocence, but I do not understand the advantages of ignorance."[7] Not to know much history diminishes a human's humanity, for history lives within us just as we live in history.

As the ancient Greek leader Pericles supposedly declared in his famous funeral oration: "For the whole earth is the sepulcher of famous men; and their story is not graven only on stone over their native earth, but lives on far away, without visible symbol, woven into the stuff of other men's lives." This quite elementary idea was taken up by the brilliant Oxford philosopher R. G. Collingwood, who argued in his book *The Idea of History* that the purpose of history is human self-knowledge, because "history is contemporary"; it lives in all of us, appropriated in thousands of ways, and emerges into consciousness only through knowledge and examination — self-examination. "Histories are as perfect," Thomas Carlyle opined, "as the historian is wise and gifted with an eye and a soul." As Ralph Waldo Emerson, sometimes called "the American Plato," once wrote in his *Essays:* "We sympathize in the great moments of history . . . because there law was enacted, the sea was searched, the land was found, or the blow was struck, *for us,* as we ourselves in that place would have done or applauded."[8] Emerson was full of the conceits of the intellectual, as when he spoke of scholars as "the eyes and heart of the world." For many "scholars," in the words of Voltaire, "originality is nothing but judicious imitation." One can, of course, be as amusing and as frivolous as Mark Twain, who in an autobiographical mood quipped, "Once I could remember anything whether it happened or not. Now I can remember only

---

7. Hutchins, cited in Keith Berwick, "What the World Needs Now Is Citizens [excerpts from a PBS interview with Robert M. Hutchins]," *The Center Magazine* 4 (1971): 25.

8. Emerson, "History," in *Ralph Waldo Emerson: Selected Essays,* ed. Larzer Ziff (New York: Viking Penguin, 1982), p. 151.

those things that didn't happen." But historians are the keepers of the social memory. Without them society suffers a kind of collective amnesia and is as helpless as an old man who has lost his way. Not to know history is like seceding from the human race.

The study of history can, of course, be carried on at various levels of complexity and depth. On the surface it serves to satisfy what Catherine Drinker Bowen has described as the Great Curiosity (the itch to know). One gains certain knowledge that is useful socially as well as in the perspective gained by an individual on his or her own life. The story is told of Benjamin Disraeli's embarrassment when at state functions — across the table from Gladstone, for example — his quite wonderful wife pretended not to remember whether the Greeks came before the Romans or not. She was a bit older than Disraeli and a great tease! On a deeper level, history can be studied on an analytical level, and so historians speak of factors rather than causes these days, in greater humility. Thus, as Jack Hexter once put it, we progress sideways. At one distinguished university the history department is known to smart undergraduates as the "cause and effects department." On the deepest possible human level, the historian and the student of history are concerned with the question of the meaning of history. One is reminded of the clever lines:

There was a philosopher with knowledge o'erweening
Who discoursed on the meaning of Meaning!
   In great glory he basked,
   Until someone him asked
To explain the meaning of the meaning of Meaning!

Christian culture, absorbing Judaism into its system, has therefore been uniquely historical, unique among world cultures. However varied the use of the word *time* in the Scriptures, Professor Oscar Cullmann in his *Christ and Time* has surely established some good points regarding the relation of the Christian religion and the importance of history.[9] Concepts were derived from the Old Testament idea of covenant fulfillment and from the New Testament concepts of *ephapax* (once and for all time), *plērōma tou chronou* (when the fullness of time was come), and *eschata,* the doctrine of the last things and times. It is necessary to assert that organizing or periodizing history cannot be done without reference to the deeper meaning of history. One cannot follow the example of medieval chroniclers — or

9. Cullmann, *Christ and Time: The Primitive Christian Conception of Time and History,* rev. ed. (London: SCM, 1962). See also James Barr, *Biblical Words for Time* (London: SCM, 1969).

even Flacius Illyricus and the Centurions and their opponents, such as Baronius — and simply march or even crawl through the centuries indifferent to the deeper substantive content of history, such as the meaning in a deeper religious or metaphysical context of the events thus recorded for human admiration or perplexity. This question comes into play quite obviously when the historian is concerned with questions such as when to terminate ancient civilization, the Middle Ages, or modern times, not to speak of postmodern times. Are we and our civilization in the end to be unravelled by postmodernist, poststructuralist, deconstructionist nihilists? Hardly!

The tripartite division of Western history into ancient, medieval, and modern developed in this way. The *trecento* and increasingly the *quattrocento* humanists became disdainful toward and demeaning of the centuries preceding their own times. From the humanists and from the late medieval reformers alike the Protestant reformers learned to speak of the medieval period as the "Dark Ages." The "Dark Ages," as Francesco Petrarch already spoke of those centuries that preceded him, contrasted badly with the age of Augustus and with the golden age and pristine purity of first-century Christianity. In contrast to the medieval period, both Erasmus, the prince of the northern humanists, and Luther, the first major reformer, thought of their own times as the dawn of a new era. Both exclaimed, though with slightly different phrasings, "We live at the dawn of a new era — at the dawn of a golden age!" The idea that there had been a long cultural caesura between classical antiquity and their day, a thousand years without a bath, gathered momentum. Dante was viewed as "the voice of ten silent centuries." Under pressure from this new Renaissance and Reformation point of view, the overall reading of history changed. In fact, both Renaissance humanist and Reformation religious historians moved away from the medieval "accounting" way of doing history to a "pragmatic" or moralistic or even a providential reading of history.[10]

The time-honored account of universal history was based upon the four kingdoms idea, derived from the prophet Daniel (on whom more later) and from the Jewish apocryphal writings as well. The *translatio imperii* served to assure the legitimacy and permanence of the Holy Roman Empire, which was to last to the very end of time. But all gave way to the tripartite division of history. The centuries between antiquity and the Renaissance

---

10. See Manfred P. Fleischer, *The Harvest of Humanism in Central Europe* (St. Louis: Concordia, 1992), pp. 17-23, 27-108; Fleischer, *Späthumanismus in Schlesien: Ausgewählte Aufsätze* (Munich: Delp, 1984); and Lewis W. Spitz, *Humanismus und Reformation als kulturelle Kräfte in der deutschen Geschichte* (Berlin and New York: de Gruyter, 1981).

came to be viewed as merely a *medium aevum,* a middle or intermediary age, a moratorium — or, dynamically conceived, as an age of transition to the new. As Adam said to Eve, "We live in an age of transition!"

The tripartite division was finally enthroned by Christoph Keller, known to historians and in the encyclopedias as Cellarius. Cellarius was a Lutheran divine with a humanistic education; around 1688, in a widely used textbook, he employed the term *Medium Aevum* or "Middle Age" for the ten centuries from Constantine the Great to Constantine XI, the poor creature whose lot it was to be emperor in 1453 when the city of Byzantium and the Hagia Sophia fell to the followers of Mohammed.

In spite of the fact that the four kingdoms or four empires reading of history — down to the fourth beast, dreadful and terrible and exceedingly strong, with great iron teeth, that devoured its victims and stamped the residue with its feet, and had ten horns (Dan. 7:7) — was strongly entrenched in the university curricula of German and other European universities for endless years, it gradually gave way. This overall view persisted in church historical writing, according to Karl Heussi, down to the eighteenth century. The first chair in history was established, not in an Italian Renaissance university, but at the new Lutheran university of Marburg, established by Prince Philipp of Hesse, and it perhaps reflected in its historical outlook the biblical orientation of the Protestants. The renowned Basel historian Werner Kaegi — who wrote the most comprehensive biography of Jacob Burckhardt, the creator of the concept of the Renaissance for modern historiography (though, so far as we know, Jules Michelet was the first to use the expression "Renaissance" in this way in the nineteenth century) — pointed to Voltaire's *Essai sur les moeurs* (1757) as the terminus of the "four kingdoms" reading of history and the triumph of the "great ages" view of history. Voltaire, as is well known, saw only four great ages in world history, two ancient and two "modern." There were the ages of ancient Athens (the Age of Pericles) and of Rome (the Age of Augustus), and the age of the Italian Renaissance and, naturally, the age of Voltaire (all developing, be it noted, in benign geographical climates before the days of artificial heating and air conditioning). Between the two ancient golden ages and the two modern golden ages in Voltaire's mind lay the dark Middle Ages, those centuries which Petrarch had labeled the times of ignorance — a thousand years without a bath! Despite the brave beginnings by Lucio Varga, Luigi Sorrento, and Giorgio Falco, there is no analysis of the concept of the *medium aevum* equivalent to Wallace K. Ferguson's *The Renaissance in Historical Thought.* More work should be done of this synthetic nature on historiography in general, but in particular more work should be done on American church history, before parish churches burn or are shaken down with their vestry libraries and records. Above all, church historians should take on the broad history of the modern church and church historiography.

The French historians refined the concept of *histoire moderne* by introducing the term *histoire contemporaine* into their books and curricula. They began, of course, with the French Revolution. Did not the French revolutionaries, after all, abandon the B.C.-A.D. system of reckoning time itself in favor of a date derived from the French Revolution, just as the pathetic and horrendously cruel and ruthless Russian one-time revolutionaries dated the history of the world from that rascal Lenin's triumphant moment? So why should not the French historical collective, and the Sixth Section (for this Section is well known to be the most prominent group of mutual back-scratchers in the historical world), adopt such quaint terminology with which to describe modern and contemporary history? At one point, not very far removed in time, at the University of Vienna, a certain Professor Benedikt concluded the only lectures on modern Europe with the Congress of Vienna (1815). The German historians as a craft seem to prefer moving directly from the Middle Ages to the Reformation, judging from the way in which the *Historische Zeitschrift* has traditionally organized its review section, and from the existence of such historical centers as the Institut für Spätmittelalter und Reformation in Tübingen. *The American Historical Review* seems to have gone the route of moving from ancient to medieval to modern Europe in its review section. American historians speak of "recent United States" or "contemporary Europe" and even employ the paralogistic term "current history," as though they were mere journalists, like all too many people in the profession who wish to ornament themselves with the name "historian."

Within the large chronological and geographical limits and divisions of history, historians have devised subdivisions, according to the great Italian Renaissance scholar Delio Cantimori, in order to reach two objectives — namely, to achieve a correspondence to a general conception of historical development, and to permit the stabilization of the peculiar characteristics of every period and to make clear the connection with the different forms of historical development.

Without the backward look one does not understand from where one is coming and certainly not where one is or ought to be going. The historian should always remember Luther's comment about theology: "So far as theology goes, a great deal of humility is called for" *(Wenn es zur Theologie kommt, eine gewisse Gescheidenheit gehört dazu)*. When it comes to history, a great deal more modesty is called for than most historians possess. In a way history is like science in that it is very overwhelming in its sheer cumulative data. As Alexander Pope put it in a famous couplet in his *Essay on Criticism:*

> One science only will one genius fit,
> So vast is art, so narrow human wit.

(ll. 60-61)

History and the humanities have in general yet another grievous problem. Lying so close to the basic human concerns of *Homo sapiens,* the fads and trends of interpretation tend to be very volatile. Professor Paul Robinson describes the "social history of ideas" that emerged in the 1960s and 1970s (Darnton, etc.) and the shift in the 1980s back to a more complex notion of the criteria by which ideas qualify for our attention.[11] In the pendular swing, there is a danger of losing or diminishing historical truth. In a seminar given at Stanford University on Leopold von Ranke and Jacob Burckhardt, the late Felix Gilbert of the Princeton Institute for Advanced Studies cautioned that historians who are self-isolated and self-congratulating, considering themselves the wave of the future, who attempt to turn social history into an ideology — whether a Marxist ideology or an ideology with even less intellectual content — are in grave danger. If one turns "social history" into an ideology, when the reaction sets in, such truth as is found by such simpleminded historians — and was not already known to nineteenth-century local and urban historians — will be lost. Once again, as Alexander Pope penned it:

> We think our fathers fools, so wise we grow;
> Our wiser sons, no doubt, will think us so.

(*Essay on Criticism,* ll. 438-39)

The profession of the historian is difficult indeed, involving great personal commitment and the investment of one's whole life in what is often the drudgery of research as well as the pleasure of writing what one finds and (one may hope) truly believes. Historians ought always to be aware of the simple fact that they are not merely cultural transmitters of the acts and thoughts of their predecessors but that they *create* culture in the minds of the young and in the minds of the general public through their books and lectures. It was the great Lord Acton who wrote: "Better one great man of history than ten immaculate historians." Historians must — and most will naturally — do their best to wrestle with the problems of

---

11. Robinson, "H. Stuart Hughes and Intellectual History: Reflections on the State of the Discipline," *Intellectual History Newsletter* 9 (Apr. 1987).

how best to write history and how best to tell the story of the past to oncoming generations. In the telling words of the late theologian Reinhold Niebuhr: "Nothing that is worth doing can be achieved in our lifetime; therefore we must be saved by hope."

As Gerhard Krüger, a noted philosopher of history, once wrote in *Die Geschichte im Denken der Gegenwart:* "History is our greatest problem. It is at one and the same time our most pressing, most all-embracing, and most difficult problem. It is most pressing because man's existence or non-existence depends upon the events of the present and the future. It is the most universal because the fate of all mankind is clearly seen to be intertwined. It is the most difficult because it deals with human freedom in the highest sense and with human destiny which is most unfathomable and incomprehensible."[12] Every human being with a past, present, and future should reflect on these things. Everyone should be his or her own historian. The historian "battles on the dark and bloody ground of learning where muddled armies clash by night." Winston Churchill's own historical writing is about on the level of Sir Robert Walpole's. Walpole once commented: "I know from long political experience that all history is lying." Sir Winston described the difficulties with which the historian must cope with grand Churchillian rhetoric: "History with its flickering lamp stumbles along the trail of the past, trying to reconstruct its scenes, to revive its echoes, and to kindle with pale gleams the passion of former days." The life of the historian is necessarily lived in the historical past and in self-conscious depth at the same time. Historians who have not thought deeply about freedom and meaning in human life and history, who have not probed the depths of human consciousness, who have not felt within themselves the pangs of finitude and the confines of temporality, cannot understand the kind of beings they are exploring in terms of their history. But if such a historian cannot identify the person, the ahistorical thinker cannot even locate a person in time.

René Descartes once described historians as people who spend a lifetime attempting to discover facts about Roman life that any illiterate serving girl in Cicero's time knew well! One is reminded of Clarence Day's clever parody in *Thoughts Without Words:*

> When eras die, their legacies
> Are left to strange police.
> Professors in New England guard
> The glory that was Greece.

12. Krüger, *Die Geschichte im Denken der Gegenwart* (Frankfurt am Main: Vittorio Klostermann, 1947), pp. 5, 30-31.

Many historians are, alas, what German university people call *Fachidioten,* specialists who know all about nothing. To think big, as one must when teaching courses in Western or world civilization, is the real challenge, as long as that thinking is rooted in basic research in a given area of history. As George Macaulay Trevelyan, the learned British historian, expressed this thought: "Clio has one mansion big enough for us all!" Harvard historian Crane Brinton stayed closer to Jesus Christ's reassurance when he wrote: "Clio has many mansions." In a discussion such as this there are many ways in which one could go. One could, for example, explore the understanding of current or recent historians and philosophers about history, Kantian philosophers pretending to be theologians such as Paul Tillich, existentialists such as Martin Heidegger in his *Sein und Zeit* or his *Holzwege,* or Karl Jaspers, a philosopher seeking to be a theologian. This essay has instead returned repeatedly to the question of division and periodization, the closest to the big question of the meaning of history, writ large.

There is many a person, as the saying goes, who does not need an introduction but who could surely use a few good conclusions. I have only one conclusion to draw, but it is all-embracing. Among those who have thought about the meaning of history, there can be no doubt, despite their pygmy detractors, that Oswald Spengler with his frightening *Decline of the West,* Pitrim Sorokin with his admonitions about a "cut-flower civilization" in *The Crisis of Our Age,* and Arnold J. Toynbee with his monumental *A Study of History,* which examines twenty-one fallen civilizations, have had the greatest impact on the public mind. My own opinion is that of St. Augustine: *Finitum non est capax infiniti.* The finite mind of the historian and the relatively historically uninformed mind of the philosopher are incapable of developing and articulating a philosophy of history. But the simple fact that a philosophy of history drawn from all the data of history, providing an outline for organization, and providing therefore a basis for prediction within reasonable limits is impossible does not mean that the historian is without recourse in this swirling vortex of the universe and overwhelming world of the past. For if there cannot be a philosophy of history, there can be and is a theology of history, a Word spoken to humankind by the Lord of history. Our honoree, Dr. Carl Henry, has through his editorial work and writings brought encouragement to many of us historians out in the secular world. He has always understood that the secular world does not mean an irreligious world, but that the liturgical words *secula seculorum* refer to the World without End, the life here and the life beyond. I am among the many thousands who are grateful to him for that.

This essay has had much to do with historians, but the question remains as to who is the Ancient of Days. For those gentle readers who have not in a long season read the seventh chapter of the prophet Daniel — a passage that has had a tremendous impact upon Western ways of thinking about history — I offer here a selection of verses from that moving book. Friedrich von Schlegel, a German philosopher, once referred to the historian as "a prophet looking backward." Here is a prophet looking both backward and forward:

> Daniel spake and said, I saw in my vision by night, and, behold, the four winds of the heaven strove upon the great sea.
>
> And four great beasts came up from the sea, diverse one from another.
>
> The first was like a lion and had eagle's wings. . . . And behold another beast, a second, like to a bear. . . . After this I beheld, and lo another, like a leopard, which had upon the back of it four wings of a fowl. . . .
>
> After this I saw in the night visions, and behold a fourth beast, dreadful and terrible, and strong exceedingly; and it had great iron teeth: it devoured and brake in pieces, and stamped the residue with the feet of it: and it was diverse from all the beasts that were before it; and it had ten horns. . . .
>
> I beheld till the thrones were cast down, and the Ancient of days did sit, whose garment was white as snow, and the hair of his head like the pure wool: his throne was like the fiery flame, and his wheels as burning fire.
>
> A fiery stream issued and came forth from before him: thousand thousands ministered unto him, and ten thousand times ten thousand stood before him: the judgment was set, and the books were opened. . . .
>
> I saw in the night visions, and, behold, one like the Son of man came with the clouds of heaven, and came to the Ancient of days, and they brought him near before him.
>
> And there was given him dominion, and glory, and a kingdom, that all people, nations, and languages, should serve him: his dominion is an everlasting dominion, which shall not pass away, and his kingdom that which shall not be destroyed. (Dan. 7:2-14, KJV)

Like all other mere human beings, historians need vision as well as the wisdom of hindsight.

God and Economics

IAN SMITH

THE WESTERN world is preoccupied with artificial economic rhythms: fluctuations in stock market indices, adjustments to interest rates, and changes in unemployment, inflation, and growth rates grip national attention. The accent granted to these and other economic indicators reflects their significance for both domestic living standards and status in the international community. Even if we are indifferent to national economic issues, we cannot escape the pervasive role that economic transactions play in our individual lives as workers, consumers, investors, and owners. It is perhaps not surprising, therefore, that these ubiquitous macroeconomic and microeconomic aspects of cultural life have generated considerable Christian commentary and reflection across the denominational spectrum.

In the evangelical tradition, the characteristic affirmation of the supreme authority of Scripture has ensured that the Bible maintains a high profile in Christian economic thinking. There is a natural compulsion to search for biblical contexts or to cite biblical proof-texts that have a bearing on economic matters. Contemporary examples of attempts to distill economic imperatives from the biblical text are numerous, diverse, and contradictory, disclosing different theological and politico-economic emphases. Indeed, the notorious lack of consensus in secular economic debate is readily paralleled in its Christian counterpart. The objective of this essay is to disentangle some of those knotty disagreements. In particular, I shall discriminate critically among the different ways in which Christian commentators on economics actually handle the scriptural data. The most influential positions will be outlined in turn and an assessment made of their validity. A final section draws attention to the key conclusions that emerge from the discussion.

Before proceeding, there are some important preliminary matters that must be dealt with regarding both the scope of the discussion and the definition of economics.

SCOPE

Much of the evangelical dialogue is pursued in the arena of "social ethics." Prominent issues include the relationship of social responsibility to evangelism,[1] and the question of which theological model best guides the way we do social ethics in a mixed society. However, the debate on whether it is the creation narratives, the Mosaic legislation, the kingdom of God, or *shalom* that provides the hermeneutical key for contemporary social ethical discussion is tangential to what follows.[2] To begin with, at least, my focus is not on the broad social ethical conversation but on economics narrowly defined.

Traditionally the major economic debate in the Christian literature has been preoccupied with which economic system — free market capitalism or democratic socialism or the social market economy or whatever — best reflects Christian principles in the allocation of scarce resources.[3] Although none of these modern politico-economic models is countenanced in the periods that constitute the biblical era, the evaluation of which modes of economic organization conform most closely to biblical norms remains a lively pursuit among Christian authors. But despite the vitality of the debate, the degree of resolution is minimal. Much discussion serves only to reveal the political prejudices of the writer.[4] It appears difficult to escape the temptation to bless a political bias by demonstrating its consistency

---

1. A recent attempt is that of J. Woodhouse, "Evangelism and Social Responsibility," in *Christians in Society,* Explorations 3, ed. B. G. Webb (Sydney: Moore Theological College/Lancer Books, 1988). A classic text is that of Carl F. H. Henry, *Aspects of Christian Social Ethics* (Grand Rapids: Eerdmans, 1964).

2. See the set of papers reproduced in *The Evangelical Quarterly* 62, 1 (Jan. 1990).

3. This point is also well made by J. David Richardson, "Frontiers in Economics and Christian Scholarship," *Christian Scholar's Review* 17, 4 (1988): 381-400. He suggests that such easily tilled and fruitful fields need some Sabbath rest.

4. On the political right, for example, W. A. Grudem surveys the biblical material and designs an optimal Christian economic system that remarkably resembles that extant in contemporary North America. See Grudem, "How an Economic System Can Be Compatible with Scripture," chap. 2 in *Biblical Principles and Economics: The Foundations,* Christians in the Marketplace Series, vol. 2, ed. R. C. Chewning (Colorado Springs: NavPress, 1989).

with carefully selected portions of Scripture. At its worst, this amounts to ideological manipulation of the Bible to suit a political interest or a confessional stance. Such misuse of Scripture is vulnerable to the Marxist critique of religion — namely, that religious ideas serve to render dominant class interests universally acceptable by affirming the prevailing socioeconomic order as divinely ordained. This sort of pitfall is, however, increasingly recognized, and appropriate warnings have been issued, as exemplified in the words of Carl Henry:

> Whoever considers the politico-economic status quo sacred or normative, or uncritically resigns himself to it, needs to reread the Bible.[5]

Interestingly, among trained economists the grand discussion of the relative merits of comparative economic systems is a more peripheral matter. Richard Lipsey, for example, in his popular undergraduate textbook *An Introduction to Positive Economics,* does not discuss the issue directly. Rather, he presumes a market model and expounds economic theory on that basis. The terms *socialism* and *planning* are not mentioned in either his index or his glossary.[6] This is not to argue that such matters are ignored by economists;[7] the point is that Christian discussion of economics tends to give disproportionate weight to this overarching and rather sterile question. In what follows, therefore, I decline to address the controversy directly, preferring instead to focus attention on less well-charted territory.

DEFINITION

Economics is a very slippery discipline to delimit. Definitions often fall into the trap of describing the research program of one of the many competing schools of thought.[8] This is not to deny that there is a textbook

---

5. Henry, "Biblical Authority and the Social Crisis," in *Authority and Interpretation: A Baptist Perspective,* ed. D. A. Garrett and R. R. Melick, Jr. (Grand Rapids: Baker Book House, 1987), p. 206.

6. Lipsey, *An Introduction to Positive Economics,* 7th ed. (London: Weidenfeld and Nicolson, 1989). The nearest Lipsey comes to the topic is in two chapters (out of forty) that discuss the theoretical cases for free markets and for government intervention.

7. See, e.g., the non-mainstream textbook by J. Robinson and J. Eatwell, *An Introduction to Modern Economics* (London: McGraw-Hill, 1973). Also, the recent moves toward economic and political liberalization in eastern Europe are inevitably generating more interest in which forms of economic organization are optimal.

8. In North Atlantic economics, the so-called neoclassicals are, of course, dominant. Hence, Richardson defines economics "as the science of decision-making under scarcity"

consensus that emphasizes the price system (supply and demand) and exchange relationships. But historically the fortunes of dominant paradigms have witnessed decline and fall. I prefer the functional definition that the content of economics is bounded by what those who label themselves economists actually reflect upon in the universities, in government departments, in industry, in finance, and in international organizations. It is the professional interests of the ordinary economist that constitute the object of my attention.[9] His or her primary function is analytical: to establish the principles on which aspects of the economic system work and to forecast and prescribe on that basis.

This definition may appear tautological and unilluminating, but it is actually much narrower than that countenanced by most non-economists, who often interlace social ethics and politics in their discussion of "economic" affairs. An example of this is the recent "Oxford Declaration on Christian Faith and Economics."[10] The overriding emphasis here on justice is largely alien to an economist's conceptual toolkit. It is a social ethical, rather than a narrowly economic, category. It has a happier home in the textbooks of political theory than in those of introductory economics (it barely gets a mention in Lipsey). However, I do not wish to argue that justice could not or should not be a conspicuous issue in the daily business of the economist (as will become clear later), but only that in practice the matter is neglected. Perhaps the lesson to be drawn from this observation is that economic categories alone are insufficient for studying social issues. Economic concerns are inevitably embedded in a larger social framework.

DESCRIPTION

From a glance at the biblical material that bears (however tangentially) on economic matters, it soon becomes clear that much, though not all, is concerned with covenantal stipulations and other moral exhortation. It deals with ethical norms that are typically given theological justification. Not surprisingly, then, most discourse in Christian economics deals with explicitly prescriptive questions: What should we do about environmental prob-

---

("Frontiers in Economics," p. 382). But Marxian, post-Keynesian, Austrian, and neo-Ricardian traditions, which might dispute this as a complete definition, persist.

9. This is defined so as to exclude the business manager. Readers interested in business ethics are referred to the text by R. C. Chewning, J. W. Eby, and S. J. Roels, *Business Through the Eyes of Faith* (San Francisco: Harper & Row, 1990).

10. Printed in *Transformation* 7, 2 (1990).

lems? How should a Christian economic system be organized? How should a Christian in business conduct his or her corporate transactions?

There is, however, a prior issue concerning the relationship of biblical revelation to the description and explanation of economic reality. So before proceeding to address the question of how the biblical material shapes economic prescription, I will examine the three main views regarding the relationship between the Bible and descriptive economics. The first and most common stance posits that scientific economic analysis is independent of any religious input; the second position argues that worldview considerations inevitably shape the agenda that is set and the categories that are applied in analytical economics; and the third and most radical conviction holds that special revelation has epistemological implications for the explanation of economic phenomena.

Disciplinary Autonomy

The first and most widely accepted position presumes disciplinary autonomy: Scripture may tell us something about the geography, history, and religion of the ancient Near East, but it has nothing to contribute directly to the understanding of modern economies. There is a gulf between specialized theory and the biblical witness. The Bible does not instruct us in macroeconomics or the theory of international trade since it is not an economics textbook. As a corollary, God concepts are redundant in scientific economic theory. In short, religion is conceived as epistemologically irrelevant for economics: economic knowledge is separable from and independent of theological knowledge, and special revelation provides no privileged comprehension of economic processes.[11]

So while economic analysis may not contradict Christianity, it is, on this view, certainly not dependent upon it. The mode of understanding is therefore entirely secular. Crises and disasters of the economic environment, such as a stock market crash or high unemployment, are so manifestly the result of mundane economic forces that they require no supernatural or metaphysical diagnosis.

The implication for the Christian economist in his or her professional capacity is that Christian witness does not manifest itself in the economic analysis but rather in the excellence of personal conduct and moral character.

11. See A. M. C. Waterman, "Economists on the Relation between Political Economy and Christian Theology: A Preliminary Survey," *International Journal of Social Economics* 14, 6 (1987): 46-68; and "Can Economic Policy Be Christian?" *Review of Social Economy* 46 (1988): 203-11.

Disciplinary autonomy is the dominant position in the day-to-day work of both contemporary secular and Christian economists. As such, it cannot be readily dismissed. Such a standpoint is echoed by Oliver Barclay in his discussion of whether there is Christian insight in mathematics. He writes:

> The fact is that Christian mathematicians have not shown themselves notably closer to the reality of God's creation in the mathematical world than other mathematicians. If they alone understood it correctly, they should do better mathematics. Not only do they not do visibly better mathematics, but what they do is indistinguishable from the mathematics done by others. The same could be said of many sciences.[12]

In the case of economics, however, the disciplinary autonomy is asymmetric. Although reluctant to permit other disciplines to trespass on the economic field, economists usually perceive no reason why economic categories, incentives, and constraints should not imperialistically dominate thinking about any and every issue without restraint.[13] After all, any social phenomenon can be conceived as human economizing activity. Take, for example, the economic theory of the church.[14] In the case of Roman Catholic ecclesiology, the pope is conceived of as the chairman of a huge multinational corporation that produces religious, educational, and social services. To quote the founding father of modern economics, Adam Smith, "The clergy of every established church constitute a great incorporation." The objective of the board of directors — that is, the church cardinals — is to maximize ecclesiastical wealth. Thus a chief task is the recruitment of priestly and episcopal labor to convince consumers that the discounted value of the future benefits of salvation exceeds their current opportunity costs — that is, their opportunities for worldly pleasure. Since the church competes at the margin in an oligopolistic market — against other religions and secular substitutes — for the allegiance of individuals, it is loathe to make frequent adjustment to its prices. Hence theological novelty must be carefully monitored to avoid disturbing the equilibrium of tradition.

---

12. Barclay, *Developing a Christian Mind* (Leicester: Inter-Varsity, 1984), p. 205.

13. The tyrannical tendency for economic categories to be exalted is made plain by R. K. McCloughry, *The Eye of the Needle* (Leicester: Inter-Varsity, 1990), chap. 4.

14. See E. J. Kane, "Pareto Optimality and the Church as an Economic Enterprise," *Kyklos* 19 (1979): 425-42; B. B. Hull and F. Bold, "Towards an Economic Theory of the Church," *International Journal of Social Economics* 16, 7 (1989); G. M. Anderson, "Mr Smith and the Preachers: The Economics of Religion in the *Wealth of Nations*," *Journal of Political Economy* 96 (1988): 1066-88.

The product mix of the company includes leisure goods (fellowship), social goods (income redistribution, Sunday school), deferred perpetuity (eternal life), and altered fate (healing miracles). These products provide a source of revenue and attract additional church members. But due to the existence of secular competitors in the product market (such as the theater, sporting events, television, and so forth) the church has an incentive to enforce a monopoly position by proscribing these substitute activities for the faithful. Alternatively the church must lower its relative prices or improve product quality with more up-beat choruses, better provision for the children, and improved car parking facilities.

And so the economic theory proceeds, accommodating all non-market, religious behavior to utilitarian calculus. Hence, while religion is claimed to be epistemologically irrelevant for economic understanding, economists tend to deny the converse; the relationship is asymmetrical.

Moreover, the disciplinary autonomy position overlooks the role of religious doctrine in the development and growth of the economic system itself. Max Weber is the most celebrated proponent of the notion that systems of religious belief shape economic outcomes. Weber argued that the Reformation emphasis on the doctrine of predestination promoted an ethic of diligence and asceticism in a calling as an objective external sign of election (2 Pet. 1:10). When applied to economic activity, this Protestant ethic fostered the development of capitalism by fathering an ethos of disciplined work and saving as a vocational duty and virtue. The implication of this well-established Weberian contention is that a complete understanding of the economic universe is by no means independent of religious ideas.

Disciplinary Interdependence

The standard response to the disciplinary autonomy view is to note that it is predicated on a strict distinction between positive and normative categories. Lipsey's textbook, for example, is concerned with *positive* economics — that is, with the scientific study of economic phenomena through the statement and testing of theories. It is concerned with facts, not values — with what "is" rather than what "ought" to be. This dichotomy is based on the positivist view that facts per se are in principle independent of values; there is a "logical gulf" between descriptive and evaluative sentences. Hence the result that Bible study is irrelevant for understanding modern economic behavior.

However, if it can be demonstrated that ethical considerations pervade economic analysis, then there is clearly scope for biblical values to shape economic descriptions. Indeed, there is now wide acknowledgment that at least in the humanities and social sciences the sharp positive-normative distinction is fallacious. In practice many economists recognize the ubiquitous intrusion of value considerations. It is difficult, for example, to remain dispassionate when advising on public policy. Also, language is replete with implicit values. While Lionel Robbins protests that surely "equilibrium is just equilibrium," as Joan Robinson points out, "disequilibrium sounds uncomfortable, goods sound good, exploitation wicked, and sub-normal profits rather sad." Furthermore, description may often be motivated by normative considerations. Poverty, for example, might be studied in order to contribute to its alleviation.

The most powerful argument against value neutrality, however, is based on the weakness of theory testing in economics. All theories are constructed within a particular vision or worldview with regard to the nature of economic reality. Neoclassicals interpret the world in terms of individuals and the market; Marxists in terms of collectivities (social groups) and power relations. As such the preferred worldview shapes the selection of problems for study and the conceptual framework. It shapes the way questions are posed, the data that are interpreted, the answers that are acceptable, the language in which the results are formulated, and the test criteria that are preferred. Thus, methodological judgments or presuppositions about what has value very powerfully invade the *context of discovery*.

This would not matter if values could be filtered out effectively through theory testing — that is, in the *context of justification*. Theories would be adopted that were most successful in the face of attempts at falsification. One would expect the best performing hypotheses, in general, to conform closest to the true worldview. In the hard sciences it would appear that we do have objective access to the empirical world through manipulative testing. Bad theories generated by defective worldviews can be filtered out.

But as is well known, economics is an inexact science; the subject matter does not display universal laws or constants. The structure of the economic universe is nonrepeatable, always changing. Consequently theory appraisal is extremely difficult, and few theories, if any, have been conclusively refuted. Since there are no decisive anomalies in the social sciences, testability fails to perform its filtering function. As a result there is a greater role for cultural and subjective factors in the formation of an economic worldview. Not surprisingly, the outcome is theoretical pluralism in economics — a pluralism that reflects different visions of social reality and therefore different judgments of what is significant. And these judgments are normative insofar as they suggest what categories and tools are necessary for accurate description. Every economic description, because of severe difficulties with testing, ultimately has to reflect a value-laden judgment that this is how the world ought to be described.[15]

So while acknowledging the positivist view that economic analysis may serve as an input into biblically based ethical discussion, the interdependency position goes further to argue that, conversely, the Bible may also serve as an input into economic discourse. It functions, for example, to set the agenda of what concerns are of special interest. This is basically the argument of Richardson.[16] He claims that some of the substance of economics is more intrinsically interesting to Christians; controversial topics such as poverty, welfare experience, income distribution, immigration, and economic development are suggested for study. Moreover, certain tools of analysis may fit a Christian's relational temperament much better than others — typically those that are more social in character, such as interviews and surveys.

There are some difficulties with such an approach. First, it is not always clear which questions are uninteresting from a Christian perspective, or, more strongly, which topics should be avoided. Donald Hay suggests that a Christian would not be too preoccupied with outcomes regarding efficiency, growth, and progress as dictated by the neoclassical research program, but rather would be concerned with issues relating to responsible stewardship and satisfying work.[17] This conclusion, of course, hinges on what is made of the biblical material, an issue considered below. Second, in practice Christians who nominally adhere to the interdependence position easily lapse into the framework of disciplinary autonomy either through neglect, because of the lack of a supportive environment, or because of professional constraints: the research agenda and tools may well be preselected. Finally, as Kenneth Elzinga laments, this agenda appears limited; it lacks a distinct Christian flavor:

> If that's all there is to Christianity and economics, i.e., caring scholars doing mainstream work on a non-random selection of topics, this will be a disappointment to those with higher expectations for the impact of Christianity upon economics. For if economics as done by Christians is to offer a new paradigm that is so bold, so useful, and so close to the

15. An extremely useful survey of the literature on this issue is provided by C. K. Wilber and R. Hoksbergen, "Ethical Values and Economic Theory: A Survey," *Religious Studies Review* 12 (1986): 208-14.

16. Richardson, "Frontiers in Economics," pp. 391-96.

17. Hay, *Economics Today: A Christian Critique* (Leicester: Apollos, 1989), p. 124.

world of reality that it will influence the discipline, this has not happened.[18]

Distinctively Christian Economic Analysis

For those concerned to operate within a more distinctively Christian paradigm, a quite radical approach is proposed. The key idea, propagated mainly by thinkers in the Dutch neo-Calvinist tradition of Kuyper, Dooyeweerd, and Van Til, is that biblical revelation transforms economic description. Ethical (biblical) categories are required to perceive reality correctly. In the words of Alan Storkey, "biblical revelation is a necessary prerequisite for perceiving our situation more truly."[19]

Biblically derived institutional norms not only show us how we are meant to live — how institutions such as the state, the family, the corporation, and the financial system should be shaped — but also provide a way of *understanding* pathological economic outcomes. Economic crises are to be understood as failures to adhere to the normative principles governing the purpose and shape of economic activity. Ethical categories, then, are imported directly into economic description. The attitudes and values exhibited in economic activity and relationships are to be questioned as part of the analysis since they are integral to the data generation process. So, for example, poverty is to be understood as a deviation from scriptural principles. More controversially, Storkey ascribes the economic performance of the West to the success of the service ethic and love of neighbor, not modern capitalism. Among other things, he also asserts that the development of new forms of service is the dynamic of company growth, and that it is egocentricity that leads to industrial unrest.

"Economic" policy proposals also become explicitly ethical: the solution to unemployment requires changed institutional values and commitments and a different way of understanding our economic relations such that a strong, positive value is given to employment. As Storkey comments, repentance may turn out to be a central economic issue. The implication is that nonnormative analyses seriously misrepresent what is going on. All true theory is Christian theory; the Bible is cognitively significant for explaining economic phenomena.

Such an approach is more common than might be imagined. Brian

---

18. Elzinga, "Comments on J. David Richardson," *Christian Scholar's Review* 17, 4 (1988): 401-5.

19. Storkey, *Transforming Economics: A Christian Way to Employment* (London: Third Way Books/SPCK, 1986), p. ix.

Griffiths, for example, notes that although inflation may be technically related to the supply of money, the fundamental problem is not the control of monetary aggregates but the addiction of Western economic democracies to consumption.[20] This creates an incentive for governments to expand the money supply in order to win elections.

One obvious merit of the Dooyeweerdian approach is that it brings biblical and ethical categories into a much higher profile. The Christian content and method are more distinctive and conspicuous. A standard criticism, however, is that the analysis ends up being rather speculative. It omits, for example, any convincing explanations of the causes of the breakdown of norms, beyond an appeal to sinful attitudes. Nor is it clear what happens to the technical analysis of economic data. Oliver Barclay is also very suspicious of the Dooyeweerdian school of thought since it tends to rely on a nonbiblical philosophical framework as the starting point.[21]

PRESCRIPTION

Whatever view is taken on the correct way to utilize the biblical records in economic description, there still remains the crucial question, so far unaddressed, of what precisely is the character of the (prescriptive) biblical witness on matters economic.

In discussions of the biblical material, certain key passages regularly appear, though their interpretation varies from author to author.[22] The creation narratives are used to mandate the creation of wealth and responsible stewardship through work. From the Mosaic law, the Jubilee legislation in Leviticus 25 turns out to be fundamental. Legislation on harvest gleanings, honest weights, tithing, slavery, loans, and the family also attracts attention. The Prophets and the Psalms offer particularly choice selections on social justice and preferential options for the poor and oppressed. The Gospels and Epistles, however, yield lower rates of return. In the synoptic Gospels, we have a few parables and sayings relating to wealth, poverty, and taxation. The New Testament Epistles

20. Griffiths, *The Creation of Wealth* (London: Hodder and Stoughton, 1984), pp. 113-14.

21. Barclay, *Developing a Christian Mind,* appendix.

22. Drawing on Hay, *Economics Today,* chaps. 1 and 2; Alan Storkey, *A Christian Social Perspective* (Leicester: Inter-Varsity Press, 1979), chap. 14; Griffiths, *The Creation of Wealth,* chap. 3; M. Schluter and R. Clements, "Reactivating the Extended Family: From Biblical Norms to Public Policy in Britain," Jubilee Centre Paper No. 1, 1986; and Christopher J. H. Wright, *Living as the People of God* (Leicester: Inter-Varsity, 1983).

have a bearing on issues related to the state, and again some discussion of personal and ecclesiastical obligations to care for those who are economically marginalized.

THE PROBLEM OF SCRIPTURAL DISTORTIONS

A very acute danger in searching for texts relevant to economics is that enthusiasm for the project can lead to unnatural exegesis. Take, for example, the parable of the workers in the vineyard (Matt. 20:1-16). Its central meaning surely has to do with the fact that the kingdom of heaven does not operate on the principles of ability or merit but on God's sovereign grace. Christian economists, while acknowledging the fundamental truths taught in the parable, typically propose secondary meanings with wider application. Brian Griffiths, for example, derives the lesson that ownership is absolute and involves total discretion. Alan Storkey understands the parable to point to a concern for unemployed workers. Alternatively one might distill lessons for union-management relationships. At best, such secondary meanings are a little strained and artificial. And some bizarre conclusions may result. One study of Jesus' parables in the context of the economic circumstances of first-century agrarian Palestine, for example, argues from the agricultural parables (the parable of the sower, the parable of the weeds among the wheat, and the parable of the mustard seed) that Jesus is implicitly advocating a collective strike by the peasantry for the sake of the kingdom of God![23]

Recognizing the dangers of eisegesis, there are basically three main approaches to handling the biblical data listed above.

(1) Minimalism

The minimalist denies that the biblical material generates much in the way of direct guidance even as prescription. According to this view, it is not possible to derive a contemporary normative economics directly from Scripture. There are two variants of this approach.

The extreme version argues that the biblical revelation is of little (even indirect) relevance for economic life, beyond personal responsibility not to steal from the taxman and to respect private property. Christianity is understood as a religion that is not immediately concerned with the structure and operation of any political, social, or economic system. This

23. D. E. Oakman, *Jesus and the Economic Questions of His Day* (Lewiston, NY: Edwin Mellen, 1986).

is an example of what H. Richard Niebuhr labeled a "Christ against culture" position, characterized by withdrawal from the world and its affairs. Such a sharp separation between the public and private spheres of life is, however, difficult to defend.[24]

The more moderate and less privatized position would accept the importance of biblical injunctions in their application to economic life but construe them in rather general terms. The stipulations are mediated through a sanctified conscience and Christian compassion, rather than through well-defined ethical theory. It is the law written on the heart that provides the motivation and justification for Christian involvement in economic affairs. So in dealing with the problem of unemployment, the moderate minimalist would be content to take "love your neighbor" as programmatic and get on with the task as earnestly and imaginatively as possible within his or her personal sphere of influence. This is the approach often adopted by socially responsible "grassroots" Christians not given to academic conversations. The ethical demands impact primarily on behavior within the Christian community as it seeks to minister as salt and light to a needy world in the name of Christ. This does not preclude involvement at the political level. Christian concern for the natural environment, for Third-World development, for the long-term unemployed, and so on is appropriately expressed in the public arena. Like the prophets of old, believers should never shrink from declaring truth to power. A prophetic witness against exploitative opulence and other expressions of social injustice cannot be divorced from the Christian faith. But perhaps the most distinctive Christian contribution is the faithful witness of the servant church as an exemplar for the world, as a social ethic itself.[25]

The important point to note is that Scripture is viewed as insufficient in its models or detail for more than, at best, very general guidance in economic prescription. Specific authoritative biblical revelation is believed to be largely absent in this field.

(2) Principles

For those who desire to pay closer attention to the guidelines of the biblical material, an approach based on a systematic formulation of derivative social

---

24. For a cogent exposition and critique see chap. 2 of Niebuhr's *Christ and Culture* (New York: Harper and Brothers, 1951).

25. As commended, for example, in the work of Stanley Hauerwas, *The Peaceable Kingdom: A Primer in Christian Ethics* (Notre Dame: University of Notre Dame Press, 1983).

principles (or middle axioms) commends itself. Acknowledging that it is not possible to pass directly from the scriptural counsels and directives to modern economic life, an inductive study of the Bible isolates certain dominant themes of relevance. There are several standard themes that typically emerge: responsible stewardship of resources; the deconcentration of wealth and decentralization of power; individual ownership of property and the need to share its benefits; the necessity and key role of work as a vocation; care for the poor and oppressed; fair prices and wages; distributive justice; and wholesome economic relationships. Many writers readily grant assent to these generic principles, though the balance of emphasis may differ from author to author.

A problem the approach immediately encounters is the one that besets the social ethics debate — that of which theme provides the hermeneutical key. Those who stress principles derived from creation tend to reach more conservative conclusions and emphases than those who rely on the prophetic call for social justice. In part, of course, the preferred theme reflects the set of ideological spectacles that are being worn.

One of the advantages of the thematic approach is that it overcomes the problem of cultural distance between a theocratic agrarian society and the secular industrial situation by seeking universal principles in God's dealings with men and women. General themes and principles can be contextualized in fresh cultural settings without losing their normative validity. The trade-off is that the degree of abstraction is necessarily quite high. As a result, proponents are usually long on conventional economic analysis and biblical exegesis, but very short on detailed prescription for inevitably complex economic problems. It is not, therefore, a terribly progressive research program in terms of policy fruitfulness. In the words of Clements and Schluter:

> [General principles] are at such a high level of abstraction as to be inadequately defined for specific application in contemporary situations.[26]

Derivative social principles also lack the twin desirable properties of uniqueness and exclusion. The non-uniqueness property refers to the fact that general principles tend not to be distinctively Christian in character; they are often observationally equivalent to the ethical imperatives of other (secular) belief systems. The non-exclusion property means that general principles may be consistent with most economic policy alternatives, even those that contradict one another. Thus the burden of proof remains on the

---

26. Schluter and Clements, "Reactivating the Extended Family," p. 25.

advocates of the principles method to demonstrate its utility for Christian economic prescription.

(3) Law

The critique of the thematic method forms a starting point for the theonomic approach that turns to the Old Testament law, at least those aspects that deal with social institutions, as a normative socio-political model for contemporary society. A theonomist is here defined broadly as anyone who subscribes to the belief that the Old Testament law continues to exercise (binding) authority over the Christian believer in terms of its covenantal stipulations — except, of course, for those sections that have been rescinded or modified in the course of salvation history. The existence of discontinuities between the old(er) and new(er) covenants is readily acknowledged by even the most extreme theonomists, such as R. J. Rushdooney, Greg Bahnsen, and Gary North. For example, Christians are no longer obliged to keep the ceremonial law (relating to the sacrificial system, the temple, and the priesthood) since these obligations have been fulfilled in Christ's redemptive work on the cross.

There are, however, major differences within the theonomic school on what else does and does not carry over into the common era. I shall focus mainly on the most plausible variant, the so-called paradigmatic approach introduced by Chris Wright and adopted by the influential Jubilee Centre in Cambridge, England.[27]

Here, the law is to be understood and applied as a paradigm in terms of the pattern of relationships between the component institutions (the local community, the state, and the extended family) and the factors of production (land, labor, and capital). The interpretation of the law is not literalistic since due account must be taken of historical and cultural context and the intention behind the laws. Yet the norms that result are tied specifically to particular institutions and fit together holistically as a model, rather than operating as general moral principles that may be applied elsewhere.

The theonomic approach is very appealing for those who wish to take all of God's revealed Word and the moral absolutes of the Old Testament seriously. The Pentateuch is also the richest biblical resource in terms of economic content, and in-depth study of it does undoubtedly prove rewarding when it comes to policy questions. Much more detailed and precise analyses and proposals have been forthcoming from the theonomists than from other Christian camps.

---

27. See Wright, *Living as the People of God.*

A favorite criticism of the theonomic enterprise cites the problem of cultural distance. Although the historical societies that hosted the biblical tradition possessed some attributes of industrial capitalism such as private property, money, public taxation, market exchange, and so on, an agrarian, tribal society knows nothing of *inter alia* complex monetary systems, global environmental pollution, and multinational enterprises.[28] Even if the Mosaic legislation is handled paradigmatically, it is difficult to conceive how the Old Testament model can be readily applied to advanced industrial societies.

The fundamental theological question that the approach raises is a salvation historical one. Does the New Testament really teach the continuity of the Mosaic law as a binding code for Christians except for those parts modified by the coming of Christ, or does it presuppose discontinuity unless reaffirmed under the new covenant?

Matthew 5:17-19 is the *locus classicus* for theonomic thought. The key to understanding these verses turns on the sense in which Jesus fulfills the law. For theonomist Greg Bahnsen, "fulfill" entails that Jesus confirms and establishes the continuing validity of the law in its precise details. There is, however, a slight inconsistency in his argument since even he qualifies verse 19 so as to exempt the ceremonial commandments, which were fulfilled in Christ.

Against Bahnsen, it is more convincing to argue that Jesus fulfilled the law and the prophets in the sense that they point to him.[29] He is the goal of the Old Testament. Jesus fulfills the Old Testament prophecies by his person and actions; he fulfills the Old Testament law by his teaching. By implication, he is its sole authoritative interpreter (hence, "You have heard that it was said, . . . But I tell you . . ." in Matt. 5:21-48). The details of the Old Testament commandments, then, are most properly obeyed by conforming to the teaching of the one who fulfills them.

The corollary of this position that I am affirming is that none of the Mosaic legislation per se is binding as independent *lex*. New covenant believers are not obliged to obey it, not one jot or tittle; on the other hand, they do fulfill it by living in conformity with the new covenant to which the old covenant points. In short, Christians live under the stipulations of the New Testament and interpret the Old christologically.

To a large extent, this approach undermines much of the theonomic

28. For further discussion see D. E. Oakman, "The Ancient Economy in the Bible," *Biblical Theology Bulletin* 21, 1 (1991): 34-39.

29. Following D. A. Carson, *Matthew,* vol. 8 of *The Expositor's Bible Commentary,* ed. F. E. Gaebelein (Grand Rapids: Zondervan, 1984).

enterprise, especially the radical version in which the details of Israel's social and political life are binding. However, this does not preclude studying the Old Testament social system as a rich ethical resource, so long as it is not appealed to as normative — that is, divinely ordained as authoritative for today. It is true that the socioeconomic laws and institutions of Israel embody those qualities of righteousness, love, justice, and compassion that reflect God's own character. Thus they are still instructive and eminently worthy of analysis. However, the fundamental question is not "How do we apply the Old Testament law?" but rather "How do we apply the teachings of Jesus and the apostles?" My point is that even if an Old Testament law (or model) can be demonstrated to be consistent with the New Testament, it is not necessarily terribly interesting. It may be very significant; it may stimulate fresh thinking; or it may be unhelpful or misleading — but it is not binding as God's will for pagan society or for God's new society, the church.

Needless to say, the status of the Mosaic law is a controversial issue that currently divides Reformed Christianity. Without the law still in force as *lex*, it might be argued that the Christian economic enterprise loses much of its cutting edge in terms of prescriptive content. After all, the difficulty of proceeding only from theologically informed general principles to detailed economic policy recommendations has already been pointed out.

CONCLUDING REFLECTIONS

This essay has assessed the ways in which Christians view the increasingly dominant economic aspects of culture. Several points worthy of attention emerge from the discussion. In general, it appears that the distinctive Christian contributions both to understanding the economic world and to detailed economic policy prescription are rather limited. Although the literature is voluminous, progress in establishing a fruitful Christian approach to economic problems remains pedestrian. Perhaps this is inevitable. The Bible does not furnish us with specific and authoritative economic models that can be directly applied to contemporary society. Some authors have disputed this observation and sought to devise a biblical economics based on the Old Testament law. However, a reliance on the Mosaic legislation to provide a blueprint for reconstructing the modern economy is theologically dubious and culturally anachronistic.

An inductive study of Scripture to formulate thematic economic principles is more defensible. The principle of responsible stewardship, for example, is commonly espoused, and this provides a powerful mandate for further Christian reflection and action, especially with regard to those urgent global economic problems with which we are all implicitly involved — namely, environmental degradation and the development of poor countries. But greater precision in specifying what the general notion of stewardship actually implies in practice is difficult to achieve. The Christian community in every generation must rely on a sanctified conscience, a renewed mind, compassion, and prayer to determine what constitute good economic works and an appropriate prophetic stance under varied circumstances. In a world in which men and women are naturally greedy and grasping, there is plenty of scope for a genuine Christian economic witness.

The Modernist Impasse in Law

Phillip E. Johnson

When President Bush nominated Judge Clarence Thomas to a vacancy on the United States Supreme Court, liberals opposed to confirming the nomination at first directed critical scrutiny to statements the nominee had made in favor of employing "natural law" in constitutional interpretation.[1] The chairman of the Judiciary Committee that had to pass upon the nomination, Democratic Senator Joseph Biden, emphasized that he too believed in the existence of natural law. Indeed, he had successfully opposed a previous Republican nominee to the Supreme Court, Judge Robert Bork, in part because Bork had denied that the Constitution protects certain "natural" rights that are not mentioned in the document itself. At that time Senator Biden had insisted, "My rights are not derived from any government. . . . My rights are because I exist. They were given to me and each of our fellow citizens by our creator and they represent the essence of human dignity."[2]

Senator Biden feared, however, that Judge Thomas might believe in

---

1. The opening salvo on the natural law issue was fired by Professor Lawrence Tribe of Harvard Law School in an article in *The New York Times*. Tribe warned readers that Clarence Thomas might employ natural law theory to hold that "abortion is murder and [therefore] its practice or counseling cannot be permitted by any state" (Tribe, "Clarence Thomas and 'Natural Law,'" *The New York Times*, 15 July 1991, p. A-15). Tribe is a frequent spokesman for liberal Democrats on legal issues. He took a leading role in the battle to defeat Judge Robert Bork's nomination to the Supreme Court.

2. "Hearings on the Nomination of Robert Bork to Be Associate Justice of the Supreme Court of the United States" (U.S. Government Printing Office, 1989), p. 97. The quotation is from Senator Biden's opening statement as chairman of the Senate Judiciary Committee.

the wrong kind of natural law. He explained the difference between good and bad natural law in a newspaper article that expanded on a theme first advanced in *The New York Times* by Harvard Law School professor Lawrence Tribe. According to Senator Biden's article, good natural law is subservient to the Constitution — that is, to positive, man-made law — and its use is therefore restricted "to the task of giving meaning to the Constitution's great, but sometimes ambiguous, phrases." Second, good natural law does not dictate a moral code to be imposed upon individuals; instead, it protects the right of individuals to make moral decisions free from dictation by either legislators or judges. Finally, good natural law is not a static set of "timeless truths" but rather an evolving body of ideals that changes to permit government to adjust to new social challenges and new economic circumstances.[3] In short, good natural law doesn't prevent us from doing anything we really want to do.

As a legal scholar, I had hoped that Judge Thomas would accept Senator Biden's challenge and articulate a vision of natural law with real content, but this was not to be. Robert Bork had debated his legal theories with the senators candidly, with disastrous results, and political strategists had concluded from that experience that the way to get confirmed is to say as little as possible. Judge Thomas took their advice and stuck to a simple set of unilluminating answers when the senators tried to probe his judicial philosophy.

The resulting stalemate illustrated the ambivalence with which our contemporary legal culture regards the proposition that there exists some objective standard of right and wrong against which human legal standards can be measured. Anyone who says that there is such a standard seems to be denying that we are morally autonomous beings who have every right to set our own standards. On the other hand, anyone who denies that there is a higher law seems to embrace nihilism, and therefore to leave the powerless unprotected from the whims of whoever controls the law-making apparatus. Either alternative is unacceptable. The safest course is to be impenetrably vague or confusing on the subject.

The Biden/Thomas exchange reflected at the partisan political level a problem that permeates the literature of legal philosophy. I call this

3. See Joseph R. Biden, Jr., "Law and Natural Law: Questions for Judge Thomas," *The Washington Post*, 8 Sept. 1991, p. C-1. This article actually lists four major points, which I have condensed to three. Senator Biden's third point was that natural law should be viewed as an evolving body of ideals rather than as a set of static "timeless truths," and his fourth point was that natural law should not "limit government's ability to respond to changing circumstances." I have interpreted these as two ways of saying essentially the same thing: that natural law is not fixed for all time, but evolves as society's needs change.

problem the "modernist impasse." Modernism is the condition that begins when humans understand that God is really dead and that they therefore have to decide all the big questions for themselves. Modernism at times produces an exhilarating sense of liberation: we can do whatever we like, because there is no unimpeachable authority to prevent us. Modernism at other times is downright scary: how can we persuade other people that what *they* want to do to us is barred by some unchallengeable moral absolute?

Yale law professor Arthur Leff expressed the bewilderment of an agnostic culture that yearns for enduring values in a brilliant lecture delivered at Duke University in 1979, a few years before his untimely death from cancer. The published lecture — titled "Unspeakable Ethics, Unnatural Law"[4] — is frequently quoted in law review articles, but it is little known outside the world of legal scholarship. I am glad to take this opportunity to bring it to the attention of a wider audience, because it is one of the best statements I know of the modernist impasse. As Leff put it,

> I want to believe — and so do you — in a complete, transcendent and immanent set of propositions about right and wrong, *findable* rules that authoritatively and unambiguously direct us how to live righteously. I also want to believe — and so do you — in no such thing, but rather that we are wholly free, not only to choose for ourselves what we ought to do, but to decide for ourselves, individually and as a species, what we ought to be. What we want, Heaven help us, is simultaneously to be perfectly ruled and perfectly free, that is, at the same time to discover the right and the good and to create it.

The heart of the problem, according to Leff, is that any normative statement implies the existence of an authoritative evaluator. But with God out of the picture, every human becomes a "godlet" — with as much authority to set standards as any other godlet or combination of godlets. For example, if a human moralist says "Thou shalt not commit adultery," he invites "the formal intellectual equivalent of what is known in barrooms and schoolyards as 'the grand sez who?'" Persons who want to commit adultery, or who sympathize with those who do, can offer the crushing rejoinder: What gives *you* the authority to prescribe what is good for *me?* As Leff explained,

> Putting it that way makes clear that if we are looking for an evaluation, we must actually be looking for an *evaluator:* some machine for the

4. Leff, "Unspeakable Ethics, Unnatural Law," *Duke Law Journal* (1979): 1229-49.

generation of judgments on states of affairs. If the evaluation is to be beyond question, then the evaluator and its evaluative processes must be similarly insulated. If it is to fulfil its role, the evaluator must be the unjudged judge, the unruled legislator, the premise maker who rests on no premises, the uncreated creator of values. . . . We are never going to get anywhere (assuming for the moment that there is somewhere to get) in ethical or legal theory unless we finally face the fact that, in the Psalmist's words, there is no one like unto the Lord. . . . The so-called death of God turns out not to have been just *His* funeral; it also seems to have effected the total elimination of any coherent, or even more-than-momentarily convincing, ethical or legal system dependent upon finally authoritative, extrasystematic premises.

Leff pointed out that it is not we who define God's utterances as unquestionably true, in the manner that we define a triangle as a three-sided plane figure. In a God-based system, God is not an idea in the human mind but a separate and controlling reality. If human reason aspires to be the judge of God's statements, it makes itself the unevaluated evaluator — which is to say that it takes God's place. In Leff's words, "Our relation to God's moral order is the triangle's relationship to the order of Euclidean plane geometry, not the mathematician's. We are defined, constituted as beings whose adultery is wrong, bad, awful. Thus, committing adultery in such a system is 'naturally' bad only because the system is supernaturally constructed."

The relationship between natural law and supernatural authority requires a bit of explanation. In the philosophic tradition of Thomas Aquinas, "natural law" is distinguished from divine law because its commands are accessible to human reason even in the absence of divine revelation. To a theist like Aquinas, the reality of a moral law was not in question. The question was how much of that law we could know from natural reason (or academic philosophy), and how much we could know only from Scripture or the church. This two-level system of reason and revelation made it possible for Aquinas to fuse the pre-Christian philosophy of Aristotle with the revelation-based doctrines of the Roman Catholic Church.[5]

To a modernist, who by definition relies only upon human authority, natural law in the Thomistic sense is no longer supportable because it would have to rest upon the unacceptable premise that nature was supernaturally

5. For an excellent brief description of the Thomistic philosophy of law, see James R. Gordley, "St. Thomas Aquinas on Law and Justice" (Legal Classics Library, 1988). This pamphlet is available from The Legal Classics Library, Ltd., P.O. Box 76108, Birmingham, AL 35253.

created. There are still plenty of people around who would like to argue that a moral code can be discerned from nature, but the modernist understanding of nature undermines their efforts. According to Judge Richard Posner, the very idea of natural law rests upon a premodern picture of nature that science has discredited:

> Even the term "natural law" is an anachronism. The majority of educated Americans believe that nature is the amoral scene of Darwinian struggle. Occasional attempts are made to derive social norms from nature so conceived, but they are not likely to succeed. It is true that a variety of widely accepted norms, including the keeping of certain promises, the abhorrence of unjustified killing of human beings, and perhaps even the sanctity of property rights, promote the adaption of the human species to its environment. But so does genocide.[6]

In other words, a certain amount of social cooperation is natural, in the Darwinian sense, because it tends to promote the survival of a tribe or kinship group. Murderous violence against outsiders is equally natural, because it promotes the spreading of one group's genes by eliminating competing genes. In fact, Darwinian natural selection is *defined* as a process by which superior varieties exterminate their inferiors, whether by attacking them directly or by competing more effectively for limited resources. It is therefore no wonder that equating what is natural with what is good — that is, trying to derive "ought" from "is" — is dismissed these days as the "naturalistic fallacy."

Modernists therefore see no merit in natural law propositions about, say, sexual morality. For example, even if one grants that homosexual intercourse or abortion is in a sense less natural than heterosexual intercourse or childbirth (because it does not further reproduction), it does not follow that "unnatural" means wrong, or even undesirable. It is equally unnatural for humans to fly in airplanes, since we are not born with wings. Rejection of the naturalistic fallacy does not necessarily mean that modernists discard natural law altogether, however. As Senator Biden's article

---

6. Posner, *The Problems of Jurisprudence* (Boston: Harvard University Press, 1990), pp. 235-36. Posner, a judge of the United States Court of Appeals for the Seventh Circuit, was formerly a professor at the University of Chicago Law School. He is renowned in legal circles as the leading figure in the "law and economics" movement, which advocates extensive use of economic concepts in legal reasoning. Posner is right that Darwinist philosophy sees nature as a scene of amoral struggle, but some observers who have looked at the evidence without Darwinist preconceptions have concluded that nature is more often "an alliance founded on cooperation." See Robert Augros and George Stanciu, *The New Biology: Discovering the Wisdom in Nature*, New Science Library (Boston: Shambhala, 1987), pp. 89-128.

indicates, modernists are much more comfortable with the idea of natural rights than with the notion of natural obligations. Because the individual human subject (Leff's "godlet") is the modernist starting point, it seems reasonable to place a heavy burden of justification upon anyone who seeks to restrain the liberty of that subject. This burden of justification is what Leff whimsically called "the grand sez who."

The assertion of rights cannot for long be separated from the imposition of duties, however. If we give X a right to do as she wants, and she wants to get an abortion, we must soon face the question of protecting her from Y, who wants to protect the rights of unborn children. If majority opinion in the legislature favors some restrictions upon abortion, and there is no specific language in the Constitution on the subject, then "pro-choice" forces have to invoke something very much like a natural law duty to get their way. "Thou shalt not interfere with a woman's right to choose abortion; indeed, thou must help to pay for abortions through tax money; more than that, thou shalt not legislate that the woman contemplating abortion must be fully informed about the potential adoptive parents who desperately want to provide a loving home for her unborn child." Sez who?

The modernist impasse, in other words, does not arise as long as all we are doing is proclaiming liberties. The problem for modernists is how to justify imposing obligations. Homosexuals have a right to be homosexuals, of course; but do employers who disapprove have an obligation to hire them? The poor have a right to public assistance, of course; but do the more fortunate and productive citizens have a right to refuse to pay when they think the tax burden has become unreasonable? The rights of all citizens must be protected, of course; but who are the citizens? What about infants, the unborn, foreigners, and animals? Who or what has the authority to tell us whom we ought to admit to the sphere of protection?

Most of Leff's lecture consisted of a review of all the unsuccessful attempts to establish an objective moral order on a foundation of human construction — that is, to put something else in God's place as the unevaluated evaluator. The asserted nonsupernatural sources of moral authority are many and varied, and each is only temporarily convincing. They include the command of the sovereign, the majority of the voters, the principle of utility, the Supreme Court's varying interpretations of the Constitution's great but ambiguous phrases, the subtle implications of platitudinous shared values like "equality" or "autonomy," and even a hypothetical social contract that abstract persons might adopt in the imaginary "original position" described by John Rawls.[7] Every alternative rests ultimately on human

7. See John Rawls, *A Theory of Justice* (Cambridge: Harvard University Press, 1971).

authority, because that is what remains when God is removed from the picture. But human authority always becomes inadequate as soon as people learn to challenge its pretensions. Every system fails the test of "the grand sez who."

Leff's lecture made a powerful impression upon a generation of legal scholars because he stated the impasse so convincingly. Most modernist thinking consists of attempts to evade the impasse with superficial resolutions. Scientific socialism can usher in a secularized kingdom of heaven by giving economic power to the proletariat. Criminal tendencies in individuals can be greatly reduced by providing education, psychiatric treatment, and economic opportunity. Public education can produce rational, self-controlled citizens who can govern themselves through liberal political institutions and free markets. Scientific technology can provide abundance and health, and it can even eventually improve the human species itself by genetic engineering. Above all, we can still know what the good *is*, however difficult it may be to achieve it. Modernist philosophy teaches that, when we lost God, we lost only a projection of the best that was in ourselves. What was real in that projection therefore remains, and only the illusion is gone.

Arthur Leff had a deeper understanding of what the death of God ultimately means for human beings. He saw modern intellectual history as a long, losing war against the nihilism implicit in modernism's rejection of the unevaluated evaluator who is the only conceivable source for ultimate premises. Leff rejected the nihilism implicit in modernism, but he also rejected the supernaturalism that he had identified as the only escape from nihilism. Here is how he concluded his 1979 lecture:

> All I can say is this: it looks as if we are all we have. Given what we know about ourselves, and each other, this is an extraordinarily unappetizing prospect; looking around the world, it appears that if all men are brothers, the ruling model is Cain and Abel. Neither reason, nor love, nor even terror, seems to have worked to make us "good," and worse than that, there is no reason why anything should. Only if ethics were something unspeakable by us could law be unnatural, and therefore unchallengeable. As things stand now, everything is up for grabs.
>
> Nevertheless:
> • Napalming babies is bad.
> • Starving the poor is wicked.
> • Buying and selling each other is depraved.
> • Those who stood up and died resisting Hitler, Stalin, Amin, and Pol Pot — and General Custer too — have earned salvation.

- Those who acquiesced deserve to be damned.
- There is in the world such a thing as evil.

[All together now:] Sez who?

God help us.

What Leff said is fascinating, but what he failed to say is more fascinating still. If there is no ultimate evaluator, then there is no real distinction between good and evil. It follows that if evil is nonetheless *real,* then atheism — that is, the nonexistence of that evaluator or standard of evaluation — is not only an extraordinarily unappetizing prospect; it is also fundamentally untrue, because the reality of evil implies the reality of the evaluator, who alone has the authority to establish the standard by which evil can deserve to be damned. When impeccable logic leads to self-contradiction, there must be a faulty premise. In this case the logical connection is clear: because God is dead, "it looks as if we are all we have." Why not reexamine the premise? Why not at least explain *why* you refuse to reexamine the premise?

By not asking that last question, Leff in effect placed the death of God in the place of God. In his system, the absence of a supernatural evaluator was a premise so far beyond question that it could not be doubted even when it pointed to a conclusion Leff desperately wanted to escape, even a conclusion he acknowledged to be *false.* If we know that totalitarian mass murder is evil and that those who acquiesced in it deserve damnation, then we know something about that absolute evaluator as well. Leff offered no reason for protecting modernism's founding premise from the brilliant skeptical analysis that he directed at everything else.[8] To a theist this must

8. Arthur Leff's intellectual crisis had a strange effect upon his scholarly career. Although I never met him, I know from mutual friends that Arthur's Yale Law School colleagues revered him because he combined an acute critical intellect with an unusual measure of humility and sympathy. According to Yale law professor Charles L. Black: "If you took to Arthur a thought of yours, he always moved it along a step. He rarely 'joined issue'; it was more in his nature to give the course of shared thought a sudden turn into some new dimension — nearly always surprisingly, always relevantly. . . . I don't think I ever heard Arthur say anything cutting or unkind about anybody. There was in this no suggestion of saccharinity. It was rather, one felt, that he was wise enough either to find some reason for charity, or to have learned, from an even greater wisdom, that charity is to be practiced even if a reason does not immediately come to mind. He carried around with him the classic Chinese maxim, that the inferior person makes demands on other people, while persons of honor make demands on themselves."

This outstanding person devoted what ought to have been his most intellectually productive years to an extraordinary drudgery. According to his wife Susan, he was haunted by what I call the impasse of modernism, in her words the realization that "there is no longer

seem indefensible, but Leff could not have done otherwise without ceasing to be a modernist. A system's ultimate premise is always beyond question; that is what it means to say that it is an ultimate premise.

The most interesting aspect of any argument is not what it explicitly states but what it implicitly assumes. A rationalistic culture teaches us to think that truth is the product of a process of logical reasoning. When we are dealing with intermediate or detailed truths, which rest on more fundamental premises, this model is correct. The model breaks down, however, when we try to apply it to the fundamental premises themselves. This is because logic is a way of getting to conclusions from premises. By its very nature, a logical argument cannot justify the premises upon which it rests. When these premises are questioned, they have to be justified by a different logical argument that rests upon different premises.

We may follow this process forever, and we will never encounter anything but another logical argument, which will itself be based upon premises. But then what is the ultimate premise, the Archimedean fulcrum on which intellect can sit and judge all the rest? If we try to answer that question by employing logic, we lapse into the absurdity of circular reasoning. Reasoning has to start *somewhere*. Any attempt to justify the ultimate starting point necessarily fails, because it only establishes a different starting point. Hence, the really important step in any argument is apt to be the unexplained, unjustified, and often unstated starting point.

For example, take the rationalist philosopher who demands philosophical proofs of God's existence. From a humanistic standpoint, which finds its Archimedean point in the self-existent human mind, the demand is perfectly reasonable. But where did this mind come from, and why should we trust its philosophical ground rules? From a biblical theistic standpoint, human reason possesses a degree of reliability because God created it in his own image. When human reason denies its basis in creation, it becomes unreason. Those who thought that they were wise in rejecting God end up as fools, carried along by every intellectual fad and approving every kind of hateful nonsense (cf. Rom. 1:19-32). Many people who live in modern

---

a reasonably obvious set of questions that will lead one, with hard work and intelligence, to produce a good piece of scholarly work." He thought that somehow he would be better equipped to return to the philosophical quandary after undertaking some Herculean labor that would compel him to master the subject of law in its entirety, "one micron deep." And so Arthur began writing a legal dictionary, at a pace so deliberate that he thought he might complete it "by the year 2075." When he died of a fast-acting cancer at the height of his intellectual powers, he had completed only the entries for the letters *A, B,* and *C.* The student-edited *Yale Law Review* devoted the entire July 1985 issue (about 400 pages) to this fragment, with the personal tributes from which the quotations in this note are taken.

times find this analysis confirmed every day by what they see on television and read in the newspapers. Then why is the biblical starting point out of the question for modernist intellectuals?

The primary answer is that modernist thinking assumes the validity of Darwinian evolution, which explains the origin of humans and other living systems by an entirely mechanistic process that excludes in principle any role for a Creator. In the words of the neo-Darwinist authority George Gaylord Simpson, the meaning of "evolution" is that "Man is the result of a purposeless and natural process that did not have him in mind." For modernist intellectuals, belief in evolution in precisely this sense is equated with having a scientific outlook, which is to say with being a modernist. The price of denying "science" is to be excluded from modernist discourse altogether. That is why "it looks as if we are all we have," even if the model for "we" is Cain and Abel.

In my book *Darwin on Trial* I explained that Darwinian theory finds its basis in the philosophy of scientific naturalism rather than in an un-prejudiced examination of the evidence. In other words, the theory that is itself the most important supporting pillar for the modernist system is itself supported by that very system, in a classic example of circular reasoning.[9] I will not repeat any of that argument here, except to observe that the continued domination of Darwinism in the face of devastating criticism from many writers is powerful evidence supporting Paul's analysis in Romans 1 of how human reason becomes folly when it rejects its own foundation in creation. The modernist impasse is a problem of the mind that has sold itself into captivity.

Can a way out be found in "religion"? Not if religious thinking itself accepts the ground rules of modernism. R. Kent Greenawalt is University Professor at Columbia University, a distinguished legal philosopher who has tried to justify a mild theism without directly challenging the modernist definition of rationality. In Greenawalt's words: "With some uncertainty and tentativeness, I hold religious convictions; but I find myself in a pervasively secular discipline."[10] In the 1986 Cooley Lectures at the University of Michigan Law School, Greenawalt defended a limited role for religious convictions in a jurisprudential culture whose ruling paradigm, called "liberalism," is roughly identical to what I have been calling modernism.

9. Johnson, *Darwin on Trial* (Washington, DC: Regnery Gateway, 1991).

10. Greenawalt, "Religious Convictions and Lawmaking," *University of Michigan Law Review* 84 (Dec. 1985): 352, 355. This article is the published version of the Thomas M. Cooley Lectures at the University of Michigan School of Law, delivered by Professor Greenawalt on 10-12 March 1986.

Some legal philosophers say that liberalism implies the exclusion of religious considerations from public life. Their reasoning is that public decisions should be made on the basis of principles and arguments accessible to all persons. This basic principle implies that common sense and science must supply all the essential factual knowledge and that standards of ethics and justice must come from secular philosophies that rest upon uncontroversial assumptions. For example, Cornell University philosophy professor David Lyons declares that to reject the idea of "a naturalistic and public conception of political morality . . . is to deny the essential spirit of democracy."[11] In the same spirit, Yale Law School's Bruce Ackerman writes disparagingly of those who want to restrict abortions "on the basis of some conversation with the spirit world." According to this influential version of liberalism, people who want to make public policy on the basis of some private knowledge of God are fundamentally undemocratic, because they refuse to share a common base of discourse with their fellow citizens.

Responding to this "religion is for private life only" position, Greenawalt argued that in some circumstances citizens of a liberal/modernist state may rely upon their personal religious values in casting votes or framing arguments. Some readers may have difficulty understanding why this argument even has to be made. All those religious citizens have to do, after all, is to invoke "the grand sez who" and then vote and argue as they like. Greenawalt conceded that citizens of a secular liberal state have a *legal* right to vote their religious convictions, but he was more concerned with when and whether they ought to exercise self-restraint in the interests of good citizenship. Model citizens do not do everything they are legally entitled to do. They do not, for example, advocate the legal subjugation of one race by another, or the establishment of a particular religion, even though such advocacy is constitutionally protected. Good citizens also decide how they will vote on rational grounds, as far as they are able. But according to modernist liberalism, religious beliefs are inherently nonrational. Does it follow that model citizens should leave their religious convictions at home (where they are relatively harmless) and base their votes and arguments on public questions on secular considerations only?

Greenawalt conceded that "legislation must be justified in terms of secular objectives." Nonetheless, "when people reasonably think that rational analysis and an acceptable rational secular morality cannot resolve critical questions of fact, fundamental questions of value, or the weighing of competing harms, they [may] appropriately rely on religious convictions

11. Lyons, *Ethics and the Rule of Law* (Cambridge: Cambridge University Press, 1984), pp. 190-91, quoted in Greenawalt, "Religious Convictions and Lawmaking," p. 358.

that help them answer these questions."[12] He assumed the modernist position that only secular reasoning can be completely rational, because he thought that "a critical nonrational element" is always present in religious belief. The presence of such a nonrational element does not disqualify religious values from consideration in lawmaking, however. Because "rational secular morality" cannot conclusively decide such important value questions as how highly we should rate the preservation of fetal life or how generously we should provide for the poor, legislators and judges as well as ordinary voters may with good conscience rely on their personal religious convictions to resolve such questions.

By implication, Greenawalt accepted the crucial modernist assumption that there exists a common secular rationality that is capable of resolving some important public issues without relying upon controversial and unprovable (i.e., nonrational) assumptions. Otherwise, the conceded distinction between "religious" and "rational secular" thinking would collapse. This is an extremely important concession. Giving modernists the power to define rationality ensures that, even if "religion" is allowed a modest place in public discussion, God will continue to be effectively excluded. The reason lies in the very basis of modernist metaphysics. "Religious belief" is a real category to modernists; so is belief in fairies. All religions are equal — equally imaginary, that is. To modernists, "God" is an idea in people's heads, not a reality outside of human subjectivity. As long as modernists make the rules, every "godlet" can undermine every theistic proposition at will by invoking "the grand sez who." The culture will still be left to choose between an intolerable nihilism and continuing to chase the illusion of liberal rationalism.

At times Greenawalt seemed to accept that illusion, but at other times he showed an awareness that it is an illusion. Here is how he explained his own understanding of rationality:

> I confess to considerable uncertainty about where rationality ends; but among rational convictions I include those that are apparent to anyone with ordinary rational faculties or that can be demonstrated or persuasively argued on rational grounds. Beliefs that humans have greater ethical capacities than leaves, and that love is more productive of happiness than hate, can be rationally established. An irrational conviction is contrary to what can be established on rational grounds. A nonrational conviction, in my sense, is a conviction that is not irrational but that reaches beyond what rational grounds can settle.

12. Greenawalt, "Religious Convictions and Lawmaking," p. 357.

When a philosopher defines his central concept only in terms of itself (rational propositions are those that appeal to rational people or that can be supported on rational grounds), it is a sure sign of confusion. Moreover, a secular rationalism that can't resolve anything more controversial than that humans have more ethical capacity than leaves is useless. The point modernist rationalism has to establish, or assume, is that a common secular rationality exists that is capable in principle of resolving the issues that actually divide people. When Greenawalt examined the most famous recent example of such a system, the rights-based liberalism of John Rawls, he clearly recognized that this basic modernist assumption is false.

> Recognizing that citizens in liberal societies have variant religious beliefs and ideas of the good, Rawls begins with premises that are widely shared by people who disagree on many fundamental questions. From these premises, he aspires to draw principles of justice whose acceptance allows political decisions to be made without reference to the fundamental religious and metaphysical beliefs that divide citizens. . . . Contrary to what Rawls supposes, he does not provide a theoretical basis for thinking that this ambition is either realizable or desirable.

But then why did Greenawalt build his defense of religious opinion on the assumption that this ambition *is* both realizable and desirable?[13] The probable answer is that he was addressing an audience of modernist liberal rationalists and wanted to persuade them that even their own philosophical system had to concede at least some room for nonrational opinions on public questions, and therefore for religious opinion. Moreover, Greenawalt is a generous-minded person who understands that it is desirable to base public discussion on as ecumenical a foundation as possible. However confused his notion of rationality may be, his intention is to persuade his adversaries by meeting them on their own metaphysical territory.

Up to a point, this way of arguing is itself an act of good liberal citizenship. If a society is to be governed on the basis of consent rather than force, it is important that the laws make sense to as many citizens as possible. To that end, we should try to justify the laws on the least controversial basis available. That is why nowadays we defend Sunday closing laws (if at all) by

---

13. When he republished his lectures in book form, Greenawalt more or less abandoned the effort to employ the categories "rational," "nonrational," and "irrational" to distinguish among belief systems. This left the basis of any principled distinction between secular and religious beliefs thoroughly mysterious. Christianity, socialism, and feminism are all alike in the sense that each has a logic of its own and attracts a wide following, while also being opposed by many well-informed and intelligent persons. See Greenawalt, *Religious Convictions and Political Choice* (New York: Oxford University Press, 1988), p. 57.

the secular purpose of encouraging a general day of rest and recreation rather than the original purpose of honoring the Lord's Day or maximizing church attendance.[14] In a more general sense, the courtesy we owe to fellow citizens argues for framing public questions in language that invites everyone to participate in the discussion on comfortable terms. It would be insensitive as well as ineffective, for example, for Christians to exhort their Jewish, Muslim, or agnostic neighbors in terms of what Jesus would want us to do. On the other hand, Christians (or religious people in general) shouldn't be excluded from the political conversation either, as they would be if only agnostic opinions could count. Greenawalt's moderate and nuanced position about the proper role of religion in secular political discourse rightly addressed these questions of political good manners.

Good manners is one thing; but giving away the authority to define rationality is something else altogether. Good citizens treat their neighbors' deeply held convictions with respect, not because they are necessarily rational, but because they are deeply held. Standards for defining rationality are as controversial as any other assumptions. What Greenawalt accepts as "rationality" is actually the irrational assumption that we can get along very well without employing any controversial assumptions about the nature of ultimate reality. This assumption is the idol of rationalism, the faith commitment that holds the tribe together. We should perhaps treat the idol gently because it is still very dear to many admirable people, but we should not bow down and worship it. Ultimate reality is still God, not the unanchored, self-validating human mind.

We are entering a time of great opportunity for affirming that centrally important truth, because the modernist idol's substance is dissolving a little more every day. In the twenty-first century, our task will be to rebuild a positive response to the human predicament that starts with the cause of that predicament: humankind's alienation from God. Before we can undertake the positive task, however, we must complete the critique of atheistic rationalism. On the scientific side, we need to continue to expose the vulnerable philosophical assumptions that provide the only real support for the Darwinian theory of evolution. On the ethical and cultural side, we need to help the public as a whole to understand that the nihilism permeating contemporary life is the inevitable consequence of apostasy. King Lear's words provide the appropriate epitaph for modernism: "Nothing will come of nothing."[15]

Secularized intellectuals have long been complacent in their apostasy

14. See Braunfeld v. Brown, 366 U.S. 1144 (1961), upholding Sunday closing laws as furthering the secular purpose of providing a uniform day of rest.
15. William Shakespeare, *King Lear,* act 1, scene 1, l. 90.

because they were sure they weren't missing anything important in consigning God to the ash can of history. They were happy to replace the Creator with a mindless evolutionary process that left humans free and responsible only to themselves. They complacently assumed that when their own reasoning power was removed from its grounding in the only ultimate reality it could float, unsupported, on nothing at all. As modernist rationalism gives way in the universities to its own natural child — postmodernist nihilism — modernists are learning very slowly what a bargain they have made. Paul foretold a time when people "will not put up with sound doctrine. Instead, to suit their own desires, they will gather around them a great number of teachers to say what their itching ears want to hear. They will turn their ears away from the truth and turn aside to myths." His instruction to Timothy for that time was to "keep your head in all situations, endure hardship, do the work of an evangelist, discharge all the duties of your ministry" (2 Tim. 4:3-5). Our ministry is to provide the sound teachers who can bring the world out of the myth of modernism and back into the path of truth.

The Christian and Politics

SIR FRED CATHERWOOD

CHRISTIANITY AND DEMOCRACY

THE CHRISTIAN FAITH compels us to respect our fellow men and women. It teaches the dignity and moral responsibility of each individual person, however poor or weak. It tells us that we are all made "in the image of God" and are all ultimately responsible to our Creator for all that we do and say.

The early church reflected this respect. But the two great churches that emerged from the Roman Empire, the Roman and Orthodox communions, reflected the imperial hierarchy rather than the simple church order of the early church. Pope and patriarch matched the emperor, the cardinals and bishops corresponded to the grandees of the Court and provinces. Not until a hundred years after the Reformation did churches come into being that gave the ordinary members the dignity Paul had given them in his greetings in the last chapter of his letter to the Romans.

Oliver Cromwell was unable to translate this feeling for the dignity of the ordinary Christian into a political system — though he certainly tried! Even in England's bloodless coup of 1689 it was a Parliament of the upper classes who compelled the king to abdicate and welcomed his daughter and her Dutch husband as joint monarchs. In Holland, too, it was the ruling classes who retained control.

It was not until the American Revolution a century after Cromwell that these principles were turned into a political system — though what was said to be "self-evident" was only so to those who had been brought up in the Christian teaching of the dignity and responsibility of the individual.

Three decades after the American Constitution, the United Kingdom of Great Britain and Ireland began the systematic extension of the franchise of the Great Reform Act of 1832 — though it took another hundred years to achieve full adult suffrage of both men and women.

Democracy moved fastest in the Protestant countries. France's Revolution of 1789 exchanged Louis XVI for Napoleon. After his defeat, the Bourbon dynasty was recalled for a short time; then there was democracy again until Emperor Napoleon III. Not until Napoleon's defeat in 1870 was democracy finally established in France — though the present constitution, established by Charles de Gaulle, gives more presidential and less parliamentary power than most other democracies.

In the nineteenth century Europe voted with its feet as millions left the rigid autocratic countries of their birth for the democratic freedom of the United States. In the first half of the twentieth century Europe's autocracies engaged in a spasm of terrible warfare. The European Community that emerged nailed democracy to its masthead, winning the hearts and minds of those still subject to dictators — Greece, Spain, and Portugal in southern Europe, and then all of the Communist countries in eastern Europe.

After World War II America introduced democracy to Japan and less directly to Israel, and the United Kingdom established the largest democracy of all in India. Despite some remaining dictatorships and continuing terrorist movements, Latin America has moved firmly over to democracy.

So despite the long history of autocracy — the persistent propaganda of the ruling classes, backed by the power of armies, police, and secret police — the Christian vision of the dignity and responsibility of the individual has had almost universal acceptance. Even in countries where it has failed, military dictators feel the need to promise free elections and are unable to justify the principle of autocratic rule.

Yet there is still a battle to be fought, especially in those Protestant countries in which this vision first appeared. It is there especially that secular humanism has most heavily undermined the Christian view of men and women made in the image of God, a foundational belief of democratic society.

THE LEGITIMACY OF GOVERNMENT

Before arguing with the secular humanists, however, we must deal with those Christians in the pietistic tradition and some of the supporters of liberation theology, who deny the legitimacy of government as part of this divine order.

In 1969, the year after the Russian tanks rolled into Prague and ended the hopes of the Czech reformers, my wife and I talked to Christian students from Czechoslovakia. They wanted to know whether it was their Christian duty to resist the Russians by force. We looked together at the letter in which the apostle Paul told the Christians in imperial Rome, where the autocratic emperor had insisted that he be worshiped, that "the powers that be are ordained of God" and should be obeyed (Rom. 13:1, KJV). At the same international students conference there were students from South America, far from any practical experience of Communism and steeped in the then fashionable "liberation theology." They found the discipline of Christian doctrine a great deal more difficult than the Czechs. So did students in Northern Ireland when I advised them that year to keep off the streets, where they would be used and then pushed aside by those who understood the streets a great deal more than they did.

Democracy has triumphed in Czechoslovakia and in most of South America without violent revolution, but in Northern Ireland it is still under threat by those who took over the streets in 1969.

It is not easy for those smarting from visible injustice to obey an unjust government. But revolution is not a Christian option. Not only does Paul say that the Romans should be loyal citizens under an unjust government, but Peter, in his first letter, says the same. And Christ himself said to Pilate, "My kingdom is not of this world. If it were, my servants would fight" (John 18:36). But in the end the Empire fell and the church survived.

The French have a saying about revolution: "Plus ça change, plus c'est la même chose" ("the more it changes, the more it's the same thing"). They rose against Louis XVI and got the Emperor Napoleon. The Germans threw out the Kaiser and got Hitler; the Russians shot the Czar and got Stalin.

The sixteenth-century French Huguenots allied themselves to a Bourbon prince who turned Catholic to gain Paris and gave them a temporary toleration, which his grandson Louis XIV later revoked.

In all the struggles following the Reformation, no Protestant leader could ignore the clear Christian teaching on the legitimacy of government, however imperfect, as a divinely ordained institution. Luther's views were so strongly expressed that he has been blamed — very wrongly — for German authoritarianism. The Huguenot apologia was the pamphlet "Vindiciae contra tyrannos," but it would have been better if they had kept the peace. Oliver Cromwell won the civil war, but soon after he died the monarchy was restored and the Puritans were banished from their churches.

The Dutch claimed their local ruler William the Silent was entitled to their allegiance rather than the distant Spanish emperor. The same argument prevailed for the Americans who followed George Washington.

But those in modern America who claim the right of resistance to a country led astray by secular humanism are on a slippery slope. Their arguments are as valid for black power and right-wing racism. The slide into conflict and chaos is only too easy.

There are no shortcuts to a just society. In democracies we all have a vote and freedom of speech. With those rights go responsibilities that we must exercise. And in the democratic business of winning hearts and minds, it is those who are seen also to care for their neighbors who go farthest.

We Christians find ourselves opposing two extremes. At one extreme are those who believe that the dark side of human nature can be restrained only by tough law and order; at the other are those who believe that human nature is essentially good, that social conditions are the root of all evils, and that Christians above all should be forgiving.

But while we can forgive someone who knocks us down and robs us, the law cannot; it must be just. Christians have to preach that crime deserves punishment, that right and wrong are absolute and not relative standards. But we must also remember that God has given all of us made in his image a conscience, a natural feeling for what is right and an idealism to which Christians can and should appeal and to which the world responds.

Even in a fallen world, people prefer truth to lies, prefer those who clearly care for them to those who despise them, those who give them a vision of a better way of life to those who offer no hope, and those whose own lives set an example to those whom they cannot respect.

It is far better to reform, through appeal to human conscience, than to react against the present moral chaos through a reactionary revolution.

Faced with societies respecting the dignity of the individual, autocracies carry the seeds of their own destruction. The spirit of innovation can only find an outlet in a free society. People can be ordered to do what has been done before, but no one can be ordered to invent an entirely new material, product, or method of production. The scientific breakthrough of the seventeenth century came naturally to a reformed Christian society. Those who decided to study for themselves the book of God's word in the sixteenth century instead of accepting all from an authoritarian church were followed by those in the seventeenth century who decided to study the book of God's works rather than accept the science of Aristotle because the church said so.

The last few years have shown that the power of an autocratic society cannot match that of a free society. Without an armed struggle, the autocracy crumbled. But were we right to prepare for an armed struggle against

Communism in case we were attacked? There have been Christian pacifists down the centuries, but the traditional teaching has been to extend the authority of the state to protect the citizens from our external as well as our internal enemies. This has been qualified by the "just war" doctrines and the prohibition against shedding "innocent blood."

It is only too easy to abuse military power. What seems perfectly justified to our own country looks quite different from the receiving end. And our own protesters are not always wrong or unpatriotic. In the spring of 1971 I stood on the steps of Woodstock Inn in Vermont beside Joseph Luns, the tall Dutch Secretary-General of NATO, who was defending American involvement in Vietnam to a small and vociferous group of students: "America is not Liechtenstein. America is a great country with great interests which it is entitled to defend."

Today's verdict seems to be that while defending 400 million citizens of western Europe from possible Communist aggression was a genuinely great American interest, which has been carried through to success, the defense of Vietnam was not nearly such a clear case and involved a great deal of "innocent blood." There have since then been other exercises of military muscle that have had even less justification, though the defense of Kuwait had almost universal support.

The end of the cold war should also bring to an end the debate on the defensive threat to kill millions of innocent citizens by nuclear retaliation against Russian cities. I once heard an Irish bishop argue, "It might be wrong to actually do it, but not to *threaten* to do it." But the military did not think much of the credibility of that position.

"LOVE YOUR ENEMIES"

One of government's primary objectives is to keep the peace and to do what it can to avoid war.

We Christians, who are told to be peacemakers, should use our powers as citizens to promote peace. In 1948, in an act of quite exceptional generosity, America gave $70 billion (in present values) through the Marshall Aid Program to friends and enemies alike, both ruined by a devastating war. This quickly restored their fortunes and, with the mutual aid institutions also set up under American leadership, resulted in the greatest increase in international trade and prosperity the world has ever known. Now with the cold war won, the industrial democracies need to give similar aid to the former Communist countries. President Walensa of Poland told the European Parliament:

The Communists have wrecked our economy and if you do not use your peace dividend to help us, in a few years some Messiah is going to stand up and tell the people that democracy does not work and that they had better follow him. Then you will have to put all the troops, missiles, tanks, and aircraft back where they were before.

President Havel of Czechoslovakia has said the same, and so has the Hungarian prime minister. The need in the former Soviet Union is even greater.

At the time of the Marshall Plan, western Europe was already recovering. Its communications, though battered, were intact. It had a skilled work force, industrialists and merchants who knew how a market economy worked, banks that could tell a good risk from a bad one, and civil servants and politicians who could translate economic needs into practical politics.

Central and eastern Europe have none of these assets. Their economies have gone into free-fall, they have poor communications, those who run their industries have been brought up to do what they were told and ask no questions, and they make little that anyone with hard currency wants to buy. Their banks do not know how to judge commercial risks, they have no experienced merchants, their politicians are novices, their civil servants have no experience of a market economy, and their work force has never experienced the discipline of working to a competitive price and quality.

Not all of this can be solved with money, but little of it can be solved without money. The sound currency needed for a successful market economy needs hard currency backing, the infrastructure needed to move food to markets needs money, so do the leaking oil-wells and pumping stations needed to fuel industry, and above all so does the immense training program needed to pass on the whole Western experience in running an industrial democracy.

All of this can be done. The Germans are doing it in the former East Germany with great dedication in a race against time, which they are determined to win. But they are helping fellow citizens. An expensive aid program from the NATO countries to help the former Warsaw Pact needs that Christian spirit of love that sprang to the rescue half a century ago.

For that half-century, Christians have been praying for their brothers and sisters behind the iron curtain who have been persecuted by anti-Christian Communist regimes and forbidden to teach their children their own faith, whose churches have been razed to the ground, who have been deprived of Christian literature, and whose pastors and leaders have been exiled to Siberia. Now, suddenly, they are all free — but for how long?

Their continued freedom depends on us. If we help the new

democratic governments that are dedicated to religious freedom to convince their people, that freedom can also bring prosperity. If we in the industrial democracies do not help them, no one else can — so we must. We should divert our arms expenditure to civil use, just as we did after World War II; if we help them to create stable and prosperous democracies, we should not need to use the resources for that level of arms expenditure again.

THE CASE OF "THE FATHERLESS AND THE WIDOW"

A second civic duty is to look after those who cannot look after themselves.

Christians do not have much difficulty in choosing political causes for which to fight. All through the Old Testament, the prophets thunder against the political leaders of the day, not only for their neglect of God, but also — in detail — for their neglect of his law.

The recurring theme of the prophets was the protection of those who could not look after themselves. In those days the loss of a father or husband could be catastrophic. The widow Naomi had lost her husband and both of her sons when she came back to Bethlehem with her widowed daughter-in-law, Ruth. They evidently had no land and no means of support; their help eventually came from a kinsman in the extended family who did have land and who married Ruth. In primitive societies the extended family is still the major buffer against personal catastrophe, but in our industrial democracies mobility of workers has scattered the extended family and the nuclear family itself is at risk. The burden has fallen on the state.

While the majority of the population felt themselves to be poor and vulnerable, political parties felt the need to look after them. But with the increase in prosperity, the majority of voters no longer feel so vulnerable, and we are much more interested in rising pay than in welfare for others. So we have begun to see a swing in political priorities away from those who are sick or out of work. This change is carried out under cover of rhetoric criticizing the abuse of welfare and urging the merits of the free market in meeting those needs previously met from the public purse.

It is true that with fallen human nature there is abuse of welfare and that, for most people, the market is the best way of allocating resources. But that is a reason for finding better ways of looking after those in need, not for shifting resources away from them.

During the eighties, beggars appeared again on the streets of London and New York, the inner cities decayed, and publicly funded hospitals found it harder to look after the sick. The rate of violent crime rose, too, and so did the number of those turning to drugs.

Governments are not altogether to blame. The churches have preached doubt instead of faith, and materialism has become the new god. Governments are reelected on the basis of their ability to increase spending power and not on the basis of moral issues. But that is all the more reason for Christians to raise these issues and to puncture the rhetoric that covers them up.

A much bigger problem is the breakup of the family itself. The rate of divorce and the number of single-parent families is rising, and with it the number of disoriented children who have no role model for a successful marriage themselves.

We are in the middle of a vast experiment in social engineering, based on totally unproved theories, which, in the name of personal freedom, has removed most of the traditional restraints on the lust and selfishness of fallen humanity. It will, of course, fail; but it will do great damage to two or three generations and, because of the backlash that is surely coming, to the very freedom that it aims to enlarge.

It is too easy for Christians to spend ourselves in frontal attack on all the positions now being claimed in the name of "freedom," and this makes us too vulnerable to the argument that we are against freedom and in favor of old-fashioned, outmoded, and constraining social structures that prevent individuals from finding and expressing their true selves.

We are in a much stronger position if we, through our churches, begin to pick up the social wreckage — the young homeless who have been turned out by a hostile stepfather, the single parents trying all alone to look after a young family, the girls under pressure to have an abortion or in trauma after an abortion, the victims of AIDS, victims of rape, and those suffering from the terrible wrench of divorce. Christians who show real care for society not only have the right to speak as experts on the causes of suffering; they also have the high moral ground from which to fight the wider battle.

This puts Christian politicians in a far stronger position. They are then able to counter social theory with expert findings on what actually happens in practice. And, since churches are far thicker on the ground than social theorists and more deeply embedded in the society around them, their findings and advice are very hard to counter. It is not easy to argue social theory against a Mother Teresa.

This is no side issue. The family, like the state and the church, is ordained by God. We are not meant to live alone, but in families. The family is the basic institution in our society. Churches rise and fall, and so do governments, but we are all born into a family. If the family could be destroyed, if society could be atomized into millions of single units, then there would be a greater destruction of God's social order than ever before. It is a fight that has to be fought and a battle that has to be won.

It is not enough to care for souls. We have to care for the sick in body too. Our Lord cared for the whole person, body and soul. He taught and he healed; he fed the soul, but, when needed, he fed the body too. Human beings had been created healthy and with sin had come sickness; both affronted him. The church produced the first hospitals, and medicine has always been part of foreign missions.

The problem today is that the advance of knowledge has given even rich societies more cures than they have funds to carry out. However much money governments pour into public health services, there is always more demand than the resources can supply. Doctors tell patients what can be done, but the resources are not there to pay for it. Private health services can look after those who are rich enough. But the Christian's special care is for those who are not rich enough. Because of advances in medicine, many more people are living longer and reaching an age when they can no longer look after themselves and need constant medical care. In our materialistic society, the very old are a dispensable minority to be put away in old folks' homes. And now the more sinister demand for euthanasia is creeping in.

Those of us who have had aged parents live with us know that they can be exhausting, but that they can also be a great joy and that it is a great pleasure to them to be surrounded by a loving family of children, grand-children, and great-grandchildren. They have lived long, have given much, and still have a great deal to pass on. They have as much right to life as anyone else, and no impatient or greedy relative should be able to ask them whether they want to live or die. The doctor and nurse should always keep their traditional role, and the old should never fear that they might turn into executioners.

A CHRISTIAN MORAL ORDER

The Tradition of Moral Order

These threats to long-established social behavior show that it is not enough for Christians to protect each pillar of the social order as it comes under attack. We have to show the need for each of these pillars as part of a whole, self-supporting, balanced moral order.

Every society needs some moral order to undergird the civil law. Law is enforceable only if more than ninety percent of society supports it, and it can deal with only a fraction of the problems that arise between people. The discipline of the family and the social discipline of the neighborhood and the workplace are all part of an underlying social order, which discourages bad behavior and promotes good behavior. The stronger the social acceptance of a moral order, the less society has to rely on the cruder and more arbitrary power of government.

Islam relies very heavily on a moral order enforced through the extended family, as do the Japanese and the Chinese. That is why conversion to Christianity is not regarded in Islamic states or in East Asia as a private affair, but as a threat to social cohesion. Tribal Africa, too, relies heavily on the extended family. No society survives for long without a generally accepted moral order to give social cohesion.

When an existing moral order is suppressed — as the Communists in Europe suppressed Christianity — the state very soon finds that it has to impose its own moral order, and since it does not carry the consent of the people, the process is unbelievably harsh and inevitably totalitarian. Finally, the people turn against it — as they turned against Communism — and as soon as the threat of force is removed they overthrow it and want to know all about the faiths so long forbidden to them.

By contrast, societies that have been built on a Christian moral order are now witnessing a concerted attempt to remove and replace it with secular humanism. Although the exercise does not carry popular support, it is strong enough to do immense damage to the cohesion of society.

Humanism will fail because it is, like Marxism, an intellectual creed that does not correspond to the experience of ordinary people and does not give any answers that satisfy them to the great questions of good and evil, health and sickness, life and death. It can dissolve the bonds that hold society together, but it cannot put them together again. It tells people outraged by crime that it is a psychological sickness that can be healed. It tells those who have no hope in this life that there is no hope after it; it tells those who live in dread of death that there is no life beyond death. It tells those who see design in nature that there is no designer, that, contrary to all human experience, order arose out of chaos. Above all, it teaches men and women, who were born to worship, that there is no God. So it cleans the house of the old, long-accepted religion, but leaves it open for the first new religion that comes along to enter and take possession (cf. Matt. 12:43-45).

Secular humanism is an intellectual's creed, held by those who believe that there is no limit to human wisdom, but it is not established in the grass roots of society. There are, of course, those who take advantage of it — husbands who want to leave their wives and children and a smaller number of wives who leave their husbands, merchants of commercial sex and of drugs, the strong who take advantage of the weak, the rich who take advantage of the poor (if we have a sexually permissive society, why not a financially permissive society?), and the armed who take advantage of the unarmed. But as the pillars of society are broken down one by one, the average citizen is bewildered and begins to be afraid.

It is the job of Christian leaders in society in both church and state to expose the rhetoric of humanism for the fraud on society that it is. It is a betrayal of the Christian faith to sail with the wind of secular opinion, as so many of today's Sadducees have done.

Why True Tolerance Needs a Christian Moral Order

Humanist rhetoric talks of tolerance, freedom, and reason. These words have great resonance in democratic societies, but we need to look carefully at their humanist interpretation, especially the humanist interpretation of tolerance.

Secular humanists' use of the term *tolerance* is especially dangerous because they are totally intolerant of any interpretation but their own. The United States was founded on the basis of religious toleration. Britain and all other Protestant countries have extended toleration to all religions. Tolerance is a Christian virtue to be protected. But tolerance is not the same as relativism, the belief that we must tolerate each other because there is no absolute truth. Christian tolerance does not remove the right of a Christian, a Jew, or a Muslim to believe that their faith is true and that others are false. It certainly does not remove our right to point out that secular humanism is as much a matter of faith as any of the others and that secular humanists certainly believe themselves to be right.

Christ taught, "I am the way and the truth and the life. No one comes to the Father except through me" (John 14:6). No claim could be more exclusive. But the Christian belief that ours is the true faith does not entitle us to impose it on anyone else. Protestants — following Augustine, the early church fathers, and the apostles — believe that the power to convert those who are dead in sin to new life in Christ can only come through the power of the Holy Spirit. A forced conversion is a false conversion. We repudiate the doctrine of "ex opere operato" by which the act of baptism alone converts, regardless of the state of mind of those baptized. All the New Testament accounts of conversion show those who became Christians as more than willing converts. Christ told the disciples that if their message was not received they were to move on to find those who would receive it. When the Jews would not accept the apostle Paul, he moved on to the

Gentiles. We are to preach the gospel in all the world, but we are not to force the Christian gospel on those unwilling to hear it.

We Christians should favor toleration because we want to fulfill this great commission to bring the Christian gospel to all the world; since we believe that the gospel carries its own power, we also believe that, in open debate, it will prevail. A strong faith demands toleration; only a weak faith demands exclusive protection from another point of view.

When Christians put forward our Christian faith as the basis for a social order, we are not insisting that our fellow citizens become Christians against their will; rather, we are putting it forward on its merits as a faith with a long and benign track record. It was the major factor in turning the savage pagan tribes of Europe into a cohesive civilization; it has been a constant, though varying, check on principalities and power; and it has encouraged the growth of democracy, education, and the dignity of men and of women.

The Scientific Method Is Founded on the Christian Moral Order

The Christian faith has also had a major effect on our relation to nature. The founding fathers of the scientific movement were Christians who believed in one orderly, benign, rational, unchangeable Creator who had given the earth and its resources to us as trustees. So they believed that the laws of his creation would be unified, orderly, rational, essentially benign, and, because he had promised it, stable until the end of time. They did not believe that we, the creatures, could know more of our Creator than he had revealed, but that their efforts should be regarded as secondary causes in a world that could be observed, measured, and tested. Their assumptions did not arise from the scientific method; they were its basis, and if they are removed, as the new paganism is removing them, the scientific explosion of the last three hundred years will be crippled.

Look at an example of modern art, perhaps in an airport lounge, and see the new pagan's world — disjointed, disorderly, irrational, unstable, and malign — and, as you step aboard, be glad that the aircraft and its navigation are still built on the principles of the scientific method.

Human Rights Are Founded on the Christian Moral Order

Look at the great United Nations declaration of human rights. Although it is expressed in secular terms, every one of its propositions is based on a Christian principle. Look back at the United States Constitution, where the same is true.

Of course the humanists — who have no track record — looking back over the uneven struggle between Christian faith and the principalities and powers, can find times when the official church became corrupt, when princes appointed themselves and their courtiers as bishops and their friends as pope, when instead of trusting in God they trusted in the sword, in forced conversions, and in the execution of heretics. But fortunately we have in Christ and in the prophets and apostles, whom he authenticated by his resurrection, a written record against which we can judge and condemn those who claimed a Christian authority that they plainly did not legitimately have.

The ultimate test of any system of belief is whether it has a built-in mechanism for putting right what has clearly gone wrong. We see it in the Old Testament history of the Jews, where, time and again, they went back to the written word of God handed down by Moses. We see it in the Christian church, where a reformer would arise, denounce the false prophets, and bring the church back again to the written word of God. So part of the track record is this self-correcting mechanism, this ability to stand up against secular trends and to establish a long line of Christian principle, the more deeply founded through two thousand years of hard-fought debate.

The Christian Moral Order's True View of Human Nature

In addition to a record of self-correction, a claim for a moral order should establish that it has a true view of human nature, that it can explain both the good and the evil in our natures and that it has a sound rationale and a workable mechanism for encouraging the one and discouraging the other.

The Christian faith does not try to avoid the problem of good and evil, which we all find within our human nature. As the apostle Paul said, "For what I do is not the good I want to do; no, the evil I do not want to do — this I keep on doing" (Rom. 7:19). The good comes from the conscience that a good Creator has given to us all; the evil comes from the spirit of rebellion against our Creator, which we have, not from God, but through our rebellious forebears and ultimately from the first man and woman.

The purpose of the social order is to school us to encourage the good and to discipline us in discouraging the bad. The family, the state, and the church are the primary social organizations for this necessary and difficult process, and any damage to them is damage to the social order.

One of the church's functions in the social order is to serve as "the salt of the earth" (Matt. 5:13), to retard the corruption in society that stems from human wickedness. This function is complementary to its primary function as "the light of the world" (5:14), which is to bring the good news that God the Father will forgive all who trust in God the Son, who has borne the punishment for our rebellion and will give us his Spirit to enable us increasingly to do what is right and avoid what is wrong. Of course, the more successful the church is as the "light of the world," the more successful it will be as "the salt of the earth." But both functions are valid, and neither is optional.

THE EXPERIMENT OF SECULAR HUMANISM

It is argued by the secular humanists that a Christian social order is no longer valid because we now live in a multi-faith society. Their argument would be more convincing if they were not also trying to impose their own social order. They hold themselves out as being somehow above the arguments among Catholic, Protestant, Jew, and Muslim. They claim that their views are based on social science, which they equate with the natural sciences in their ability to establish a workable thesis by practical experiment. But the mysteries of good and evil behavior do not yield so easily to external objective experiment. Human beings cannot be programmed like a computer. There is the utterly unexpected in all of us, for both good and ill. And we are all different. People are not like plants and rocks; you can plot the melting point of steel, but you cannot breed a poet. There is no secure base, as there is in natural science, from which to conduct external and repeatable experiments. Nor can any person experiment, for instance, between sleeping around and a monogamous relationship, for the two are mutually exclusive.

What we do know is that after a full generation the social experiments of the secular humanists are ripping society apart. They cannot produce a stable replacement moral order, and society cannot afford to allow the experiment to run any longer. If Christianity is only one point of view, then so is secular humanism. But Christians, Jews, and Muslims all have a written record of their moral order and centuries of experience of its application to very different social conditions. They are organized in social groupings with some experience of obtaining a stable social order within their own membership. The humanists have no agreed moral order and no organization through which they can deliver broad assent among a majority, and their track record of application to the social order is both brief and destructive.

Nor is it true that Christians, Jews, and Muslims create a "multi-faith vacuum" that only the humanists can fill. Christians and Jews share the same moral law; we differ only in its interpretation. And the Muslims share our belief in one God, a written moral law, and the centrality of the family. There are other old faiths in the Western world, but none with the same record. In almost every major issue, these three faiths stand together against secular humanism.

The moral order in every society should be explicit; it should be able to prove itself and show in practice what it can do to help maintain a social order. It should be organized at the grass-roots level across the country and should be able to deliver support and extend influence at every level of society. And it should be supported from below by ordinary citizens and not imposed from above by the elite. The Christian faith can answer all of these criteria — the humanists, none.

SAVING SOCIETY FROM CORRUPTION

The secular humanists talk of freedom. But freedom does not come by abolishing the laws and customs of society. That simply gives freedom to those who have against those who have not; to the rich against the poor; to the strong against the weak; to the influential against the nobodies; to the clever and plausible against the innocent and gullible; to those who know how to exploit our greed, lust, and temper against those of us who cannot keep them under control.

Freedom is as hard to achieve as unpolluted air in a city center. It requires law and discipline. Freedom to walk the streets or to sit on a park bench without fear of attack requires a strong moral code that is widely accepted. But it also requires a police force backed by a law that is enforced without fear or favor. Freedom from want in old age requires savings that hold their value, uncorrupted by inflation, pension funds that can be trusted because those who manage them are subject to regulation and inspection.

Freedom between the sexes requires a moral code that removes the fear of harassment and rape, of seduction through promises that can be broken without social or legal consequences. Freedom between husband and wife can only be achieved if each is sure of the other's commitment, and it is the more secure if it is conducted in a society that gives that commitment strong social support and gives breach equally strong social disapproval. The greatest freedom in marriage is found within a strong, loving mutual commitment.

Freedom between the generations requires mutual respect and mutual obligation from which neither side will walk out.

A free market requires honesty and transparency so that those dealing with each other know what they are buying and selling. That requires not only enforceable law but also a degree of honesty that creates trust between buyer and seller. Those who want to allow sexual permissiveness are not so keen on financial permissiveness. But moral corruption is not so easily confined. The sexual permissiveness of the eighties was matched by spectacular financial scandals. At the political level, it was also a decade in which the United States was turned from the greatest creditor in the world to its greatest debtor, and in which Britain spent its North Sea oil bonanza.

When there is corruption in society, it reaches right to the top, and politicians start to buy votes with public money. Bribes involve a perversion of judgment. A richer majority is bribed at the expense of a poorer minority; the present generation is bought off at the cost of a debt burden on future generations. Policies are judged not on their long-term benefit but on their short-term fiscal cost.

But perhaps the most dangerous corruption of democracy is the power of populism, the temptation to buy votes with prejudice against minorities and foreigners. We sometimes forget that Adolf Hitler's National Socialist Party was popularly elected and that prejudice against Jews and foreigners was a part of the appeal that brought Hitler votes in a country in which the great majority still went to church.

Populism can be as effectively presented today as it was in Europe sixty years ago, and Christians who refuse to get involved in politics are especially vulnerable because they have never had to allow their prejudices to be challenged in public debate with those of another point of view. To us our prejudices are self-evident truths, so we never question them. Our friends and neighbors hold them, and so do all the other "sensible folk" we know. We never see our circle from the outside.

Populism is encouraged in the United States by the development of the Constitution, which allows the president to be elected by 200 million people who can only know him in populist terms, rather than as the Constitution evidently intended (and as is the rule in other democracies) by the legislators with whom he has to deal.

Looking back a hundred years, we wonder that Christians of that time can have been so taken over by the spirit of the age. Looking at our country from the outside, through the eyes of a Christian from Russia, Japan, India — or even Spain — we suddenly see the extent to which our country's secular assumptions have infiltrated our Christian thinking. Indeed, one of the great advantages of an international Christian conference, especially among the young, who are far franker than their elders, is the way in which we can peel off each other's layers of national prejudice, so that, unprejudiced, we are able to study God's Word to discover what it actually says.

THE CHRISTIAN CITIZEN

Democracy not only brings privileges; it also brings duties. Democracy makes the citizens, collectively, the final arbiters of their country's government, and that is a weighty responsibility. Nothing is so frustrating to a politician as the people who say that they do not propose to vote, in a tone that implies that they are above the political debate. We are our brothers' keepers; we are responsible for our neighbors. Christ taught us to pray that God's will be done on earth as it is in heaven. If God cares for what is done on earth, so should we. If he tells us to pray for governments and for his will to be done, surely we should not be above doing what is in our power to help the object of our prayers. "Faith without deeds is dead," as James tells us (2:26).

We may feel that our vote does not make much difference, but that is not how the politician sees it. Maybe half of those who are eligible to vote do not do so. That doubles the value of our vote at once. Maybe half to three-quarters of those who do vote do so through ingrained habit or prejudice. If you think before you vote, then you are the marginal voter who makes all the difference. If you go to meet candidates and question them, you are one of a very small minority who will, with their questions, set the tone of the campaign and influence the pledges that are made and the action that has to be taken on those pledges. We should not leave this task to church leaders. Church and state have been ordained by God as separate institutions, with separate officers. The preaching of eternal truth should not be mixed with political views, which are based on our state of secular knowledge and experience, and qualified by political judgment as to what can be legally enforced and what cannot. The pulpit gives Christian citizens their moral base. It is then our civic responsibility to apply it as best we can.

We should certainly, as responsible citizens, try to decide which are the major issues on which, as Christians, we need to fight, and we should take care not to be unduly swayed by well-funded one-issue lobbies. The one-issue, tunnel-vision lobby is the despair of the politician. There are times when, reading the mail, nothing seems to matter so much as "animal rights." I am in favor, as every Christian should be, of consideration for animals; but there are more urgent and more human matters on which it is harder for lobbies to raise funds, and which do not find their way so easily to the top of the political agenda. As citizens we should aim for a balanced political agenda, headed with what really *does* matter and with what *can* be done politically if we all see the need.

We should also be able to show how the Christian moral law is very obviously aimed at the general good. This enables us to put together coalitions that are far wider than the church and that help us make a much more effective case than we could on our own.

In Britain, the Keep Sunday Special Campaign put together a winning coalition of chain stores (whose costs for seven-day trading would rise far more steeply than sales), small shopkeepers who would be put out of business by chain stores forced to increase market share to cover the extra costs, and the labor unions, whose members — especially women — wanted a day off when all the family could be together. It produced the only major defeat of the Thatcher government in eleven years.

We should not be worried, as Christians, by such coalitions of interests with those who do not hold our faith or theology. Democracy is the rule of the majority, and a majority must consist of people with very different views who are committed to work together. Christian moral law is, I believe, the "Maker's instructions" on how his creation *can* work together harmoniously. It is the most broadly accepted moral law because, in my view, it is the one that is really true to human nature and therefore the one to which people most readily respond. For instance, women naturally see pornography as offensive to female dignity because, whether or not they believe in God, the great majority feel instinctively the dignity that God has given them.

Interest coalitions are not usually enough on their own to change established laws, to make new laws, or to resist change. Our politicians are people under heavy daily pressure who have little time to think through the problems that confront them. So they reach for available solutions, not just to moral problems, but to administrative problems and to counter-arguments put by those opposing change.

For instance, I received a lot of letters from Christians opposed to euthanasia ("mercy" killing) on moral grounds. Then came the counter-flow of letters from those in favor of euthanasia on grounds of compassion, to relieve the terminally ill of unnecessary suffering. Neither side has so far dealt with the problems the politician would face. The medical profession is dedicated to the preservation of life. Can it also be given a counter-responsibility for killing? And although the argument is only for voluntary euthanasia, who can be sure that undue pressure will not be put on the old by relatives who are weary of caring for them or impatient to get their money?

So Christian doctors, nurses, and others who care for the old need to get together to work out advice to government, advice that embodies both a moral case and its application to the argument. If it gives politicians a well-founded position that they can defend in public debate, then they are far more likely to take it up and act on it. For instance, Christian support of hospices for the terminally ill not only gives some experience of a better way of bringing dignity to painful death, but it also gives those involved in it a moral authority that cannot be ignored.

In some countries, Christian graduates have formed professional fellowships in their respective professions — medicine, law, teaching, business, and others — so that they can look at ethical problems and try to come to agreement on the Christian principles that should guide them. They provide a very valuable resource for the rest of their profession and for all Christians in public life.

PARTY POLITICS

A lot of Christians will go as far as this, but stop short of endorsing one party. Those who have to go into the pulpit are right to draw that line. Parties rise and fall, and a church should not be dragged down by public opposition to the party they have openly supported. Even for the men and women in the pew, it may be better to be an expert adviser available to all who ask.

But there comes a time, as it certainly came to me, when an issue arises that seems so fundamental to the future of your country that you feel that all your advice is worthless if the issue goes the wrong way.

Of course, you cannot fight on a party platform, or support it as an activist, unless you are in broad agreement with it. But political parties are coalitions bracketing a fairly wide span of different views, and most parties allow a free vote on moral issues.

The British and American electoral systems are based on the electoral district rather than the national party. That gives the party member a degree of independence from the party machine. What matters is your relation with your local party. There you have to build up trust, and if you do a good job for your district, they will tolerate a degree of independence from a party line. As another old hand once told me, "Just tell them that your thinking is a bit in advance of the party and that they will all shortly catch up with you!"

There are those who cannot believe that a Christian can succeed in politics. If we measure success by the power to impose our views, the power of great office, then perhaps not. The Christian standard of success must be the ability to serve those who trusted and elected us. The Christian, above all, should be able to inspire trust and should want to serve.

A Christian in politics should also be able to inspire trust in colleagues that they will not be let down, that they are being told the truth, that a job undertaken will be done — trust that there is no hidden agenda in the discussion, that no lobby is steering the argument.

If, in the end, there is a crisis of conscience, Christians must never live for politics; we must be able to risk our position to oppose something to which we cannot in Christian conscience agree. But before that happens we should try to persuade our colleagues, and, if we cannot do that, our supporters. The chances are that, if we have served them well, they will back us through thick and thin; but if not, and if we are quite clear that the issue is one of conscience, then we have done all we can and we should resign gracefully.

But a Christian should be a fighter for good causes, not a quitter. The campaigns for the abolition of slavery and for the nineteenth-century reform of working conditions are stories of great patience and persistence. The political leaders of these campaigns did not tire and they did not quit. But they also did not make unnecessary enemies. They had friends everywhere, even among those who disagreed with them. They were courteous and patient, surviving setbacks better than some of their followers. And after long years, they won the argument.

Joseph, Moses, David, Daniel, and Nehemiah were rulers greatly used by God. We cannot all be what they were, but we can all learn from them. All had terrible setbacks. All were at one time or another in despair. We know that both Moses and David made mistakes. What all had in common was absolute faith in God and in his word. And all were men of prayer. The great prayers of Moses and David have come down to us, dialogues between God and men who, in facing apparently insoluble crises, knew all the same that they would trust God and his word. The God they trusted is also our God. May he raise up such people for our generation too.

Literature in Christian Perspective

Leland Ryken

NEARLY HALF a century has passed since Dorothy Sayers declared that "the Church as a body has never made up her mind about the Arts."[1] Actually, the status of literature in the church is not quite this uncertain. Literature has never seemed crucially important to most laypeople and clergy, or even to most Christian intellectuals. The task of formulating a Christian poetic (philosophy of literature) has been the domain almost exclusively of teachers of literature and a coterie of readers for whom literature is an overwhelmingly important part of life.

In terms of practice, then, the church *has* made up its mind about literature: literature is a peripheral concern in living the Christian life. A leading theme of Christian apologists for literature has accordingly been that literature *ought* to be much more central than it is in the Christian church — that in fact literature is a leading but unexamined influence in nearly everyone's life and in culture as a whole.

Nor has there been such drastic disagreement among those who think and write about the relationship of Christianity to literature as may at first appear. This is concealed by the way in which each successive generation of literary scholars feels obliged to create a new critical vocabulary and agenda of interests, accompanied by a disparagement of earlier theories. At any given time, therefore, a Christian approach to literature is likely to be an assimilation of currently popular literary theory

---

1. Sayers, "Towards a Christian Aesthetic," in *The New Orpheus: Essays Toward a Christian Poetic,* ed. Nathan A. Scott, Jr. (New York: Sheed and Ward, 1964), p. 4. Originally delivered as an address in 1944.

with Christian belief.[2] There is nothing pernicious about this practice, so long as it produces a genuinely Christianized version of a given theory. It is only natural that a Christian approach to literature would incorporate the best literary theory as derived from the discipline of literary criticism. After all, the Christian doctrines of natural revelation and common grace should lead us to expect that some of the truth about literature will be empirically derived from the study of literature itself.

A definite pluralism thus characterizes attempts to formulate a Christian philosophy of literature, and it would be inappropriate to speak of *the* Christian approach to literature. There is no single Christian approach. Whether a critic agrees with a given Christian approach is likely to depend on the critic's degree of sympathy with the literary theory onto which a Christian perspective is being grafted.[3] While a greater consensus than this may be desirable, it is futile to expect it.

What we can hope for instead is agreement on the Christian principles that need to be integrated with literary theory. Underlying the shifting winds of Christian literary theory are enduring constants, just as bedrock theological premises remain while the agenda of theological interests and the terms in which those interests are expressed change with time. For purposes of this essay I have attempted to deal with the issues at the level of deep structure that literary scholars would agree are the essential considerations, regardless of their preferred approach to literature. I have likewise isolated the aspects of the Christian faith that are relevant to the literary enterprise, regardless of how a given person might apply them.

What, then, are the premises that enter any theory of literature? I offer the following as a list of essentials: (1) There is a form of discourse

2. The following sequence of books integrating Christianity and literature during the second half of the twentieth century will show both constant factors and the ways in which the changing face of literary theory has affected Christian critics: Finley Eversole, ed., *Christian Faith and the Contemporary Arts* (Nashville: Abingdon, 1957); Roland M. Frye, *Perspective on Man: Literature and the Christian Tradition* (Philadelphia: Westminster, 1961); Nathan A. Scott, Jr., ed., *The New Orpheus;* Nathan A. Scott, Jr., ed., *The Climate of Faith in Modern Literature* (New York: Seabury, 1964); Giles B. Gunn, ed., *Literature and Religion* (New York: Harper, 1971); G. B. Tennyson and Edward E. Ericson, Jr., *Religion and Modern Literature* (Grand Rapids: Eerdmans, 1975); Leland Ryken, *Triumphs of the Imagination* (Downers Grove, IL: InterVarsity, 1979); Leland Ryken, ed., *The Christian Imagination: Essays on Literature and the Arts* (Grand Rapids: Baker, 1981); Leland Ryken, *Windows to the World: Literature in Christian Perspective* (1985; repr. Dallas: Word, 1990); Clarence Walhout and Leland Ryken, eds., *Contemporary Literary Theory: A Christian Appraisal* (Grand Rapids: Eerdmans, 1991).

3. A comprehensive Christian assessment of the leading contemporary schools of criticism can be found in Walhout and Ryken, eds., *Contemporary Literary Theory*.

that possesses properties that set it apart from other discourse in such a way that we can speak of "literature."[4] (2) One aspect of literature consists of form, beauty, technique, or creativity, and this aspect is self-rewarding as a form of enjoyment, entertainment, and aesthetic enrichment. (3) The content of literature has a lot to do with human experience, as distinct from abstract thought or ideas. (4) This should not, however, lead us to minimize the importance of perspective in literature and its interpretation, nor to deny that values and ideas are *part* of the literary enterprise, nor that works of literature make truth-claims that need to be evaluated. (5) As a stimulus to a response, literature is always a potential moral influence and is therefore subject to moral evaluation. Christian literary critics would agree on an additional premise: a Christian approach to literature requires us to integrate each of these concerns with relevant Christian data.

Although I have chosen the foregoing anatomy of issues as the structural scheme for this essay, a few additional signposts will clarify the exploration I am about to undertake. A Christian philosophy of literature entails two things — a general defense of literature (a rationale for its importance in a Christian's life) and a methodology for relating one's actual reading or writing of literature to the Christian faith. It is also useful to remember that the literary writer's task is threefold — to present human experience, to offer an interpretation of that experience, and to create form/technique/beauty. A complete Christian approach to literature takes all three into account. Finally, it is a time-honored principle of literature (first articulated by the Roman writer Horace) that literature has two main functions — to teach and to delight, to be useful and to entertain. The Christian faith has something to say about both of these dimensions, and any Christian philosophy of literature is deficient if it slights either of them.

While some Christian theorists base their aesthetic theory on a specific theologian or theological tradition, such aesthetic theories are of rather local interest, inasmuch as their credibility depends on the degree to which a reader finds the theologian or theological tradition viable.[5] I am interested in something more foundational and universal than a given theologian — namely, the Bible. We should not forget that Christianity is a revealed religion and that this revelation is the source of Christian belief.

---

4. Recent literary theorists generally deny that literary texts possess distinctive traits, but the practice of these theorists belies their claims: they continue to use the word *literature* to isolate a body of writing that falls into this category, to exclude texts that fall outside this category, and to teach and write about the standard literary texts.

5. Norman Reed Cary surveys some theologically based philosophies of literature in *Christian Criticism in the Twentieth Century: Theological Approaches to Literature* (Port Washington, NY: Kennikat, 1975).

I

> Literature will yield to . . . anyone . . . what it has
> to give only if it is approached as literature.
>
> — F. R. Leavis, *The Common Pursuit*

To speak of "literature" is to imply that it has identifiable traits that set it apart from other forms of discourse. This may seem self-evident, but it is not. Through the centuries Christians have tried to turn literature into something other than what it is, and the record of literary theorists is not much better. T. S. Eliot's dictum that poetry should "not [be] defined in terms of something else" is always in need of reiteration.[6] The first step toward a Christian approach to literature is to let literature be literature. Like other aspects of God's creation, it has its own integrity. As we will see, several perennial fallacies and one prominent strand in contemporary literary theory stand in the way of our acknowledging this.

What characterizes the phenomenon that we call literature, and what constitutes its inherent integrity? Literature consists of words, first of all. Yet when Christians talk about literature, it would be easy to get the impression that literature consists of ideas. It does not. When a poet lamented his inability to write poetry even though he was "full of ideas," the French poet Mallarmé responded, "One does not make poetry with ideas, but with *words*."[7]

A proper respect for language is thus a prerequisite to producing and understanding literature. Christianity itself pushes us toward such a respect because it is a revealed religion whose authoritative truths are written in a book. The very fact that God trusted language to communicate the most important message that exists puts Christianity on a collision course with recent theories that deny the ability of literature to communicate a definite or knowable meaning.[8]

---

6. Eliot, *The Use of Poetry and the Use of Criticism* (Cambridge: Harvard University Press, 1933), p. 147.

7. Mallarmé, cited in Paul Valéry, "Poetry, Language and Thought," in *The Modern Tradition: Backgrounds of Modern Literature,* ed. Richard Ellmann and Charles Feidelson, Jr. (New York: Oxford University Press, 1965), p. 77. Valéry's own formula is likewise useful: "Poetry is an art of language."

8. The most obvious exemplar of the "prison house of language" position is known as deconstruction. Its methodology is to reduce literary texts to a system of contradictions, with a view toward demonstrating that texts do not communicate a discernible or definite meaning.

Stated this baldly, my proposition no doubt seems simplistic. But one thing we need to recognize is that literary theories point toward a larger worldview. Moving in the other direction, a worldview impinges on literary theory, and although a Christian worldview is remarkably adaptable in accommodating a range of literary theories, it sets boundaries that exclude some of them. The Christian worldview asserts a meaningful order to the universe and the ability of humans to discern and communicate that meaning in language, however imperfectly. Of course, the Fall affected language as well as the human intellect, and variability of interpretation remains a fact of literary and biblical interpretation. But this is different from a thoroughgoing skepticism about the ability of language to communicate ascertainable meaning at all.

The bigger obstacle to letting literature be literature among Christians has generally been a naive belief that literature is somehow a direct rendition of reality. But literature is always life at the remove of art and the imagination, a feature that classical literary theory acknowledged with its view that literature is an imitation *(mimēsis)* of life. Literature is an artificial world having its own characteristics and its own integrity as a world created by human subcreators.[9]

The crucial point here is that the world of literature is a construct of the imagination. This world of the imagination adheres to conventions that are always to some degree unlifelike and often openly fantastic.

The world of the imagination, for example, is made out of words and is therefore different from the tangible world in which we live. Fiction is a staple of literature, in poetry no less than in narrative. A work of literature is always selective in a way that the experiences of real life never are. Literary tragedy, for example, is often praised for being true to life, but it does not portray catastrophe as it normally happens in life. In the words of C. S. Lewis, it omits "the clumsy and apparently meaningless bludgeoning of much real misfortune and the prosaic littlenesses which usually rob real sorrows of their dignity," presenting instead suffering "that is always significant and sublime."[10]

---

9. I borrow the term *subcreator* from J. R. R. Tolkien, though the concept is as old as the Renaissance poet Sir Philip Sidney. Tolkien's formulation is this: "What really happens is that the story-maker proves a successful 'sub-creator.' He makes a Secondary World which your mind can enter. Inside it, what he relates is 'true': it accords with the laws of that world" ("On Fairy-Stories," in *Essays Presented to Charles Williams,* ed. C. S. Lewis [1947; repr. Grand Rapids: Eerdmans, 1966], p. 60). The critics whom I have found most useful in establishing the world of the literary imagination as a world having its own integrity are Northrop Frye and C. S. Lewis.

10. Lewis, *An Experiment in Criticism* (Cambridge: Cambridge University Press, 1965), pp. 79, 81.

Literature also heightens experience beyond what we find in real life — through selectivity, through highlighting, through juxtaposition. The characters we meet in stories are more heroic or more villainous than we ordinarily find in real life. They are also simpler, and their motivations are clearer. Stories and poems have a self-containedness that experiences in real life do not. Speaking of poetry, how often in real life do people speak in regular meter and rhyme? Literature is patterned around archetypes such as the journey or quest or initiation in a more obvious way than we feel life to be organized. In these and additional ways, literature defamiliarizes life.

Christians have traditionally found it difficult to grant integrity to this world of the imagination and have responded in two directions. One tendency has been to discredit imagination and fantasy as being untruthful, frivolous, a waste of time, dangerous escapism, and something to be left behind with childhood. The other tendency has been to suppress the imaginary element in literature and to act as if literature is a direct replica of life, in effect abolishing the world of the imagination and merging it with empirical reality.

Both of these responses misinterpret the nature of literature. Literature is built on a great paradox: it is a make-believe world that reminds us of real life and clarifies it for us. The eighteenth-century critic Samuel Johnson noted that the imitations of literature "are not mistaken for realities, but . . . bring realities to mind."[11] This is similar to artist Pablo Picasso's great aphorism that "art is a lie that makes us realize truth."[12] Consider yet a third statement of the idea: "it is the function of all art to give us some perception of an order in life, by imposing an order upon it."[13] The order that it imposes is the order of the imagination.[14] It is no wonder that Northrop Frye claims that "the constructs of the imagination tell us things about human life that we don't get in any other way."[15]

11. Johnson, "Preface to Shakespeare," in *Criticism: The Major Statements*, ed. Charles Kaplan (New York: St. Martin's Press, 1975), p. 264.

12. Picasso, *The Arts*, May 1923.

13. T. S. Eliot, *On Poetry and Poets* (New York: Farrar, Straus and Cudahy, 1957), p. 93. It is impossible to overstate how much analytic mileage one can get out of this statement. On the one hand, it leads us to scrutinize the order that the imagination has imposed on reality in a story or poem. On the other hand, it leads us to ask what this imagined order tells us about life in our world.

14. For more on the order that the imagination imposes on reality, see my discussion in *Triumphs of the Imagination*, pp. 75-98, and in *Windows to the World*, pp. 35-62.

15. Frye, *The Educated Imagination* (Bloomington: Indiana University Press, 1964), pp. 124-25.

One strand in a Christian approach to literature, then, is a respect for the ability of the imagination — even the fantastic imagination — to embody the truth. There is no valid reason for the perennial Christian preference of biography, history, and the newspaper to fiction and poetry. The former tell us what *happened,* while literature tells us what *happens.* Both are forms of truth. Francis Schaeffer once wrote that "Christian artists [and we could add readers] do not need to be threatened by fantasy and imagination. . . . The Christian is the one whose imagination should fly beyond the stars."[16]

The example of the Bible, which is central to any attempt to formulate a Christian approach to literature, sanctions the imagination as a valid form of expressing truth. The Bible is in large part a work of imagination. Its most customary way of expressing truth is not the sermon or theological outline but the story, the poem, and the vision — all of them literary forms and products of the imagination (though not necessarily the fictional imagination). Literary conventions are present in the Bible from start to finish. Narrative is the dominant form of the Bible as a whole. Metaphor and symbol abound. And what could be more fantastic than some of the details in the visions of the prophets and the book of Revelation?

In sum, a Christian approach to literature must begin where any other literary theory begins — by determining the properties of literature and granting literature the right to be true to its identity. Jesus and the writers of the Bible did not distrust the literary imagination. They told stories and spoke in metaphor. They did not share a common disparagement of literature as being "just stories" or "just poems." They also trusted literature to make its point by literary means instead of feeling an obligation to Spell It Out.

II

As image-bearer of God, man possesses the possibility both to create something beautiful, and to delight in it.

— Abraham Kuyper, *Lectures on Calvinism*

Literature is a form of knowledge, but it is also an art form — the creation of technique and beauty for the sake of entertainment and aesthetic enrich-

16. Schaeffer, *Art and the Bible* (Downers Grove, IL: InterVarsity, 1974), p. 61.

ment. A Christian approach to literature includes an endorsement of the pleasure-giving aspect of literature. It should stand as a corrective to the prevailing utilitarian spirit of a technological society, though in fact Christians have often perpetuated the utilitarian outlook.

Faced with the charge of the nonusefulness of literature, Christian apologists for literature have tried to meet the argument on its own terms, showing that literature is useful after all. It teaches truth, apologists say; it moves people to good moral behavior. While there is truth in these arguments, there is something inherently wrong about ignoring the pleasure-giving aspect of literature. To defend literature solely for its usefulness is to overlook why most people go to literature in the first place.

A Christian approach to literature should not denigrate or ignore literary form in deference to content. It should instead defend the nonutilitarian, human creativity, beauty, and pleasure. A defense of each of these can be rooted in biblical example and doctrine.[17]

The doctrine of creation forms a good starting point. God himself is a creator, and the world he created is a world that is beautiful as well as utilitarian. This creative God made people in his image — that is, with a capacity for creativity and beauty. It is no wonder that Christian defenders of the arts have made much of creativity.[18] Christian poet Chad Walsh writes that writers can see themselves "as a kind of earthly assistant to God . . . , carrying on the delegated work of creation, making the fullness of creation fuller."[19]

The example of the Bible confirms the importance of literary form and beauty. If the *message* of the Bible were all that mattered, there would have been no good reason for biblical poets to put their utterances into intricately patterned verse form, or for biblical storytellers to compose masterfully compact and carefully designed stories. In God's economy, the writers of the Bible did not have something better to do with their time and ability than to be artistic to the glory of God. The writer of Ecclesiastes speaks for other biblical authors as well as for himself when he tells us that he arranged his material "with great care," and that he "sought to find pleasing words" (Eccles. 12:9-10, RSV) or "words of delight" (12:10, KJVn.).

---

17. For more on these subjects than I can say here, see my comments in *Windows to the World*, pp. 63-81, and in *The Liberated Imagination: Thinking Christianly about the Arts* (Wheaton, IL: Harold Shaw, 1989), pp. 65-96.

18. The standard source is Dorothy Sayers's book *The Mind of the Maker* (1941; repr. Cleveland: World, 1956). Sayers pushes the analogy between divine and human creativity too far, but her main thesis is sound: people create because God creates and because God made people in his image.

19. Walsh, "The Advantages of the Christian Faith for a Writer," in Ryken, ed., *The Christian Imagination*, p. 308.

This biblical endorsement of literary creativity is matched by its respect for beauty. When God formed paradise, the perfect human environment, he "made to grow every tree that is pleasant to the sight and good for food" (Gen. 2:9, RSV). God's design for human life, in other words, is aesthetic as well as utilitarian. The word *beauty* and its variants appear more than six dozen times in the Bible, in an overwhelmingly positive sense. In the Old Testament, beauty is an important part of worship.

The Bible affirms pleasure and enjoyment as thoroughly as it does creativity and beauty. The God-centered passages in the book of Ecclesiastes (e.g., 3:12-13 and 5:18-19) encourage a zestful enjoyment of life. The example of Jesus reinforces this spirit, since one of his habitual activities was attending dinner parties. On one occasion he kept a wedding party going by turning water into wine, a gesture of festivity that in no way detracts from the way in which the miracle also demonstrated Christ's messianic fulfillment of Old Testament ceremonialism. The classic passage is 1 Timothy 6:17, which tells us that "God . . . giveth us richly all things to enjoy" (KJV).

How can a person read literature to the glory of God? One answer to this question is, By enjoying the beauty that human creativity has produced, recognizing God as the ultimate source of this beauty and creativity. We do not need to defend literature, as most people have done, solely on the didactic grounds that it teaches us. Literature has a reason for being quite apart from that. In a Christian worldview, literature exists for more than our enjoyment, but not for less. Valuing literature on the pleasure principle is part of a bigger picture as well — leisure as part of the stewardship of life, a topic addressed elsewhere in this book.

III

> Poets are always telling us that grass is green, or thunder loud, or lips red. . . . This is the most remarkable of the powers of Poetic language: to convey to us the quality of experiences. . . .
>
> — C. S. Lewis, "The Language of Religion"

Along with the Christian doctrine of creation, the doctrine of the incarnation has most often been invoked in Christian philosophies of the arts, with the Christian sacraments close behind. It is not hard to see why the incarnation has loomed so large in Christian thinking about literature: in the words of

C. S. Lewis, literature "too is a little incarnation, giving body to what had been before invisible and inaudible."[20]

Although the terminology has differed from age to age, literary theory through the centuries has agreed that the subject of literature is human experience. The thing that sets literature off from philosophy and the "thought" disciplines is that it embodies human experience in concrete form rather than in the form of abstract propositions. Literature gives the example rather than the precept. It embodies experience in event and character, in image and metaphor — in other words, with a certain indirectness.

Modern criticism has been right to insist that the presentation of human experience in concrete form is a type of knowledge — knowledge different from what the "idea" disciplines give us but no less important to us as we grapple with reality and seek to understand it. Literature does not give us information but a living through of an experience. In the words of fiction writer Flannery O'Connor, "Fiction writing is very seldom a matter of saying things; it is a matter of showing things."[21]

The writer's task is (to quote Nathan Scott) "to *stare*, to *look* at the created world, and to lure the rest of us into a similar act of contemplation."[22] Novelist Joseph Conrad said something similar: "My task . . . is, by the power of the written word to make you hear, to make you feel — it is, before all, to make you *see*."[23] Flannery O'Connor quipped, "The writer should never be ashamed of staring."[24]

The Christian doctrine of the incarnation and the sacraments have provided a convenient analogy to literature, and perhaps even a sanction for it, though this pathway has led to some loose thinking about literature and the arts.[25] Like the incarnation of Jesus and the sacraments, literature embodies meaning in concrete form. In fact, to borrow a motto from the New Critics of mid-century, in all of these phenomena the form *is* the meaning.

20. Lewis, *Reflections on the Psalms* (New York: Harcourt, 1958), p. 5.

21. O'Connor, *Mystery and Manners,* ed. Sally Fitzgerald and Robert Fitzgerald (New York: Farrar, Straus and Giroux, 1961), p. 93. This is one of the truly important books on Christianity and literature.

22. Nathan Scott, Jr., *Modern Literature and the Religious Frontier* (New York: Harper, 1958), p. 52.

23. Conrad, *The Nigger of the Narcissus* (New York: Collier, 1962), p. 19.

24. O'Connor, *Mystery and Manners,* p. 84.

25. I am referring to the "how to be religious without really trying" syndrome that *equates* literature with the sacraments and therefore treats literary experience as automatically religious or even Christian in nature.

I have taken this excursion into the incarnational nature of literature and the kind of knowledge that it gives (an experiential knowledge of life as we live it) because they have important ramifications for thinking Christianly about literature. Let me mention four of these.

First, Western culture generally — and the Christian subculture specifically — has had an unwarranted tendency to think that abstract ideas and facts are the only valid type of knowledge that we possess. Literature challenges that bias, and so does the Bible. The Bible is not a theological outline with proof-texts attached. It is an anthology of literature more than anything else. When asked to define "neighbor," Jesus refused, telling a story instead (the parable of the good Samaritan). Our fund of important knowledge is not limited to ideas but includes the characters and events of stories and the images and metaphors of poetry as well. In a startling challenge to our customary thinking in this regard, C. S. Lewis claimed that it is "a mistake to think that our experience in general can be communicated by precise and literal language and that there is a special class of experiences (say, emotions) which cannot. The truth seems to me the opposite."[26]

Second, the incarnational nature of literature has important implications for settling the usual question of whether a given work of literature tells the truth. One of the levels of truth in literature is truthfulness to human experience and external reality. Literature overwhelmingly tells the truth at this level. Writers are sensitive observers of reality. It is part of their craft to be such. Too many debates over the truthfulness of a piece of literature have been a great waste of effort because the participants were talking about different types of truth (truthfulness to human experience vs. ideas that might be true or false).

A third significance of the incarnational nature of literature is that this aspect of literature is one of the common bonds of the human race. The portrayal of human experience binds people together even when ideas push them apart. Christians are a minority in their society and as such are subject to all the tendencies of other minorities: a sense of alienation from culture as a whole, an in-group mentality and vocabulary, an inclination to concentrate on their distinctives and to slight what they have in common with all people, and a "we-they" outlook on the world. The experiential content of literature can be a beneficial corrective. It leads not only to a sympathetic understanding of others but to self-understanding as well. In reading literature, we see ourselves — including what Augustine called the dark corners of the heart.

26. Lewis, "The Language of Religion," in *Christian Reflections*, ed. Walter Hooper (Grand Rapids: Eerdmans, 1967), p. 138.

Finally, the incarnational nature of literature, combined with its power to influence society, should lead us to question a common assumption that a person's worldview consists only of ideas. A person's worldview has a "mythology" as well as an ideology. It is a world picture as well as a worldview. This is to say that it contains images, symbols, stories, and characters as well as ideas.

People are as much symbolic creatures as rational ones. A noted theologian has said that we are "image-making and image-using creatures, . . . guided and formed by images in our minds," adding that a person "grasps and shapes reality . . . with the aid of great images, metaphors, and analogies."[27] Christians live out their lives in an awareness of specific images — God as shepherd, Jacob and Esau, the good Samaritan, the cross — as well as ideas. The imagination is a leading ingredient in our picture of truth, and literature provides much of the content of our imagination. We appropriate truth by story and image as well as by idea. We understand the nature of providence by the story of Joseph and by the pastoral images of Psalm 23 as well as by a theological definition in the Westminster Confession or in Berkhof's *Systematic Theology*.

To sum up, literature offers a kind of experiential knowledge and truth that everyone needs. Literature and the Bible alike tell us that we live by more than abstract ideas. When we fail to acknowledge this, we are in danger of knowing both ourselves and our world a great deal less well than we need in order to live as we ought and can.

IV

All writers . . . must have, to compose any kind of
story, some picture of the world, and of what is right
and wrong in that world.

— Joyce Cary, *Art and Reality*

Literature does more than present human experience; it also interprets that experience. If one type of literary truth is representational truth based on the reality principle, another type is perspectival truth, consisting of ideas. At this level literature embodies implied ideas and makes implicit truth-claims.

27. H. Richard Niebuhr, *The Responsible Self* (New York: Harper, 1963), pp. 151-52, 161.

The question of meaning in literature has always been somewhat problematic. Earlier centuries viewed literature as a branch of rhetoric or persuasion and made extravagant (and often unsupportable) claims for literature as a teacher of truth and moral influence. In the middle of the twentieth century, literary theory was so preoccupied with literature as the embodiment of human experience that the ideational dimension of literature was slighted. More recently, deconstruction and related forms of skepticism have questioned the ability of literature to convey ideational meaning.

It is perhaps salutary to be reminded, then, that writers themselves intend to communicate meaning. A specimen statement is novelist Joyce Cary's claim that "a reader must never be left in doubt about the meaning of a story."[28] Equally convincing is Gerald Graff's observation that "there are two good arguments for . . . accepting the claim that literary works make assertions. Briefly put, the arguments are that authors intend assertions and readers can scarcely help looking for them."[29] The assumption of meaning is simply one of the conventions of literature — in fact, one influential literary critic labels it "the rule of significance" and calls it "the primary convention of literature."[30] Writers, after all, are on the lookout not only for good story material but also for stories in which (to use the words of the nineteenth-century French poet Baudelaire) "the deep significance of life reveals itself."[31] The assertions that literature makes about life fall into three categories: reality (what really exists), morality, and values.

Writers intend meaning, and their works are a carefully contrived system of persuasion to get the reader to accept their view of the world. Literature is affective. In the words of David Lodge, "The writer expresses what he knows by affecting the reader; the reader knows what is expressed by being receptive to affects."[32]

The Christian tradition has never been able to make up its mind about whether the persuasiveness of literature is good or bad. Augustine granted that literature is a teacher, but he regarded this as bad because it teaches

28. Cary, *Art and Reality* (Garden City, NY: Doubleday, 1961), p. 132.

29. Graff, "Literature as Assertions," in *American Criticism in the Poststructuralist Age,* ed. Ira Konigsberg (Ann Arbor: University of Michigan Press, 1981), p. 161.

30. Jonathan Culler, *Structuralist Poetics: Structuralism, Linguistics, and the Study of Literature* (Ithaca: Cornell University Press, 1975), p. 115. Culler's formulation is that we should read a work of literature "as expressing a significant attitude to some problem concerning man and/or his relation to the universe."

31. Charles Baudelaire, as quoted by J. Middleton Murry, *The Problem of Style* (London: Oxford University Press, 1922), p. 30.

32. Lodge, *Language of Fiction* (London: Routledge and Kegan Paul, 1966), p. 65.

error rather than truth. Renaissance poet Sir Philip Sidney thought literature the most important of all disciplines because it moves people to virtue. Both viewpoints are right: literature can persuade readers toward an acceptance of either truth or falsehood.

What this means is that Christian readers must be discerning and self-conscious about their responses as they read. A Christian approach to reading literature is a continuous testing of the spirits to see if they are from God. All of which gets us to the topic of assessing the intellectual and moral viewpoint of the literature that we read.

The keynote was sounded in a justly influential essay by T. S. Eliot, who wrote near the end of the essay, "What I believe to be incumbent upon all Christians is the duty of maintaining consciously certain standards and criteria of criticism over and above those applied by the rest of the world; and that by these criteria and standards everything that we read must be tested."[33] At the outset of his essay Eliot spoke of how "literary criticism should be completed by criticism from a definite ethical and theological standpoint."

Several things are implied by Eliot's theory. One is that, before we assess the truth or error of a work of literature, we must let the work be itself as a work of literature. I would go so far as to call this a moral duty that we owe to a writer. Furthermore, self-forgetfulness — getting beyond ourselves and our limited range of experience — is one of the chief rewards of reading literature. In fact, a degree of initial detachment from a work of literature is exactly what makes it useful for clarifying our own experience, for the simple reason that we cannot see something well if we are too close to it.

But self-forgetfulness must be followed by self-consciousness about who we are as readers. Once we have isolated the implied assertions of a literary work, we need to assess them by ordinary methods of philosophic and theological analysis. Works of literature can assert false ideas as well as true ones, and their artistic greatness does not guarantee their philosophic or moral truthfulness. In the words of Francis Schaeffer, "Art may heighten the impact of the world view, in fact we can count on this, but it does not make something true. The truth of a world view presented by an artist must be judged on separate grounds than artistic greatness."[34]

33. Eliot, "Religion and Literature," as reprinted in Ryken, ed., *The Christian Imagination*, p. 153.

34. Schaeffer, *Art and the Bible*, p. 41. T. S. Eliot makes the same distinction between form and content: "The 'greatness' of literature cannot be determined solely by literary standards; though we must remember that whether it is literature or not can be determined only by literary standards" ("Religion and Literature," p. 142).

Assessing the truth-claims of literature — its ideational content — is a comparative process in which the implied statements of the work are compared to what the Bible and Christian doctrine say on the same subject. Of course, we must remember that much of the content of the Christian faith is something that it shares with other religious and philosophic viewpoints. We can profitably picture two circles, one representing Christianity, the other representing other philosophic traditions. The two circles have a large overlapping area of agreement. This is the inclusively Christian element in a work of literature. There is also potential for exclusively Christian content in a work, as well as anti-Christian content.

Although the scheme I have outlined is simple in theory, in practice it requires the best intellectual effort of a reader. It also requires continuous reflection on what the Christian faith says on a wide range of subjects. This is the point of intersection between theology and literary criticism — the point at which a Christian critic must become a theologian as well. Christian theology, moreover, is eventually more specific than theism. Its view of life encompasses specifically New Testament interpretations on such issues as sin, atonement, forgiveness, redemption in Christ, the moral life, the church, and eschatological hope.

If we want to see what a full-fledged Christian worldview looks like in literature, we can profitably consider the models provided by such classic Christian writers as John Milton, John Donne, George Herbert, Gerard Manley Hopkins, Fyodor Dostoyevsky, Leo Tolstoy, and T. S. Eliot. In general, these writers combine faithfulness to human experience and excellence of technique with the interpretive bias of Christian theology and ethics. But I need to add two cautions here: Christian writers themselves should not be viewed as being exempt from the kind of theological assessment that I am urging; and on the other side, writers who are only nominally Christian or who make no profession of personal Christian faith at all can write works that measure up to the criteria of inclusively and even exclusively Christian viewpoints.

The intellectual usefulness of literature is not that it necessarily tells us the truth about an issue but rather that it serves as a catalyst to thinking about the great issues of life. If this is true, we can also see how misguided has been the frequent assumption that it is the task of Christian literary criticism to show *that* works of literature are Christian. The task is rather to assess *whether* and *to what degree* works are Christian in their viewpoint. Christian enthusiasts for literature too often seek to baptize every work of literature that they love.

I need to add another caution as well. Even when we judge a work of literature to be deficient in truth when measured by a Christian viewpoint, we should not dismiss the work wholesale. There are other aspects for which we can commend it. We can always be rapturous over the technique and beauty of a well-crafted story or poem. We can also value and affirm its truthfulness to life and human experience, even if the interpretive slant is wrong. As Christian readers we are free to approve part of a work without endorsing all of it, and conversely we can disagree with part of it without devaluing it entirely. On all of these matters the record of Christians is not as good as one would wish.

V

Moral standards . . . are as relevant to literature as they are to life itself.

— Keith F. McKean, *The Moral Measure of Literature*

Although the moral dimension of literature was slighted during the ascendancy of the so-called New Criticism in the middle of the twentieth century, more recent developments (chiefly the rise of Marxist and feminist criticism) have put the question conspicuously back on the agenda of literary scholarship. For Christians it probably never left the agenda, just as it was a major issue throughout the history of literary criticism. Yet it is a subject not very well understood in Christian circles.[35]

When I speak of morality of literature, I do not mean simply its ideational content. Morality deals specifically with human behavior, especially one's dealings with other people. The moral aspect of literature has to do chiefly with the models of human behavior portrayed in literature and the influence of literature on the behavior of readers.

We approach the subject through a cloud of misunderstanding, so let me pause to clear the pathway. First, *no* effect of literature is automatic. Even reading the Bible does not produce automatic results. The mere portrayal of immoral action in literature does not, therefore, make the work itself immoral, nor does it mean that reading the work is immoral. Nor is it true that moral literature presents only exemplary characters and behavior. The Bible itself follows a pattern of embodying moral viewpoints in the portrayal of immoral behavior.

I should also pay my disrespects to a viewpoint common in Christian

---

35. For a more extended discussion on the morality of literature than I can undertake here, see chap. 7 of my book *Windows to the World*.

circles that moral literature is literature that *moralizes*. Great literature never moralizes. The morality of literature is determined chiefly by three factors, which I will discuss in order of increasing importance.

The least reliable index to a work's morality is its subject matter, even though this is often the chief criterion applied by Christians when they object to works of literature. The mere portrayal of evil is not by itself a moral statement. Such subject matter may be offensive to a refined or Christian sensibility, but by itself it is less important than is usually assumed. The qualification I would make to this is that the images that we take into our consciousness become part of us. The strategy of literature is to give form to our own feelings and impulses. These good and bad inner impulses are to some degree latent, waiting to be activated by external stimuli. Moral literature can awaken good impulses, and immoral literature can awaken bad ones.

More important than subject matter by itself is the moral perspective that writers build into their works. When writers portray human experience, they always suggest an attitude toward it; even silence or neutrality suggests an attitude. Literature is a calculated strategy to get readers to approve of some things and disapprove of others. Moral literature can therefore be defined as literature that recommends moral behavior, while immoral literature is literature that offers immoral behavior for approval. Of course, Christianity has its own standards of what is moral and immoral, and it is these standards that a Christian reader must apply to works of literature.

By far the strongest determinant of the morality of a work of literature is the response of the individual reader. The mere words on a page are a potential stimulus, but a reader's response determines the direction that the stimulus will take. The same book can have moral and immoral effects on different readers. Moral readers can assimilate a work in a moral way contrary to the writer's intention and a work's perspective. The moral impact of literature depends ultimately on the reader.

Christian readers therefore need to monitor their own moral responses to the literature they read. As they do so, they can remember that the only effective form of censorship is self-censorship.

VI

It is the whole person who responds to a poem or novel; and if that person is a believing Christian, then it is a believing Christian who judges. . . . Literary criticism is as much a personal matter, as much

the product of a personal sense of life and value as
literature itself.

— Vincent Buckley, *Poetry and Morality*

Recent literary theory has championed the idea of interpretive communities
— readers who share an agenda of interests, beliefs, and values. Christian
readers and writers are one of these interpretive communities. Everyone
sees the world and literature through the lens of his or her beliefs and
experiences. Christians are no exception. As an interpretive community,
Christians should not apologize for having a worldview through which they
interpret the world and literature.

What, then, ought to characterize Christian writers and readers? What
does the Christian faith offer to writers and readers? My answers to these
questions will cast a retrospective look over the territory I have covered.

I begin with a caution: Christians are not necessarily better writers
and readers than other people. The Christian faith does not privilege its
adherents in that way. What Christianity provides instead is an agenda of
concerns and working premises.

The most basic of all these presuppositions is the Christian view of
authority and truth. Christians believe that the Bible and the system of
doctrine derived from it are authoritative for thought and practice. Christian
involvement in literature, therefore, begins with a belief that the Bible and
its doctrine will determine how we should view literature itself and will
provide a standard by which to measure the intellectual content and morality of literature.

This is a way of saying that the Christian faith provides the right
perspective from which to view the world of literature. One of the things
that this perspective clarifies is the contradictions that we find in literature
itself. The doctrines of common grace and general or natural revelation
explain how unbelieving writers can produce works of truth and beauty.
We do not have to inquire into a writer's orthodoxy in determining whether
a novel or poem is worthy of praise. On the other side, the doctrines of the
Fall and sin explain the abuses of literature that we see — the espousal of
error, immorality of content and effect, degradation of subject matter, and
deficiency of form.

The Christian faith also assures writers and readers of the importance
of their enterprise. Christians believe that this is their Father's world. God's
creation, including the creatures in it, have meaning and importance because God made them. The world is therefore worthy of the writer's
portrayal and understanding and love. The same doctrine assures Christian

readers that their interest in the portrayal of human experience in literature is not frivolous but essential.

Something similar is true of the enjoyment of literary creativity and beauty. God made people capable of creating. Art is God's gift to the artist (see especially two passages about the beautifying of the tabernacle in Exod. 31:1-11 and 35:30–36:2). This should deflect the ultimate praise from the subcreator to the Creator. The very form in which God inspired the writers of the Bible to write shows that the gift for literary composition bears God's imprint. The Christian reader is equally assured that enjoying the products of human creativity is one of the things that God intends for the human race.

For these and other reasons, the Christian imagination should be a liberated imagination. A certain lack of inhibition with regard to literature ought to follow from what I have said. Christian writers and readers alike are free to revel in literature — in its ability to capture human experience, in its capacity to express truth, in its potential to provide the occasion for artistic enrichment and enjoyment. Christians should feel free to be themselves as they pursue literature.

If the Christian faith assures us of the worth of literature, it also spares us from making an idol of it. There are more important things in life than producing and enjoying literature. As Chad Walsh puts it, "Art is not religion. A writer is not a god or godling. There is wisdom and illumination but not salvation in a sonnet."[36]

Christians should neither undervalue nor overvalue literature. Literature is not exempt from artistic, moral, and intellectual criticism. Yet its gifts to the human race are immeasurable: artistic enrichment, pleasurable pastime, self-understanding, clarification of human experience, and, in its highest reaches, the expression of truth and beauty that can become worship of God. Martin Luther said about the study of literature that "by these studies, as by no other means, people are wonderfully fitted for the grasping of sacred truth and for handling it skillfully."[37] This conviction has not burned as brightly in Protestantism as Luther would have wished.

I began this essay by saying that thinking about the place of literature in the Christian life has been the concern of a minority of Christians. I conclude by saying that I believe that the Christian worldview ought to make this situation intolerable. Literature in some form enters every per-

---

36. Walsh, "The Advantage of the Christian Faith for a Writer," p. 308.

37. Luther, *Luther's Correspondence and Other Contemporary Letters,* trans. and ed. Preserved Smith and Charles M. Jacobs (Philadelphia: Lutheran Publication Society, 1918), 2:177.

son's life, whether at a popular level (television drama or the movies) or at the level of literary classics. People who read the Bible regularly have still more exposure to literature. Christians generally should value their literary experiences more than they do, should seek to upgrade the quality of those experiences, and should read literature with more self-awareness, thoughtfulness, and enjoyment than has been customary.

Living Art:
Christian Experience and the Arts

EDMUND P. CLOWNEY

As CHRISTIANS we are committed to truth and goodness; what about beauty? Can theology aid us in understanding aesthetic experience? Is it possible to deepen our appreciation of the arts without endorsing what we suspect to be critical snobbery?

The Bible does not speak about art at all, in the sense in which we most often use the term. We may forget how recently that use began. When the Declaration of Independence was written the words *art, industry, democracy, class,* and *culture* were not yet being used in their modern sense.[1] The political revolutions in America and France and the Industrial Revolution in England brought about not only a change in Western culture but also a new way of speaking of culture. Before that change, painting was thought of as a craft.[2] The long corridors lined with portraits in the great houses of Britain were not begun as museum galleries. The paintings were hung to remember ancestors, not to exhibit artists' works. As André Malraux has observed, the modern attitude to "art" has created a "museum without walls."[3] Not only do we stack museums with historic "works of

1. Raymond Williams, *Culture and Society 1780-1950* (New York: Penguin, 1961), pp. 11-19.
2. R. G. Collingwood, *The Principles of Art* (New York: Oxford University Press, 1958), pp. 5-6.
3. Malraux, *The Voices of Silence,* trans. Stuart Gilbert (Princeton: Princeton University Press, 1978), part one, "Museum Without Walls," pp. 13-127. See Nicholas Wolterstorff, *Art in Action: Toward a Christian Aesthetic* (Grand Rapids: Eerdmans, 1980), p. 204. Wolterstorff devotes an illuminating chapter to "Malraux's Humanistic Alternative" to a Christian position.

art" stripped of their original purpose; we have come to think of the ceiling of the Sistine Chapel or even the cathedral at Chartres as a "work of art." Art critics serenely ignore the religious motivation of museum paintings and display professional outrage at anyone who might dare to offer a moral objection to "artistic" pornography. Painting, sculpture, photography, music, poetry — that which we call "art" has become an end in itself; indeed, it is given an absolute value that not only resembles religion but also demands religious commitment.

Christo, the Bulgarian-born environmental artist, in 1991 master-minded the erection of thousands of giant umbrellas: 1,760 yellow ones in California, and 1,340 blue ones in Japan. The wind uprooted one of the 480-pound parasols in California and flung it against a young woman, killing her. A Japanese worker was electrocuted when lifting one umbrella with a crane that touched a power line. Christo's comment: "The beauty, the tragedy, the joy is part of that project."[4] The sacrifice of unwilling martyrs is offered to the goddess Art.

But if beauty is not to be deified, is Deity beautiful? We catch glimpses of what we find to be beautiful in the world, yet beauty seems to defy analysis. "Beauty at the same time shows and hides itself; it shows itself through a fine work of art, but it cannot be definitively revealed by it because it always exists above that through which it appears."[5] Plato could appeal to the elusiveness of beauty in order to describe beauty as an ideal reality in which the world of sense participates. Calvin Seerveld has perceived the unbiblical assumptions of the Platonic and Aristotelian concepts of beauty.[6] He warns against deifying beauty or making artistic "inspiration" divine revelation. But does the Bible offer a different way of relating our experience of beauty to God, our Creator and Redeemer?

THE LIVING GOD REVEALS HIS BEAUTY

In his works of creation, God reveals himself. Creation, according to Genesis, is not an emanation from God's Being; it is the work of his Word. He speaks and it is done; he commands and it stands fast. That work, extrinsic to himself, meets with his repeated approval: "And God saw that it was good" (Gen. 1:10, 12, etc.). The Lord contemplates with satisfaction

4. Christo, cited in *U.S. News & World Report,* 11 Nov. 1991, p. 26.
5. Jean Brun, *Les rivages du monde* (Paris: Desclée, 1979), p. 115.
6. Seerveld, *A Christian Critique of Art* (St. Catharines, Ontario: The Association for Reformed Scientific Studies, 1963), pp. 32-39.

the form of his creation. In the garden where God put the man he had formed were "trees that were pleasing to the eye" as well as "good for food" (Gen. 2:9). The beauty of the trees in Eden echoes as a superlative in the oracle Ezekiel received. There Assyria is imaged as a cedar of Lebanon, whose beauty is "the envy of all the trees of Eden in the garden of God" (Ezek. 31:9).

The visual beauty of the garden displays the order given to creation by the Spirit and the Word of God. God orders by division: he divides light from darkness, the waters above the firmament from those below it, the land from the sea. He orders by creating living forms marked off "according to their kinds" (Gen. 1:25). Creation formed by God's Word has its own language that delights those with ears to hear (Ps. 19:1-2).

Abundance as well as order marks creation. Life appears in abounding forms; the seas, the earth, and the heavens teem with the munificence of God's design. We are told of the treasures in the land of Havilah: gold, aromatic resin, onyx. Rich resources await the hand of the human creator made in God's image. The gold used in the furnishings of the tabernacle and worn on the forehead of the high priest is gold provided by God for the inspired craft of Bezalel and Oholiab (Exod. 35:30-35).

God expresses joy in his creation as he pronounces it good. The human pair, made in the image of God, may share his joy in the order and beauty of creation. God does not simply pronounce them good as a part of his creation; he blesses them as the heirs and lords of creation. They are to continue God's work of ordering what he has made. Its riches are theirs as God's gift, to explore, to conserve, to develop.

In the fall, the sin of Adam and Eve violates their relation to the created order as well as to the Creator. The serpent wants the woman to see the beauty of the trees as evidence of the malice of the Creator, who denies what he appears to offer (Gen. 3:1, 5, 6). The fruit is desirable but forbidden; God creates beauty, but he tantalizes his creatures by denying the desires he has kindled. God is not to be trusted, for he fears the independence of humankind come of age. Eve can judge for herself; she need not take God's word for it.

The folly of Eve and of Adam is apparent. Neither they nor the serpent could create the trees of the garden, nor the beautiful fruit of the tree of knowledge. Far less could they create or even gain access to the tree of life, reserved for the obedient Son of God. Grasping equality with God, they became dupes of Satan, doomed to death — the very separation from God they had presumed to hazard.

But God spared our first parents and their created world, though under a curse. Adam and Eve were driven from the garden, but they were given a promise: God would reverse the relation they had initiated between themselves and the serpent. Enmity would replace alliance; the Son of the woman would crush the head of the serpent and bear the wound of that victory. Even the flaming swords of the cherubim guarding the gate of the garden signaled a promise of hope. There was yet a gate of God on earth; the Lord was present, and his purpose would be accomplished: the tree of life would yet bear fruit for the sons and daughters of Adam and Eve.

The creation that was spared for Adam and Eve was renewed for the family of Noah after the flood. The olive leaf in the beak of the dove and the rainbow set in heaven marked the limit that God set to his judgments. Human wickedness would not bring destruction to this planet until God's full purpose was realized. At the last, God would bring in a new order of transcending glory. That new order was foreshadowed in the pattern of God's tabernacle in the wilderness. There, in the earthly sanctuary that pictured the true and heavenly dwelling of the living God, the flowering almonds of the garden gleamed in gold, and the cherubim no longer guarded the gate with flaming sword but spread golden wings over God's throne of mercy.

To the beauty of the garden and of the temple is added the beauty of the city where God had set his name: "From Zion, perfect in beauty, God shines forth" (Ps. 50:2); "It is beautiful in its loftiness, the joy of the whole earth. . . . Mount Zion, the city of the Great King" (Ps. 48:2). The beauty of the Lord's dwelling anticipates the final blessing of his coming when all will be restored and the curse will be removed.

With the new order will come new life — bounty in nature such that plowmen and reapers will overtake one another (Amos 9:13), and peace in God's mountain such that the wolf will live with the lamb (Isa. 11:6). The destruction that fills a world of sin will cease, and the groaning of creation will end in joy (Rom. 8:22-23). The beauty of God's creation will not end in a wasted planet, but in a renewed world to be described as a garden, a temple, a new Jerusalem come from heaven.

God's revelation of beauty in the physical creation points to the spiritual beauty revealed in his salvation. God's image-bearers are to serve him in the harmony of personal delight, finding joy in his creation, in one another, and above all in the Lord their God. To sinners, God's salvation brings hope for beauty restored. Even the rebellious are not left without signs of God's goodness. The first flowering of culture recorded in the Bible is not in the line of godly Seth, but in the line of fratricidal Cain. Metalworking produces a sword, and with it comes poetry — Lamech's hymn of boastful vengeance. Jubal is the father of all who play the harp and flute (Gen. 4:21).

In Sumerian mythology, the elements of culture are direct gifts of the gods, sometimes by way of the birth of appropriate deities — deities of cattle breeding or plant farming, for example.[7] One poem tells how the city of Erech gained the laws of culture — including the arts, crafts, music, and musical instruments — when its patron goddess Inanna stole them from the god Enki, the lord of wisdom, in his watery abyss.[8] In Genesis, by contrast, culture is a human achievement, for humankind bears God's image. For that reason, humankind in rebellion against God is still capable of cultural and technical triumphs. Cultural success, indeed, became a source of pride. The builders of Babel used their advanced technology in firing clay bricks to build not only a city but also a tower to heaven, a structure designed to accommodate God's descent to their cultic specifications. God did descend, but in judgment. He curbed the unity of rebellion by scattering the nations. That judgment showed divine mercy, for among the scattered peoples God placed his own people to bear his salvation.

Clearly, the Bible does not present God's people as the architects of a bigger and better Babel. Israel did not excel in architecture, painting, or sculpture. Their calling was to the worship and service of God, according to his commandment. When Solomon built the temple that marked the high point of divine blessing, he imported the skills of Tyrian contractors. The temple must excel in beauty to represent the dwelling of God on earth. Israel did not possess the craftsmen capable of such work. At this time, God did not again inspire a Bezalel and Oholiab with his Spirit. Rather, since God is the God of all the earth, and since Solomon's reign of peace raised the witness of Israel before the surrounding nations, it was fitting that the holy house of God should be shaped by the hands of gifted Gentiles. It must be a house of prayer for all nations, gathered in to behold God's glory.

Yet Israel did not lack artistic gifts. God's worship required thankful confession of his saving deeds and praise hymned to his majesty. The art of Israel was the art of narrative, of poetry and song, of reflective wisdom, and of prophetic proclamation. Israel did not leave a treasure of representations of the created world, but of poems brimming over with delight in the beauty of fruitful fields, grazing sheep on the hillsides, and the grandeur of clouds rimmed with light or rolling with thunder.[9] Yet these descriptions

---

7. Claus Westermann, *Genesis 1–11: A Commentary,* trans. J. J. Scullion (Minneapolis: Augsburg, 1984), pp. 26, 27; Samuel N. Kramer, *The Sumerians: Their History, Culture, and Character* (Chicago: University of Chicago Press, 1963), pp. 115, 116.

8. Kramer, *The Sumerians,* pp. 116, 160-62.

9. See Gerhard von Rad, *Old Testament Theology,* vol. 1: *The Theology of Israel's Historical Traditions,* trans. D. M. G. Stalker (New York: Harper & Row, 1962), pp. 364-68.

do not glorify nature; nor are they crafted to draw admiration for the poet. The poetry and history of Israel celebrate the works of the Lord, the God of the covenant. Israel's inspired poets are not delighted with their own delight; their delight is in the Lord. It is this religious center of the life of the people of God (or better, of those whom God raised up to witness to that life) that shapes the understanding of beauty in the Old Testament. Beauty is not comprehended as an abstraction.[10] Yet when the author of the apocryphal book The Wisdom of Solomon speaks of God as the author of the greatness and beauty of creation, he only expresses what the praises of Israel have always declared (Wisd. of Sol. 13:5).

How, then, does the Old Testament present God's revelation with respect to beauty? An extensive vocabulary describes what is perceived to be beautiful, although the terms may often have other nuances and may better be rendered "glory," "majesty," or "pleasantness." Since we are particularly interested in beauty as related to the Lord, we may think especially of terms for beauty related to worship. The dwelling of God with his people in the tabernacle offers a vivid reference point. The Lord's presence was signaled by the cloud of glory that rested over the tabernacle. It was this cloud that led Israel through the wilderness: a pillar of cloud by day and of fire by night. The Lord revealed himself in the beauty of glory, seen in the billowing cloud that filled the viewer with awe.

A second form of beauty displayed at the tabernacle was the beauty of design and craftsmanship: the beauty of the twisted colors in the woven curtains of God's tent, of the gold-embroidered robes of the high priest, of the golden furniture of the holy place. Israel was called to worship the Lord in the "beauty of holiness" (Ps. 29:2; 96:9, KJV); the priests were to enter the holy place in holy array. If the first form of beauty reflected the awesome majesty of the divine presence, the second form reflected the wisdom of the Lord. The craftsmen for the temple were filled with God's Spirit of wisdom for their work (Exod. 31:1-11; 35:30-35).

A third form of beauty may best be expressed by the blessing in the divine name pronounced by the high priest as he emerged from the holy of holies on the Day of Atonement. It is this beauty of delight that draws the Psalmist to desire the courts of the Lord and to yearn for the blessing of God's presence there (see, e.g., Ps. 84:2). The praises of Israel respond to a spiritual beauty of loveliness, the beauty of God's grace.

The terms for beauty in the Old Testament are applied to the Lord and to his deeds. This is clearly true of the first form of beauty, the beauty of glory or of majesty. A term for towering height *(ga'ᵃwāh)* describes the

---

10. von Rad, *Old Testament Theology,* 1:365n.21.

column of smoke that rises from the bolt of God's wrath (Isa. 9:18[17]). In the Song of Moses at the Red Sea, the same root is doubled to describe the towering glory of the Lord: "I will sing to the LORD, for he is *highly exalted*" (Exod. 15:1). The cloud of God's glory had led them to and through the sea and had been a wall of defense against the pursuing chariots of Egypt. "In the greatness of your *majesty* you threw down those who opposed you" (Exod. 15:7). Israel surely had a clear but terrifying image of the transcendent majesty of God. The association of God's majesty with the clouds is frequent in the poetry of the Old Testament: "There is no one like the God of Jeshurun, who rides on the heavens to help you and on the clouds in his *majesty*" (Deut. 33:26; see Ps. 68:32-34). That exalted majesty is so identified with the Lord that he can be said to be "robed in majesty" (Ps. 93:1 = LXX Ps. 92:1: "clothed with beauty").

Alongside the image of the majesty of height and exaltation there is the majesty of light, the splendor of God's glory. Light is naturally associated with the glory-cloud of God's presence. The Lord comes from Sinai and shines forth from Mount Seir (Deut. 33:2). When the Holy One came from Mount Paran, "His splendor was like the sunrise; rays flashed from his hand" (Hab. 3:4). "From Zion, perfect in beauty, God shines forth" (Ps. 50:2). A fire devours before him, and a tempest rages about him. The location of God's splendor on Zion is between the cherubim; from his mercy seat he causes his face to shine upon Israel (Ps. 80:1, 3; 89:15). The brilliance of the Lord's majesty shines in the fire of his judgment as well as in the blessing of his regard (Ps. 94:1). The beauty of God's splendor contrasts with the resplendent beauty that filled the king of Tyre with pride, bringing the judgment by which his own fire consumed him (Ezek. 28:14-19). The Lord's splendor outshines all creation, human or angelic (cf. Job 40:6, 10).

> The sun will no more be your light by day,
>   nor will the brightness of the moon shine on you,
> for the LORD will be your everlasting light,
>   and your God will be your glory.
>
> (Isa. 60:19)

In the Psalms especially, the terms for majestic beauty are blended in praise:

> Honor and majesty are before him;
>   strength and beauty are in his sanctuary.
>
> (Ps. 96:6, RSV and NKJV)

The term *tiph'ārāh* in this verse is well translated "beauty," for the term is often used in that sense, not only to describe beautiful clothing and jewelry (and even the beauty of a carved image — see Isa. 44:13), but also to speak of "glory" in a sense that suggests beauty: the term is used to describe a crown of beauty or glory (Prov. 16:31); Wisdom bestows a "garland of grace" and a "crown of splendor" (*tiph'ārāh*, Prov. 4:9); God's people will be a crown of beauty, a royal diadem in the hand of God (Isa. 62:3); and, conversely, "In that day the LORD Almighty will be a glorious crown, a beautiful wreath for the remnant of his people" (Isa. 28:5).

One may well observe that the use of the many Old Testament terms to describe the glory, majesty, and splendor of the Lord does not parallel our use of the term *beauty*, nuanced as the latter is by Greek idealism and by contemporary aesthetics. The Greek translation of these terms in the Septuagint may be seen as a Hellenizing — intentional or not — of the Hebrew mind. Isaiah and the Psalmists do not think of Yahweh in the image of Apollo. Yet we will miss the force of Israel's praise of the majestic glory of the Lord if we think of it as falling outside our conception of aesthetics; indeed, we would be excluding one of the major dimensions of aesthetic understanding. Trivialized and mannerist art may lose sight of the infinite transcendence that alone can give life ultimate meaning, but the revelation of God's supreme glory presents the reality that cannot be escaped, even when it is suppressed in despairing rage.

The complexity of human response to the divine glory makes art criticism a perilous enterprise, easily exploited by pontificating experts.[11] Visitors to Amsterdam's Stedelijk Museum may have been amazed to learn that Barnett Newman's giant abstraction *Who's Afraid of Red, Yellow and Blue III* was evaluated at $3.1 million. Many presumably saw only a huge panel of carefully blended red paint with a thin blue border on the left. After a vandal slashed it, they may have been the more incredulous to learn that the restorer, Daniel Goldreyer, was paid a fee of $300,000 and then was accused of having done the job with alkyd paint rather than oils and a paint roller instead of a brush.[12] No critic, apparently, was able to detect any difference in the appearance of the restored canvas. Why should this simple abstraction be evaluated so highly? Unless the painting exhibits merely the self-deceived standards of an elitist subculture, the rationale

---

11. Calvin Seerveld rather floridly warns, "Art — doing, viewing, or buying it — *can* make a man a prig, parasite, a nauseating, self-satisfied, elegant bore" (*A Turnabout in Aesthetics to Understanding* [Toronto: Wedge, 1974], p. 11).

12. See the article in *Time*, 6 Jan. 1992, p. 64.

must be found in some sense of the numinous, of sensate splendor, that the painting evokes. In this respect it does not differ from an aching sense that many more people would feel in viewing an Andrew Wyeth painting, one in which the simple form of an open window and a blowing curtain draws one toward the infinite reach of the sky beyond.[13] Wyeth may be viewed as a mere illustrator by many who lack his skill; they may find his paintings to be evocative only of nostalgia. Indeed, these paintings may not be great art — but they are art, not simply exercises in painting, for they speak the language of the ultimate question.

The second aspect of the Old Testament conception of beauty is the beauty of design. This aspect is also drawn into relation with the Lord. The cloud of God's presence soared above the tabernacle in the beauty of majesty, but the tabernacle itself reflected a heavenly pattern that brought together in workmanship the fruitful beauty of Eden (the gold almond blossoms of the lampstand) and the splendor of the angels (the figures woven into the curtains, the gold cherubim on the mercy seat). Terms for glory are used to describe God's dwelling: the radiance of God's presence shines forth from Zion, his holy hill (Ps. 50:2); in the great day of God's glory, the nations will bring in their treasures, and God will beautify his sanctuary with cedars, the glory of Lebanon, along with pine, fir, and cypress (Isa. 60:13).

Personal ornaments of many kinds were worn in the ancient Near East, and the clothing of the high priest was richly decorated.[14] Designs were woven into his apron or skirt ("ephod").[15] The names of the tribes of Israel were engraved on two onyx stones on his shoulder straps, and on precious stones mounted on gold filigree in his breastpiece. The skirt of the ephod was trimmed with yarn pomegranates alternated with bells of gold (Exod. 28:31-35). In the turban of the high priest was a gold plate with the inscription "HOLY TO THE LORD" (Exod. 28:36). While all of these directions are rich in symbolism, express or implied, they also use elaborate artistic skill to make the ceremonial statements. Umberto Cassuto reminds us that in Canaanite legend a god built the temple, and that the qualities there attributed to the deity for the work are here God's gift to his workmen (Exod. 31:1-11).[16] God's gift of wisdom is needed, for the beauty of the

13. Wyeth, *Wind from the Sea* (1947), in *Andrew Wyeth* (Philadelphia: Pennsylvania Academy of the Fine Arts, 1966), no. 25, p. 26.

14. T. C. Mitchell, "Ornaments," in *The Illustrated Bible Dictionary,* ed. J. D. Douglas, part 2, pp. 1121ff.

15. See Umberto Cassuto, *A Commentary on the Book of Exodus* (Jerusalem: Hebrew University, Eng. trans. 1967), pp. 373-74.

16. Cassuto, *Commentary on the Book of Exodus,* p. 402.

tabernacle is *designed*. Bezalel is "to make intricate designs" and then to execute those designs in gold, silver, bronze, gems, and wood carving (Exod. 31:4-5). God himself first plans and then executes his designs (Jer. 33:2); so, too, he calls Bezalel and Oholiab to devise the intricate details that will translate the divine pattern into the metal, gems, fabric, and wood of the tabernacle. Bezalel's inspiration does not produce creative frenzy but reflective design.

God is to be worshiped in the splendor and beauty of holiness, for the rich design of his sanctuary symbolizes his wisdom (Ps. 96:9), wisdom that shows his splendor and beauty in his works of creation and in redemption (Ps. 90:16).

Beyond the awesome brightness of the glory-cloud and the intricate designs of the tabernacle there is a third kind of beauty that the Old Testament traces to the Lord: the beauty of delight. In Psalm 90, that delight is contrasted with the bitter emptiness of life under the curse. Life is but a breath in contrast with God's eternity; under the doom of his judgment, it is a sigh, a moan. A generation is commanded to return to death in the wilderness because God has set their iniquities before him. But to the God who said "Return to dust!" (Ps. 90:3), Moses, the man of God, cries out,

> "Return, O LORD! How long?
>   And have compassion on Your servants.
> Oh, satisfy us early with Your mercy,
>   That we may rejoice and be glad all our days!"
>
> (Ps. 90:13-14, NKJV)

The psalm ends in benediction:

> And let the beauty of the LORD our God be upon us,
>   And establish the work of our hands for us;
>   Yes, establish the work of our hands.
>
> (v. 17, NKJV)

Life in the wilderness, life under the curse, may be transformed by the intervention of God's faithful love. Not only will he give meaning to the work of our hands in a wilderness where no trace remains; he will reveal to our children his glory (*hāḏār*, glory suggesting the beauty of his design), and he will crown us with his own beauty, the loveliness of his grace. The term in verse 17 that the New King James Version renders "beauty" *(nōʿam)* is used to describe the land of Issachar (Gen. 49:15). David applies it to Jonathan in his threnody over the death of his friend (2 Sam. 1:26). In the Song of Songs it describes the beauty of the King's beloved: "How beautiful you are and how pleasing, O love, with your delights!" (Song of Sol. 7:6, where this root is joined with *yāphîh,* another term for physical beauty; see also Ps. 45:11).

The delight evoked by beauty is found in praise to the Lord (Ps. 147:1), because God himself is its source. David cries:

> One thing I ask of the LORD,
>   this is what I seek:
> that I may dwell in the house of the LORD
>   all the days of my life,
> to gaze upon the beauty of the LORD
>   and to seek him in his temple.
>
> (Ps. 27:4)

It is the Lord alone whom the Psalmist seeks, and it is in the Lord that he finds the supreme delight of his life. Here is the heart of Old Testament worship. When God threatened to withdraw his presence from the midst of rebellious Israel, Moses prayed to behold God's glory (Exod. 33:18). God caused not merely his glory but also his goodness to pass before Moses, and he proclaimed his name, the God of grace and faithfulness. God did not withdraw; he would dwell in the tabernacle among his people, that they might delight in his forgiving mercy (Exod. 34:9).

It is this mercy that makes the Lord's presence a delight rather than a devouring flame of holy wrath, so that Moses can make it his crowning blessing: "Let the beauty of the LORD our God be upon us" (Ps. 90:17, KJV).

This psalm, like the conclusion of Deuteronomy, points to the ultimate blessing. After God kept his promises under David and Solomon, and after he brought his judgments on apostate Israel, the blessing of the latter days would come. God would renew the spared remnant of Israel and the nations. In that day every pot in Jerusalem would be like a temple vessel and "HOLY TO THE LORD" would be on the horses' bridles (Zech. 14:20-21). The feeblest citizen of Jerusalem would be like King David. What then of the house of David? "The house of David will be like God, like the Angel of the LORD going before them" (Zech. 12:8). God himself must come to keep his promises.

When God, the true Shepherd of Israel, comes to gather his scattered sheep, the Prince will also come, the Son of David (Ezek. 34:24). The Son to be born will bear the divine names: "Wonderful Counselor, Mighty God, Everlasting Father, Prince of Peace" (Isa. 9:6). David prophetically understands that his Son must be his Lord:

The LORD says to my Lord:
"Sit at my right hand
until I make your enemies
a footstool for your feet."

(Ps. 110:1; cf. Matt. 22:41-46)

The Messianic promise appears in other psalms that celebrate the glory of the Son and King (Pss. 2; 45; 72; 80). It is not surprising that in Psalm 45 the glory of the King is celebrated with terms for beauty; what is suggestive is the parallel with expressions of the divine beauty and glory.[17] The King is "the fairest of the sons of men"; he wears his sword "with glory and majesty" (Ps. 45:2-3, RSV; LXX "in your beauty and your loveliness").

The celebration of the glory of the King as a bridegroom in Psalm 45 is expanded in the symbolism of the Song of Songs. The Song in its erotic poetry is more than a celebration of love. It celebrates the love of the King, whose position is that of the Lord's Anointed. In the pattern of the biblical history of redemption, Solomon, the son of David, is a typical figure, anticipating the fulfillment of God's Messianic promise to David. Since Jesus claimed to be the bridegroom (Mark 2:19; Matt. 25:1; John 3:29; cf. Eph. 5:25), the early church fathers Hippolytus and Origen did not hesitate to find in him the spiritual beauty that his bride, the church, desires.[18]

Reflection on the beauty ascribed to the Lord in the Old Testament points to parallels in the witness of the New Testament to Jesus. In the Transfiguration the beauty of "Majestic Glory" (2 Pet. 1:17) shone from the face and robes of Christ before the cloud appeared (Matt. 17:2). Moses stood on the mountain with him and saw the glory of God, not in a glimpse of his back (cf. Exod. 33:21-23), but in the face of Jesus Christ. Moses' face had shone with borrowed glory when he came down from Mount Sinai (Exod. 34:29), but the face of Jesus shone with his own glory, the glory that he had with the Father before the creation of the world (John 1:14).

The New Testament also presents Jesus in the beauty of holy array. In the book of Revelation he appears among the lampstands of the heavenly sanctuary, belted with gold and robed as the royal Priest (Rev. 1:13). Not

---

17. The Messianic reference of Psalm 45 was recognized in the Targum as well as by the Christian church. See Georg Bertram, "καλός in Christological Statements in the Early Church," in *Theological Dictionary of the New Testament*, 9 vols., ed. Gerhard Kittel and Gerhard Friedrich, trans. Geoffrey W. Bromiley (Grand Rapids: Eerdmans, 1964-74), 3:554; see Heb. 1:8.

18. Bertram, "καλός . . . ," p. 554n.77.

only is he the Son of Man, given eternal dominion by the Eternal; his attributes are those of the Ancient of Days: hair as white as snow, eyes blazing with the fire of the throne (Rev. 1:14; cf. Dan. 7:9, 13-14). The beauty of design in the tabernacle points to the fulfillment of the divine plan in Jesus Christ, who is the Wisdom of God (1 Cor. 1:30; Col. 2:3). God's Spirit of wisdom given to the designers of the tabernacle enabled them to build an earthly sanctuary, like in pattern to the true. Jesus, the Priest of the heavenly sanctuary, bears the Spirit to accomplish the plan that the design of the tabernacle symbolized.

The beauty of divine grace is also found in Christ. The desire of Moses to know God is fulfilled in Jesus. Philip said to him, "Lord, show us the Father and that will be enough for us" (John 14:8). Jesus answered, "Don't you know me, Philip . . . ? Anyone who has seen me has seen the Father. . . . Don't you believe that I am in the Father and the Father is in me?" (John 14:9-10). In the Word become flesh, the grace of the Father is revealed. The divine grace and truth of which Moses wrote has come in Jesus Christ (Exod. 34:6; John 1:14, 16-17).

The "Branch of the LORD" is indeed beautiful and glorious (Isa. 4:2), more than "outstanding among ten thousand" (Song of Sol. 5:10). He is the royal bridegroom to whom the apostle Paul would present the church as a pure virgin (2 Cor. 11:2) in the day when "our eyes will see the king in his beauty" (Isa. 33:17).

The beauty of Christ's grace, however, is a beauty that shines through hideous disfigurement. The grace of the Lord of glory is lifted up at Calvary. Those who see him are appalled: "his appearance was so disfigured beyond that of any man and his form marred beyond human likeness" (Isa. 52:14).

> He grew up before him like a tender shoot,
>   and like a root out of a dry ground.
> He had no beauty or majesty to attract us to him,
>   nothing in his appearance that we should desire him.
> He was despised and rejected by men,
>   a man of sorrows and familiar with suffering.
>
>   (Isa. 53:2-3)

In the history of the Christian church and its art, there has always been tension between conceiving of Christ as handsome in his manhood or hideous in his suffering.[19] Early representations of Christ in the catacombs pictured the Good Shepherd as a beardless youth in the tradition of

---

19. See Bertram, "καλός . . . ," pp. 552-56.

Roman painting. In the Middle Ages, a Gothic Christ showed the agony of suffering. Contemporary illustrators have outdone Sallman in presenting a popular Christ who is not only a handsome Aryan but an advertiser's model: buoyant, vivacious, without a sorrow or care. It is also left to our time for devilish hatred to paint an obscene Christ — not a sin-bearer, but a vile sinner, as corrupt as blasphemy can conceive.

To resolve the tension between our vision of the King in his beauty and the Servant in his agony we may not eliminate either scriptural picture. Rather, we must appreciate the spirituality of the beauty of the Lord. The apostle Peter reminds Christian women that their beauty is not that of braided hair and gold jewelry, but "that of your inner self, the unfading beauty of a gentle and quiet spirit, which is of great worth in God's sight" (1 Pet. 3:3-4). Peter's words apply directly to his conception of the beauty of Christ, whom he had seen and loved. It is the meekness and gentleness of the suffering Christ that Peter holds before the church as the pattern for their living (1 Pet. 2:21). The "inner self" (1 Pet. 3:4; "hidden man of the heart," KJV) is the new creation, united to Jesus Christ, displaying his beauty. New Testament spirituality does not deny the beauty of God's creation, nor does Peter deny that clothing or jewelry can be beautiful. He knew well enough the divine ordering of the jewels of the high priest. The point, rather, is the paradox of the incarnation and of the suffering Savior. Peter's values had been overturned by the cross. He had condemned the purpose of Jesus in going to the cross as shocking folly, but he had found that it was the wisdom of God. The transcendence of God's plan made foolish the wisdom of the world, made useless the power of the world, and made irrelevant the treasures of the world. Human-centered ideals of beauty cannot conceive of a standard that makes the Greek image of Apollo insignificant. The beauty of God revealed in the grace of the cross opens a delight that surpasses all other aesthetic experience as the rising dawn surpasses the shadows it dispels.

THE PEOPLE OF GOD ENJOY HIS BEAUTY

In fellowship with God, we perceive the beauty of the divine fullness. The transcendence, the richness, and the goodness of God's fullness are revealed in the Bible.

The Transcendence of God's Revealed Fullness

The overwhelming majesty of God's glory evokes awe and wonder by its very reality. All worship includes "realization." We recognize the "thereness" of the Almighty Creator. "Hallowed be thy name" is more than a petition that God hallow his name in creation. It desires that God hallow his name in his own being — that he be God. Contemplation of the Lord in awe engages not only reflection and surrender but also the supreme delight of our existence.

God's reality opens for us created reality as well. We wonder at the "thereness" of the world about us. Jean-Paul Sartre has poignantly described the nausea that overwhelmed his character Roquentin as he looked at a stone.[20] The horror was simply that the stone was *there.* He had no relation to it, no control over its existence. It threatened him by its reality. Even the thought of the deep roots of a chestnut tree, unseen and untraced, could awaken the same revulsion. Sartre's insight is profound. The nausea he describes is the horror of unbelief, the dark void that opens with the conviction that God is dead. It is the polar opposite of another emotion: the delight a believer finds everywhere in creation when he or she has come home to God. One of the commonest experiences of a newly converted person is to see as for the first time a tree, a hillside, a flower, or even a stone. Reality triggers joy, for creation points us to the transcendent Creator.

Otto von Simpson describes how the Christian Platonists who inspired the builders of the Gothic cathedrals viewed light. For them physical and spiritual light existed in an unbroken hierarchy of being. "At the basis of all medieval thought is the concept of *analogy.* All things have been created according to the law of analogy, in virtue of which there are, in various degrees, manifestations of God, images, vestiges, or shadows of the Creator. The degree to which a thing 'resembles' God, to which God is present in it, determines its place in the hierarchy of beings."[21]

Analogy is indeed a key to aesthetic experience and is basic to our knowledge of God, but analogy requires difference as well as similarity; if identity is affirmed, and limited only by degree, the Christian doctrine of creation has been exchanged for the hierarchical chain of being in Neoplatonism. The face of a friend will give a newborn Christian more delight than the surface of a stone, but the source of delight in both flows from the experience of living fellowship with God the Creator. It is the transcendence of God's fullness that excites the ultimate awe of a creature

20. Jean-Paul Sartre, *Nausea.*
21. von Simpson, *The Gothic Cathedral: Origins of Gothic Architecture and the Medieval Concept of Order,* Bollingen Series 48 (Princeton: Princeton University Press, 1974), p. 54.

made in his image. The wonder of aesthetic experience echoes the awe found in the presence of God, who is not only One but Three, not only Judge but Savior, not only Lord but Servant.[22]

The Patterns of God's Revealed Fullness

God's fullness becomes the source of beauty in the rich patterns of his revelation. Aesthetic experience is an experience of surprise. We perceive more than we had expected. But the "more" is not just more of the same. Surprise arises because we discern variety in kind, but variety that is linked by analogy, by relation. Classical Greek philosophy long ago perceived that beauty joins diversity in unity. Even the notion of harmony does not fully explain the surprise. The wonder arises as we sense analogy operating across the boundaries of distinct modes of thought and experience. A Bach fugue is full of marvelous surprises as its melodic and rhythmic structures, captivating in their own composition, are also blended contrapuntally to construct fresh harmonies. Yet even the richness of Bach's music gains a new dimension when he designs it to accompany words from the Gospel of Matthew. When those words are sung, yet another dimension is added.

To some extent, all aesthetic experience is multidimensional. To diagram the mere mechanics of a bird's flight or a stag's leap might be an exercise limited to the perspective of physics, but to watch a soaring eagle or a bounding deer is to sense an "extra," a suggestive display of power, ease, and symmetry that far exceeds the plotting of muscle contraction and leveraging.

Calvin Seerveld rightly finds the key to aesthetics in "allusiveness," for without the crossing of boundaries through analogy the discovery distinctive to aesthetic experience would not occur. Since structures of analogy pervade all our experience, affective as well as cognitive, we may chart areas of potential links indefinitely.[23] Neo-Kantian scholar Suzanne Langer has distinguished between presentational and discursive symbolism. The presentational symbolism of a painting offers its message as a whole to an

---

22. Jonathan Edwards held that "the beauty of the divine nature does primarily consist in God's holiness . . . the beauty of his moral attributes," so that delight in God must begin with a delight in his holiness, rather than any other attribute. His point was that there could be no by-passing of the holiness of God in the religious affections, so as to be delighted with his power or goodness without knowing his judgment and salvation. One who knows the holiness of God may then also delight in his power and loveliness (Edwards, *Religious Affections*, ed. John E. Smith [New Haven: Yale University Press, 1959], pp. 256-58).

23. See Wolterstorff's discussion of "fittingness" in relation to left and right placement on a scale of opposites in *Art in Action*, p. 109.

intuitive grasp, but it may also invite sequential analysis. The discursive symbolism of a literary piece marches in linear fashion, yet it may also create a world that becomes intuitively known.

The rich literary art in the Scriptures displays the wealth of allusiveness in which God's revelation is given. Symbolism appears not only in metaphorical language but also in the elaborate patterns of the Old Testament ceremonial cultus. It is also evident in the accounts of redemptive history and in the shaping of redemptive history itself. Design in the pattern of the tabernacle points to the larger design of God's wisdom in his plan for the redemption of sinners.

Just as the majestic glory of God provides the transcendent fullness that alone can explain the deep wonder of profound aesthetic experience, so, too, the wisdom of God is the fountain of our joy in order, in pattern and design. There is more here than the thrill of discovery; there is the sense of ultimate meaning as well as of ultimate power, but there is also the sense of the infinite richness of those patterns of meaning. We may fault Augustine for following the Platonists in reducing the order of aesthetics to mathematical order, although the application of those harmonic principles to Gothic cathedrals remains impressive. Yet Augustine's reflections on measure, on the order of creation, and on time and eternity are continually carried on before the triune God who is the Source of all wisdom and truth.

The Goodness of God's Revealed Fullness

The abounding glory of God overwhelms us with awe; the infinite wisdom of God fills us with amazement; finally, the measureless love of God melts our hearts with delight. Divine beauty would be dreadful in majesty, and threatening in its all-encompassing order, were it not for the sweetness of divine grace. The apostle Peter recalls the cry of the Psalmist: "Taste and see that the LORD is good" (Ps. 34:8; 1 Pet. 2:3). In the experience of divine love the redeemed child of God finds delight that surpasses all human ecstasy.

Not only is the presence of the Lord the pinnacle of all aesthetic delight; it is also that which makes delight possible. Even in a world under the curse, God has not withdrawn the tokens of his goodness, nor has he abandoned the world to the total absence of his goodness that forms hell. Yet the dim and broken awareness of the true delight that remains apart from Christ cannot be compared to the joy that floods our hearts when the Holy Spirit pours out on us the love that God had for us even when we were his enemies (Rom. 5:5).

God himself is the fountain of that delight, as the monks of St. Athos were eager to confess at the end of the first Christian millennium. They sought to prepare for the beatific vision by climbing "Jacob's Ladder" in ascetic discipline, but they knew that only God could open the gates of heaven. Eastern Christian mysticism knew well the rapture of tasting that the Lord is good, but somehow it missed the promise to every believer and forgot that the devotion that responds to grace does not so much seek to gain delight as to give delight to the Lord of grace. The love that is kindled by God's love seeks not its own delight but brings tribute to the Beloved.

The joy of God's love does not draw us away from the world where we serve him. Rather, we taste his goodness in every gift that comes from the Father of lights. Since the fullness of God's love appeared in the gift of his only begotten Son, our response of love turns not only to him but also to his purposes in the world he came to save.

For that reason, our vision of God in the triumph of his grace leads us to a vision of the world as the theater of his redemption. In the worlds of art no less than in the other dimensions of life our calling is to bring glory to the Lord. J. R. R. Tolkien, author of the *Lord of the Rings* trilogy, was once rebuked for writing "escapist" literature. He cheerfully acknowledged that his epic was escapist but observed that the escape he offered was escape from illusion, from a secularist dream world that has lost the distinction between good and evil.

Our aesthetic response to the revelation of the divine beauty must always first be receptive. We are creatures in God's image, and we cannot ignore his revelation in the natural world, nor in the world of human culture that image-bearers construct. Contemporary art is often world-denying and sometimes defiantly world-destroying.

Further, we are stewards in God's covenant. In art we are responsible to God and to others. Art is doxological and ministering. Although art reflects a distinct aspect of human experience, it is not for its own sake. Since the source of aesthetics is in God, art is for his sake. Apart from reference to God, art readily becomes idolatry, an idolatry that can self-destruct into nihilism. Since all Christians are stewards in God's covenant, all are called to a life-style of joy in the revelation of divine beauty. Artistic expression is not an elitist pursuit, encoded for a restricted circle of initiates. It cannot be limited to what we speak of as "the arts," for its root is spiritual and the highest art is the exercise of what Jonathan Edwards called the "religious affections." Gifts in the "arts" vary vastly; highly gifted artists will always find their most appreciative audiences among those who are most familiar with the history and "language" of their world of expression.

Yet every Christian is called to share his or her own vision of God's glory. In art as in theology, gnosticism is unchristian.

Our aesthetic response is also creative. Life-style artistry explores in freedom the richness of styles and of media that are offered in our cultural setting. It has tasted the thrill of allusiveness; it affirms, imagines, explores. The history of Christian hymnody shows that those gifted in God's praise are not always major poets or musicians. Yet the same devotion that delights in a child's praise will be driven to bring to the Lord the best we can offer — better than repetitive incantations or heedless words to half-remembered echoes of musical scales.

When we catch the aesthetic dimension of doing all to the glory of God, we will be sensitive to dress and to etiquette, to house furnishings and flower arranging. Creativity always requires discipline. An artist knows the dialogue of creativity, for in the creative process the limitations and uniqueness of the medium result in a transformation of one's original vision. The ultimate dialogue is the fellowship of the creature with the Creator, found not so much in the display of artistic genius as in a simpler way: Jonathan Edwards walking in the fields in meditation, singing forth his praises to the Lord.

Christ and Culture:
The Christian and the Media

LARRY W. POLAND

MOTHER TERESA sat in the New York television studios of the *Morning Show* for an interview with a man she could see only on a television screen. Malcolm Muggeridge, the man who had taken her to the interview, described the interviewer on the television monitor as a man with "a drooping green moustache, a purple nose and scarlet hair." Muggeridge narrates the dramatic moment that followed as Christ and the media met in a clash of cultures:

> It was the first time Mother Teresa had been in an American television studio, and so she was quite unprepared for the constant interruptions for commercials. As it happened, surely as a result of divine intervention, all the commercials that particular morning were to do with different varieties of packaged food, recommended as being non-fattening and non-nourishing. Mother Teresa looked at them with a kind of wonder, her own constant preoccupation being, of course, to find the wherewithal to nourish the starving and put some flesh on human skeletons. It took some little time for the irony of the situation to strike her. When it did, she remarked, in a perfectly audible voice: "I see that Christ is needed in television studios." A total silence descended on all present, and I fully expected the lights to go out and the floor manager to drop dead. Reality had momentarily intruded into one of the media's mills of fantasy — an unprecedented occurrence.[1]

The Scriptures were written and Jesus taught in a relatively media-free environment. Apart from the oral tradition handed down from genera-

1. Muggeridge, *Christ and the Media* (Grand Rapids: Eerdmans, 1977), pp. 48-49.

tion to generation, word-of-mouth communication of current events, publicly read edicts, primitively hand-produced scrolls, and chiseled stone records, mass media were nonexistent.

Imagine the contrast if Moses, at the foot of Mount Sinai nearly 3,500 years ago, had addressed a couple of million Jews immersed as we are in electronic media. Suppose the television cameras had been rolling as Moses descended to witness the orgies of the Israelites (Exod. 32:15-20). Would the debauchery that angered Moses have been at least partly perpetuated by prime-time television and hard-core pornography on video? Would the dancing and pagan revelry have been stimulated or passed along by MTV? Would the Israelites have been hiding contemporary counterparts to *Playboy, Hustler,* or ten thousand worse titles under the carpets of their tents?

Would Moses have had difficulty getting a hearing for his angry pronouncements because many of his constituents were wearing Walkman cassette players or were tuned to another television channel, as they commonly were seven to nine hours per day? Would the post-golden-calf-destruction commentary by the television news team have featured a psychologist and a liberal Levite pontificating that the action by Moses was merely evidence of his legendarily poor anger management? Would they have been piously calling for sympathy for a man whose adult rage was certainly more the result of the childhood trauma of being abandoned and raised by those who were not his real people than justifiable rage over the violation of Yahweh's righteous law?

Project the current immersion of mass media onto the public ministry of Jesus. How would Christ have handled the constant harassment of television field producers with their minicameras dogging him day in and day out in an effort to record his miracles for skeptical viewers in Judea, Samaria, and the uttermost parts? What would have been our Lord's response to a battalion of investigative reporters trying to prove his miracles fraudulent and relying on the false testimony of "former believers" who had "seen the light" and now were denouncing the professed Son of God as a fake and a phony? What would have been our Lord's response if, while he was traversing the countryside teaching and healing, the big-city theaters were showing a hideously distorted biographical portrayal of his life called *The Last Temptation of the Nazarene,* one that undermined his character and claims?

Malcolm Muggeridge suggests that the media establishment would quite likely have posed the fourth temptation for Jesus. He postulates that a wealthy Roman tycoon passing through Galilee might have heard Jesus teach and observed his spell-binding effect on his audiences. The tycoon might then have tried to get him to come to Rome to enter show biz, with absolute confidence that Jesus would agree. "How could he possibly refuse what would enable him to reach a huge public, right across the Roman Empire, instead of the rag, tag and bobtail lot following him around in Galilee?"[2] Jesus, of course, would reject this fourth temptation as he did the other three.

The question for believers in the media-saturated — some feel media-dominated — world of the twenty-first century is this: What are the temptations and assaults that the church of Jesus Christ faces from the media and how ought they to be handled?

DEFINITION OF TERMS

As preparation for examining this question, let us define some terms. For the sake of this essay I am defining the media as the community of people who control and operate the instruments of mass communication, especially film, television, radio, video and audio recordings, and print — book, newspaper, and magazine publishing. I am excluding reference, somewhat arbitrarily, to other dimensions of the arts, music, theater, and entertainment, except as the people in these fields share common influence with or are part of the power structure of the media, as I have defined the term. I am also excluding those communications industries that do not generate or control the content of messages but merely convey the messages of others — entities such as telephone, satellite, cable, facsimile, and computer industries.

I am taking the liberty of using *media,* which is a plural of *medium,* as a singular, collective noun when referring to the broad community of media establishments, and as a plural when describing the many forms of communication that make up the broad community. For the sake of simplicity, I am lumping together several industries into a "media community" whose leaders would vehemently object to being tied to other components of what is actually a very diverse family of communities.

This working definition of the media focuses on the *people* who control and operate the media, rather than on the *instruments* of mass communication, for the simple reason that I view the instruments to be morally and spiritually neutral. I do not subscribe, for example, to theories like those reportedly advanced by some well-meaning believers at the advent of radio and television that these media are inherently evil instruments because they pass through the air, and Lucifer is the "prince of the

2. Muggeridge, *Christ and the Media,* p. 41.

power of the air" (Eph. 2:2, RSV). Since people and power structures of the world system are not morally and spiritually neutral, these constitute the focus of my attention in this discussion.

DISTINCTIVE ATTRIBUTES OF CURRENT MEDIA INFLUENCE ON BELIEVERS

The strangeness of my earlier illustrations of Moses and Jesus dealing with the pressures of the media was due in large part to the anachronism of a technological feature in a pre-technology culture. In this regard, the influence of media on the moral and spiritual climate of a civilization is distinctive from most other influences. Pick any one of a hundred phenomena with which we struggle in modern life, and you will find that in both Old and New Testaments believers struggled with the same phenomenon, even if in somewhat different form. Issues dealing with war, adultery, violence, heresy, greed, prostitution, exploitive relationships, thievery, murder, covetousness, idolatry, or sexual perversion in our society have direct counterparts in Scripture. But where are the references to the unique impact of the mass media on godly values? Where are the narratives describing or the instructions warning about how the human heart can be enslaved by the enemies of our souls through exposure to satanically inspired rock music or the vicarious sexual experiences we may share through film, television, or sexually explicit literature?

Scripture provides guidance in dealing with these challenges only by principle or by extrapolation. For example, if King David was tempted to adultery by viewing a naked beauty from his rooftop (2 Sam. 11), we can infer that viewing such a sight in a film, on television, or in print might also be dangerous to one's moral purity and marital fidelity, even if the object of the lustful covetousness is far less accessible.

A second distinctive feature of media-related spiritual and moral issues is that they are of very recent origin. If we assume that the age of humankind is in the *thousands* of years — to say nothing of those who believe that *millions* of years would be a more appropriate definition — mass media–related issues have been with us for only a tiny fraction of human history. Through personal research I arbitrarily identified thirty-six inventions that I feel have made present mass communication possible — inventions such as the moveable type press, the telegraph, the transatlantic cable, photography, the typewriter, the telephone, the phonograph, the motion picture, audio recording, radio, television, etc. I discovered that all of them but one, Gutenberg's press, were invented within the last 155 years! The recency of mass communication means that it is providing new challenges to the church of Jesus Christ, challenges never before faced.

A third feature that makes media-related moral and spiritual issues distinctive is the proximity to evil that the media now make possible for believers. There was a time when, if you were to see a prostitute, you had to travel to a part of the community in which prostitutes operated. Not so now with television. For most of human history in most cultures, to see a naked body you would have to invade the privacy of another human being or be admitted to a private situation in which nudity was entertainment. Not so now with videos, pornography, and cable television. If you wanted to carry on a sexually explicit conversation with an immoral person, you would have to find a person with those values and establish enough of a relationship to share intimate talk of this kind. Not so now with so-called phone sex.

From time immemorial, if you were to see a person brutally killed, you would probably have to enter some kind of mortal combat such as warfare or travel to view gladiatorial games. Not so now with "R" rated movie channels on television and "reality" news programs. To observe a sex act, you would probably have to be a participant in it; and perverse sex acts were nearly impossible to view, even for the more determined. Not so now with "adult" videos and magazines. If you desired instruction in violence, sexual perversion, or occult practices, it would have been difficult to acquire. Not so now with "uncensored" bookstores and libraries. For the first time in the history of the human race, most of these evils are as close as the walls of our own homes, and certainly not more distant than a few blocks or miles.

Moreover, for the first time in the history of the Christian faith these evils have invaded the homes and personal environs of believers. Followers of Christ now have nearly the same access to these evils *without pursuing them* as the most morally perverse unbelievers who pursued them aggressively in the past. The mass media have made these evils nearly omnipresent in our society. The late Rev. Morton Hill, founder of Morality in Media, made this point by declaring of pornography, "It's no longer downtown; it's downstairs."[3]

Lest the reader get the impression that this essay is merely an exercise in media bashing, let me affirm my appreciation for the spectacular benefits offered to us by the media. I appreciate the expansion of global awareness;

---

3. Hill, cited in Jerry R. Kirk, *The Mind Polluters* (New York: Thomas Nelson, 1985), p. 31.

the insights into other cultural, educational, social, and political arenas; the benefits of wholesome entertainment and inspirational programing; and the marvelous ability to communicate messages instantly and globally.

I have not missed the fact that it is due to the marvelous advances of media technology that this may well be the generation in which the Great Commission of our Lord is fulfilled. It is, after all, the era in which reportedly one out of every three of the world's inhabitants saw or heard part of the most recent Olympic games. It is the era in which the most widely translated and widely viewed motion picture in the history of film-making is the film *Jesus*. It is the era in which Christian short-wave broadcasting layers the earth with the gospel many times over. In America alone, the church operates 322 Christian television stations and 1,350 Christian radio stations.[4]

I see the value of these vehicles for propagating God's Word, and I do not wish to return to the state of communication in the seventeen or eighteen hundreds. Rather, my purpose is to identify dynamics of the media that cause significant conflict with the person, message, and work of Jesus Christ. By my definition, the media is the *community of people* who control and operate the instruments of mass communication. It is this community's values and evangelistic zeal for an anti-Christian worldview that draw me into an adversarial relationship with much of the media. So, without apology, I will make this conflict my focus.

THE CONFLICT

Exposure and Experience vs. Innocence

Building on my assertion that the media have brought evil closer to the believer than it has ever been before, I now observe the first face-off between the media and biblical values, the media's assault on innocence. God's Word places an extremely high value on innocence. Its pursuit is a virtue and its retention is a command. The media, on the other hand, exult in exposés, revelations, titillations, and innocence-stealing probes into the bizarre world of even the most perverse sinners. A glance at the themes and lists of guests on daytime talk shows for any given month will document this point. Favorite expressions of the media community are "Don't knock it if you haven't tried it" and "How can you criticize something you

---

4. *The Directory of Religious Broadcasting,* 14th international ed. (Parsippany, NJ: National Religious Broadcasters, 1991), p. 10.

haven't even seen?" This reinforces the media's high value on "experiencing" and "seeing" things — however debauched or impure — as a prerequisite for making moral judgments.[5]

In his wise counsel to Philippian believers, the apostle Paul sets biblical guidelines that bear on the believer's media consumption. Things that are true, noble, right, pure, lovely, admirable, excellent, and praiseworthy are to be the focus of the faithful Christian's thinking and reckoning (Phil. 4:8). This directive obviously eliminates the false, ignoble, unrighteous, impure, unlovely, despicable, mediocre, and damnable, declaring them unsuitable for the Christian's consumption and meditation. Yet much of the content of contemporary media fits one or more of the adjectives from this latter list. God directs his people to "set before [their] eyes no vile thing" (Ps. 101:3). Obedience on this point ensures a wonderful innocence about evil. We must remember that Noah's son Ham was cursed, it appears, both for his lack of respect for his father and for his intentional surrender of innocence in viewing Noah's "nakedness" (Gen. 9:20-27). His brothers, more discreet and virtuous, approached their father backwards with a garment to cover him, thus guarding their innocence (Gen. 9:23). The apostle Paul puts to death the communication philosophy of tabloid journalism and daytime talk shows by declaring that it is "shameful even to mention what the disobedient do in secret" (Eph. 5:12). If this injunction were obeyed by the media, it would kill a whole genre of television and radio programs and all the supermarket tabloids!

In response to this assault on Christians' innocence, the church has no alternative but to develop more aggressive strategies for protecting innocence, especially the innocence of children, through (1) moral suasion of those seeking to steal it, (2) aggressive defensive action — even legal action — against unbelievers who are undermining it, and (3) tighter management of media consumption in the Christian home. This last defense certainly cannot coexist with the "there-was-only-one-scene-that-was-bad" argument I hear articulated even by the leadership of the church in describing the moral content of media products they have consumed. Is anyone less dead if he or she takes poison in a series of small doses rather than in one large dose?

---

5. The media used this argument to powerful advantage against believers who protested the release and distribution of *The Last Temptation of Christ* by Universal Pictures in August of 1988. See my book *The Last Temptation of Hollywood* (Redlands, CA: Mastermedia International, 1988), pp. 148-70, for documentation of this point.

The Increasing Influence of the Media in Defining Truth

There is one grand foundation on which the Christian life and message rests. It is the ultimate, comprehensive, and objective truth that expresses the character of God (John 3:33), is personified by Jesus (John 14:6), and liberates every human who accepts it and applies it (John 8:32). The tragedy of unregenerate men and women is that they, like Pontius Pilate, lose sight of the lighthouse of ultimate, objective truth and are dashed to pieces on the rocks of their own off-course notions and values.

The character of our Savior is glorious in that he never departed in the slightest from truth, faithfulness, and integrity in his relationship with the Father or in his relationships with others. There was never the slightest confusion in his mind between what was real and what was illusory, between what met the test of universal truth and what was idolatrous and sham. Conversely, the disaster of humankind is epitomized in the words of Saint Paul describing the mortal stage in human devolution: "They exchanged the truth of God for a lie" (Rom. 1:25).

Probably in no other generation has such a small contingent of people had such enormous influence in shaping a culture's definitions of truth and error, right and wrong, purity and impurity — even reality and unreality — as does the media establishment in America today. My assertion that this is a *small* group is based on eleven years of working with professionals in film and television in Hollywood and New York and at least three years of research to identify the power brokers who control these two media. Originally I estimated that seven hundred people control three-fourths of film and television. After research to identify those individuals by name, my organization's staff reduced that number to about five hundred.

Admittedly, if one includes the power brokers of every local broadcast entity and print periodical, adds the leadership of cable television outlets and magazines, and digs deeper into these structures to the functionary level, the number can climb into the thousands or tens of thousands. Even so, we are talking about a number that is between one thousandth and one ten thousandth of the United States population. This tiny minority controls the content and messages of the ubiquitous media. This micro-society chooses what we see and what we don't, determines the character of the people portrayed as heroes and goats, puts the laugh tracks on content it thinks should be funny, gives world events the "spin" it wants them to have, and filters out spiritual realities that do not fit their worldview. They even create pseudo-news "media events" that would not be "reality" (that is, wouldn't exist) if the media were not there to cover them.

The influence of the media can be measured in a number of ways. If we assume that people are influenced by the messages they see and hear (an assumption that billions of dollars of advertising money supports), the media are influential in that they captivate the American public's attention so much of the time — between seven and nine hours each day through television and videos alone. That is the amount of time the television set is on each day in the typical home, with each person averaging four hours of actually watching it![6] This means that, to some extent, those who program television are helping to decide what Americans in nearly every age bracket *think about,* if not what they actually *think,* for several hours daily. Television viewing has become the second most time-consuming activity of Americans (after sleep). Even third graders spend an average of 1,170 hours per year watching television, while they spend only 900 hours per year in school.[7]

But the influence of the media in moral and spiritual terms can be better measured, I believe, in the extent to which they have been successful in redefining truth. C. S. Lewis's elder devil Screwtape counsels novice demon Wormwood:

> Think of your man as a series of concentric circles, his will being the innermost, his intellect coming next, and finally his fantasy. You can hardly hope, at once, to exclude from all the circles everything that smells of the Enemy: but you must keep on shoving all the virtues outward till they are finally located in the circle of fantasy, and all the desirable qualities inward into the Will.[8]

The prince of darkness has used the media to push God's truth from Lewis's inner circle of "the Will" outward to the "circle of fantasy" in this culture. Commonly today, a person who espouses absolute moral standards, questions the notion of a woman's "reproductive right to choose," challenges the rightness on a moral plane (or even the wisdom on a practical plane) of homosexual or lesbian behavior, opposes the taking of sacred life from a terminally ill patient (or from one whose "quality of life" is not to his or her liking), or condemns the horrors of pornography is viewed by the media as having all the credibility of the Tooth Fairy. Such a person assuredly must be an illegal alien from Fantasyland!

I have taken the liberty of substituting "the media" for "history" in Herbert Schlossberg's summary of the present state of morality:

6. S. Robert Lichter, Stanley Rothman, and Linda S. Lichter, *Watching America* (New York: Prentice Hall, 1991), p. 3.

7. Advertisement for Texas Instruments in *Time,* 1 Apr. 1991, p. 27.

8. Lewis, *The Screwtape Letters* (New York: Macmillan, 1960), p. 37.

In the late twentieth century, bereft of the biblical limitations by a generation that has turned away from Christian faith, [the media] pursues its mad career, running amuck with saviors making rules that they crown with divine status. [The media] thus dechristianized has no moral limitations. "Right" is a moving target, propelled by the march of facts and sentiments. Theft, homosexuality, pornography, genocide, and torture were wrong yesterday, but tomorrow who can say? . . . A society that cannot tolerate a judge beyond history will find that it can tolerate anything else.[9]

This state of being could never have occurred if the church had been aggressive in proclaiming, teaching, evangelizing, and discipling the populace and the younger generation in the truth of God's Word. Americans not only get most of their news from television; they also get a significant percentage of their convictions about truth and error from the media. The mandate for the church in the face of this increasing "redefinition of truth" by the media, which is really a proselytizing to lies, is to proclaim — as God's prophets always have — "Thus saith the Lord!"

The Media's Assault on the Means of Spiritual Growth

There are certain disciplines of the Christian life that are indispensable for the person who pursues a love relationship with the Savior; they are absolute essentials for Christian growth and maturity. These disciplines are undermined or destroyed by the media in its attempts to fulfill its objectives. Like a jealous husband who is furious at someone attempting to seduce his wife, one would think that believers would burn with indignant rage at attempts to impair or steal the deep and intimate relationship they enjoy with their Beloved (as in Prov. 6:32-36). On the contrary, it seems that many believers, like the foolish youth in Proverbs, take the fire of the media into their bosoms and expect not to be burned (Prov. 6:27).

And what are these disciplines of faith that the media so effectively undermine? First, there is the freedom of the mind and spirit to communicate with the Beloved, freedom resulting from the absence of other distractions. C. S. Lewis declares that it is easy to avoid God in our time and place:

> Avoid silence, avoid solitude, avoid any train of thought that leads off the beaten track. Concentrate on money, sex, status, health and (above all) on your own grievances. Keep the radio [and television] on. Live in

9. Schlossberg, *Idols for Destruction* (Nashville: Thomas Nelson, 1983), p. 37.

a crowd. Use plenty of sedation. If you must read books, select them very carefully. But you'd be safer to stick to the papers [and magazines]. You'll find the advertisements helpful; especially those with a sexy or a snobbish appeal.[10]

Prayer, worship, meditation, praise, thanksgiving, and petition all require one precondition — freedom of the mind and spirit from distractions of the world, the flesh, and the devil. One can receive no guidance, acquire no peace or assurance, admit no instruction, and bear no rebuke or correction unless the mind and spirit are freed sufficiently from the voices of the world to hear the voice of God. While the prime condition for these dynamics of the Christian walk is solitude, to some extent they may be acquired "on the run" if the environment is sufficiently free from noise, or if the decibel level of the noise is low enough to hear the whisper of the still, small voice above it.

This is one point at which the media war against our souls. If a human mind is not involved in processing (1) the commercial messages that support the medium or (2) the content that is designed to keep that mind "locked on" until the next commercial message, that mind is — to the media — unproductive. And when a dollar is to be made (in the words of a television public service message), "a mind is a terrible thing to waste."

But God has prioritized those things that are of transcending value: "The world system is in the grip of obsolescence with its entire bag of superficial desires, but doing the will of God never goes out of style."[11] Certainly few believers would deny that God wants his children to pursue the benefits of faith just listed — prayer, worship, meditation, praise, thanksgiving, petition, guidance, peace, assurance, instruction, rebuke, and correction. But honest believers must admit that these spiritual pursuits are nearly impossible in a society in which even many believers are incurable "mediaholics." They stay tuned to one or more forms of the media from rising to bedtime. They carry media with them to former sanctuaries of silence like the beach and the woods. They strap media to their sides and to their ears during recreation and exercise. They furnish their homes with more instruments of the media than toilets, as if the former were more necessary to life functions than the latter.[12]

As believers in Christ permit it, the noise of the media drowns out

10. Lewis, "The Seeing Eye," in *Christian Reflections,* ed. Walter Hooper (Grand Rapids: Eerdmans, 1967), pp. 168-69; bracketed words added.

11. Free paraphrase of 1 John 2:17.

12. For an expansion of the concept and functional definition of a "mediaholic" see my booklet *Profile of a Mediaholic* (Redlands, CA: Mastermedia International, 1986).

all meaningful conversation with their Lord, all meditation, all devotional thought and communication. This deafening cacophony is the objective of hell's minions. In the words of Screwtape, all of space and time in hell has been occupied by noise: "Noise, the grand dynamism, the audible expression of all that is exultant, ruthless, and virile — Noise which alone defends us from silly qualms, despairing scruples, and impossible desires. We will make the whole universe a noise in the end."[13]

A second assault on the means of spiritual growth by the media is the offensive against righteous, interpersonal communication, Spirit-based fellowship, and loving interaction. Charles Colson decries the radical individualism in our culture and the extent to which the media have contributed to making us isolated passive receptors. He describes much of the church as "sofa-loads of expressive individualists reclining in their living rooms, nibbling chocolates and reveling in TV-induced tears, testimony and titillation."[14] To the extent that this portrayal is true, it is tragic, since the life of the Christian is sustained through intimate, spiritual interaction in the body of Christ and through the burden-bearing that comes from deep, interpersonal communion (Heb. 10:25; Gal. 6:2). In particular, Christian family relationships should be characterized by Spirit-filled, harmonious communication, praise-and-thanks-filled interaction, joyful prayer, and mutual submission to one another (Eph. 5:15–6:4).

Most followers of Christ fail to appreciate the success of the enemy in shutting down interpersonal communication in the family and in the small group through the media. I remember years ago making a home call for the church I was attending, a call to deal with some very serious situations in the family. The host and hostess welcomed my friend and me at the door and offered us a seat in the living room, in which also sat the blaring television set. I can still recall my growing frustration as we tried to carry on serious conversation with family members who not only did not turn off the television set but did not even turn down the volume. One of the children ignored us completely, and the adults regularly glanced past us at the television in an obvious effort to pick up snatches of the programing as well as bits and pieces of our conversation. When it was time to leave and it was suggested that we have prayer, our hosts still made no effort to kill the television. Stunned, I asked if it would be possible to turn off the set so that we could pray. After giving me a disgruntled, nonverbal response, the host directed the child to turn it down, not off. While I kept my eyes closed during the prayer, I wouldn't bet a lot of money that the

---

13. Lewis, *Screwtape Letters*, pp. 113-14.
14. Colson, *Against the Night* (Ann Arbor: Servant Books, 1989), p. 103.

family members did. Our request clearly was an offense. We were interfering in the family's relationship, not with each other, but with the media.
And *that* relationship took precedence.

Few believers recognize that the media have created instruments that
demand attention — even at the expense of attention to the human beings
in our lives, and regardless of the content being communicated. Even before
the age of television, Henry David Thoreau understood this danger: "We
are in great haste to construct a magnetic telegraph from Maine to Texas;
but Maine and Texas, it may be, have nothing important to communicate."[15]
Thoreau understood that once the telegraph was constructed its mere availability would demand that communication be carried on. He knew that
every communication medium is designed and empowered to create its
own definition of discourse and will engage someone regardless of the
content of the communication. Computer bulletin boards and citizen band
radios are filled with people communicating useless drivel just to speak,
hear, and be heard.

The compelling power of television, the queen of the media — or
perhaps I should say "whore," since that is the ultimate exhibitionist — is
that it *demands* to be watched. This should be understandable to Bible-
believers, since God has told us that "the eye never has enough of seeing"
(Eccles. 1:8). The television image offers more than three million dots per
second, of which the viewer is able to accept only a few dozen.[16] Every
3.5 seconds or less (usually less) the image is changed, demanding attention
to the new image.[17] So, rapid new image by rapid new image, television
seduces its viewers to keep watching lest they miss something — again,
regardless of the content.

An entire culture of believers and unbelievers alike has become more
or less addicted to watching television. I have seen no study that indicates
that there is any statistically significant difference in the number of hours
of television watched or in the types of programs watched between those
who profess to be Christians and those who do not.

The consequence of this phenomenon is that homes with one or more
television sets have one or more rooms in which no significant, quality,
interpersonal communication takes place among family members when the
set is on. Add to television the radios, stereos, compact disc players, and
periodicals in the home, and the "static" from the world system via the

15. Thoreau, *Walden* (Boston: Houghton Mifflin, 1957), p. 36.
16. Marshall McLuhan, *Understanding Media: The Extensions of Man* (New York:
McGraw-Hill, 1964), p. 273.
17. Neil Postman, *Amusing Ourselves to Death* (New York: Penguin, 1988), p. 86.

media can jam all spiritual communication lines. Interpersonal sharing can become an irritant because it interferes with one's involvement with the media ("Leave me alone! I'm *trying* to watch this program!"). This is why some family psychologists recommend never putting a television set in a room where intimate communication commonly takes place, such as the dining room or the bedroom.

A further consequence is that young people from the mass media/television/video generation seem to be incapable of creating meaningful social interaction in small groups without the crutches offered by the media. Blaring sound recordings and/or fast-paced videos or television are the sine qua non of social events, even in many church groups. "Having a party of friends in? Rent a video!" seems to be the firmly established pattern. Charles Colson declares:

> It's significant to note how television, the most popular mass medium of our day, reflects and reinforces individualism. Through brief, loosely connected sensations that play on temporary but vivid emotion, television thoroughly engages an audience of one, making personal relationships unnecessary.[18]

The church must respond to this media threat with stronger exhortations to heads of homes and heads of groups to manage and restrict media consumption so that it does not stifle the very processes that sustain spiritual life. Furthermore, the church must provide tools — seminars, classes, practical materials such as how-to guides, checklists, and other materials, and accountability systems — for lay leadership, parents, and youth so that nothing is left to the imagination as to how to protect believers from the corrosive effects of media on Christian and family values.

The Media's Success in Disarming the Guardian of the Believer's Spirit

The Scriptures are clear that all believers have a sacred duty to station a guard at the entrance to their spirit to protect themselves from attacks by the enemies of the soul. Like a sentry in wartime, under no circumstances must this guard be permitted to sleep. In Proverbs we are told that "discretion will protect you, and understanding will guard you" (Prov. 2:11); we are also told to guard the instruction we have received, "for it is your life" (Prov. 4:13), and "above all else, guard your heart, for it is the wellspring of life" (Prov. 4:23).

18. Colson, *Against the Night*, p. 40.

Jesus often exhorted his followers to be on their guard against the enemies of Christ (Matt. 10:17), against false prophecies (Mark 13:22-23, 33), against sins such as greed (Luke 12:15), and against the hypocrisy and carnality of corrupt religious leaders (Matt. 6:5, 16). The apostle Paul commands believers to be on their guard and to stand firm in the faith (1 Cor. 16:13). Biblical prohibitions against everything from divination and occult practices to drug use, from drunkenness to the careless use of spiritual gifts, are designed to keep the guard at the door of our spirits vigilant and active.[19] Anything that results in a surrender of control of the believer's spirit (which is to be under the control of the Holy Spirit) to any substance or alien spiritual influence is lethal to the Christian. With these thoughts as a backdrop, the potential dangers of the media take on a new light.

In his book *Four Arguments for the Elimination of Television,* Jerry Mander cites research that indicates that the interaction between the television screen and the viewer is such that it frequently bypasses the viewer's consciousness. In 1975 a team of researchers at the Center for Continuing Education, Australian National University at Canberra, delved into the neurophysiology of television viewing.[20] The researchers concluded that very little cognitive, recallable, analyzable, thought-based learning takes place while watching television:

> The evidence is that television not only destroys the capacity of the viewer to attend, it also, by taking over a complex of direct and indirect neural pathways, decreases vigilance, the general state of arousal which prepares the organism for action should its attention be drawn to [a] specific stimulus. . . . The continuous, trance-like fixation of the TV viewer is then not attention but distraction.[21]

The researchers went on to report that the human response to the repetitive light-stimuli of television viewing (flickering light, dot patterns, limited eye movement), accompanied by a static physical state, causes "habituation." In this state the left brain's "common integrative area" goes into a kind of holding pattern, and viewing "is at the conscious level of somnambulism."[22] Mander concludes: "if the [researchers] are correct, . . . then television information enters unfiltered and whole, directly into the memory

19. See 1 Cor. 14:31-33. Even in the exercise of spiritual gifts, the spirit of the one using the gift is to be subject to that person alone as opposed to entering an altered state of consciousness or spiritual control that might give entry to seducing spirits.

20. Mander, *Four Arguments for the Elimination of Television* (New York: William Morrow and Company, 1978), p. 205.

21. Mander, *Four Arguments,* p. 206.

22. Mander, *Four Arguments,* pp. 206-7.

banks, but is not available for conscious analysis, understanding, or learning. It is sleep teaching."[23]

I can personally attest to a mental, physical, and spiritual numbness that overtakes me during long periods of watching television, even when viewing content that should be stimulating and exciting — like New Year's Day parades and football games. I have noted that I experience similar subconscious effects from long periods of listening to secular music and viewing secular films as well — feelings of spiritual dullness and lifelessness.

Far worse, I have caught myself (1) picturing impure or lascivious scenes — and fantasizing about them — from movies or magazines I viewed decades ago, and (2) singing lyrics to songs that I never intentionally learned and would declare that I do not know, songs that contain moral and philosophical messages I despise for their contradiction to God's Word and God's ways. Through the media, thoughts and ideas, images and visions have entered my subconscious mind that are destructive to my soul's health and well-being.

Not only do the media get their content past the guard and into the minds of Christians through subconscious communication; they are also relentless and persuasive instructors in paganism at the conscious level. I remember hearing a former commissioner from the Federal Communications Commission declare, "All television is educational television. The question is merely, 'What is it teaching?'"

Since television, radio, newspapers, and magazines are commercial enterprises in this country, they are almost totally underwritten by the advertising dollars of people trying to sell goods or services to the clients of each medium. As a result of this reality, the dominant message and motivation of the media is consumerism. Where no legitimate human need exists, a need is "created" in order to sell products and services. One analyst insists that advertising exists *primarily* to purvey things human beings do not need, for if people really did have a basic human or survival need for such things, they would surely find them with or without advertising![24]

Ben Stein, in his classic work *The View from Sunset Boulevard,* makes it clear that there are other messages being given once the "Buy! Buy! Buy!" message is uncompromised.[25] His research into the media observed "uncanny homogeneity" in the values of media's elite, and he identified a body of

---

23. Mander, *Four Arguments,* p. 207.
24. Mander, *Four Arguments,* pp. 126-27.
25. Stein, *The View from Sunset Boulevard* (Garden City, NY: Anchor Press/Doubleday, 1980).

common perspectives coming through media, many of which are in opposition to biblical truth. Here is a sampling of some of those common perspectives:

- high-level police are bungling and corrupt, but a few rare heroes at lower levels do exist;
- rebels — whether kids, students, cops, private investigators, or feminists — are heroes;
- businesspeople are hard, evil people, and those from big business are the worst;
- most crime is violent and is committed among whites rather than among poor ethnics, where in real life a disproportionate amount of crime is committed;
- responsibility for crime is seldom placed on the criminal and is more commonly placed on "society" or the "evils in society";
- military officers are stiff, hypocritical, impressed with their own importance, and bungling;
- the rich are superficially lovely but scheming and unhappy people who will stop at nothing to exercise their affluent power;
- ministers are sinister, hypocritical, or benignly harmless but irrelevant figures;
- sexual activity is beautiful, desirable, morally neutral, and acceptable, with few, if any, restraints;
- religion is a non-issue in life and is essentially irrelevant.[26]

Stein makes a point that I can support from twelve years of working with media leaders in Hollywood and New York: these views come through media content because they *are* the personal views of media's producers, writers, and executives who control the creative processes. Jesus declared, "Out of the overflow of the heart the mouth speaks" (Matt. 12:34). We could apply that to media: "Out of the overflow of the heart a person writes, produces, directs, and creates media products."

The danger for the media-immersed Christian is that he or she unconsciously begins to tolerate and then to embrace the values of the media, which are commonly at odds with those of the typical American and deeply opposed to biblical values.[27] To protect itself, the Christian church must

26. Most of these statements summarize the contents of individual chapters in Stein's book. Therefore no page numbers are given.

27. For two fine studies on the extent to which the values of the media's power brokers are dissimilar from those of the average American and in conflict with those of the biblical Christian, see S. Robert Lichter, Stanley Rothman, and Linda S. Lichter, *The Media Elite* (Bethesda, MD: Adler and Adler, 1986), and also their book *Watching America*.

reduce the quantity of media consumed and increase the moral quality of the content of the media that is consumed. Furthermore, it is essential that parents raise their children with a low view of media consumption as a legitimate leisure-time activity and that they teach them how to discern the messages of the media and the biblical response to those messages.

DEALING WITH THE MEDIA AS A COMMUNITY OF PAGAN PEOPLE

Christians must deal with the media as people — pagan people. Pagan they are: ninety-three percent seldom or never attend a religious observance of any kind, and they are significantly less likely to pray or read sacred writings than the general populace.[28] My initial definition of "media" focused on the community of people who control and operate the media, not on instruments, technologies, or even messages. People are behind the media; therefore, a change in the values of the people who run the industry would result in dramatic changes in the content, values, messages, styles, and responsibility taken by various segments of the media. When one is confronted with such an all-pervasive, powerful, and pagan influence in our society and in the church, three stratagems become possible.

The first stratagem is the mobilization of aggressive, national response and protest to hold the media leadership accountable for what they do, to raise a standard of righteousness in society and in the media, and to pressure the media to change its content in the direction of this standard. A host of political and moral action groups and organizations have chosen this approach.

While I believe there is a clear biblical mandate for proclaiming God's law and "seasoning" society with the salt of Christian values, I also believe that, by themselves, these efforts will fail. The media are restrained by protest and boycott efforts only so long as the pressure from those efforts is sufficiently irritating, costly, or problematic to cause them to alter their decisions. The minute the pressure lets up or the level of difficulty for the media drops to that of a minor irritation it reverts to "business as usual." Furthermore, there are some segments of the media that, because of structural diversity, are virtually untouchable by this stratagem; the film industry, the music industry, and the pornography industry are the best examples.

One day as I sat in the office of a network vice president he very casually announced that his company had just received 250,000 cards from a Christian organization protesting its program content. When I asked him

28. Lichter, Rothman, and Lichter, *Watching America*, p. 14.

what effect that campaign had had on his network, he indicated, "Not much. One letter from a responsible person like you whom we know and trust would do more good." Clearly the campaign had had very little effect; no program changes were made. The largest and most broadly based Christian protest in the history of film or television, the conflict over the film *The Last Temptation of Christ*, makes the point. While achieving stunning successes in other areas, the protest did not keep that film or other equally evil films from being produced and released.

A second stratagem is that of establishing a "Christian media industry" to harness the potential power of the technology for kingdom objectives and to compete with the secular media power structure with redemptive motivations and products. A multibillion dollar industry has arisen in Christian radio and television broadcasting, program production, cable and direct broadcast linkups, Christian and "crossover" music, and Christian bookselling. While there is biblical warrant for proclaiming good news by every means possible, these "Christian media industries" have not made a significant dent in the power, values, or content of the secular media establishment, which continues to hold a virtual monopoly. By some media trade estimates, all of Christian television reaches less than four percent of the nation's television viewers, and these are largely within the Christian fold. Similar statistics could probably be mustered for the Christian radio, music, and bookselling industries.

Furthermore, the elite of the "Christian media" have often perpetuated such strange, irrelevant, or subculturally distinctive stereotypes of Christianity that nationally they have been more the object of ridicule than of serious consideration or influence. Add to this the exploitable corruption of a handful of Christian media leaders, and it becomes clear that this stratagem is not going to have significant impact on the secular media power structures. In fact, in the national survey that became the basis for the book *The Day America Told the Truth*, televangelists ranked third from the bottom in the category "Americans grade professions for honesty and integrity" — between organized crime boss and prostitute![29]

Charles Colson has little respect for the nature of the Christian media. He judges that

> the church has been crippled from within by an invasion of barbarian values and habits. Nowhere is this more evident than in the electronic church, where lavish ministries compete for audience share and viewer

---

29. James Patterson and Peter Kim, *The Day America Told the Truth* (New York: Prentice-Hall, 1991), p. 144.

dollars as surely as network programs vie for ratings and advertising dollars. . . . Much of the electronic church has given in to the prevailing moods of the culture it purportedly exists to confront.[30]

The third stratagem, and the one I view to be more central to the biblical mandate (and consequently more effective), is the establishment of a powerful Christian presence among the secular media establishment. This, I believe, must be accomplished through (1) the mobilization of specific prayer for media's leaders;[31] (2) the evangelism of media professionals at every level of media influence; (3) the discipleship of existing Christian professionals in media to equip them for a more powerful witness and a more redemptive use of their media skills; (4) the networking, support, and mobilization of committed believers in media for significant spiritual impact; and (5) the penetration of the media power structure by trained, committed Christian professionals.

In the sixties Joseph Bayly wrote *The Gospel Blimp* as a parody of one Christian family's attempt to reach its neighbor and the community for Christ.[32] In that book evangelistic attempts become more and more ludicrous until a blimp is purchased to broadcast the gospel to the community and drop "gospel bombs" (tracts wrapped in colored cellophane) on the town. In the end, all of the sophisticated but impersonal attempts fail. The neighbor is finally won to Christ by loving care and personal witness.

I can attest to the power of loving care and personal witness in creating an impact on the media. A number of years ago an NBC vice president prayed with me in a Burbank restaurant inviting Jesus Christ into his life. He was one of a handful of individuals with authority over the content of all of the network's programing. Less than ninety days after his decision, I visited this new believer in his office. He tossed a script across the desk to me and asked me to look it over. It had red pencil marks through foul language, impure scenes, and even through the program's title. The executive said, "I've become a lot more conservative in what I'll approve since I became a reborn Christian."

I have often reflected on that incident, the natural result of the working of the Spirit of God. It was not the result of protest, boycott, or competing Christian media structures. It was an incremental step toward solution

30. Colson, *Against the Night,* p. 102.

31. "The Media Leader Prayer Calendar" is a nationally distributed list of media leaders tied to a calendar for daily prayer. It is available from Mastermedia International, 330 North Sixth Street, Suite 110, Redlands, CA 92374.

32. Bayly, *The Gospel Blimp* (Grand Rapids: Zondervan, 1960).

through a loving, personal witness to the gospel of Christ. I conclude that the church's mandate in dealing with the media is the same as it has been with all other hostile groups, from Roman polytheists to intellectual Greek philosophers — to proclaim the good news in the power of the Spirit and to disciple those who respond to Christ in God's transforming Word. That, after all, is one of the main reasons we Christians are here!

A Dialogue with "Prof"
on Christianity and Science

CHARLES B. THAXTON

"CHRISTIANITY and science have nothing to do with each other." This comment came from Jon, an American university student studying in Prague. We viewed this beautiful historic city from Karluv Most, Charles Bridge, as we walked and talked on a lovely spring morning. "Furthermore," he said, "even if they did I wouldn't want to admit it because science gave us fallout, napalm, and acid rain."

Ah. The cynicism of American youth. I believe that this cynicism is not a little responsible for students' inability to think, and thus for declining S.A.T. scores. It is not more money for school facilities and technical aids that will increase real learning (though I am not opposed to these things). The antidote is truth. Christians have a firm foundation for truth and worthwhile reasons to pursue it. Students must be given reasons to believe.

"I've heard it all before," Jon glibly recited. "You can't have science without a firm conviction that the world is really there, and we Christians know it is really there because God told us in the Bible. We know the world is orderly and structured to conform to our mathematics and theory construction because God is a rational God who made the world by his power

I wish to thank Fieldstead and Company of Irvine, California, for a grant that has enabled me to be in Prague, Czechoslovakia, for the years 1992 and 1993, as I lecture on origins and history of science to students throughout eastern Europe and the former Soviet Union. Some of the material used in this dialogue was published as an essay entitled "Christianity and the Scientific Enterprise," in *Veritas Reconsidered*, September 1986, Special Edition in Celebration of Harvard University's 350th Anniversary.

out of nothing and made us in his image. We are reasoning beings because God is."

"Sounds okay to me," I replied, remembering that Jon was not the average student. I urged him to go on.

"Both reason and sensory experience are divinely given tools for probing the world and knowing it. There is a uniformity of cause and effect, so we can reason about it. Thus we don't have the epistemological problem the atheistic humanist or new ager has."

I was very impressed with Jon. "Where did you learn that?" I asked.

"In a special course I had last summer. We used J. P. Moreland's book *Scaling the Secular City*.[1] Ever heard of it?"

"A fine book," I said. "Anyway, what is wrong with that answer?"

"It's so trite," he said. "Atheists and Hindus live in this world too and do science and get Nobel prizes. How many Christians get Nobel prizes?"

Jon seemed agitated now. Seeing I was about to respond, he quickly added, "If we've got the truth, how come the other guys get the prizes?"

He was right, of course. We Christians have lost our great cultural influence. As a friend once put it, we people of faith are salt, but we seem to have become blocks of salt on Sunday mornings instead of granulated salt that is sprinkled throughout society during the week.

"You raise a good point," I told him, ready to press on with the question of whether Christianity has anything to do with science.

Then Jon interrupted, "It's only philosophy, you know. Ideas. Science will get done regardless of what we believe. Besides, who wants to be associated with Christianity when all the best scientists are atheists?"

Jon had raised several ideas that were worthy of discussion. Was there a significant connection between Christianity and science? Does the atheist have a legitimate basis for his activities as a scientist? Is it true that our beliefs have no bearing on science? However, I sensed that his main concern was the noticeable lack of visible Christian heroes in the world of science. So I asked, "Are you sure about that, Jon, that all the best scientists are atheists?"

"Well," he said, "I've never heard of any famous scientists who are Christians, or of any Christians who got Nobel prizes. It seems like all the scientists you ever hear about are atheists, people like Carl Sagan, Isaac Asimov, Tim Ferris, Jacob Bronowski, David Attenborough, Richard Dawkins, and all the guys interviewed on 'NOVA,' and in the National Geographic specials. They're all atheists."

"There you have it," I said. "All you have ever *heard* about are atheists. Maybe the problem is not the lack of Christians who are scientists,

---

1. Moreland, *Scaling the Secular City* (Grand Rapids: Baker, 1987).

even famous scientists, but that you haven't heard about them."[2] I could tell this was a new thought for Jon.

He asked, "What do you mean? Are there really any famous scientists today who are Christians? Has any gotten a Nobel prize?"

I assured him that there have been in the twentieth century many believing scientists, even some Nobel prize winners. I produced a list that included Dorothy Hodgkin, famous British crystallographer and Nobel prize winner; Charles Coulson, the famous mathematical physicist; Sir Robert Boyd, the pioneer in upper atmosphere X ray physics; Werner von Braun, the rocket pioneer and a leader of the early American space program; Francis Collins, the discoverer of the cystic fibrosis gene; Allan Sandage, the famous astronomer at Mount Palomar Observatory . . .

"Tell me, Prof," his affectionate name for me, "how come I've never heard of these people before?"

As our conversation revealed, there was a practical and psychological problem behind his apparent cynicism. Where are the visible Christians who are doing anything in the area of science? Since we Christians are suffering from a public relations problem, many young people are disillusioned with the relevancy of Christianity in the scientific area.

Excusing himself to go say hello to a friend, Jon stopped off at a sidewalk snack bar and returned with two dishes of ice cream. We continued our discussion. Since I knew that Jon was interested in the massive changes going on in Russia and Eastern Europe, I asked him to tell me why he thought the students there were so eager to learn. I had mentioned the great interest students showed in my lectures on science and its history on my visits to Romania and Poland in the spring and summer of 1990 and 1991.

"That's easy," said Jon. "The people have lived under totalitarianism. Information was controlled so that people learned only what the government wanted them to learn. They are now free and eager to know something besides propaganda."

I asked if he thought something similar might have happened in the United States.

"No way," said Jon. "We don't live under totalitarianism. We are free and can read and learn anything we want to."

"That's right," I said. "So how come you've never heard about the Christians who are scientists?"

---

2. Jon had raised an important question. We Christians are many, and we are not fairly represented in the ranks of the first-rate scientists — i.e., those who get the prizes — as Jon said. An excellent discussion of this problem can be found in John A. McIntyre, "Calls of Ivy," *Christianity Today* 34 (5 Nov. 1991): 31-34.

Jon paused, and then said thoughtfully, "Surely you're not suggesting mind control."

"Not that," I said. "Something more effective." I reminded him of the Greek myth about an island on which grew a tasty plant. However, eating and digesting it required more energy than was received from it. Those who liked the taste and refused to leave the island quite literally ate themselves to death. The freedom of the West, I suggested, has created an environment in which those who lack discipline to take in more nourishing mental food, and who are guided by their taste alone, can in a figurative way choose to entertain themselves to death.[3] "Mind candy is addictive," I added.

We finished our ice cream and walked to a nearby park. Jon mulled over what had just been said. A few birds were quarreling over a piece of bread that a passerby had thrown their way. Children were barely audible in the distance. We sat on a park bench overlooking the Vltava River, with a wonderful view of the awesome castle dominating the landscape, breathing in the warm spring air. Jon turned and said, "Okay, Prof. I understand that there are famous scientists who are Christians and that certain truths may be hidden from us in our entertainment culture. You may be right about all the distractions that have kept me from — "

I interrupted, "You mean all the things you allowed to distract you from learning. They didn't keep you from it. You allowed it to happen."

"Yes, freedom of choice," Jon mused. "But you can't get around the fact that science gave us the bomb, the polluted environment, and the other destructive things, so — "

I interrupted again. "Are you sure that science is the culprit? Earlier you were just as convinced that all the scientists are atheists."

"Well, technology then," said Jon.

"Even technology," I said. "Science is a tool for probing and knowing the world, as you put it earlier. And technology is also a tool for doing what we want. People decide what they want," I continued, "and then other people use technology to get it for them."

"Don't tell me, Prof. Ethics, right?" questioned Jon. "You're talking about ethics. Before we were talking about science, and now it's ethics. Ethics doesn't have anything to do with science, any more than Christianity does."

A decided edge appeared in Jon's tone, and it was clear he was quite perturbed by the topic. "Anyway, if you're right," continued Jon, "then Christianity *is* the culprit. It gave us science and technology, which have given us all these destructive things. Take CFCs [chlorofluorocarbons], for

3. See Neil Postman, *Amusing Ourselves to Death: Public Discourse in the Age of Show Business* (New York: Penguin, 1985).

instance." Jon was quite animated now. "They seemed such a wonderful thing in the early days."

"You mean back in the fifties?" I asked.

"Yeah, back in the fifties. Everyone could ride around in air conditioned cars — "

"You mean because of using CFCs as a refrigerant in air conditioners," I added.

"Yeah. And girls could use their hair spray. And now forty years later we find out we're committing suicide. Just great. More things for quicker dying through chemistry. Give me a break, Prof. You had me going there for a while, with all that business about Christians who are scientists. If that's really true, then Christians are part of the problem and not the solution. At least the atheist scientists like Sagan are doing something about our polluted environment and the ozone depletion. Don't you see? In a few years we won't even be able to go to the beach anymore. All because of this wonderful connection between Christianity and science. Well, no thanks. Give me good old humanism that fights the evils of the day. No, I don't want to hear any more. Besides, I'm late. I have an appointment at the embassy. See ya."

And Jon ran off through the park.

Though he left instead of seeing the discussion through, I rationalized his sudden exit. It was important for Jon to take time to reflect and assimilate the new thoughts and material. His desire to know and to find out was strong. I have found that many young people are like Jon. They may have a testy demeanor, but underneath they have tender hearts, wanting the truth and needing love. It takes patience and time to listen and talk.

"Hi, Prof." It was Jon a week later coming out of the Metro station at Karlovo Namesti near Charles University on a bright sunny spring morning.

"This time I'll buy the ice cream if you have an hour. There's an outside cafe open not far from here. Is that okay?"

"Sure," he said. "Lead the way."

We sat at a table with a view of cathedrals, castle spires, and government buildings on a hillside, ordered ice cream and strawberries from the menu, and enjoyed the cool breeze. I was silent, waiting for Jon to take the lead. With some concern showing in his voice he said, "Prof, I'm about to graduate."

"Wonderful," I said, wondering to myself if it could really have been so many years since we had first met. "What will you do now?"

"That's a problem. I'm not sure. I'm getting a degree in history, but I'm unclear where to go or what to do with it."

"A degree in history?" I questioned, probably showing my puzzlement. "I thought you were studying physics."

"I started out in physics," said Jon, "but in the middle of my second year I changed to history. I guess I'm not as good at it as I thought I was. Anyway, it's too late now. I graduate a few weeks after I return to the States. I'm only here for one semester to take courses in European history." There was a troubled, almost forlorn sound to Jon's voice — even, I thought, a touch of regret.

"Do you want to talk about it?" I asked.

"Prof, do you remember when I was in high school, and I won the physics award at the county science fair?"

"Certainly I do. We were awfully proud of your accomplishments, too."

"Well," Jon continued, "a lot has happened since those days." I was concerned now, and I listened as Jon unfolded his story.

Something *had* happened, sadly a much too common story. Jon had made a Christian commitment during high school, and he showed much interest in spiritual things and in learning about the Bible. He had shown through practical example that he had understood the central core of the gospel. In every way his life was exemplary. His parents had done a very commendable job of instilling godly values. His pastor was impressed with Jon's commitment and willingness to help whenever called upon. His teachers at the local high school saw much promise in his future. He received awards from his peers as well as academic awards. What was most vivid in my memory of those days was Jon's intense desire to learn everything he could about science, not just physics, which was his special interest. Surely something had happened to bring such uncertainty to Jon, to create such an open hostility regarding any connection between Christianity and his beloved science, and, at this late juncture of his college career, to cause him to doubt his future.

As he recounted the story it became clear. By degrees Jon's worldview as a Christian had been narrowed during his college days, not by any identifiable specifics, but more by the whole experience. Jon admitted that very few of his professors ever openly ridiculed his faith as a Christian, or ever said or did anything that could be called anti-Christian. "It was more subtle than that," said Jon, and many who have gone to college know what he meant. Slowly, step by step, his previous strong beliefs had succumbed to the eroding, relativizing experience of life in the university, which has been so aptly described by Allan Bloom as "the closing of the American mind."[4]

Gradually, for Jon, Christianity lost any claim to intellectual credi-

---

4. Bloom, *The Closing of the American Mind* (New York: Simon and Schuster, 1987). For a Christian look at the same problem see Ronald Nash, *The Closing of the American Heart* (Dallas: Probe, 1980).

bility in the modern world, dominated by burgeoning social problems. "I see Christianity like an Indian reservation," he said. "It's a subculture that has its own religious rituals with little relevance to broader society."

"So about all Christianity has to offer is personal morality and salvation?" I asked, really only making a comment.

"That's about it, Prof. I just don't see how Christianity has anything to do with the modern world."

"And personal morality, any problems there?"

"Prof, I guess I've blown it there too. Not that I'm proud of it, but, well, Prof, you wouldn't understand."

"Oh, Jon, what you've experienced is more common than you know." Reminding him that I had gone to university too, I began to tell him some of my own story.

When I was a student back in the 1960s, derision was heaped upon Christianity whenever it was mentioned in the classroom. Serious thinkers, I was led to believe, had replaced mythical, old-fashioned Christian thinking with a far superior, more scientific view of reality. Christianity and science were seen as necessarily in conflict. Like most other Christian students during those days, I remained silent, intimidated by the superior knowledge of my professors. It was only several years later, after an intense struggle in my own Christian faith, that I developed confidence in Christianity and could see its relevance to science.

At Harvard in 1971 I had the good fortune of listening to Professor Reijer Hooykaas, noted historian of science from Holland, deliver a series of lectures that would significantly change my intellectual course. Hooykaas had developed the provocative thesis that Christianity significantly and positively influenced the rise and development of modern experimental science.[5]

I remember my reaction well. As a Christian I wanted to believe him, but my scientist side was more skeptical. Hadn't scholars thoroughly examined every area of supposed Christian influence and dismissed Christianity from being a credible intellectual position? I could not bring myself to accept an argument that ran counter to the dominant perspective of my education to that point. I had a Christian heart, but a pagan mind.

Still, Hooykaas's argument fascinated me. Being a postdoctoral fellow gave me freedom to design and begin a reading program to examine his claims. I was surprised to find that other scholars had also recognized that a distinctly Christian worldview had inspired early scientific inves-

5. See Hooykaas, *Religion and the Rise of Modern Science* (Grand Rapids: Eerdmans, 1972).

tigation. Stanley Jaki, for example, wrote *Science and Creation*.[6] Of that work one reviewer commented:

> Although we seldom recognize it, scientific research requires certain basic beliefs about the order and rationality of matter, and its accessibility to the human mind. . . . [T]hey came to us in their full force through the Judeo-Christian belief in an omnipotent God, creator and sustainer of all things. In such a world view it becomes sensible to try and understand the world, and this is the fundamental reason science developed as it did in the Middle Ages in Christian Europe, culminating in the brilliant achievements of the seventeenth century.[7]

Alfred North Whitehead added:

> In the first place, there can be no living science unless there is a widespread instinctive conviction in the existence of an *Order of Things*. And, in particular, of an *Order of Nature*. . . . The inexpugnable belief that every detailed occurrence can be correlated with its antecedents in a perfectly definite manner . . . must come from the medieval insistence on the rationality of God. . . . My explanation is that the faith in the possibility of science, generated antecedently to the development of modern scientific theory, is an unconscious derivative from medieval theology.[8]

According to Loren Eiseley, the origin of modern science was due to

> The sheer act of faith that the universe possessed order and could be interpreted by rational minds. . . . The philosophy of experimental science . . . began its discoveries and made use of its method in the faith, not the knowledge, that it was dealing with a rational universe controlled by a Creator who did not act upon whim nor interfere with the forces He had set in operation. The experimental method succeeded beyond man's wildest dreams but the faith that brought it into being owes something to the Christian conception of the nature of God. It is surely one of the curious paradoxes of history that science, which professionally has little to do with faith, owes its origins to an act of faith that the

6. Jaki, *Science and Creation* (Edinburgh and London: Scottish Academic Press, 1974).

7. P. E. Hodgson, review of Jaki's *Science and Creation,* in *Nature* 251 (24 Oct. 1974): 747. The best book by Jaki on the role of Christianity in the origin of science is *The Road of Science and the Ways to God* (Chicago: University of Chicago Press, 1978).

8. Whitehead, *Science and the Modern World* (New York: The Free Press, 1967), pp. 3-4, 12-13.

universe can be rationally interpreted, and that science today is sustained by the assumption.[9]

Melvin Calvin, Nobel laureate in chemistry, wrote:

> The fundamental conviction that the universe is ordered is the first and strongest tenet. As I try to discern the origin of that conviction, I seem to find it in a basic notion discovered 2000 or 3000 years ago, and enunciated first in the Western world by the ancient Hebrews: namely, that the universe is governed by a single God, and is not the product of the whims of many gods, each governing his own province, according to his own laws. This monotheistic view seems to be the historical foundation of modern science.[10]

Perhaps Christianity had played a greater role in the development of modern science than I had imagined. I wanted to know more.

"You know, Prof," Jon interrupted, "I'm sorry to be such a skeptic, but doesn't it take more than the fact that science originated in Christian Europe where people believed in God to show that anything specifically Christian was connected to the origin of science?"

Of course, Jon had asked an important question that needed attending to, and before I could respond, he continued: "Despite what these scientists and philosophers have said, I still have difficulty believing that Christianity produced science."

"Jon, you've raised an excellent point," I said, "and before I respond I would like to clear up a misunderstanding. I'm not suggesting that Christianity *produced* science, but only that an essential ingredient for the origin and development of modern experimental science came from Christian thought."[11]

---

9. Eiseley, *Darwin's Century: Evolution and the Men Who Discovered It* (Garden City, NY: Anchor, 1961), p. 62.

10. Calvin, *Chemical Evolution* (Oxford: Clarendon, 1969), p. 258.

11. It has been maintained by some that the views of Hooykaas and Jaki represent an indefensible extreme position if they are saying that the fundamental successes of seventeenth-century science are owed to Christianity. See, e.g., the collection of essays edited by David C. Lindberg and Ronald L. Numbers, *God and Nature* (Berkeley: University of California Press, 1986). Without presuming to speak for Hooykaas and Jaki, who have acquitted themselves well without any help from me, I believe it is important to qualify the claim so as to make clear that there were many factors involved in bringing us science. In claiming a distinctly Christian role, perhaps I should make clear that I am referring to specifically biblical, non-Greek ideas — such as creation by an omnipotent Creator — and the implications those ideas had for bringing reform to the methodology of inquiry into nature.

"Well," said Jon, "even with this qualification, how come modern science didn't start in the early days of Christianity — say, back in the third or fourth century? Why did it take 1500 years? Isn't that an argument against Christianity having a profound and positive influence on the origin of modern science?"

"Good question," I said. "Now let's be more specific. By Christian influence, I don't mean just what Christians say. I mean particularly those ideas that are unique to the Bible."

"I'm not sure I follow you, Prof," said Jon.

"To understand the ideas I'm referring to and how they accomplished the task, you have to know some history. Are you up for an overview? How about next Saturday, same place, same time?" I asked.

"Okay, next week," said Jon, "and I'll buy ice cream."

"Next week, then," I said. "Bye for now."

In the space of our brief conversation, Jon had shown signs of genuine interest in the possible connection between Christianity and science. I was encouraged. He had already shown familiarity with much of the relevant terminology for a meaningful discussion. Jon's problem, as he expressed it, was that he just didn't see any relevance to the question.

"Vanilla with strawberries, right?" Jon had already ordered the ice cream when we met at Karlovo Namesti the next Saturday. "I can't believe I'm spending Saturday morning at a history of science lecture, and not even getting credit for it," he laughed. "But I do want to know. Do it, Prof."

"Okay," I said. "Let's start with the Greeks. . . ."

Many Greeks viewed nature as a living organism imbued with attributes of divinity. Nature was eternal and self-existent, not created. Nature was impregnated with final causes, with divine purposes, and as such was self-revealing. These purposes had only to be apprehended by the mind — hence the significance placed on intuiting axioms and principles from which all particular truths could be derived by deductive reasoning. It followed from this view that for many Greeks knowledge of nature and reality rested on the authority of the "system builders": Euclid in geometry, Galen in anatomy, Ptolemy in astronomy, Plato and Aristotle in philosophy, etc. As a corollary to this view of truth, sensory experience did not lead to new knowledge. It could only provide illustrations for what was already known through reason. Sensory experience was no more relevant to the Greek science of nature than it was to Euclidean geometry. Although the pre-Socratics held rather more diverse views, the tendency was toward a science of nature that was not experimental. This Greek conception of nature and reality led them to distrust the senses. So, following in the footsteps of Plato, many philosophers in the twelfth century taught "that the senses were deceitful and reason alone could give truth."[12]

The dominant view of reality in medieval Europe was essentially Greek, having been co-opted by the church and adapted for Christian service. It offered no motivation to investigate nature by observation and experiment. To the Greeks, reality consisted of forms and essences, not material things. In a world where ideals subordinate material reality, observing "what is" becomes less important than reasoning "what must be."

The medieval world picture inherited from the Greeks was that of a vast hierarchy of beings extending from the deity in the empyrean heaven at the outer edge of the universe, through a graded series of angels inhabiting the ten concentric crystalline spheres surrounding the central earth, to the levels of human beings, animals, and plants on the earth itself, which formed the system's cosmic center.

A sharp qualitative distinction separated the terrestrial and celestial domains of the universe. Not only were the two domains composed of different types of materials; they also had different motions. The terrestrial environs consisted of earth, air, fire, and water, each with rectilinear motion (down toward the center of the earth) that had a beginning and an end. The heavenly bodies (above the moon) were composed of a more perfect fifth essence and possessed eternal circular motion.

According to ancient mechanics, motion was maintained only as long as there was a constantly applied push. As Herbert Butterfield said, "A universe constructed on the mechanics of Aristotle had the door half-way open for spirits already. . . . Intelligence had to roll the planetary spheres around."[13]

Medieval Christians were attracted to this Greek picture of the world. An authority-based hierarchical system with God in his empyrean above the moon was easy to visualize. The angels mentioned in the Bible could push the planets around — not a hard job since celestial bodies were made of the very light fifth essence.

"This basically Greek view reinforced the church's teaching about the importance of humankind too," Jon interjected. "It gave human beings a psychological boost."

"Yes," I said. "It has been said that such a conception gave human beings in the Middle Ages a truly cosmic sense of their importance."[14]

---

12. A. C. Crombie, *Medieval and Early Modern Science,* 2 vols. (Cambridge: Harvard University Press, 1963), 2:4.

13. Butterfield, *The Origins of Modern Science* (New York: The Free Press, 1957), p. 19.

14. Although the point would have diverted the conversation, it should also be added that the conception of an earth-centered system adding to the psychological sense of human

The linchpin for this medieval cosmology was Aristotle's view of motion through a constantly applied mover. But as Butterfield remarks, "It was supremely difficult to escape from the Aristotelian doctrine (of motion) by merely observing things more closely. . . . [I]t required *a different kind of thinking-cap,* a transposition in the mind of the scientist himself."[15]

Late medieval Christianity supplied just such a transposition of thought through a greater familiarity with Scripture and an emphasis on the doctrine of creation. Through the advent of the printing press the ideas of Scripture were much more widely disseminated. People could discover for themselves in their own languages that both Old and New Testaments regarded the material world as substantial, real, and good. A premium was placed on the value and essential trustworthiness of sensory experience, especially in some of the more prominent authority-based passages. For example, after Moses reiterates the ten commandments, he reminds the people that he is not the authority. The commandments on stone did nothing more than permanently record the message all the people heard. Says Moses, "You heard the voice" (Deut. 5:23). The Hebrews had an empirical test for identifying a false prophet (18:22). John introduces his first epistle with an empirical emphasis: "we have heard, . . . we have seen . . . , our hands have touched" (1 John 1:1). Jesus said to the disciples after his resurrection, "Touch me and see" (Luke 24:39).

The church had emphasized the doctrine of creation from the first century onward. Though this teaching affected the official vocabulary, it did not successfully overcome the way most people thought about nature. For the most part, people continued to think of nature in the old Greek

---

well-being and dignity is surely mythology. In the medieval scheme the flames of hell were thought to lie beneath our feet, at the center of the earth. So how could residing on earth's surface be thought to elevate psychologically one's sense of worth and value? This idea has always puzzled me, despite the fact that it has been cited in numerous works. I can only guess that it must be an explanation in retrospect, coming from minds that fail to understand that, according to Christianity, our dignity arises from who we are — image-bearers of the Creator — and not from any relation of human beings to the earth or of the earth to space. If anything, the human sense of well-being should have been enhanced by the adoption of a sun-centered universe — but then this doesn't fit the mythology. The mythology is that humankind, influenced by the Christian worldview, underwent great psychological trauma with the scientific revolution. If anything, the earth-centered universe, with human feet just above the flames of hell, served to keep human beings in a state of perceived unworthiness and vulnerability — in need of grace. With this in mind I can well believe humankind would have experienced relief with the scientific revolution. See the essay by C. S. Lewis, "Dogma and the Universe," in *God in the Dock: Essays on Theology and Ethics,* ed. Walter Hooper (Grand Rapids: Eerdmans, 1970), pp. 38-47.

15. Butterfield, *The Origins of Modern Science,* pp. 16-17; emphasis added.

ways, as a living organism that could be known through its self-revelation via intuition and deduction. However, as the Middle Ages progressed, more and more people began to read the Bible in their own languages. There began a fresh appreciation of what the words of Scripture were telling about nature — namely, that if nature is created, as is revealed in Scripture, then there is no particular reason to expect that nature is what the Greeks have told us it is. And if nature is fundamentally different from the dominant Greek model, then there is no particular reason why the methods one uses to inquire into nature and to know it must be the Greek methods. So it was the perceived *fact* of creation, not merely the doctrine about it, that was the key to understanding how belief in creation influenced the rise of modern science. According to M. B. Foster, "The modern investigators of nature were the first to take seriously *in their science* the Christian doctrine that nature is created."[16]

Francis Bacon (1561-1626) maintained that finding new facts required new methods. He set out to reformulate scientific method to give the empirical, inductive process a more central place. If nature is created, then we must inquire into nature by asking different kinds of questions than the Greeks asked. In fact, Lord Bacon, who was a lawyer and a follower of Calvin's theology, had studied the same Renaissance law as had Calvin. Calvin had revolutionized the study of the Bible by introducing a new way of asking questions, an inductive method he had learned from studying law. If the Bible is the book of God's Word, reasoned Calvin, then we must ask questions that can be answered by going directly to the Bible, allowing the Bible to speak to us. Bacon applied the same inductive method to the inquiry of nature, maintaining that we must put our questions directly to nature, the book of God's works.[17] Part of the genius of modern empirical science was precisely its use of recurring natural events to provide observable checks on hypotheses. No more would scientists content themselves with speculative reason unchecked by sensory experience.

"I think I understand," exclaimed Jon. "You are saying that all those years before the people had the Bible, they didn't really know the value of experience. The whole Greek system of thought was based on authority.

16. Foster, "Christian Doctrine of Creation and the Rise of Modern Natural Science," *Mind* 43 (1934): 446; emphasis his.

17. I owe this exposition of Calvin and Bacon as lawyers and the role of Renaissance law and its method of asking questions to Thomas Torrance, whom I heard in a lecture series at Princeton Theological Seminary in the early 1970s. Different portions of the lectures can be found in various titles by Torrance, including *Space, Time, and Incarnation* (New York: Oxford University Press, 1969); *God and Rationality* (New York: Oxford University Press, 1971); and *Theological Science* (New York: Oxford University Press, 1969).

In the Middle Ages the people, still without the Bible, remained subject to the authority of Aristotle in their views about nature, even though Christianity was officially in power, and the church leaders had the Bible. But as the people began to find out for themselves what the Bible said, it was a sufficient force to counter the hold Aristotle had had over their minds."

"Jon, there are points here to discuss, but that is basically the way it seems to me. We could usefully trace the contribution of Thomas Aquinas, for instance — initially advanced against considerable opposition. But what you have said rightly summarizes broad streams of medieval thought. A created world is contingent upon the will of the Creator, and it need not necessarily conform to our a priori reasoning about it. This, I believe, is the historical basis for the early scientists' reliance on observation, using the five senses and experiment in order to gain new knowledge. Galileo and Kepler, and other early modern scientists, were encouraged to rely on experience because the Bible taught it. But notice that this wasn't doing away with authority. It was the people's belief in God as the ultimate authority, and in the Bible as derived from him, that allowed them to rely on experience as a better authority with regard to nature than the words of Aristotle, the priest, or even interpretations of the Bible."

"Wait a minute, Prof. Even the Bible? That's a bit radical, even for me."

"Even Jesus," I reminded Jon, "said not to take just his word for something, that it too required corroboration of two or more witnesses."[18]

That is why I believe the wisest course when confronted by problematic passages in the Bible or supposed conflicts between scientific theories and the Bible is to avoid an interpretation that is based on a single Bible verse or a limited set of observations. Science has always been a conservative body, slow to change an opinion, but it moves when enough weight is at hand. I believe it is the same with the church's interpretation of the Bible.

"Anyway," I continued, "take another example, say Galileo Galilei (1564-1642), and I think you can see what I mean. Galileo was another pioneer of modern science who valued sensory experience in the acquisition of knowledge. Galileo's discovery of the laws of projectile motion, combining mathematics and experiment, was a lasting contribution to science. He could test his ideas about how balls roll down inclined planes, how pendulums swing, how objects behave in free-fall, and how a cannonball travels in a parabolic trajectory. The new view of motion was based on experience.

18. See John 8:17 where Jesus cites Deut. 19:15: "A matter must be established by the testimony of two or three witnesses."

"In his letter to the Grand Duchess Christina in 1615 Galileo argued that, unlike some Bible scholars were known to do, it is impossible for professors of the experimental sciences to change their opinions at will.[19] There is an empirical check on our ideas about nature. Furthermore it was Galileo's view that 'all of the verses of Scripture are not obliged to function as rigorously as every law of nature.'[20] Our opinions about nature must fit nature, and arguments about nature must be settled by nature. Therefore, recurrent nature provides a more sure authority for our views of nature than that derived from the various interpretations of Scripture. He was not opposed to the Bible. He felt strongly, however, that God did not intend that we abandon sensory experience, logic, and intellect. There were Scripture twisters[21] in Galileo's day, and they would often find some verse in the Bible to support the reigning Aristotelian view of the world. But in science, disputes would be settled by going to nature. The problem is still with us, of course, and Galileo — and another great early scientist, Kepler — believed that the Bible was freeing them from the shackles of Aristotle."

Johannes Kepler (1571-1630) was an early modern scientist who corresponded with Galileo, and he also had problems with those who would use Scripture to support the Aristotelian status quo, instead of relying on experience. Kepler wrote, "In all science there is nothing which could prevent me from holding an opinion, nothing which could deter me from acknowledging openly an opinion of mine, except solely the authority of the Holy Bible, which is being twisted badly by many."[22]

Kepler is an excellent case study because he was at the threshold or even caught between two regimes of science, the ancient Pythagorean (animistic Aristotelian) and the modern. Since Kepler is at a pivotal position in the history of science, between the ancient and the modern, one of his biographers has described him as "the Watershed."[23] His works pioneered in the development of modern science, showing the value of depending on experience instead of authority — whether of a religious tradition, a holy

---

19. Galileo, "Letter to the Grand Duchess Christina." An incomplete English translation of the famous letter may be found in *Discoveries and Opinions of Galileo,* trans. Stillman Drake (Garden City, NY: Doubleday, 1957), pp. 175-216.

20. Galileo, *Discoveries and Opinions of Galileo,* p. 183.

21. For a helpful study of this topic see James W. Sire, *Scripture Twisting* (Downers Grove: InterVarsity, 1980).

22. Kepler, quoted by Gerald Holton, *Thematic Origins of Scientific Thought: Kepler to Einstein* (Cambridge: Harvard University Press, 1973), p. 86.

23. Arthur Koestler, *The Sleepwalkers: A History of Man's Changing Vision of the Universe* (New York: Macmillan, 1959). The section dealing with Kepler was later published separately as *The Watershed* (Lanham, MD: University Press of America, 1985).

book, or reason — to settle scientific questions. For example, Kepler once abandoned a thoroughly worked-out theory of planetary motion because it disagreed with empirical observation by only eight minutes of arc in the orbit of Mars. Some have thought it was taking observation a bit too seriously. But Kepler was convinced that the true picture of the heavens would agree with the observations and entail physical causes. He therefore believed that this eight-minute discrepancy was pointing the way to a revised understanding of astronomy.

Kepler had been deeply influenced by the Pythagorean intellectual tradition, and he never completely broke with it. The Pythagorean influence on Kepler was more than just his reliance on their mathematical achievements. The early Kepler viewed the planets themselves as intelligent beings moving on their own. He even referred to the "mind" of the planet and wondered whether the planet could be aware of the laws of nature. Thus Kepler has been numbered among the neo-Pythagoreans of the Renaissance. Kepler did not mean, however, that the planets exercised will and could act on their own volition. Rather, this "mind" was more like a computerized homing device, which could calculate orbital positions and keep on track, but could not alter the instructions of its mission. Kepler was a man in process, whose thought and vocabulary at the time of writing *Mysterium Cosmographicum,* his first book, was still significantly informed by the old animistic tradition of the Pythagoreans who believed that the universe was a divine, living being.

Kepler shows how far he had moved away from this Pythagorean notion in a letter to Herwart von Hohenberg (dated February 10, 1605), which he wrote a few years later, near the completion of his *Astronomia Nova:* "My aim is to show that the heavenly machine is not a kind of divine, live being, but a kind of clockwork."[24] He was quite jubilant over his discovery that "nearly all the manifold motions are caused by a most simple, magnetic, and material force, just as all motions of the clock are caused by a simple weight. And I also show how these physical causes are to be given numerical and geometrical expression."[25]

Before Kepler the tradition of science had little use for empirical observation. After him, science would be unthinkable without it.

Recognizing the implications of a created nature opened the door for emphasizing the importance of sensory experience. Empirical scientific methods follow directly from belief in a created and therefore contingent nature. Not until the end of the seventeenth century would Newton reach

24. Holton, *Thematic Origins of Scientific Thought,* p. 72.
25. Holton, *Thematic Origins of Scientific Thought,* p. 72.

a new understanding of physical reality. In the meantime, a certain sense of delight and fascination came in exposing cracks in the Aristotelian edifice.

The voyages of discovery in the fifteenth century not only opened up the New World with new trade routes; they also gave empirical proof that ancient knowledge was both incomplete and in many instances wrong. The explorers contradicted the ancients by experience. Once a "transposition" in thinking occurred, allowing for meaningful experiential checks on ideas, the new empiricists found the universe replete with evidence repudiating the ancient cosmology.

In 1572 a new star appeared in the skies over Europe. The star remained visible for a year and a half, even in the daytime. The star hovered clearly above the moon. Yet according to established Aristotelian views, the heavens were supposed to be changeless. Some of the learned professors refused to acknowledge the new star, calling it an optical illusion. But for everyone else it was clear evidence that the Aristotelian system was in deep trouble. What's more, the evidence was empirical.[26]

Another blow to the Aristotelian picture came with the comet of 1577. The comet not only signaled more change in the heavens; since it must have passed through the supposedly impenetrable crystalline spheres, its appearance contradicted Aristotle's view of the heavens. Many, such as Tycho Brahe, were encouraged actually to deny the existence of the crystalline orbs.

Copernicus had taken the bold first step in refashioning the world picture. He put the sun at the center in his system, thus making the earth just one of the planets. Copernicus did keep to circular motion for the planets, however. Later, Kepler would discover on empirical grounds that the orbits were elliptical.

By the end of the seventeenth century Newton had synthesized the work of Copernicus, Tycho Brahe, Kepler, and Galileo by achieving a unity of heaven and earth, all equally subject to mathematical analysis. Newton banished the Aristotelian terrestrial/celestial dichotomy that had dominated intellectual thought for nearly two thousand years.[27]

---

26. This may be yet another example of a scientific anomaly that goes unrecognized or unacknowledged because there is no satisfactory new conceptual framework within which to place it and thus give it compelling explanation. See Alan Lightman and Owen Ginerich, "When Do Anomalies Begin?" *Science* 255 (1992): 690-95.

27. Admittedly this is something of a simplification. Cartesian thought was a dominant force in France, and advocates of Newton's insights regarding optics found they had to confront it. Cf. Henry Guerlac, *Newton on the Continent* (Ithaca: Cornell University Press, 1981).

The modern scientific enterprise was now ready to explore, by means of the senses combined with mathematics, the structure and ongoing operation of the universe. Surely it can be said that Christian thought had done much, not only to inspire this new form of inquiry, but also to shape its methods.

"Prof, that is an impressive sweep of history," said Jon, "but it raises a question."

"What's bothering you now?" I asked.

"How did we go from a vital Christian influence for the origin of modern experimental science, as you claim, to the world of science and technology today, where on every hand, it seems, what is touted is the triumph of materialism?"

It seemed we were finally at the question Jon wanted answered from our first meeting. To answer, however, would require a further historical excursion to understand something of the role ideas play in the changing kaleidoscope of history.

"Are you up to the task, Jon?" I asked.

"Sure, Prof, I'm into this now. Continue."

So I did. Ideas are like seeds that require soil, water, and nurturing before they grow and bear fruit. There seems to be a cultural soil in which some ideas germinate and flourish while others languish and die. As we have seen, the European mental soil was right for the development of experimental science, which sprang up among people convinced that nature was freely created by an omnipotent Creator. Although we did not go into the matter, the empirical science of nature never took root and flourished in other cultural milieus, including the ancient civilizations of Babylonia, China, and India. In these places science was "stillborn."[28] In Europe the philosophy of nature changed from viewing nature as a living organism to recognizing nature to be a created, inert, and passive medium, which had received its form and structure from the Creator. The method of inquiry underwent a commensurate change to be consistent with the new philosophy of nature. Modern experimental science resulted, and it has flowered for four hundred years.

However, the seeds for undermining confidence in the thought structure of Christianity, which played this positive role in birthing science, were also planted in the same European soil. The irony is that in part they were planted by none other than Isaac Newton, who gave us the great vision for the modern world in his *Mathematical Principles of Natural*

---

28. Jaki, *Science and Creation*, p. viii: "In a world history that had witnessed at least half a dozen great cultures, science had as many stillbirths."

Philosophy[29] and who consciously hoped his work would turn many toward Christianity.[30] These seeds for undermining Christian faith would have a profound effect in generations following Newton, but they also had a devastating impact on Newton himself.[31]

"Newton was a Christian, wasn't he?" asked Jon.

"Yes," I said, "but Newton was not orthodox in his faith. He started out wanting to understand in practical terms the omnipresence of God — that is, how God could be everywhere at once. This question was very much in Newton's mind as he synthesized the work of Copernicus, Tycho Brahe, Kepler, and Galileo, and as he added his own contribution in his great synthesis. What made it philosophically devastating for Christian belief, and I believe even for his own faith, was not his view that nature behaved mechanically, but his view of space."

"Go slow here, Prof. I want to make sure I get this," said Jon.

"Okay," I replied. "Newton's solution to the problem of God's omnipresence was simply to make space = God.[32] You can see the problem, I think, if you consider Newton's definition of density."

"You mean, mass per unit volume, or M/V?" queried Jon.

"Correct. Now according to Newtonian physics, what is the connection or relation between matter and space?" I asked.

---

29. Newton, *Sir Isaac Newton's Mathematical Principles of Natural Philosophy and His System of the World*, ed. Florian Cajori, trans. Andrew Motte (Berkeley: University of California Press, 1934 [orig. 1687]).

30. Newton wrote in a letter to Richard Bentley, "When I wrote my treatise upon our Systeme I had an eye upon such Principles as might work with considering men for the beliefe of a Deity and nothing can rejoyce me more than to find it usefull for that purpose." Cited in Margaret C. Jacob, "Christianity and the Newtonian Worldview," in *God and Nature*, p. 244.

31. For a discussion of the heterodox views of Isaac Newton, see the essay by Richard S. Westfall, "The Rise of Science and the Decline of Orthodox Christianity: A Study of Kepler, Descartes, and Newton," in *God and Nature*, pp. 218-37.

32. Some have questioned this equation, space = God, as I have stated it here. However, it is clear that David Brewster, one of Newton's students, thought Newton meant this. And others thought so too. See, for example, Jonathan Edwards's essay "Of Being," in *The Works of Jonathan Edwards*, vol. 6: *Scientific and Philosophical Writings*, ed. Wallace E. Anderson (New Haven: Yale University Press, 1980), pp. 202-7. This was probably written when Edwards was in graduate school and had read Newton. He states plainly, "space is God" (p. 203). Others, such as Thomas Bradwardine and Nicole Oresme in the fourteenth century, held that space existed independently and God filled it, as is noted by Edward Grant in his essay "Science and Theology in the Middle Ages," in *God and Nature*, p. 57. Newton gets credit for the great achievement of unifying physics. So it is only fair that he also bear blame for giving us a picture of the world that made it so difficult to consider Christianity a credible perspective. Of course, there were many predecessors who paved the way for this unintended consequence.

"I don't know, Prof, I can't think of any relation."

"Nor could anyone else," I said. "In fact, Newton defined density such that there was no relation between matter and volume."

"I must be dense myself, Prof, because I still don't get it," commented Jon.

To help make the point, I told Jon the story about Albert Einstein's first visit to the United States. Einstein had become famous because of his epoch-making theories, beginning in 1905. When he arrived in New York, journalists crowded round to interview the great physicist who had dared to question Isaac Newton. One journalist wanted to know what was the essential difference between his new views of physics and those of Newton. Einstein answered by noting that if you gathered all the matter in the universe into a ball and threw it away, in Newton's formulation you would still have space left. But, said Einstein, in the new view, if you throw away all the matter you don't have any space left either. In other words, in Newton's view there was no relation between matter and space, and in Einstein's view they were so tied together that if you destroyed one you destroyed the other too.

I went on to explain that the great Christian message begins with "The Word [divine *Logos*] became flesh and dwelt among us," the startling claim of the Johannine prologue, and . . .

"I get it," exclaimed Jon. "If space is God and there is no relation between matter and space, as required by Newton's physics, then how could the *Logos* become flesh and be born in Bethlehem?"

"Absolutely correct," I said. This anti-Christian conclusion seemed to follow directly from Newton's physics, and although it was not specifically expressed by Newton, it was there for any who cared to look at the philosophical implications. If physics were literally true as he formulated it, then how could there be an incarnation? And of course Newton eventually denied the incarnation and Christ's deity, though he did not publicize this; hence his denial of the orthodox Trinitarian view of God.[33]

It also followed from the Newtonian view of space that miracles generally must be denied, because they also required divine action across the great conceptual chasm between God (= space) and matter. Once a

---

33. Of course, historians have shown that there were many religious influences on Newton, not least a number of works in the Arian tradition that he carefully read. Cf. the forthcoming study by Professor Betty Dobbs (Cambridge University Press). Despite what I have said about Newton and his lack of orthodoxy, brought about by acting on his own theories of the world, Margaret Jacob has written, "Yet all the evidence we possess about Newton's own religiosity confirms his theistic and providential understanding of God and his biblical sense of history" ("Christianity and the Newtonian Worldview," p. 246).

chasm was set up separating God and the world of matter, the logic soon played itself out. And of course the great miracle of God's communicating to finite material human beings by revelation must also be denied. How can Newtonian physics, which explains and predicts so much, be wrong? And only if his physics were wrong, it seemed, could the orthodox Christian faith be viewed as credible.

These unintended consequences of Newtonian physics made it easier to be a Deist and did much to usher in the Enlightenment, and today many educated people still see Christianity as intellectually untenable. Of course, many maintained an orthodox faith, but it seemed to a growing number of people that faith had to be held against reason and evidence. In an amazing turnabout, Christianity, the religion of truth, was repudiated by many in the name of truth.

"Prof, that's quite a story. But surely not everybody was concerned with the doctrine of omnipresence. Even if Newton made space equal God, I don't see that everybody who learned Newton's physics had to do the same and draw these philosophical conclusions."

"Jon, you're quite perceptive," I said. "You raise an excellent point. Most people were not sitting up nights trying to puzzle out the great problem of omnipresence that plagued Newton, but many were greatly troubled by his physics. Do you know why?"

"No," said Jon, "why was it?"

I continued. For more than a thousand years before Newton's revolution in physics, Christians viewed the world in terms of a celestial/terrestrial dichotomy, with heaven above and earth below. If you had asked anyone in the Middle Ages where God lived, he or she would have pointed upward, toward heaven. The problem created by the painstaking labors of Copernicus, Kepler, Galileo, and Newton was that the achievement of a unitary world of heaven and earth, with mathematics applicable equally everywhere, seemed to leave no place for God.

This should not have been a problem because the Lord had instructed the people not to make images of him. The children of Israel had a struggle throughout history with this, but they eventually learned to put away idols. The church has had its struggle with this issue too. Though it was not worshiping idols, it still wanted to know where Jesus was, in a quite literal way, now that he had ascended into heaven. That is the point of the dichotomy of heaven above and earth below. It gave a visual image of where to place God.

Despite the warning in Scripture, Newton quite plainly set out to solve this great problem of where to put God. He interpreted quite literally the verse in the Acts of the Apostles where it is written, "In him we live and move and have our being."[34] Newton, who mathematized the old Platonic view of space as a container, thought he had solved a great theological problem, showing exactly how it was that God was near at hand to each one of us as Scripture says.

Most people, however, weren't able to grasp the conceptual point about space as readily as Newton did. Instead, nearly everyone thought of it in visual terms. They simply noticed that according to his physics there was no more heaven *up there*. For them it seemed that heaven must be *out there;* somewhere beyond the limits of infinite space is where God is, they thought. It had an eerie feel to it, and most people could not possibly imagine how a God so far away could hear their prayers, or even care that they were there. As numerous commentators have pointed out, it seemed that earth was but a tiny speck floating in the cosmic void, and we seemed to be alienated and alone, left to define our own existence, chart our own course, and guide our own destiny. The cozy little universe with God close at hand ready to hear and answer our prayers was no more.[35]

An infinite universe, with God residing beyond the boundary of space, created the same effect as I developed on Newton's view of space. The great chasm between God and the world was not viewed conceptually, however. God, whom we cannot see, was imagined in more visual terms to be infinitely far away, beyond the rim of space. Surely there could be no incarnation, no miracles, no revelation, and no prayers ever heard, let alone answered. We are so far removed from God that he could not extend an outstretched hand to help if he wanted to, and how could anyone know if he wanted to . . . ? Cynicism followed. One of the best examples in literature that shows the implications of Newton's view is the famous piece by Bertrand Russell:

> That man is the product of causes which had no prevision of the end they were achieving; that his origin, his growth, his hopes and fears, his loves and his beliefs, are but the outcome of accidental collocations of atoms; that no fire, no heroism, no intensity of thought and feeling, can preserve an individual life beyond the grave; that all the labors of the ages, all the devotion, all the inspiration, all the noonday brightness of human genius, are destined to extinction in the vast death of the solar

---

34. Acts 17:28. See the General Scholium in Newton's *Mathematical Principles,* p. 545. This is cited by Gary B. Deason in his essay "Reformation Theology and the Mechanistic Conception of Nature," in *God and Nature,* p. 184.

35. For an exposition of the "up there" and "out there" vocabulary as it relates to the Newtonian worldview, see John A. T. Robinson, *Honest to God* (Philadelphia: Westminster, 1963), pp. 9-18.

system, and that the whole temple of man's achievement must inevitably be buried beneath the debris of a universe in ruins.[36]

"Prof, you're not very encouraging with this story of how we arrived at the modern world," said Jon. "I wanted to know the path from Christianity's role in the birth of science to today, when so many find it hard to believe the Bible, but I didn't expect your story to reinforce the doubts I already had. This is depressing."

"If you feel the despair and the lack of hope through this exposition," I explained, "then you understand something of why art, music, literature, and philosophy in the twentieth century have also tended toward despair. It is the mark of the twentieth century."

Then Jon asked, with more than a little concern in his voice, "Is there any answer to this, or are you just educating me to the hopelessness of it all?"

"Jon, do you remember the story I told you earlier about Einstein's description of the difference between his and Newton's views of physics?"

"Yes," said Jon, "in Newton's formulation, if you threw away all matter in the universe you'd have space left, but in Einstein's there wouldn't even be space left."

"Exactly," I said. "Well, Einstein was Jewish, and later he embraced the pantheist views of Spinoza. Even so, the great lesson learned by Judaism, to put away the images, had been deeply embedded, perhaps unconsciously, in Einstein. For the views of Einstein also solved the great theological problem introduced by Newton."

"I'm not getting this, Prof," said Jon.

"Stay with me just a bit and I think you will," I replied. "Einstein gave us a famous equation."

"You mean $E = mc^2$," said Jon.

"That famous equation contains within it," I said, "with additional information provided in Einstein's general theory of relativity and refinements others added later, the basis for showing that the physical world — including matter, energy, space, and time — had a true beginning."[37]

"That is amazing, Prof," exclaimed Jon. "That's just what the Bible says. And to think it came from a man opposed to belief in a personal God."

"Yes, it is amazing," I agreed.

36. Russell, "A Free Man's Worship" [orig. 1903], reprinted in *Why I Am Not a Christian*, ed. Paul Edwards (New York: Simon and Schuster, 1957), p. 107.

37. For a fuller exposition of Einstein and developments in cosmology see Hugh Ross, *The Fingerprint of God* (Orange, CA: Promise Publishing, 1989).

"So exactly how does this solve the problem of despair?" asked Jon.

"It shows that something that is non-material, non-spatial, non-energy, and non-temporal began everything," I said.

"But what is the difference between something that is non-material, non-spatial, non-energy, and non-temporal being there — and nothing at all?" asked Jon.

"This Something had the information and power to create something out of nothing," I responded. "Materialists truly are at the end of their rope with this one. They would like to give a rational answer to the problem, and they can't find one. They simply say that out of nothing something came. They have given up the quest."

"But Prof, even if the materialist doesn't have a rational answer, it doesn't mean that theists are right."

"You are correct, Jon," I said. "Remember about the *Logos* (Word) becoming flesh and dwelling among us?" I asked. "The *Logos*, God's Agent in creation, has information, and that is the missing ingredient in physics, as well as in biology. Fong made a profound statement a few years ago at an origin of life conference: 'The question of the ultimate source of information is not trivial. In fact it is the basic and central philosophical and theoretical problem. The essence of the theory of Divine Creation is that the ultimate source of information has a separate, independent existence beyond and before the material system, this being the main point of the Johannine Prologue.' "[38]

"Prof, every answer you give raises more questions for me." Jon paused, smiled, and asked, "What about the E word — you know, evolution?"

Well, we did discuss the E word. I pointed out that although the subject of evolution has been one of the most contentious issues the church has ever faced, it is one that we are better able to address today than a century ago. The church was overwhelmed by this issue in the last century because it failed to notice that the dominant worldview of the culture had either already abandoned theism for naturalism or was well on the way in the process. The significance of this is that the church continued to act and react as if the issue were about *facts*, when in fact it was about something else. It was about the overall frame of thought that gives the facts their meaning. I explained to Jon how I too had struggled with the issue of evolution. It took several years before I learned to discern the difference between science and metaphysical naturalism masquerading as science.[39]

38. P. Fong, "Thermodynamics and Statistical Theory of Life: An Outline," in *Biogenesis, Evolution, Homeostasis,* ed. A. Locker (New York: Springer-Verlag, 1973), p. 105.
39. I recommend interested readers to dip into the waters of Phillip Johnson's *Darwin*

It used to be assumed that the only legitimate way to discuss the question of origins in a scientific area was to speak in terms of a natural process, which most have taken to be tantamount to naturalism. It has been widely believed that opposing this automatically meant escaping science entirely and entering the realm of religion and the supernatural. Now, with the recognition that the same methods of science that have uncovered various natural processes are also revealing intelligent design,[40] the opportunity for an alternative approach is available. Instead of attaching philosophical labels — for example, "naturalism" or "theism" — to results of empirical inquiry, it is acceptable to speak in terms of natural and intelligent causes.[41] Whether a further philosophical argument is given that the result is naturalistic or theistic, as in the case of apologetics,[42] it is no part of the scientific discussion proper. The tragedy is that when the distinction between science and apologetics is not recognized, it allows for the culturally dominant philosophy to masquerade as science, and efforts to counter it are labeled as "attacks from the lunatic fringe." Thus it is naturalism that is culturally acceptable and dominant today, and theism that is the "lunatic fringe."[43]

---

on Trial (New York: Regnery Gateway, 1991). Though Johnson is not a scientist (he is a law professor at the University of California), his writing on scientific subjects is remarkably clear and even witty. There is a veritable storm brewing over this book because many Christians have managed to come to terms with Darwin. See, e.g., Johnson's 1992 Founder's Lectures at Trinity Evangelical Divinity School and the response by Howard J. Van Till, professor of physics at Calvin College (currently available only on tape). The issue revolves around this question: Can one hold the natural cause view of Darwin without also embracing naturalism? Johnson argues that establishment scientists *do* mean naturalism when they speak of Darwin's theories. Johnson is not satisfied that theistic evolutionists — or, as he calls them, "theistic naturalists" — have done anything substantially different.

40. Almost any recent popular book on astronomy or cosmology will illustrate my point. So prevalent is the information indicating intelligent design that some have concocted fantastic explanations. None is more fantastic than various descriptions of the anthropic principle, which is a naturalistic way to account for intelligent design features of the universe, including life and human beings. The best single reference is John D. Barrow and Frank J. Tipler, *The Anthropic Cosmological Principle* (New York: Oxford University Press, 1986).

41. This approach is taken in the high school biology supplement by Dean Kenyon and Percival Davis, *Of Pandas and People* (Dallas: Haughton, 1989).

42. An excellent example of naturalistic apologetics, using science in support of naturalism, is Carl Sagan, *Cosmos* (New York: Random House, 1980). Sagan divulges his apologetic purpose at the very beginning of the television series when he says, "The cosmos is all that is or ever was or ever will be" (p. 4).

43. A perfect example of this is the fact that the new booklet *Teaching Science in a Climate of Controversy* (published by the American Scientific Affiliation, P.O. Box 668, Ipswich, MA 01938), which recognizes the legitimacy of natural process origins within a theistic philosophical framework, is lumped together with the young earth creationists by

We discussed many questions regarding fossils, biochemical similarity among all living creatures — especially the universality of the genetic code — the origin of life, and other standard questions about evolution,[44] as well as the fact that it is still true that most of our brightest minds continue to embrace naturalistic perspectives.

Eventually Jon said, "You know, Prof, it's too bad more people don't know these things about the connection between Christianity and science."

"Yes," I agreed. "It is too bad."

"If only more teachers could show students the connection," said Jon, "then maybe more students could be salvaged for Christ, recover the joy of learning, and collectively regain a great cultural influence — and they wouldn't turn to the emptiness of naturalism."

"Yes," I agreed. "If only there were more teachers."

Jon reflected a while, and then asked, "Prof, do you think I'd be a good teacher?"

---

the science establishment and its publications. See *The Science Teacher* 54 (Feb. 1987): 8, and 54 (Sept. 1987): 64, 66.

44. For a thorough critique of Darwinism see Michael Denton, *Evolution: A Theory in Crisis* (Bethesda: Adler & Adler, 1986). For an analysis of origin of life research see Robert Shapiro, *Origins: A Skeptic's Guide to the Creation of Life on Earth* (New York: Summit Books, 1986). A more technical analysis is C. Thaxton, W. Bradley, and R. Olsen, *The Mystery of Life's Origins* (New York: Philosophical Library Publishers, 1984).

The Uneasy Conscience of the
Human Race: Rediscovering Creation
in the "Environmental" Movement

LOREN WILKINSON

IN CARL HENRY'S eighty-year lifetime more momentous changes have occurred than during any comparable time in history. That period has seen two world wars, the tripling of the human population, and advances in technology that have linked humanity (like it or not) into a global community. Such changes have made us uniquely aware of living in a single human *world*, and some of Dr. Henry's most important writings have been those urging Christians to take part in that world socially, politically, and intellectually. His has been a voice urging us not to retreat from the challenges of the modern world but to challenge, transform, direct, and (if necessary) oppose it through the knowing and living of a fully biblical Christianity. He has encouraged Christians to think theologically within the horizon of the modern but not to be limited by that horizon, as God's Word is not limited by it. Thus he has encouraged a recovery of the full strength of historic Christianity, not its compromise.

The need for such deep theological thinking to challenge a new era has by no means passed. For out of the momentous changes accompanying modernity has emerged one change in particular that challenges modernity itself, as well as a Christianity that is all too comfortable within it: that change is the appearance in the last two decades of "the environmental movement." If a characteristic of modernity has been a growing awareness of living in one human *world*, a characteristic of the environmental movement has been an awareness of living on and in one *earth*, in which the supreme importance of the human world and its programs is being radically called into question; thus it is an essentially *postmodern* movement, and it presents particular challenges to a Christianity that has formed its apologetic and its theology in a dialogue with modernity.

The problems with which the environmental movement is concerned have given rise to a whole discipline — "environmental ethics" — with its own *Journal of Environmental Ethics* and dozens of serious books trying to bring ethical principles to bear on what is essentially a new human awareness — that of ethical responsibility for a whole planet and its range of living and non-living things.

One such book is by the Australian philosopher Warwick Fox. Titled *Toward a Transpersonal Ecology: Developing New Foundations for Environmentalism,* it is typical of environmental ethics not only in its moral seriousness and high scholarly quality but also in its tacit assumption that the Western tradition has little to contribute to the building of those new foundations because of (in his words) "the assumption of human self-importance in the scheme of things."[1] (Significantly, Fox's book has on its cover a painting depicting Burmese Buddhist cosmology.) Fox begins his book with a litany of the problems that, he feels, require the development of an environmental ethic. We have heard them before, but we can profitably hear them yet again:

> . . . terrestrial pollution; the pollution of freshwater and marine environments; atmospheric pollution (ranging from local effects to such global concerns as acid rain, the greenhouse effect, and the depletion of the ozone layer); the unintended consequences of the widespread use of biocides . . . ; the long-term containment of highly toxic chemical and nuclear wastes; the hazards associated with nuclear testing and nuclear power generation; the immediate, mid-term and long-term devastation that would be caused by a nuclear war and the nuclear winter that would follow such a war; the hazards associated with releasing genetically engineered organisms into the environment; the degradation and depletion of fisheries, forests, croplands, and grazing lands and the related issues of topsoil erosion, desertification, and urban expansion or citification; the destruction of wilderness; the destruction of nonhuman habitat (whether wilderness or not); the extinction or threatened extinction of particular plant and animal species and, more generally, the astonishing rate of these extinctions; the cruelties inflicted upon nonhuman animals in the course of factory farming and scientific study; the degradation and extinction of aboriginal human cultures; and finally, the plethora of problems associated with exponential human population growth.[2]

1. Fox, *Toward a Transpersonal Ecology* (Boston: Shambala, 1990), p. 10.
2. Fox, *Toward a Transpersonal Ecology,* pp. 3-4.

These problems are real, and they are among the most serious consequences of modernity. But as challenging to Christians as the problems are the proposed solutions. It is frequently argued today that since the modern world has been shaped by the scientific and technological applications of ideas nourished by Christianity, the environmental threats of modernity are *caused by* dangerous flaws in those Christian ideas.

Here are some of those environmentally dangerous ideas attributed to Christianity, which, many argue, need to be replaced by something more environmentally benign (we will have occasion later in this essay to judge if these ideas are indeed Christian, and if so, whether they are as environmentally pernicious as they are alleged to be):

- creation by a transcendent (i.e., detached) and patriarchal God;
- creation of human beings in God's image (thus elevating the human to a status infinitely above everything else in creation);
- the giving of "dominion" to human beings, thus providing license for whatever they want to do with creation;
- a doctrine of the "fall of nature," which sees natural processes (including death) as intrinsically evil;
- a doctrine of salvation in which human beings alone are promised "eternal life," thus making the rest of creation only a backdrop or a means for human salvation;
- a view of history that encourages the destructive notion of progress;
- a short time-scale that impedes appreciation of evolution, and hence of ecology;
- the encouragement of science and technology through the desacralization of creation, faith in its intelligibility, and an affirmation of the appropriateness of human dominion over it.

These are among the principal environmental charges leveled against Christianity.[3]

We need, however, to recognize that although these charges are part of a vigorous criticism of Christianity, they do not amount to a criticism

---

3. I have not specifically documented these charges. Most of them are touched on in Lynn White's famous essay "The Historic Roots of Our Ecologic Crisis" (which was given in an address to the American Association for the Advancement of Science in 1966, was first printed in *Science* 155 [10 March 1967], and has been endlessly anthologized since then). White was the first to make clearly the charge that "Christianity is the most anthropocentric religion the world has ever seen" and "bears a huge burden of guilt" for environmental problems. The ideas have since been repeated uncritically in many places, usually with less thoughtfulness than they were advanced by White.

of religion in general. Quite the contrary: environmentalist criticisms of Christianity are increasingly accompanied by a call for new religious attitudes, as a way of resisting the earth-destroying machine of secular modernity. (And that machine is usually portrayed as being a product of Christendom's devaluing of nature and elevation of human beings.) "Environmentalism" thus contains a criticism not only of modernity but also of Christianity — and a call for new faiths (or a return to old ones) that will honor the earth. Among the religious alternatives being seriously explored today (mainly for environmental reasons) are goddess religion, Wicca, Taoism, Buddhism, and various forms of native spirituality. All of these are rooted in an understanding of "environment" that is supposed to transcend the dangers of the Christian view of creation.

THE EMERGING CONCEPT OF "ENVIRONMENT"

The word *environment* is an attempt to replace earlier ways of thinking of the earth, embodied in yet other names for it. The oldest of those names (still commonly used) is "nature." The word has a bewildering variety of meanings,[4] but the most potent of these reflects an ancient proclivity to personify and deify nature into a vague but fecund force: "Mother Nature." The word is still in common use (and in modern times it has had to bear the added weight of the paradox of *evolution,* considered not simply as a process of change but as "Evolution" in the quasi-religious sense of random change that is at the same time purposeful and directed). In ancient times and throughout the Middle Ages the idea of Nature as sacred, a mysterious and nurturing mother, seems to have discouraged both science and technology; in any case it has too many spiritual and pantheistic connotations for hard-headed modernity. So in the last couple of hundred years "nature" has often come to be spoken of simply as "matter," for the purpose of study, or, from a strictly economic viewpoint, as "natural resources." It was thinking of the earth as "resources" that impelled much of European expansion and empire-building and that underlies modern economic thought.

4. These are summarized very well in C. S. Lewis's fifty-page chapter "Nature," in *Studies in Words* (Cambridge: Cambridge University Press, 1960), pp. 24-74. Lewis speaks of the enduring meaning of "Great Mother Nature" and observes that it "has proved a most potent sense down to the present day. It is 'she' who does nothing by leaps, abhors a vacuum, is *die gute Mutter,* is red in tooth and claw, 'never did betray the heart that loved her,' eliminates the unfit, surges to ever higher and higher forms of life, decrees, purposes, warns, punishes and consoles. . . . [O]f all the pantheon Great Mother Nature has, at any rate, been the hardest to kill" (pp. 41-42).

The earth's principal value, in "resource" thinking, is to provide raw material for human activity.

But if "nature" seemed inadequate because it suggested too much reverence for the earth, "resources" proved inadequate for the opposite reason. In the twentieth century the danger of regarding the earth merely as "resources" came home with a vengeance — starting, in the New World, with problems of erosion and siltation, and leading in the dust-bowl years to the "conservation" movement. But to many thoughtful observers of our relationship to the earth "conservation" itself was too narrow a concept, for it still implied that the main value of soil, water, animals, and plants was to be conserved intact for human use. Thus in the forties there emerged — especially in the work of Aldo Leopold — the first popular articulation of the broad principles of ecology. With a poet's eloquence and a biologist's grasp of ecological principles, Leopold — and later, Rachel Carson, followed by many others — described the earth as an intricate network of relationships of living things exquisitely related to their environment. Thus, by the sixties, John Muir's homespun insight from early in the century ("When you try to pick anything out by itself you find it hooked to everything else on the planet") was confirmed by poet-biologists such as Leopold and Carson, and "ecology" and "environment" began to be household words.[5]

This new awareness of interconnectedness was given dramatic confirmation in the photos of the earth from space. These photographs have become almost iconic in their power to evoke a picture of the earth as *one* thing, the infinitely complex environment for living things. Out of this awareness, rejecting both the pantheism of "nature" and the selfish anthropocentrism of "resources," has come the current word of choice for the earth and everything in it: "the environment."

Yet it is a curiously inadequate word. One problem, of course, is its abstraction. It is as peculiar to call our home planet "the environment" as it would be to call our house "the environment." Though the word is intended to suggest connectedness, its very abstraction disconnects us from any emotional involvement.

But the real problem with the word lies deeper, and it emerges when we ask, *whose* environment? Here there are only two options. First of all, we can mean *our* environment: everything is considered as a support for human civilization. This seems to be the understanding that most people express when they speak, for example, of an urgent need to "clean up" or

5. *Ecology* is a "household" word in a double sense, since it is the study of the *oikos* or "household" of life.

"preserve" *our* environment. But clearly this usage is only a slightly more sophisticated form of regarding the earth as resources: air, plants, animals, and water are considered as valuable resources for us because they sustain human beings. But though many people do use the word in this way, it is clear that a richer and more subtle use is usually intended.

This more sophisticated use of the word *environment* rejects the "speciesism" of the human center and sees human beings as one node in the dynamic network of living and non-living things. Since sophisticated environmental awareness can hardly be separated from evolutionary understanding, this higher use of the word *environment* means something like the following: as a human being I am only one genetic expression of one species that is involved in harmony with all other living things; in fact, I am a part of that network; it is my body, myself, so I have a responsibility to preserve and enhance "the environment" because, ultimately, "the environment" is myself.

This is the conclusion reached by Warwick Fox in the study of environmental ethics quoted above, *Toward a Transpersonal Ecology*. In that study Fox quotes the founder of "Deep Ecology," Arne Naess:

> Care flows naturally if the "self" is widened and deepened so that protection of free Nature is felt and conceived as protection of ourselves. . . . Just as we need not morals to make us breathe . . . [so] if your "self" in the wide sense embraces another being, you need no moral exhortation to show care.[6]

And Fox makes this observation:

> This has the highly interesting, even startling, consequence that ethics (conceived as being concerned with moral "oughts") is rendered superfluous! The reason for this is that if one has a wide, expansive or field-like sense of self then (assuming that one is not self-destructive) one will naturally (i.e. spontaneously) protect the natural (spontaneous) unfolding of the expansive self (the ecosphere, the cosmos) in all its aspects.[7]

As Fox makes clear through abundant citation of the current literature, this is the emerging consensus of "environmental ethics": knowledge is virtue — in this case, a knowledge that nature, the earth, the environment, *is* ourselves. We are not *in* nature; we *are* nature. When we know that, we will act with environmental carefulness.

---

6. Arne Naess, "Self-Realization: An Ecological Approach to Being in the World," quoted in Fox, *Toward a Transpersonal Ecology*, p. 217.

7. Fox, *Toward a Transpersonal Ecology*, p. 217.

There are three reasons why this conception provides an inadequate foundation for "environmental" ethics. The first is logical, and it involves the often-recognized impossibility of moving from "is" to "ought." The whole environmentalist premise is that a change in our behavior is needed. Fox lists a long litany of environmental issues (which I quoted earlier) and repeatedly uses the word *problems* to describe them. But strictly speaking he cannot call them "problems," for on his premises they are simply the way the evolutionary process is unfolding. Here is a blunt statement of the implications of that process in a book by Daniel Kozlovsky entitled (paradoxically) *An Ecological and Evolutionary Ethic*:

> You are an animal, part of a natural process, part of the evolution or convolution of the universe, part of the living fabric of this earth, part of a process whose origin was inevitable in the bonding potentialities of this planet's atoms. . . . You are merely one specimen of one of the millions of living forms, no more important, no more beautiful, no more meaningful than the rest. You are the result of the historic pathways that your gene pool has followed in its complex and intricate journey from simple living stuff to yourself. . . . The only meaning that you have is found in that pathway, just as the only meaning of all other living human forms is to be found in their pathways.[8]

If there is no goal outside the flux of evolutionary change in which life and consciousness have appeared, there can be no "solution" and indeed no problem. Nor can Fox use with any consistency words like *cruelty* and *degradation* to describe anything that happens in that evolutionary flux. If we are simply a part of the process that we are calling "the environment," and if there is no *outside* to that process, we have no reason to lament, denounce, or seek to change anything in the process. It is futile, in such a framework, to imply a direction in which we ought to move or a problem we ought to solve. Lewis put it well in a stanza from his satiric "evolutionary hymn":

> Far too long have sages vainly
> Glossed great Nature's simple text;
> He who runs can read it plainly,
> "Goodness = what comes next."
> By evolving life is solving
> All the questions we perplexed.[9]

8. Daniel Kozlovsky, *An Ecological and Evolutionary Ethic* (Englewood Cliffs, NJ: Prentice-Hall, 1974), p. 109.

9. C. S. Lewis, "Evolutionary Hymn," in *Poems,* ed. Walter Hooper (New York: Harcourt, Brace and World, 1964), p. 55.

The other two problems with "environment" as a foundation are empirical — or at least phenomenological. In the first place, the announcement that ethical concern for nature is an illusion based on a false sense of separation simply does not match our experience. Though we need (desperately) to be reminded of our connectedness to the earth, it is futile to deny our awareness that we are *other* than nature. Surely it is significant that the beached whale, the oil-soaked grebe, and the spotted owl are *objects* of human concern, but neither they nor any other nonhuman creatures exhibit concern for us. This may seem trivial and obvious, but it is important. Conscious human concern for other creatures is not a matter of our being part of them, but a function of the profound and troubling *difference* that our consciousness creates — and it is a difference central to human nature, not just a late effect of alienating modernity.

Finally, we must face the awkward fact that even when we know that something is good for us, we often do not do it. Knowledge of the good — even of a good *for us* — does not necessarily lead to doing that good. We could point to obvious things like smoking and over-eating, as well as to the various subtle forms of physical and psychic self-destruction that our era has perfected. We have far too much evidence that even when we know the good for ourselves, we don't do it; we have little evidence that an increase in knowledge about our interconnectedness with nature will change our behavior.

CHRISTIAN RESPONSES TO ENVIRONMENTALIST CRITIQUES

As Christians have become aware of the scope both of environmental problems and of these diverse (but mainly non-Christian) reactions to the problems, they have tended toward one of four responses.

The first response accepts as accurate most of the description of Christianity we have outlined above, placing much emphasis on the fallenness of nature, on the fact of human dominion, and on the resourcefulness of human ingenuity in finding new ways of solving problems. Those Christians who respond in this way deny, however, that environmental problems are serious. Rather, they regard the media attention given to such supposed problems as yet another thinly disguised socialist attempt to limit human freedoms by impeding the growth of a free market economy. This is the approach taken (for example) by Calvin Beisner in *Prospects for Growth: A Biblical View of Population, Resources and the Future.* His approach is systematically to debunk reports of environmental crises and to oppose anything that would limit the growth of human population or the application (through technology) of human ingenuity. His overarching goal for the use of the earth is expressed in these words:

> Consistent with the dominion mandate's insistence that the earth, with everything in it, was made for man, not man for the earth, the goal of resource management would be to increase the degree to which the world serves man. . . . Within the limits of God's moral Law, any use of resources that serves people is permissible; the more efficiently it serves them the better it is. But any policy-maker who thinks he can determine in advance what uses are best is a sad victim of *hubris*. Freedom, not constraint, must be the rule here.[10]

A second Christian response accepts the reality of environmental problems, but sees them as a grim but ultimately hopeful sign that the last days (and hence the second coming and the establishment of God's kingdom) are almost upon us. This response draws heavily on dispensationalist eschatology, premillennialism, and teachings about a pre-tribulation "rapture" of believers. Though environmental abuse is certainly not encouraged by those who take this approach, they show little long-range concern for the future of the earth, for they believe that it will shortly be destroyed and replaced by God's new creation. Probably the best-known single work here (though it is more a reflection than a cause of widespread attitudes in American conservative Christianity) is Hal Lindsey's *Late Great Planet Earth*.[11]

The third Christian response accepts both the reality of environmental problems and the accuracy of the environmentalist characterization of Christian beliefs. Those who take this approach argue that we need to purge the Christian tradition of environmentally dangerous ideas, even if they have long been regarded as central to the faith. And we need as well to search the Christian tradition for resources that will enable us to meet the challenge posed by the emerging "new story of the earth." This will, they argue, entail a thorough but long-needed revision of orthodox theology.

Here the loudest voice is probably that of the Dominican scholar Matthew Fox, head of the Institute in Culture and Creation Spirituality. Fox argues that we need to move away from an Augustinian theology obsessed with sin and the fall toward a more creation-based theology of "original blessing," with an awareness of the "cosmic Christ." Unfortunately, he seems to reduce the "cosmic Christ" to a principle of cosmic

---

10. Beisner, *Prospects for Growth* (Westchester, IL: Crossway Books, 1990), p. 168. The book was published in conjunction with the Fieldsted Institute, Irvine, CA.

11. Lindsey, *The Late Great Planet Earth* (Grand Rapids: Zondervan, 1970).

interconnectedness, and he condemns salvation through Jesus as "christo-fascism."[12] A more moderate (but no less heterodox) voice in this call for a thorough revision of Christianity is Thomas Berry, a Catholic monk whose *Dream of the Earth* argues (much after the manner of Teilhard de Chardin) for a recasting of the Christian story in terms dictated by current under-standings of cosmology and evolution.[13]

There is a fourth Christian response, and it is much more in line with the example that Carl Henry's theological work has set. This approach takes seriously the integrity and value of the created world, and it takes no less seriously the broad stream of orthodox Christian understanding ex-tending back through the Reformation, the Middle Ages, and the church fathers, and into the New and Old Testaments of the Bible. It is also an approach that recognizes that Christian orthodoxy is rarely a confirmation of the culture — and also rarely a total rejection of it; rather, Christian orthodoxy requires us to sift and evaluate.

In the remainder of this essay I would like to consider some central Christian doctrines that are of particular importance for the environmental movement. Often the parts of these doctrines that pertain to creation have been neglected over the centuries, so I will be drawing heavily on early Christian thought. It will become clear that, when understood in its full biblical force, Christian theology has a great deal to say to and for the environmental movement — not only correcting and refuting its judgment of what Christian teaching is, but also providing rich resources for a theology of care for the earth. I will touch briefly on several doctrines and texts. But all center around a more robust doctrine of creation that takes seriously both God's transcendence and his immanence, and that affirms a thoroughly Trinitarian faith in God as Creator and Redeemer.

THE TRANSCENDENT AND IMMANENT CREATOR

Though we cannot affirm too much the transcendence of God, we often do so to the exclusion of God's immanence, his *closeness* to creation. We

---

12. Among Matthew Fox's more important works are *The Coming of the Cosmic Christ* (San Francisco: Harper & Row, 1988), and *Original Blessing: A Primer in Creation Spirituality* (Santa Fe, NM: Bear and Co., 1983).

13. Berry, *The Dream of the Earth* (San Francisco: Sierra Club Books, 1990). See also his *Befriending the Earth: A Theology of Reconciliation* (Mystic, CT: Twenty-third, 1991), and also his earlier books *Teilhard in the Ecological Age* (Chambersburg, PA: Anima, 1982), and *Management: The Managerial Ethos and the Future of Planet Earth* (Chambers-burg, PA: Anima, 1980).

have defended so ardently the Genesis account of creation "in the beginning" that we overlook the abundant biblical testimony of God's continuing, upholding care for the whole cosmos. Indeed, one of the tragedies of our time is that, while our whole society is crying out for a concept of the earth as "creation" (a cry expressed in the environmental movement), Christians have diminished that concept by their endless squabbling over its "how" and "when." We have neglected to wonder at the "that" of creation *now*.

On the whole the poets have done better at glorying in God's closeness to creation than have the theologians. Thus the poet Gerard Manley Hopkins proclaimed in the first line of one sonnet: "The world is charged with the grandeur of God";[14] and in the last lines of another he exclaimed:

> All things counter, original, spare, strange;
>   Whatever is fickle, freckled (who knows how?)
>   With swift, slow; sweet, sour; adazzle, dim;
> He fathers-forth whose beauty is past change:
>   Praise him.[15]

A result of the theological neglect of God's immanence has been a kind of Christian deism that pictures God as far off, breaking through only in occasional miraculous events. Thus we have seen the Incarnation not as "the Word . . . without [whom] nothing was made," but only as a kind of divine rescue mission, necessary to save God's image-bearers, human beings, from a cursed and doomed creation (like a child from a burning house).

The biblical picture is of a much closer relationship between Creator and creation. God is presented as everywhere present to his creation, but nowhere confused with it — a closeness that would be impossible were it not for his infinite greatness. Hopkins (who, though a great poet, was also no mean theologian) puts this paradox very well:

> God is so deeply present to everything that it would be impossible for him, but for his infinity, not to be identified with them or, from the other side, impossible but for his infinity so to be present to them. This is oddly expressed I see; I mean a being so intimately present as God is to other things would be identified with them were it not for God's infinity, or were it not for God's infinity he could not be so intimately present to things.[16]

14. Hopkins, "God's Grandeur," in *Poems of Gerard Manley Hopkins*, ed. W. H. Gardner and N. H. Mackenzie (London: Oxford University Press, 1967), p. 31.

15. Hopkins, "Pied Beauty," in *Poems*, p. 70.

16. Hopkins, *Sermons and Writings of G. M. Hopkins*, ed. Christopher Devlin, S.J. (London: Oxford University Press, 1959), p. 128.

Two texts make the point well. One is Psalm 104, which is loosely patterned after the order of Genesis 1. Unlike Genesis 1, however, many of God's creative acts are here presented not as taking place in some archetypal beginning but as happening continually, *now:*

> He makes springs pour water into the ravines;
> . . . .
> He waters the mountains from his upper chambers;
> . . . .
> He makes grass grow for the cattle,
>   and plants for man to cultivate —
>   bringing forth food from the earth.
> . . . .
>
> These all look to you
>   to give them their food at the proper time.
> . . . .
> When you send your Spirit,
>   they are created,
>   and you renew the face of the earth.
>
> (vv. 10, 13, 14, 27, 30)

This is certainly not pantheism (a heresy to which Christians sometimes fear an emphasis on God's immanence will lead). For the Psalmist never confuses Creator and creation, but sees God's goodness and self-giving love as present *here* and *now*. In the New Testament, Paul in his sermons to the pagan world takes seriously the pagan recognition of the overflowing goodness of creation, but he turns it back to its proper source: the God who (in Paul's words to the Athenians) "is not far from each one of us. 'For in him we live and move and have our being'" (Acts 17:27-28). In another pagan setting, at Lystra, Paul urges the people to turn to "the living God, who made heaven and earth and sea and everything in them" (14:15). But Paul goes on to make clear that this Creator is not distant in space or time:

> [H]e has not left himself without testimony: He has shown kindness by giving you rain from heaven and crops in their seasons; he provides you with plenty of food and fills your hearts with joy. (14:17)

The biblical picture of creation is also a trinitarian one, and the challenge of the environmental movement may well drive us to rediscover the neglected doctrines of the *Creator Spiritus* and of a *biblical* "cosmic Christ." Our tendency to associate God the Father with creation, and the other two persons of the Trinity with salvation and sanctification respectively, has contributed to a skewed emphasis on the transcendence of the Creator. For though we do indeed experience the Son and the Spirit in the Christian life, we tend to think of them as related to creation only in the subjectivity of individual men and women. Thus we tend to think of our intimacy with God in terms of those persons of the Trinity whom we suppose have much to do with us but little to do with the rest of creation. We forget that the "Spirit of God" who moved on the face of the deep in Genesis 1, and who "creates" the beasts from the dust in Psalm 104, is the same Spirit who bears witness with ours, the same Spirit with whom Christians pray to be filled.

Likewise we need to recognize the involvement of the Son in creation. Many texts speak of this "cosmic Christ" (including, perhaps, Proverbs 8, that strange glimpse of "Wisdom," which has traditionally been associated with the pre-incarnate Christ). But the clearest texts are well-known New Testament passages: John 1, which speaks of Christ as the Word "through [whom] all things were made" (v. 3); Colossians 1, which speaks of Christ as the one "by [whom] all things were created," the one in whom "all things hold together" (vv. 16-17); Ephesians 1:10, which speaks of Christ as the fulfillment of all things, and of God's purpose "to bring all things in heaven and on earth together under one head, even Christ"; and Hebrews 1, which speaks of Christ as the one "through whom [God] made the universe," who is "sustaining all things by his powerful word" (vv. 2-3). Yet these writers speak of Christ not as some cosmic abstraction; this is indeed "Jesus our Immanuel," God with us, the Word made flesh — in John's words, "That which was from the beginning, which we have heard, which we have seen with our eyes, which we have looked at and our hands have touched" (1 John 1:1). And we need to recapture the fact that repeatedly the writers speak of Christ's relationship not just to human beings but to "all things" that are the concern of the environmentalists as well.

Contrast this rich picture of an immediate and giving Creator with the typical impression in the environmental movement of what Christians are supposed to believe. The following passage, taken from an anthology of "ecofeminist" literature, is fairly typical. The author refers to the concept of divine immanence and calls it

a concept foreign to those raised in Judeo-Christianity. The view that we've grown up with is that the divine and matter are separate and that matter is really dangerous. The material world belongs to the devil. What's under your feet is closer to hell.[17]

We can easily criticize the shallowness of this author's understanding, but we have to acknowledge the likelihood that she picked up her impression of God's relationship to the world not from reading the Bible but from listening to and watching Christians. It is not surprising therefore that, dimly grasping the goodness of God in creation, many in the environmental movement turn from the shallow and deistic notion that they associate with Christianity — but turn unwittingly as well from the full picture of God given in the Bible, and thus end up with some form of pantheism or nature worship.

REDEMPTION

Just as we have let a diminished picture of creation obscure the full sweep of the biblical doctrine of creation, so also we have focused on only part of the biblical doctrine of redemption and have left out God's concern for the renewal of all creation. There is a curious historical narrowing of our understanding of the scope of redemption that has undoubtedly contributed to the general impression that Christians' notion of salvation leaves creation behind. Frederick Dillistone, in his study of various understandings of the atonement, describes this irony:

> the smaller the dimensions of man's world, the more wide-ranging is likely to be his systematic account of reconciliation. As his world expands, so his system seems to contract. When the limits of his universe have vanished into far-off distances, his concentration of concern tends to be focussed upon the small-scale world of the isolated inner self. Such a sequence can certainly be seen in the history of theories of the Atonement.[18]

For a thousand years Western Christian theology has been hampered by an understanding of the atonement that has been too narrowly focused on legal metaphors of justification, and that has neglected the equally

17. Susan Griffin, "Curves Along the Road," in *Reweaving the World: The Emergence of Ecofeminism,* ed. Irene Diamond and Gloria Feman Orenstein (San Francisco: Sierra Club Books, 1990), p. 87.

18. Dillistone, *The Christian Understanding of Atonement* (Welwyn: James Nisbet, 1968), p. 406.

biblical teaching of salvation as *restoration* —or, to use an English translation of Paul's term in Ephesians 1, as "recapitulation."

This was the understanding of the atonement that was central in Irenaeus, whose closeness to the apostles (though certainly no guarantee against error!) gives his second-century theological articulation great weight.

It may be that the challenge of the "environmental movement" will lead us to rediscover truths about the atonement first articulated by Irenaeus. Certainly the fact that he is being defended today by heterodox Christian thinkers such as Matthew Fox should not dissuade us from learning from his thought; rather, we should restore it to the center of a fully orthodox and biblical theology.

Irenaeus places the victory of Christ within the purpose and intention of creation (as does the whole biblical story). The whole point of Christ's work on the cross is, for Irenaeus, the *restoration* and *completion* of God's work in creation.

> For the Lord, taking dust from the earth, moulded man; and it was upon his behalf that all the dispensation of the Lord's advent took place. He had Himself, therefore, flesh and blood, *recapitulating in Himself not a certain other, but that original handiwork of the Father,* seeking out that thing which had perished.[19]

Irenaeus stresses here what is obscured in the more recent Western understanding of the atonement — that is, the fact that we are redeemed not simply by a sinless man, the perfect victim, but by God himself, *our Creator.* If we take seriously the New Testament passages that link Christ to creation, we must take seriously as well the implications of the atonement for the whole creation. Irenaeus puts eloquently this summing up and restoring of all things in Christ:

> For the Creator of the world is truly the Word of God: and this is our Lord, who in the last times was made man, existing in this world, and who in an invisible manner contains all things created, and is inherent in the entire creation, since the Word of God governs and arranges all things; and therefore He came to His own in a visible manner, and was made flesh, and hung upon the tree, that He might sum up all things in Himself.[20]

19. Irenaeus *Against Heresies* 5.14.2, in *The Ante-Nicene Fathers,* vol. 1: *The Apostolic Fathers with Justin Martyr and Irenaeus,* ed. Alexander Roberts and James Donaldson (1885; repr. Grand Rapids: Eerdmans, 1975), p. 541; emphasis added.

20. Irenaeus *Against Heresies* 5.18.3, pp. 546-47.

Nor is this understanding of the atonement as "recapitulation" peculiar to Irenaeus. As Gustaf Aulén points out in *Christus Victor*, it was central to the theology of all the fathers:

> To mention only the most important names, Origen, Athanasius, Basil the Great, Gregory of Nyssa, Gregory of Nazianzus, Cyril of Alexandria, Cyril of Jerusalem, and Chrysostom.[21]

Athanasius's words put very eloquently the same link between Christ and creation that Irenaeus saw:

> We will begin, then, with the creation of the world and with God its Maker, for the first fact that you must grasp is this: *the renewal of creation has been wrought by the Self-same Word Who made it in the beginning.* There is thus no inconsistency between creation and salvation; for the One Father has employed the same Agent for both works, effecting the salvation of the world through the same Word Who made it at the first.[22]

When we grasp the awesome fact that we are redeemed by our Creator (the Word in whom "all things hold together") it will be easier for us to see that God's kingdom is not concerned just with human salvation, but with (in a phrase repeated fully five times in Col. 1:15-20) the reconciliation of "all things" to himself. And such a recognition will give new meaning to our often repeated prayer: "Thy kingdom come, Thy will be done, *on earth* as it is in heaven." The whole *earth* is intended here (in the kind of minute detail that the new science of ecology is beginning to show us), not just the world of the human heart or the world of human affairs.

SIN, HUMAN NATURE, AND STEWARDSHIP

But how is God's purpose for the reconciliation of all things related to the pervasiveness of sin — and to the actions of sinful human beings? One of the most persistent environmentalist critiques of Christianity is that Christians regard the world as cursed and of little worth in view of the drama of human salvation. As we have seen, many Christians concur in this view. Their argument is that, through human sin, creation is irreparably fallen,

21. Aulén, *Christus Victor: An Historical Study of the Three Main Types of the Idea of the Atonement* (New York: Macmillan, 1931), p. 53.

22. St. Athanasius, *On the Incarnation*, translated and edited by a Religious of C.S.M.V. (Crestwood, NY: St. Vladimir's Orthodox Theological Seminary, 1953), p. 26.

shot through with pain and death; but God chose to save his image-bearers *out of* fallen creation to live eternally with him, while creation (subjected to "futility" through human sin) is consigned to destruction.

A far more biblical view is that creation is fallen *through* human sin and will be redeemed *through* human redemption. The earth is not objectively "cursed," but it is fallen because its human head is fallen. This is implicit in the wording of Genesis 3:17: it is not so much that the ground is cursed "because of you" but "with respect to you." That this is the intended meaning becomes clearer in verse 18: "It will produce thorns and thistles *for you*"; thorns and thistles were a part of God's good creation, but they have become a curse because of the nature of our alienation. The human relationship to the earth has become one of enmity, cross-purposes. Thus creation waits (in the language of Romans 8) "in eager expectation for the sons of God to be revealed" (v. 19).

Many Old Testament texts present the same picture of a close relationship between human sin and the health of the land. Perhaps the most vivid is in Hosea:

> There is no faithfulness, no love,
> no acknowledgment of God in the land.
> There is only cursing, lying and murder,
> stealing and adultery;
> . . . .
>
> Because of this the land mourns,
> and all who live in it waste away;
> the beasts of the fields and the birds of the air
> and the fish of the sea are dying.
>
> (4:1-3)

What these texts suggest is that, far from human redemption being a *deliverance from* our embeddedness in the rest of creation, it is the beginning of redemption *for* that creation. Human beings are presented as *mediators* between creation and God. Here once again the Eastern Orthodox tradition has understood this most clearly. Vladimir Lossky declares:

> In his way to union with God, man in no way leaves creatures aside, but gathers together in his love the whole cosmos disordered by sin, that it may at last be transfigured by grace.[23]

23. Lossky, *The Mystical Theology of the Eastern Church,* translated by members of the fellowship of St. Alban and St. Sergius (London: James Clarke & Company, 1957), p. 111.

And Bishop Kallistos Ware says of the human task in creation:

> Made in the divine image, microcosm and mediator, man is priest and king of the creation. Consciously and with deliberate purpose, he can do two things that the animals can only do unconsciously and instinctively. First, *Man is able to bless and praise God for the world.* . . . Secondly, besides blessing and praising God for the world, man is also able to *reshape and alter the world.*[24]

To the environmentalists it is a kind of heresy to say anything good about the human ability to "reshape and alter the world," although this ability reflects the picture of human nature presented in the Bible — for example, in the notorious Genesis 1:28 command to have dominion, as well as in the lofty picture in Psalm 8 of human beings with "all things under their feet" (v. 6, NRSV). It also reflects the reality of the human experience in the world: as fellow creatures with other things, but also separate from them and having power over them. The alienation of sin has caused that separateness to be expressed in domination and destruction. We are used to seeing this alienation in our relationship with people. We need to realize that in our relationship to creation, as well as in our relationships with other people, power should be used for caring. Through the restoration accomplished in Christ, our creative, dangerous, but God-given powers of dominion can become restoring, healing powers, leading to an enhancement of what God has made, to an unfolding of the Creator's purpose. To quote Kallistos Ware again:

> the fact that man is in God's image means that man is a creator after the image of God the Creator. This creative role he fulfills not by brute force, but through the clarity of his spiritual vision; his vocation is not to dominate and exploit nature, but to transfigure and hallow it.[25]

Which brings us to yet another biblical doctrine that the environmental movement is helping us to rediscover — that is, the fact that we are *stewards* of creation. This picture of the human task as a priestly, preserving, and unfolding activity, in which the Creator's image-bearers are responsible both *for creation* and *to the Creator* is a biblical view. Yet the concept of "stewardship" is used increasingly in the secular world to speak of our responsibility for creation. Sadly, only half of the concept is usually used:

24. Ware, *The Orthodox Way* (Crestwood, NY: St. Vladimir's Seminary Press, 1979), pp. 68-69.

25. Ware, *The Orthodox Way,* p. 69.

responsibility *for* creation, but not responsibility *to* any Lord other than creation itself. We Christians need to recover the concept of stewardship. Yet we have diminished this concept almost as much as we have that of "creation," by limiting it only to stewardship of monetary wealth — and that usually only in the context of giving to the church. As Douglas John Hall puts it in his book entitled (significantly) *The Steward: A Biblical Symbol Come of Age:* "Our first responsibility as Christian stewards today may be to become better stewards of the stewardship idea itself!"[26]

THE SABBATH

As we come to the end of this discussion of ways in which the environmental movement is influencing us to rediscover some key biblical doctrines, it is appropriate to consider the Sabbath. Centuries of unhelpful legalisms regarding what is and is not appropriate to do on the Sabbath have obscured the central fact about the fourth commandment: it is fundamentally a call to rest and rejoice with God over creation and God's work in creation. Here we have much to learn from Jewish attitudes toward the Sabbath.

We forget, too, that the culmination of creation in the biblical account is not (as is so often supposed) the creation of man and woman; it is rather the Sabbath rest in which all of creation is experienced as complete, as good, and as an object of joy. We can hardly expect to remember creation adequately if we forget the Sabbath. As Jürgen Moltmann puts it:

> on the sabbath and through it, men and women perceive as God's creation the reality in which they live and which they themselves are. The sabbath opens creation for its true future. On the sabbath the redemption of the world is celebrated in anticipation.[27]

In the celebration of the Sabbath, a limit is drawn to human activity. Thus we are reminded of our creatureliness, of the fact that our very existence is a gift from God. At the same time, we are regularly invited back into our flawed human priesthood, our privilege of offering creation back in thankfulness to the Creator. To quote Moltmann again:

> The celebration of the sabbath leads to an intensified capacity for perceiving the loveliness of everything — food, clothing, the body, the soul

---

26. Hall, *The Steward: A Biblical Symbol Come of Age* (New York: Friendship Press, 1982). See also the recently revised edition of the book (Grand Rapids: Eerdmans, 1990).
27. Moltmann, *God in Creation* (London: SCM, 1985), p. 266.

— because existence itself is glorious. Questions about the possibility of "producing" something, or about utility, are forgotten in the face of the beauty of all created things, which have their meaning simply in their very selves.[28]

Nor should we think of the Sabbath as an outmoded Jewish celebration. The Jewish Sabbath and the Christian feast of the Resurrection — one celebrating the old creation, the other looking forward to its restoration, through Christ, in the new — are closely related. A final practical suggestion from Moltmann:

> It would be a useful practical step in this direction if the *eve* of Sunday were allowed to flow into a sabbath stillness. The Saturday evening devotions which are held in many congregations, and which many Christians like to attend, always unconsciously and involuntarily contain something of the rest and happiness of Israel's sabbath. After the week's work one comes to rest in God's presence, sensing on this evening something of the divine "completion" of creation. Worship on Sunday morning can then be set wholly in the liberty of Christ's resurrection for the new creation.[29]

*　　　*　　　*

The "environmental movement" challenges the confident modernity of this century in which Carl Henry has been such a persistent and articulate voice for faithfulness to the gospel and to the ethic it contains. As the century draws to a close we need to hear the confused voices from the environmental movement as what they often are: an intimation of the fact that we are creatures and stewards. The environmental movement is an ethic looking for a religion — indeed, a religion looking for God. We need to recover, from Scripture and the richness of the Christian tradition, deeper doctrines of creation and redemption. Then, as Paul did in Athens, we can say to our contemporaries (who are beginning to catch a glimpse of their stewardly task as God's image-bearers): "What you worship as something unknown I am going to proclaim to you" (Acts 17:23).

28. Moltmann, *God in Creation*, p. 286.
29. Moltmann, *God in Creation*, p. 296.

Bioethics: The Twilight
of Christian Hippocratism

NIGEL M. DE S. CAMERON

SIR EDWARD CREASY'S *Fifteen Decisive Battles of the World*[1] may seem
to reduce human history to the military engagements that, since Marathon,
have marked the high- and low-water marks of imperial power. Yet there
was nothing antecedently inevitable about the victory of Miltiades over
Datis, and part of the virtue of this sort of history writing is the lesson it
teaches that a well-fought engagement can really make a difference. When
our grandchildren come to write their intellectual and social histories there
can be little doubt as to the decisive significance of current discussion of
bioethics in determining the shape of post-Christian Western society, and
it is a thousand pities that the contemporary evangelical movement shows
so general a disinterest in serious engagement in this discipline.[2] Widespread recent recruitment of evangelicals to the pro-life cause has had no
parallel in the vigorous academic field of inquiry that in the past two
decades has taken the leading edge of bioethical thinking far beyond the
horizons of the abortion debate. And vigorous it has proved to be. The
burgeoning of bioethics as an academic/professional discipline is a recognized phenomenon in the academic world, plainly measurable in publishing, academic appointments, international conferences, and the establishment worldwide of scores of "centers" and other institutional
expressions of commitment to this new field. Perhaps the best of all
barometers is the appearance of new journals, and here progress has been

---

1. Creasy, *The Fifteen Decisive Battles of the World* (1851); various reissues.
2. There are notable exceptions, including Carl F. H. Henry himself and, especially,
Harold O. J. Brown. Recent writers include Allen Verhey and John Frame.

spectacular, with a constant stream of fresh announcements.[3] Evangelical participation in the mainstream bioethics community has been modest, with a modesty unbecoming those who have such a stake in the outcome of the community's thinking.[4] Evangelical investment in bioethics institutions has been almost nil.[5]

Explanations are generally elusive, though not entirely so. One factor has been the widespread evangelical unease with philosophy, the lingua franca of the bioethics world. Another lies in the forgivable but ultimately disastrous desire of evangelicals for simplicity at all costs. The pro-life movement offers a necessarily simplistic account of the crisis in contemporary medical-scientific values by fastening exclusively on the status of the fetus as its sole public policy concern (though the question of euthanasia has started to awaken an adjunct interest, if no more). The pro-life movement can hardly be faulted for its political savvy (a single-issue focus is almost required for effectiveness), though a deeper awareness of the public policy issues that will confront evangelicals ten or twenty years down the road would have given a three-dimensional quality to campaigning concerns, as well as helping to prepare the constituency for the next campaign and the next-but-one. Pro-life organizations — evangelical and other — have shown scant interest in sponsoring the kinds of research that would help them develop their own thinking beyond the demands of the immediate political agenda.

A further factor, affecting the evangelical constituency more broadly — and perhaps especially its existing educational and other institutions — is the uncertainty and, at points, deep disagreement that have marked its response to key questions such as abortion.[6] There has been some development here, since evangelical opinion was much more divided and uncertain twenty years ago on that issue than it is today. But as euthanasia and the various dimensions of our new capacity for genetic manipulation rise up the political-moral agenda, further division and uncertainty within

3. There is a new announcement every few months, though evangelicals have yet to launch a technical journal.

4. Very few evangelicals are to be found at the international conferences that have become determinative of the development of the bioethics community. It is of course true that evangelicals who are interested in these questions tend to be associated with evangelical schools, which in turn may be less interested in funding such participation — which raises the institutional question afresh.

5. Modest exceptions are the Lindeboom Instituut at Ede in the Netherlands and the fledgling Centre for Bioethics and Public Policy in London. Trinity Evangelical Divinity School is in process of launching an M.A. track in bioethics.

6. For example, members of the (British) Christian Medical Fellowship offered two conflicting responses to their government's advisory body on embryo research issues.

the community appear inevitable. Indeed, our failure to develop institutions within and among which these questions could be addressed is storing up all manner of difficulty in articulating an evangelical position on issues that have yet to be posed. This is not least among the reasons why such institutional development is now urgent.

But the intention of this essay is no more to explain the parsimony of the evangelical imagination than to lambaste it. There is limited though growing evidence that the situation is at least beginning to right itself, with a handful of evangelicals participating in bioethical debates and interpreting bioethics to the evangelical community. What is particularly urgent, if this development is to be sustained, is the need for appropriate institutions to be established so that a self-sustaining evangelical mind can develop, sketching broad perspectives for its community, defining options on particular controverted questions, and giving effective voice to evangelical concerns in the twin arenas within which the crucial discussions are in progress: public policy debate, and behind public policy debate — and sinisterly and depressingly determinative of it — debate within the international bioethics community.

Yet what of bioethics itself? Its phenomenal growth has been widely observed. As the supremely interdisciplinary discipline, it stands at the confluence of the biomedical sciences, law, philosophy, theology, and, of course, ethics itself as analyst and would-be arbiter of the contested terrain in which most "bioethicists" — who have themselves set out from one of the traditional disciplines — have established for themselves a multidisciplinary bridgehead in the land of values, science, and medical practice. This, of course, is not some arcane country, but the place where men and women live; and the fateful character of contemporary bioethics lies precisely in its occupation of that part of the intellectual landscape where a new understanding of what it means to be human is being fashioned and tested. So the Christian stake could hardly be higher.

How then should we understand the establishment and rapid growth of this most interdisciplinary of disciplines? There are two coincident factors that together begin to offer an explanation. The first factor is the "revolution" in medical technology. This is actually not one but a cluster of developments — developments in drug therapy, surgery, the technology of life-support systems, and parallel developments such as the general appropriation of information technology. These developments have combined to lengthen the reach of medical science, and they have also combined to add increasingly expensive items to the menu of clinical options. Expectations have been raised and often met, fueling an inflation of demand. Consequent crises in resourcing have been one result. Attempts at resolution have, of course, taken different forms within different health-care systems, but resultant rationing in such procedures as renal dialysis and neonatal special care has been universal — whatever its method — and has given public focus to ethical conflicts. At other times it is the availability of new biological techniques — supremely, *in vitro* fertilization — that has raised new issues. In other cases, different issues are prominent: abortion, of course, continues for the public and politician alike to be the most significant bioethical issue of our day, and though it is safer and more widely available than ever before, it is nothing new. The next big storm is brewing over euthanasia. Though this question is intersected by special concerns over the use of technology — which enables many patients, whether accident victims or terminally ill, to survive when previously they would have died — the practice, like that of abortion, is as old as human society.

The prominence of these life issues in contemporary bioethical discussion gives the lie to the widespread assumption that the bioethics boom is simply the fruit of revolutionary progress in the development of medical technology and the hard questions it has forced upon us. The second level of explanation is more fundamental, and it lies in the breakup of the ethical consensus in Western society. The medical culture to which we have fallen heir dates back before Christ to the Hippocratic physicians of ancient Greece, though it was early recognized by Christians as congruent with their own special values and came to exercise a mesmeric influence down many centuries of health care in Judeo-Christian (and also, though distinctly, in Islamic) society.[7] Central to that medical culture has been the sanctity of life. (Proscriptions of both abortion and suicide-euthanasia lie side by side in the Hippocratic Oath with principles such as confidentiality and the germ of the idea of what we now call a profession.)[8] Medical values

---

7. This thesis is further sketched in my book *The New Medicine: Life and Death After Hippocrates* (Westchester, IL: Crossway, 1992).

8. The Hippocratic Oath reads as follows (translation by W. H. S. Jones in his book *The Doctor's Oath* [Cambridge: Cambridge University Press, 1924], with minor alterations and added headings):

The Covenant

I swear by Apollo Physician, by Asclepius, by Hygeia, by Panaceia, and by all the gods and goddesses, making them witnesses, that I will carry out, according to my ability and judgment, this oath and indenture:

Duties to Teacher

To regard my teacher in this art as equal to my parents; to make him partner in my livelihood, and when he is in need of money to share mine with him; to consider his offspring equal to my brothers; to teach them this art, if they require to learn it,

have not been isolated from those of society at large, though the relationship is complex and medicine has maintained — or has been expected to maintain — the highest values held in general esteem.[9] The Hippocratic profession was from the start a moral calling, and its most characteristic feature was its inseparable blending of its distinct moral values and medical technique, strikingly illustrated by the prohibition in the oath from teaching medical skills to any persons who have not already first committed themselves to the Hippocratic values. Part of the special importance of current developments in medical values lies in the role of medicine as an index of wider social change in the double move both away from Hippocratic-Judeo-Christian values and, at the same time, away from *any* consensus values. For it is not that some new religion has usurped the old; the post-Christian society is developing as a kind of anti-society in which consensus values — the substructure of every other society, past and present — have been displaced by a value anarchy that seeks its validation and strives for social cohesion through models of autonomy alone, as if pluralism were a unifying "ism" like any other. Just as medicine once served as standard-bearer of

---

without fee or indenture; and to impart precept, oral instruction, and all the other learning, to my sons, to the sons of my teacher, and to pupils who have signed the indenture and sworn obedience to the physicians' Law, but to none other.

Duties to Patients

I will use treatment to help the sick according to my ability and judgment, but will never use it to injure or wrong them.

I will not give poison to anyone though asked to do so, nor will I suggest such a plan. Similarly I will not give a pessary to a woman to cause abortion. But in purity and in holiness I will guard my life and my art.

I will not use the knife either on sufferers from stone, but will give place to such as are craftsmen therein.

Into whatsoever house I enter, I will do so to help the sick, keeping myself free from all intentional wrong-doing and harm, especially from fornication with woman or man, bond or free.

Whatsoever in the course of practice I see or hear (or even outside my practice in social intercourse) that ought never to be published abroad, I will not divulge, but consider such things to be holy secrets.

The Sanction

Now if I keep this oath and break it not, may I enjoy honour, in my life and art, among men for all time; but if I transgress and forswear myself, may the opposite befall me.

9. The relation of medicine and society is most helpfully discussed in Eliot Freidson, *Profession of Medicine: A Study in the Sociology of Applied Knowledge* (New York: Harper & Row, 1970).

all that was best in the old society, so it is coming to exemplify the new in its ambiguity and growing incoherence.

CHRISTIAN HIPPOCRATISM

The Western medical tradition owes its origins and its character to a striking fusion of pagan and (Judeo-)Christian notions. The enduring association of Hippocrates of Cos and the practice of medicine in the Christian/post-Christian West offers telling evidence of the welcome that the church extended to this product of pagan antiquity. There is some evidence of Christian attempts to bowdlerize the pagan oath[10] (an approach adopted with much more success within Islam, where also Hippocratism was welcomed and became the standard of medical values);[11] but it was the original, overtly pagan form of the oath that was adopted into and remained the standard of Christian medicine.

There is much uncertainty as to the origins of the oath and its historical connection with Hippocrates himself. He was the most famous of all the physicians of antiquity, and his name is associated with a considerable library of writings on ethical, clinical, dietary, and other medically related issues, conventionally referred to — with unintended humor — as the Hippocratic *corpus.* Scholarly opinion locates some of this material after his time, and there seems good reason to believe that, however formal or informal it may have been, there was a Hippocratic "school" associated with the name and memory of Hippocrates of Cos that sought to perpetuate and develop his thinking.[12]

More than one historical reconstruction has been offered,[13] but the most influential (it was actually cited by the court in *Roe v. Wade* in a curious attempt to relativize the significance of the Hippocratic tradition) remains that of Ludwig Edelstein, a distinguished historian of medicine

10. See Jones, *The Doctor's Oath,* pp. 23ff.

11. See M. Ullmann, *Islamic Medicine* (Edinburgh: University of Edinburgh Press, 1978).

12. Little is known with any certainty about Hippocrates of Cos (460-377 B.C. are the years most often suggested for his life; he died old, some say a centenarian). Jones summarizes what we do know in *The Doctor's Oath,* with the authority of the editor of the Loeb edition of the *corpus.*

13. For references see the most recent scholarly study in English of the Hippocratic tradition (though its chief interest does not lie in Hippocratic *ethics*), Owsei Temkin, *Hippocrates in a World of Pagans and Christians* (Baltimore: Johns Hopkins University Press, 1991), p. 21n.16.

who in 1943 published a monograph on the oath in which he sought a location for its values and its understanding of medicine within the religious and philosophical schools of Greek antiquity. Edelstein searched the religious-philosophical options of the period for one in which the declared values of the oath would find a home. He found it in the school of the Pythagoreans, about whom not much is known, though we do know that they held some distinct opinions on some of the highly controversial issues on which the oath displays a distinctive view (especially abortion and what Edelstein calls suicide-euthanasia, both of which were commonly approved in the Greece of antiquity but forbidden in the oath).

Edelstein's Pythagorean identification of the early Hippocratics may or may not be correct. But the significance of his work has been to repristinate Hippocratic medical values as those of a reforming minority. This is important for two reasons. First, before his monograph there was a tendency for writers to laud the values of the oath as self-evidently true, a collection of statements of the obvious.[14] Second, we have inherited Hippocratic medicine as consensus medicine, for so it has been for many centuries during which few have dissented from its understanding of human dignity and the role and calling of the physician. Edelstein's work reminds us of the highly controversial character of human values, of which the dissonant ethical voices of Greek antiquity offer us a paradigm; and it reminds us of the calling of the first Hippocratics and the challenge they faced as they sought to commend and practice their very distinctive values in a society that marched to a different drum. In other words, Edelstein's thesis repristinates Hippocratism as a dissident medical creed, and the oath as (to use his term) a "manifesto" for the humane medical values it advocates. Since the wheel of medical values is set to turn full circle as we emerge into a post-Hippocratic medical culture, this rediscovery is timely.

The readiness with which Christians embraced Hippocratic medicine, and even its plainly pagan oath, underlines its fundamental congruence with a Christian agenda for medical values. That is perhaps most evident in the stress that the oath places on the sanctity of human life. The explicit prohibition on medical killing (whether in abortion or in medically assisted suicide) and the patient-first emphasis (Hippocratic philanthropism) outline a nonmanipulative, servant role for medicine and energetically distinguish between medicine as healing and medicine as anything else. The old, pre-Hippocratic medicine — like the post-Hippocratism emerging today — did not make these distinctions. Moreover, the context of these distinct ethical commitments was theistic, even if its theism was pagan. The key

14. Jones, *The Doctor's Oath*, offers a good example.

to the significance of theism for the oath lies in the fact that it was an *oath*. How far we have moved from a medical culture in which the transcendent ethics of Christian Hippocratism set the context for clinical practice is sadly evident in the fact that of the many influential modern restatements of (more or less) Hippocratic medical values, starting with the definitive Declaration of Geneva of 1948, which sought — on behalf of the World Medical Association — to reinstate the Hippocratic basis of international clinical practice after the sorry story of Nazi medicine, not one is actually cast in the form of an oath; and no one seems to have noticed. For the first Christians, this pagan medical ideology, which sought to limit the physician's role to that of healer and which did so explicitly *coram Deo,* was immensely attractive. What is more, by its nature the oath declares medicine to be, first and foremost, a matter of moral commitment;[15] this is made explicit in its own prohibition on the passing on of medical skills to those who have not first accepted its values. The understanding of medicine that is gaining currency today — as essentially a set of skills that may or may not be acquired alongside this or that code of values — is anathema to the oath, which joined together technique and value, the "life" and the "art" of the Hippocratic practitioner, in an indissoluble union that has characterized not simply the idea of medicine but, at its best, the idea of a profession. Thus Hippocratism was adopted into the church, *mutatis mutandi,* as the basis for the Christian practice of medicine. And it is for these same reasons that the Christian stake in Hippocratism is today so great.

It has been common for evangelicals to dismiss the significance of bioethics as simply an intra-professional discussion, important no doubt for physicians, but no more important for the rest of us than ethical discussions within the many other professional communities. But this dismissal arises out of a naive misunderstanding of the significance of medicine. The subject matter of contemporary bioethics is only incidentally related to the professional responsibilities of the physician. That is part of the reason why *bioethics* or *biomedical ethics* is generally used in place of *medical ethics* as the generic term for the discipline (in North America, at least). Bioethics treats of fundamental human values; generally these values involve a medical or medical-scientific component, but at several removes from the "old" medical ethics, which majored in medical etiquette — addressing such questions as whether or not it is proper for a physician to form a liaison with a patient, for example. Not that these areas are unrelated; the Hippocratic Oath addressed them both (and its doctrine of medical

---

15. For a contemporary echo, see especially the work of Stanley Hauerwas — e.g., his book *Suffering Presence* (Notre Dame: University of Notre Dame Press, 1986).

confidentiality, for example, remains fundamental and unchallenged). But the farther the center of controversy moves from professional etiquette, the greater is its impact on public policy discussion and matters that affect us all at the most profound level. So abortion and euthanasia are, of course, issues with vital medical dimensions, but none would deny that they are chiefly moral and social questions and that, at the level of principle, they are not for the medical profession to resolve.

This is, indeed, one reason why the discipline of bioethics has developed, and why it has developed alongside and not as a department of medicine. But that leads us to recognize the universality of the questions that are being raised under this head. Rather curiously, part of the reason for and part of the result of the underdeveloped state of bioethical discussion within the evangelical community lies in the conservative character of evangelical medicine in this respect. The medical mainstream has been more open, and has been open for a longer period of time, to nonmedical participation in bioethical discussion than has evangelical medicine. In the light of evangelicals' overt religious and moral commitments, this is surprising, and its explanation is probably to be sought in sensitivity in areas like abortion over which evangelical opinion has itself been divided (especially twenty or more years ago, when bioethics was in its infancy and the structure of much later discussion was being decided).

The subject matter of bioethics is humankind; man, male and female, made in the image of God. That is the starting point of Christian reflection, and that is also the point at which contemporary secular bioethical discussion makes contrary assumptions about the nature of the being who is the subject of argument. Human being is made in the *imago Dei,* and while the content to be given to this fundamental biblical concept is the subject of continuing discussion,[16] it is bearing the divine image and likeness that marks off human being from all other kinds of created being and declares human life to be "sacred" or to possess "sanctity." The use of these religious terms to indicate the inviolability of human life (whether in general, or more specifically as technical terms in bioethical discussion) is no accident, and it reflects precisely the Christian theological tradition. The import of Genesis 1:26 — "Let us make man in our image" — is spelled out in 9:6: the capital sentence awaits those who take human life, since it is made in the image of God; human life, that is, is sacred and inviolable because of its intimate connection with God himself, who is its Creator.

Yet men and women are mortal, condemned to death by sin, the

16. Helpfully and most recently summarized by Gerald Bray in *Tyndale Bulletin* 42, 2 (1991): 195-225.

effects of which are universal; and it is in this dialectic of sanctity and mortality that the calling of the physician and, indeed, the task of the bioethicist lie. For the believer there is an irreducible ambivalence in his or her attitude to death, the last enemy whose gloomy portal is also the gate of life. Yet for the unbeliever, too, there is ambivalence, and it is the ambivalence of the unbeliever that has dominated and continues to dominate bioethical discussion of issues on the boundaries of life. The unbeliever has no resurrection hope and for that reason may strive to hold on to what remains of life at all costs, since it is all there is. But if there is no resurrection hope, there is also no resurrection judgment, no accountability, no notion that life is God's to give and God's to take away, no confidence in divine providence and comfort. So the unbeliever may move from fear of death to fear of dying — or fear of continuing alive in conditions of distress — and may opt for that control over dying that has always been available in suicide and its medical surrogates.

What is more, unbelievers may take to themselves power over the dying of others, with that same lack of accountability to resurrection judgment and with exclusive concern for comfort in the here and now (whether their own or that of the "other"), whether the "other" is an unborn child or a demented and costly parent, and whether the means is the abortionist's instrument or the withdrawal of the food and drink that sustain the chronic and incompetent sick. Much of contemporary secular bioethics may be understood as a life-and-death struggle between the desire to hold on to life because it is all there is and the increasingly stronger desire to take control of death to make life easier. In some cases the easier life and the eased death are predicated of the same person, and thus it may be the patient who seeks and who takes hold of the keys. But more and more, the life made easier and the death that makes it so are distinct, the keys of death seized not by a patient in anguish (for very, very few now need die like that) but by a relative or a physician or an insurer or an administrator, whose life will be easier (emotionally, financially, . . .) because that other life is over. That is, of course, the typical pattern with abortion (there are some few indicators that could be claimed to suggest that the child herself would be happier dead, but they are few), and that pattern is increasingly becoming the dominant pattern for euthanasia. Life is cheap because death is cheap, and the medical decision-making process becomes the theater of a power-play in which the race is to the strong, and patients' rights — vaunted as the justification for breaking the mold of rigid Hippocratic values — have become a Trojan horse for the entry of extraneous interests into decisions concerning the life and death of the patient. It has never been plainer that Hippocrates was the patient's friend.

ISSUES IN DEBATE

The list of topics addressed in current bioethical discussion grows every month as technology advances and ethical options open wider. Cryopreservation, fetal brain tissue implants, the immense array of genetic possibilities — clearly this is not a single-issue debate, and for that reason there are questions on which a Christian response will not yet have come to a clear focus. But at the heart of the contemporary scene lies the abandonment of the Christian-Hippocratic conviction of the sanctity of human life. Many of the particular questions being explored around the margins of technological possibility and ethical acceptability are options only because of that denial of the central tenet of our medical culture. So our focus must continue to lie here, in the sanctity-of-life doctrine that imparts such dignity to the individual and that stamps the calling of the physician with such an ideal of disinterested service — without both of which our medical tradition lies in tatters.

Beginning-of-Life Issues

We have already noted the major, if somewhat belated, evangelical engagement in the pro-life movement. This has not always reflected unanimity among evangelicals on at least some of the abortion options, but it does reflect a mainstream evangelical commitment on one side of the debate rather than the other. In the United States, as in other countries, evangelical medical opinion has been the most divided, both with respect to abortion itself and when confronted with related questions such as that of deleterious research on the human embryo. That does not augur well for the coming round of debate on euthanasia, for which — as with abortion twenty years ago — evangelical opinion is thoroughly ill-prepared, and which is also destined to move rapidly beyond intellectual reflection into the marketplace of public policy and legal change. Indeed, we may well see a rerun of the abortion awakening, in which the intellectual struggle *followed* political-legal decisions and an evangelical mind was achieved altogether too late. We have already noted that among the most striking features of the contemporary debate on life issues is its lack of novelty: the religious-philosophical discussion and the medical practice both go back through classical society into primitive times, and indeed both abortion and euthanasia are practiced today by primitive peoples as well as in technological societies. While these questions may have taken on fresh perspective, in themselves they are unconnected with the new technological and other resources of contemporary medicine. Indeed, it is worth remarking that the Hippocratic repudiation of these practices was in the context of a primitive medical culture; the clinical and other resources available in modern Western society for the care of unwanted children, the handicapped, and the chronic and terminally sick are incomparably greater. Yet it is now that the turnaround in the ethical consensus has taken place.

The abortion argument began as an argument about when life begins, and that is a question on which Christians have a highly distinctive answer. For there is a series of biblical indicators that together come to a particularly — indeed, even a surprisingly — sharp focus in answer to our question. In fact, the debate has moved on, and it is now much more the debate that some of us have feared it would become: a debate about when life, which has very plainly already begun, may legitimately be taken. This is a more logical though also a more sinister debate, in which the continuity of fetal and born human life has ceased to tell against abortion and has begun to tell in favor of euthanasia. The self-evident and substantially Hippocratic assumptions of a generation ago have given place to radical questioning. In the pro-life syllogism (human life is sacred, fetal life is human life, therefore . . .), the focus has shifted from the minor to the major premise.

Broadly, Christians have taken two kinds of approaches to the determination of a biblical position, both alike recognizing the uniform character of Christian opposition to abortion on all but extreme therapeutic grounds from the earliest days of the church (our first evidence is in the *Didache*).[17] One approach has noted that there is no explicit reference to abortion in Old or New Testament as something to be commended or condemned, though in a famously difficult passage (Exod. 21:22-25) we find casuistic discussion of the penalty due for causing a miscarriage. More than one interpretation of the text is possible,[18] but even on the conventional reading its relevance to the procuring of abortion is very remote; for it outlines a case in which two men are brawling, heedless of the fact that a pregnant woman is nearby, and as a result of reckless but accidental injury to her she miscarries. The result is a fine for those responsible. It is hard to see how they are responsible for anything other than brawling recklessly near a pregnant woman. They are certainly not responsible for procuring an abortion. And, as we need to be reminded, the limited range of criminal sanctions possible in Old Testament society meant that a fine could be an

17. The *Didache* is a very early statement of post-apostolic Christian practice, dated to the first half of the second century or before.

18. The New International Version reads: "If men who are fighting hit a pregnant woman and she gives birth prematurely but there is no serious injury, the offender must be fined. . . . But if there is serious injury, you are to take life for life . . ." (Exod. 21:22-23).

appropriate penalty for a relatively serious offense. The suggestion of some interpreters that if the fetus were fully human the death penalty would have been appropriate is extraordinary.[19]

A very different approach seeks guidance not first of all in the matter of abortion, looking for legislation and arguing from silence, but with respect to the nature of unborn human life.[20] There are several different lines of argument in this approach. First we have the significance of the creation of humankind in the *imago Dei,* as we have already noted. The context of this statement lies in the taxonomy of the created order that is found in Genesis 1. (Whatever else this chapter says, it does set out such a taxonomy.) The implication is plain: wherever humankind is found, wherever this species that we call *Homo sapiens* is met, there is one who bears the divine image. The image is co-terminous with the biological constitution of humankind. This is in truth a very striking statement, for not only does it bear momentous implications for the dignity of both women and men, but it also declares in principle the equal dignity and value of every human life — irrespective of color or creed, moral worth or depravity, age or sickness, mental impairment or genius: all who share in the genetic constitution of the human race bear that inestimable dignity that is bestowed by God in their creation in his image.

A second line of argument picks up the manner in which, within the Old Testament especially, the process of generation is addressed. Abraham begat Isaac. The point at which one generation was succeeded by the next was (surprise, surprise!) the point of generation, the point of begetting. In light of what has been said about the taxonomy in Genesis 1 — and in light of what I shall say next about the incarnation — this argument has particular force. So, from the very beginnings of human biological existence, that being is by definition a new member of *Homo sapiens,* who in common with all mammalian species begets and reproduces himself and herself — the product of human conception is no *tertium quid* but the next generation of the species.

A third line of argument addresses the incarnation of Jesus Christ. Much use has been made in support of the full humanity of the fetus of biblical references to unborn human life, especially in Job, in some of the prophets, and in certain of the psalms. These texts are by no means ir-

19. In his influential book *Abortion: The Personal Dilemma* (Exeter: Paternoster, 1972), R. F. R. Gardner introduces this text as the "one clear reference to abortion in the Old Testament" and comments: "it would seem fairly obvious that in any case the text implies a difference in the eyes of the law between the fetus and a person" (p. 119).

20. This line of argument is laid out at more length in my contribution to *Abortion in Debate* (Church of Scotland Board of Social Responsibility; Edinburgh: Quorum Press, 1987), pp. 1-19.

relevant, but they pale beside the narrative of the birth of Jesus Christ. For the point of incarnation is plainly put at the point of his virginal and supernatural conception. There is no separation made between his biological beginnings as Mary's conceptus and the mysterious overshadowing of the Holy Spirit. In the case of Jesus we have an open-and-shut case for the highest possible view of the earliest stage of fetal life. Incarnation took place in embryo. This raises many questions, though in terms of orthodox theology it is straightforward. Jesus' humanity is patterned after our humanity, sin only apart; so the character of his own unborn human life is also the pattern of ours. If we find it hard to imagine a zygote possessing the dignity of one who bears the image of God, we have only to cast our minds to the miracle of the incarnation. The problem lies, not in the unimaginable genetic complexity and completeness of the zygote, but in the altogether limited imaginative faculty that we are able to bring to bear on the subject.

The coupling of these suggestive biblical-theological arguments with the striking fact of Christian opposition to abortion from the earliest days of the church, and until very recently in an unbroken tradition, leads us to an enthusiastic endorsement of the Hippocratic refusal to participate in abortion that was, until lately, the orthodoxy of the Western medical tradition. And if the debate moves on to the possibility of using human embryos for deleterious research, the grounding of our argument against abortion in the decisive character of conception-fertilization already gives us our answer. If human life is sacred right from its biological beginnings, then we stand face-to-face with that which bears the ineffable image of its — her, his — Maker.

End-of-Life Issues

No more than a generation ago, euthanasia — however it was dressed up — was regarded as at best the preserve of cranks and at worst as subversive, with ideological overtones of fascism. This issue is now at the very heart of the public policy debate on health care and human values. Although it has not yet been made the subject of a political-legal revolution that compares with *Roe v. Wade* and the abortion legislation that marked a similar path in most industrialized and many other countries during the 1960s and 1970s, there is widespread public support for voluntary euthanasia in most Western countries. That support depends critically on fears and misunderstandings, but it has offered cover for a succession of legal and political moves toward a positive euthanasia policy in many countries. These moves have opened increasingly liberal approaches to case law in marginal situations and have prepared public opinion for more general legal change. The high-water mark of these developments in the United States is the so-called Patient Self-Determination Act of 1991, which obliges hospitals and other institutions receiving federal funding to inquire of patients on admission whether they have a "living will"; in Europe it is the *de facto* legalization of voluntary euthanasia in Holland, where statute has still to catch up with a permissive public policy in which prosecuting authorities and courts have conspired with the major medical bodies to give doctors a license to kill their patients.[21] As we have already noted in more general terms, from the standpoint of history the most curious feature of this movement away from the sanctity-of-life doctrine is the degree to which the resources needed to sustain those who are handicapped or chronically or terminally ill have so dramatically increased just at the moment when opinion is shifting round to favor killing. An excellent example of a fundamentally different approach is hospice care, a recent development in geriatric and palliative medicine that has sought "death with dignity" in supportive community care of the dying, joining expertise in drug therapy and pain control with associated medical and nursing skills.[22] Yet euthanasia is cheap, and the central place that cost containment holds in current discussions has given a major fillip to the euthanasia trend, as the Patient Self-Determination Act shows. With the ethical framework of which the sanctity of life was a key element now in flux, the desire to limit costs will place increasing pressure on end-of-life choices and may well be the deciding factor in legislative moves toward voluntary euthanasia. And if the key pressures at the level of legislation will be financial, it seems clear that the Chinese walls that alone separate the "voluntary" and the "involuntary" will not long survive (any more than this distinction has proved reliable in the sub-legal and informal euthanasia context of the Netherlands).[23]

It is important to note some of the distinctions and connections that characterize this discussion before we return to biblical-theological comment. The overt justification for the modern euthanasia movement is that of patient self-determination: patient autonomy is to replace Hippocratic paternalism, as it is perceived, giving patients the right to "medically assisted suicide" or "aid in dying," as its proponents variously term it. In fact what

---

21. See Richard Fenigsen, "A Case against Dutch Euthanasia," *Hastings Center Report*, Special Supplement (Jan./Feb. 1989); reprinted in *Ethics and Medicine* 6, 1 (1990): 11-18.

22. See Cicely Saunders, "Euthanasia: The Hospice Alternative," in *Death without Dignity: Euthanasia in Perspective*, ed. Nigel M. de S. Cameron (Edinburgh: Rutherford House, 1990).

23. See Richard Fenigsen, "The Report of the Dutch Governmental Committee on Euthanasia," *Issues in Law and Medicine* 7, 3 (1991): 339-44.

they seek is a curious amalgam of suicide and homicide; the decision, they say, should lie with the patient, and if the patient requests death the attending physician should be obliged to comply and bring it about. This is not actually assisted suicide but homicide with consent, homicide at the victim's request; it actually partakes of the moral problematic of both suicide and homicide. And its rooting in the patient's act of free decision, on which whatever defense is offered must wholly rest, is deluged in difficulty. For what kind of free choice on this most fundamental of human questions is someone who is by definition a patient able to make? Who can assess the pressures on one who is, say, chronically sick, who is trying to double-guess her relatives to decide whether they would really prefer her dead, who is juggling financial uncertainties and perhaps knows that her children's hope of a legacy entirely depends on her dying sooner rather than later? These are typical of many questions that can be raised about the simple coherence of the euthanasia project, aside from ethical critique.

There is then the question of the alleged distinction between this voluntary, patient-autonomy euthanasia and involuntary killing, which of course most euthanasia advocates seek to disown. Aside from the psychological difficulty of envisaging free choices for and against euthanasia in a family, in a hospital, indeed in a society that formally endorses this as an option, there is a basic logical difficulty. What is to be the ground on which the physician is obliged to bring about death? There are two possible answers: either the simple expressed desire of a person who seeks death, perhaps qualified by its repetition on successive occasions or before successive physicians, or an expressed desire coupled with a certain medical condition. If the latter, the question arises how those who satisfy the medical criteria but do not express a wish to die will ultimately be treated, especially when they are incompetent. The pressure to move from voluntary to "nonvoluntary" (in the case of the incompetent) and ultimately to a full involuntary euthanasia policy will be unstoppable. (For example, there might be federal withdrawal of medicaid and medicare, insurance exclusions, and so forth if a "voluntary" decision for euthanasia is not made.) On the other hand, if no medical criteria are set down, the policy is simply a charter for suicide: the jilted teen and the postnatal depressive will have nothing to bar their way. The basic problem, of course, lies in the assumption that it can be good to will one's own death and that any community that accepts that proposition as part of its understanding of the rights of the individual can flourish. There is no third way: the acceptance in principle of medical killing will resolve itself either in the encouragement of arbitrary decisions for suicide or in the creation of classes of persons for whom the choice to die is regarded as reasonable; and if the latter, then those in that class who do not choose to die will be marginalized at best, and at worst will be killed for their unreason and their claim on community resources. It is a truly frightening prospect.

Over against this option for death the Christian sets Job's dictum, "The LORD gave and the LORD has taken away; may the name of the LORD be praised" (1:21). Job refuses the urgings of his wife to "curse God and die" (2:9). He lays hold on the providential purposes of the good God who has given him life, and he trusts him for aid as it becomes harder to live and as death looms bitter-sweet on the horizon of his pilgrimage.

This is not to say that there are no hard choices to be faced. One reason why our failure to develop an evangelical bioethics is so serious lies squarely here: we have yet to form a community within which appropriate biblical-theological responses to real, hard questions can be formulated. Yet the beginnings of that culture lie in the old medicine of Christian Hippocratism and in the application of its principles to new situations. In accordance with those principles, futile treatment has never been good treatment. The well-advanced dying process is the place for palliation, not invasive and distressing procedures initiated to please relatives or on the advice of the hospital attorney or to pursue some tacit experimental purpose. How we define futility in a sanctity-of-life context may be radically different from a quality-of-life evaluation, but Christian Hippocratism has always recognized that there is a time to die.

KEY QUESTIONS FOR AN EVANGELICAL BIOETHICS

The agenda is as long as the road is untraveled, yet several key questions stand out that require address from a biblical-theological perspective. First and most broadly, we need to develop a biblical theology of medicine. The field of medicine offers a prime example of the theological-hermeneutical challenges that confront evangelicals today, since the practice of medicine and the questions raised in the discussion of medical values are of prime importance to the church. Yet where Scripture touches on this subject, it does so almost entirely indirectly.

If life is sacred because God has made us in his own image, and if death is nonetheless universal in fallen human experience, what is the place of medicine? The hope of humankind is the hope of the resurrection of the body, and that bodily resurrection — in its imaging yet transcending human experience before the mortal consequences of the fall — gives rich significance to those anticipations of the resurrection of the body that we find in the New Testament, supremely in the healing miracles of Jesus. It is common to see "natural" medical healing as quite other than the healing of a miracle; yet both alike stay the progress of mortality and thereby offer broken and anticipatory witness to the eschatological abolition of death. A biblical theology of medicine will be eschatologically oriented.[24]

Second, we must address the question of health-care provision at the extremes of human existence: the anencephalic baby, for example, or the patient in a persistent vegetative state. The pressure is on (and it has been felt by some evangelicals already) to adopt essentially quality-of-life criteria in these cases that would be vigorously repudiated if they were applied more generally. If we move in just a little from the margins, we stumble over the curious medicalization of the giving of food and drink (symbolized in the use of the labels "nutrition" and "hydration" for these elemental human requirements), a major step — unwitting or not — in the generation of opportunities for medical killing and a potent threat to the sanctity-of-life position. It is hard to exaggerate the importance of such bellwether questions as the evangelical mind crystallizes in the flux of current discussion.

Finally, the fundamental technological development of our time lies in the field of human genetics. The unlocking of ever greater proportions of the genetic code has begun to realize an ultimately enormous range of manipulative possibilities affecting the very nature of the human species. The harvesting of these developments will begin in earnest just as the values of post-Hippocratism have established themselves in mainstream medicine. The generation of appropriate Christian responses will require the resources of a major intellectual community, but such a community in this field has scarcely begun to develop.

THE PROBLEM OF CONSENSUS

Despite the fundamental significance of the sanctity of life for the assumptions that govern bioethical discussion, and despite the central place that beginning-of-life and end-of-life issues hold on the public stage today, there is yet another kind of issue that we must address — that of consensus in medicine. We have already noted that the scene has been set for the incipient breakup of the Christian-Hippocratic consensus. Many particular substantive questions are on the agenda, not because society's mind has all of a sudden changed, but because the prevailing consensus — and with it, the *idea* of a consensus — has begun to crack. Abortion began to be defended,

24. I have developed this theme somewhat in an appendix to *The New Medicine*, cited above in n. 7, and in a forthcoming issue of *Christian Scholar's Review*.

irrespective of the merits of traditional arguments pro and con, as a concomitant of the right of privacy or the rights of women. Euthanasia is on the agenda as an exercise in self-deliverance, the final act of patient autonomy. Curiously enough, academic bioethics has concerned itself less and less with these and other similar substantive ethical questions, and increasingly with questions of procedure. Of course, these questions are not unrelated. Procedural questions may well also, in themselves, be of ethical interest. But the weight that is now placed on the establishment of procedures that will allow individuals of diverse ethical convictions to determine their treatment regime is a declaration of despair. Its implication is that there will be no new consensus and that the only area in which we can seek agreement with one another is in the determination of the procedures of disagreement. This can be illustrated no better than in the title of the milestone congressional legislation of 1991 to which we have already referred: the Patient *Self-Determination* Act. Whatever the cost-containment concerns that may lie behind this and similar legislation elsewhere, the question we must keep asking is this: Why do we need procedures laid down in federal law that assume that we no longer share a community of values in terminal care? Is there no longer a medical *community,* representative of the broader community, infused with the values of centuries of humane clinical experience, whose judgment that wider community can trust? There are many partial answers; but at root we recognize, on the one hand, the undeniable and general fragmentation of community values, though we also recognize, on the other hand, that it is in the interest of a (morally) liberal minority on the leading edge of that fragmentation to give the impression that things have gone farther and faster than they actually have. This in turn is deeply influencing the move to pluralism. The societies of Europe and North America are actually much more cohesive — in fact, much more "societies" — than many of their glib interpreters suggest; and that is particularly true in the field of bioethics, where the purveying of half-truths about the significance and state of incipient pluralism is proving catalytic and has actually helped to give birth to the discipline.

So should I have a living will? The answer to this question lies buried in the complexity of Christian-Hippocratic tactics in an age in which Hippocratism is proving to be "biologically tenacious" (a chilling phrase that some bioethicists have applied to patients who refuse to die when they "should"), and yet an age in which, equally certainly, a post-Hippocratic medical culture is in the making. Originally a clever ploy in the armory of euthanasia advocates, this coyly named advance directive permits the patient to decide ahead of time the principles according to which treatment decisions should be made should the patient become incompetent, so that these decisions are not left in the hands of relatives, physicians, hospital administrators, or — ultimately — the courts. Perhaps our response should be that drawing up a living will offers Christians a wonderful opportunity to ensure Christian-Hippocratic canons of medical care right to the last. Yet, aside from many practical problems that the use of the living will poses, every time someone draws one up another nail is knocked in the coffin of consensus. That may not be an argument against using the living will in the United States, where one evidence of the weakness of the consensus is the degree of involvement of the judiciary in clinical management decisions; but it is an important argument against their general introduction in some other jurisdictions (e.g., in the United Kingdom) where there is still a substantial consensus in medical values and considerable confidence in physicians as interpreters of the best in the humane medical tradition.

This raises the question of tactics. Part of the naiveté of sections of the pro-life movement has lain in the assumption that, with the striking down of *Roe v. Wade* or equivalent watersheds in other parts of the world, all would somehow be well. Liberal abortion is a symptom of the diseased character of contemporary medical ethics; it is not the disease in itself. Political advocacy on those bioethical issues that break surface in public policy discussion is vital, but it must be part of a grand strategy by which political and other initiatives must be judged — everything down to my own initiative or lack of it in exercising patient "self-determination" and drawing up an advance directive.

The key lies in an awareness of the state of fragmentation of the consensus, on the one hand, and a rediscovery of the origins and logic of Hippocratism on the other. Nothing must be done that makes it easier for the bioethics community to point the finger and cry "pluralism"; we must seek to shore up and draw attention to the elements of consensus, which are, incidentally, far more in evidence in our society and in the health-care professions than among bioethicists themselves. And yet we must also begin to look ahead to the day when the prophecies have come true and we enter an age of truly post-Hippocratic medicine. As we focus on this developing situation, we seek to apply our general principles of Christian community and witness. We must be dissident, and we must be prophetic; we must maintain our own distinctive community while never entirely dissociating ourselves and our community from the wider community of which we remain indissolubly a part. And that is where the rediscovery of Hippocratic origins has a special and challenging relevance. For if the first Hippocratics were dissidents and prophets, protesting the inhumanity of the medical culture of their day and leading the way to a better one, there are footsteps in which we can follow.

Human Sexuality: A Psychiatric
and Biblical Perspective

Armand M. Nicholi, Jr.

Sexuality is a profound, pervasive aspect of the human experience. If we consult Webster's *New Collegiate Dictionary,* we come away with little more understanding than that with which we began: "Sexuality *n.:* the quality or state of being sexual: *a.:* the condition of having sex *b.:* sexual activity *c.:* expression of sexual receptivity or interest esp. when excessive." As you can see, Webster's is less than helpful and perhaps reflects the confusion that characterizes our concept of sexuality in the latter decade of the twentieth century.

A few general comments might help to define sexuality more clearly. Sexuality, first of all, contributes to our identity as living beings. We are either male or female — and we have little choice. Our genetic makeup, the particular combination of x and y chromosomes, determines our sexual identity. These genes and certain chemical substances called hormones — their relative presence or absence in the body — determine how masculine or feminine we appear physically and the intensity of our sexual desire. On the other hand, gender identity — that is, the inner sense or picture of ourselves as male or female — is largely determined by social and psychological forces. Gender identity is usually formed primarily in infancy and childhood, and it differs from what we refer to as the biologically determined sexual identity. So biologically our genes and hormones determine our outer sexual identity — that is, the appearance of our bodies — while social and psychological factors such as our early life experiences

---

This chapter is a revised draft of the Dwight Lecture delivered at the University of Pennsylvania.

determine our gender identity — that is, our inner picture of our sexual selves. Sometimes our sexual identity conflicts with our gender identity: some people may inwardly feel that they are different than how they outwardly appear and may want to alter their outward appearance. Thus we have transvestites who alter their outward appearance by dressing like the opposite sex, or transsexuals who desire to alter their appearance through hormone injections and surgery.[1]

Sexuality infuses our lives with excitement and pleasure. Within the context of a relationship of love and permanent commitment — that old-fashioned state we call marriage — sexuality provides what might be the most fulfilling and most purely pleasurable of human experiences. Paradoxically, sexuality may also become a monstrosity and cause considerable pain and suffering.

Sexuality in the 1990s is above all openly and freely discussed. We have scrutinized it with all the tools of modern science and technology. We know a great deal about sex. We have accumulated a reservoir of knowledge about the anatomy, physiology, neurology, endocrinology, biochemistry, pathology, genetics, sociology, and psychology of human sexuality. For the first time in history, human sexuality has been studied from before birth up to and including old age. These studies include large systematic statistical surveys such as those conducted by Kinsey and his group in the 1940s and 1950s.[2] They also include laboratory and clinical studies such as those conducted by Masters and Johnson in the 1960s and 1970s. Masters and Johnson observed and recorded close to 14,000 sexual acts carried out under a wide variety of conditions.[3] Research in endocrinology has given us knowledge of a wide variety of birth control methods. Research in neurology has given us knowledge of the close association between sexuality and certain centers in the lymbic system of the brain.

Living in the 1990s exposes one to open, explicit displays of sexuality. Movies, video cassettes, plays, novels, prime-time television, and magazines in adult bookstores as well as supermarkets expose the individual to all forms of sexuality. They display adultery, fornication, group sex, homosexuality, sex with children, and a variety of other perversions as normal and natural aspects of everyday experience.

1. *Diagnostic and Statistical Manual of Mental Disorders,* 3d ed., revised (Washington, DC: American Psychiatric Association, 1987); *A Psychiatric Glossary,* 4th ed. (Washington, DC: American Psychiatric Association, 1980).

2. A. C. Kinsey, W. B. Pomeroy, and C. E. Martin, *Sexual Behavior in the Human Male* (Philadelphia: Saunders, 1948).

3. W. H. Masters and V. E. Johnson, *Human Sexual Response* (Boston: Little, Brown, 1966).

With all the facts we have accumulated about sexuality and with all of the daily exposure to every expression of it, we still know and understand little. Human sexuality remains a mystery and an area of great confusion. The more we learn about sexuality, the more it seems to escape our grasp of it. Dr. Lewis Thomas, one of the more innovative thinkers in modern medicine, wrote in the *New England Journal of Medicine* a statement that might very well apply to our understanding of sexuality:

> The only solid piece of scientific truth about which I feel totally confident is that we are profoundly ignorant about nature. Indeed, I regard this as the major discovery of the past 100 years of biology. It is in its way an illuminating piece of news. It would have amazed the brightest minds of the 18th century enlightenment to be told by any of us how little we know and how bewildering seems the way ahead. It is this sudden confrontation with a depth and scope of ignorance that represents the most noteworthy contribution of 20th century science to the human intellect.[4]

A great deal of the confusion concerning sexuality centers around standards of sexual behavior. People appear more confused than ever about what sexual conduct is in their best interest. What about premarital or extramarital sex? What's wrong with it? If two people really love and care for one another, why hesitate? What about two strangers who find themselves attracted to one another physically? Why not express these feelings? Is it not natural and normal? What about homosexuality, which we hear and read about so widely today? Is a homosexual born a homosexual? Is homosexuality inherited, like the color of one's eyes? Or does it result from certain family constellations, from certain environmental influences? Is homosexuality a sickness? Is it pathological? Or is it merely a variant of normal sexuality? Can one who is exclusively homosexual ever become exclusively heterosexual? Does modern psychiatry shed light on these questions?

For generations, social scientists kept telling us that our society was too inhibited sexually and that repressive rules and reluctance to speak openly about sex caused unnecessary sexual problems. Once we established a free, open, and uninhibited attitude toward sex, we were told, our problems in this area would disappear and we would arrive at a sexually healthy and happy society. We have indeed developed an open attitude. We can now talk about sex more freely, and that may indeed be healthy. But the freedom to speak has been extended to a license to act. We have become confused over what, if any, standards of sexual behavior exist. Consequently, we don't need to look far to know that all is not health and

4. Thomas, *New England Journal of Medicine* 296 (1977): 327.

happiness in the realm of human sexuality. Clinical experience indicates that the new sexual permissiveness appears to have led us not to health but to illness. We see an annual rate of over a million illegitimate teenage pregnancies a year.[5] In Massachusetts, where I reside, the number of live births overall has decreased forty percent since 1960, but the number of births to unwed mothers has increased ninety-two percent.[6] The new sexual freedom also does not appear to contribute to the stability of families. The divorce rate has skyrocketed nationwide since the onset of this sexual revolution.[7] Neither does the new sexuality appear to lessen the incidence of sexual disorders. Sex therapy clinics have mushroomed throughout the nation during this time for the treatment of an endless array of psychosexual disorders: the so-called sexual dysfunctions, such as inhibited sexual desire; gender identity disorders, such as transsexualism; paraphilias, such as transvestism; pedophilia, engaging in sexual acts with children; exhibitionism; voyeurism; and so forth. There appears to be a higher incidence of sexual pathology than ever before. One statement we can make for certain is that the new sexual freedom has by no means abolished our sexual problems.

In addition, pornography abounds in our society; some two hundred million pornographic magazines are sold every year. The sexual abuse of children in childcare centers has filled newspapers over the past two or three years. Crimes have increased to the point that our cities are no longer considered safe.

Another characteristic of sexuality in the nineties is the epidemic of new and deadly venereal diseases. Highly resistant forms of gonorrhea and herpes make miserable the lives of those afflicted and puzzle the doctors trying to cure them. And no discussion of sexuality today could avoid mentioning *the* venereal disease of the nineties — Acquired Immune Deficiency Syndrome (AIDS). This disease, unknown before the 1980s, has preoccupied and terrified the country.[8] Because of the panic and confusion

5. W. Baldwin, "Trends in Adolescent Contraception, Pregnancy, and Childrearing," in *Premature Adolescent Pregnancy and Parenthood,* ed. E. R. McAraney (New York: Grune & Stratton, 1982); S. B. Levy and W. N. Grinker, *Choices and Life Circumstances — An Ethnographic Study of Project Redirection Teens* (New York: Manpower Demonstration Research Corp., 1983).

6. A. M. Nicholi, Jr., "Children and the Family." *Report of the Massachusetts Governor's Advisory Committee,* 1980.

7. J. Wallerstein, "The Impact of Divorce on Children," *Psychiatr. Clin. North Am.* 3 (1980): 455-68.

8. S. H. Landsman, H. M. Ginsburg, and S. H. Weiss, "Special Report: The AIDS Epidemic," *New England Journal of Medicine* 312 (1985): 521-25; H. M. Ginsburg and L. Gostin, "Legal and Ethical Issues Associated with HTLV-III Diseases," *Psychiatr. Annals* 16 (1986): 180-85.

that has surrounded this disease, even within colleges and universities, let me give a brief outline of what we know at this time.

We know the cause of AIDS — a virus known as HTLV-III or Human T-cell Lymphotrobic virus, type III — now simply known as HIV. We know that in the Western world the disease is almost exclusively confined to the homosexual population, with almost ninety percent of cases occurring among sexually active homosexual and bisexual men and among intravenous drug users. We know that the first case of AIDS was described in 1981, that in the U.S. about 1,000 cases a month are now being reported, and that by May 1987 the total number of cases reported exceeded 40,000. We know that death usually occurs within two years after the onset of symptoms; the death is by no means an easy one, and the rejection of the person once the illness is known by family, friends, and homosexual lovers is even more painful. We know that the vast majority of cases in the U.S. have thus far occurred in four cities — New York City, Los Angeles, San Francisco, and Miami, with about forty percent occurring in New York City. We know that for every case reported there are about fifty others who carry the virus; thus there are an estimated one million people in the U.S. who have been infected with HTLV-III but have not yet developed symptoms of the disease, more than ten million worldwide. We know that people afflicted with the disease have a variety of symptoms — early symptoms of weight loss, chronic fever, diarrhea, and swelling of the lymph glands, and late symptoms that include a dementia that resembles Alzheimer's disease. We know that the general population, because of their panic over this epidemic, have changed their attitudes toward homosexuals. Before the epidemic, close to a third of the population reported that the homosexual life-style was acceptable. Researchers now report a marked decrease in that number. They also report that many homosexuals have altered their life-styles because of the disease. Medical articles have recently pointed out that patients with AIDS often fail to receive sympathetic support and assistance normally afforded to the ill because of the public's association of the disease with homosexual "fast lane sex," and also because some segments of the population see it as "an act of divine retribution for the practice of unnatural sexual acts." So the victims of this disease suffer enormously, not only from the disease itself, but also from a panicked and sometimes irrational reaction among part of the population.

What we don't know yet about the disease is this: We do not yet know of a vaccine to prevent its spread, nor do we know of prophylactic treatment for those who are infected with the virus but not yet ill, nor do we know of an effective treatment once the infected person begins to experience symptoms.

What about sexuality with regard to the single individual living in the

1990s? Perhaps the most economical way to give more psychiatric perspective to this area is to quote from a textbook of psychiatry — *The New Harvard Guide to Modern Psychiatry*. In that text I wrote the following:

> For many youth today, the sexual freedom of our culture exacerbates a conflict-ridden issue. Because of the early onset of puberty, the individual is biologically ready for coitus at a considerably earlier age than his counterpart of a century ago. Yet his psychological and social readiness is considerably delayed. Many factors account for this delay, not the least being that the long years of education required to prepare for most careers today prolong emotional and financial dependence on the family and make early marriage difficult. In addition, he has been reared in a permissive society. In this society the mass media, for purposes of exploitation, tend to keep sexual impulses at a high pitch and to encourage their free expression. The adolescent, especially the older adolescent, has an intense need not only for sexual expression but also for guidelines on how best to conduct this aspect of his social life. As part of his struggle for identity, he seeks a moral framework for his life and desires to know not only what behavior is expected of him but also what behavior is in his best interest. When he turns to the adult world, he often finds more confusion than enlightenment. Even when he turns to the medical profession, he may receive conflicting messages. For example, the Group for the Advancement of Psychiatry's publication *Normal Adolescence* (1968)[9] raises the question of whether premarital intercourse fosters healthy psychological development in the adolescent. The author speaks of traditional sexual standards that discourage intercourse outside of marriage as 'a set of taboos and prohibitions which historically may have been appropriate but today seem inappropriate in the light of medical scientific advancement.' Modern medicine, the authors imply, has made invalid the concerns upon which these standards were probably based — concerns about venereal disease, illegitimate pregnancy and its destructive impact on the family. Even the more unsophisticated young people, however, realize that these concerns not only remain extremely relevant today but present a greater problem to our society than at any time in the past. This kind of information has made many adolescents feel disillusioned and misled by proponents of the new sexual permissiveness and confused as to where to turn for reliable guidelines on how to conduct their lives.[10]

9. Group for the Advancement of Psychiatry, *Normal Adolescence* (New York: Scribner's, 1968).

10. Nicholi, "The Adolescent," in *The New Harvard Guide to Modern Psychiatry*, ed. A. M. Nicholi, Jr. (Cambridge: Harvard University Press, 1988).

Dr. Helena Deutsch believes this new sexual freedom has failed to keep its many promises. She states that young people caught up in this new freedom "suffer from emotional deprivation and a kind of deadening, as a result of their so-called free and unlimited sexual excitement," and that "the spasmodic search for methods by which to increase the pleasure of the sexual experience indicates unmistakably that the sexual freedom of our adolescents does not provide the ecstatic element that is inherent — or should be — in one of the most gratifying of human experiences." She goes on to say, "The inadequacy . . . of the sexual experience as such is expressed not only in their needs for drugs but also in the increasing interest they show in sexual perversions." Deutsch refers to the new sexual freedom as creating "a psychological disaster" and interfering with "the development of real tender feelings of love and enchantment." She also refers to the "social and personal catastrophe of illegitimate motherhood" among young girls and expresses the fear that this phenomenon will increase. That fifty percent of teenage marriages end in divorce within five years makes these findings no less disturbing. Deutsch points out that teenage pregnancies are "compulsive" and that sexual instruction and modern contraceptives will do little to prevent them.[11]

Many who have worked closely with young people over the past decade have realized that the new sexual freedom has by no means led to greater pleasure, freedom, and openness, more meaningful relationships between the sexes, or exhilarating relief from stifling inhibitions. Clinical experience has shown that the new permissiveness has often led to empty relationships, feelings of self-contempt and worthlessness, an epidemic of venereal disease, and a rapid increase in unwanted pregnancies. Clinicians working with college students began commenting on these effects as early as twenty-five years ago.[12] They have noted that students caught up in this new sexual freedom found it "unsatisfying and meaningless." In my own study of college students, I found that, although their sexual behavior by and large appeared to be a desperate attempt to overcome a profound sense of loneliness, they described their sexual relationships as less than satisfactory and as providing little of the emotional closeness they desired. They described pervasive feelings of guilt and haunting concerns that they were using others and being used as "sexual objects."[13] These students' experi-

11. Deutsch, *Selected Problems of Adolescence* (New York: International Universities Press, 1967).

12. See S. L. Halleck, "Psychiatric Treatment of the Alienated College Student," *American Journal of Psychiatry* 124 (1967): 642-50.

13. Nicholi, "A New Dimension of the Youth Culture," *American Journal of Psychiatry* 131 (1974): 396-400.

ences underscore Freud's observation that, when sexual freedom is unrestricted, "love [becomes] worthless and life empty."[14]

Another area of confusion and distortion in the 1990s concerns homosexuality. How does modern medicine generally, and psychiatry specifically, view homosexuality? The American Psychiatric Association defines homosexuality very briefly and simply as "a preferential erotic attraction for members of the same sex."[15] Let's focus on three questions that cause a great deal of confusion: (1) Is an individual born a homosexual? (2) Is homosexuality an illness or merely another form of normal sexual behavior? (3) Can one change from being exclusively homosexual to being exclusively heterosexual?[16]

Is a homosexual born that way? No scientific evidence supports this conclusion. Some suggestive evidence that genetics may play a role has been derived from studies of twins, but the overwhelming evidence appears to be that environmental factors such as early parental and peer reactions contribute to a child becoming homosexual. The Harvard Medical Mental Health Letter refers to a series of studies demonstrating how environmental factors contribute to development of homosexuality. It states that in some cases both heredity and environment may play a role. The bulk of clinical research in this area, however, indicates that homosexuals are not born that way; rather, they develop their condition as a result of early and in many cases later life experiences.

Is homosexuality an illness? How does psychiatry answer this question? Well, if one looks at the American Psychiatric Association's *Diagnostic and Statistic Manual of Mental Disorders,* one finds homosexuality listed as a disorder, an illness. It is listed, however, under the heading "Ego Dystonic Homosexuality." By that term the manual implies that homosexuality is an illness only if the individual is unhappy with his homosexuality. Thus we have the puzzling and confusing situation that if you are homosexual and you don't like being that way, then you are sick. If you are homosexual and enjoy being homosexual, then you are well. Many psy-

14. Sigmund Freud, "On the Universal Tendency to Debasement in the Sphere of Love," in *Standard Edition,* ed. J. Strachey (London: Hogarth Press, 1961), vol. 11.

15. *A Psychiatric Glossary.*

16. See C. W. Socarides, "Sexual Politics and Scientific Logic: The Issue of Homosexuality," *The Journal of Psychohistory* 10, 3 (1992); *Homosexuality* (New York: Jason Aronson, 1978); *The Homosexualities,* ed. V. D. Volkan (Madison, CT: International Universities Press, 1990); M. L. Pattison and E. M. Pattison, "Ex-Gays: Religiously Mediated Change in Homosexuality," *American Journal of Psychiatry* 137, 12 (1980): 1553-69; and C. W. Socarides, "Homosexuality — Basic Concepts and Psychodynamics," *International Journal of Psychiatry* 10, 1 (1972): 118-25.

chiatrists think this to be utter nonsense. In the revised DSM-III the term *homosexual* was removed altogether.

The way this all came about is a long and involved story, and I will outline it only briefly.[17] On December 16, 1973, the National Gay Task Force and the Board of Trustees of the American Psychiatric Association (APA) announced at a joint news conference that homosexuality would no longer be considered an illness. Only those who felt "disturbed" over their homosexuality would be considered ill. Hundreds of members voiced alarm over this change, and several hundred members signed a petition protesting the change. The issue was put to a vote by all the members of the APA, and the referendum lost by a small majority, with about fifty-eight percent of the membership voting. Before the vote, a letter that had been drafted by members of the National Gay Task Force had been sent out to all of the members of the APA. However, the letter was signed by three physicians who were then running for the presidency of the APA. This letter was worded in such a way as to suggest that if the member voted against the change, he would be voting against the civil rights of homosexuals. Because psychiatrists tend to feel strongly about civil rights, many members supported the change for that reason. The only important point here is that the decision to remove homosexuality from the category of illness was based not on new scientific findings, as many have been led to believe, but on political considerations. Of course, most psychiatrists think the notion of voting an illness out of existence is absurd. They argue that if this were possible we could quickly get rid of all our illnesses by simply voting them out of existence. Many doctors also consider absurd the notion that if you are bothered by your homosexuality, you are ill, and if you're not bothered by it, you're well. Many of the most severely psychotic people have no awareness of their illness. A person in a manic phase of a manic-depressive psychosis may be grossly and overtly psychotic and yet be absolutely content, if not elated, with his or her condition. I don't think that anyone *really* believes homosexuality is normal. From my clinical experience, no homosexual, whether he accepts or rejects his homosexuality, really feels *or* thinks he is normal. A man who finds himself in a cold sweat whenever he is in the presence of a woman or a woman who experiences uncontrolled diarrhea when in bed with a man knows that something about their condition is not normal. And certainly no physician who has ever treated homosexuality for any sustained period of time thinks homosexuality normal.[18]

The question of whether or not a person who is exclusively ho-

17. For more discussion, see Socarides, "Sexual Politics and Scientific Logic."
18. See any of the sources listed in note 16.

mosexual can ever become exclusively heterosexual can be answered very quickly. There's a great body of medical and scientific evidence that change can be accomplished both through psychotherapy and through other methods of treatment. Among these other methods are religious self-help group movements. One such movement is called the Ex-Gay Movement, and a recent study of participants in this movement was done by Dr. E. Mansell Pattison, chairman of the Department of Psychiatry at the Medical College of Georgia. In a survey of members who have successfully completed treatment in this movement, Dr. Pattison documents fifteen people he evaluates carefully, documenting their change from exclusive homosexuality to exclusive heterosexuality. Dr. Pattison presented his research at the annual meetings of the American Psychiatric Association and published his findings in the *American Journal of Psychiatry*.[19] His findings, together with the research of many other clinicians and investigators, make invalid the charge "Once a homosexual, always a homosexual."

When we speak of sexuality, we inevitably encounter the issue of morality. Because sexuality involves relationships above all, we must, if we are to broaden our understanding of sexuality, consider the rules for human relationships. Morality is very simply a code of rules or principles of conduct — rules that pertain to how we treat others, to justice and fairness and honesty, to what goes on between people. Scholars have long written about the fact that our society is in a moral and spiritual crisis. Why are the words *spiritual* and *moral* so often used together? *Spiritual* usually refers to faith and to a person's relationship with his or her Creator. Biblical faith involves a transforming relationship with this Creator that brings one's behavior under God's judgment. So the Old and New Testaments have for thousands of years been a guide to how to conduct one's life. Abraham Lincoln said of the Bible, "Nothing short of infinite wisdom could by any possibility have devised and given to man this excellent and perfect moral code." If the Scriptures are indeed the perfect moral code, and if they are what they claim to be — that is, inspired by God, the comprehensive equipment for resettling the direction of a person's life — then we might profit from seeing what Scripture says about this vast and confusing area of human sexuality.

If we wish to take an overview of the biblical perspective of sexuality — especially as spelled out in the New Testament documents — we can find no one who expresses that view with more economy than the British scholar and critic C. S. Lewis. He writes that this ethic is simply, "Either

19. Pattison and Pattison, "Ex-Gays: Religiously Mediated Change in Homosexuality."

marriage, with complete faithfulness to your partner, or else total abstinence."[20] Lewis goes on to say that this sexual code is so difficult and in such conflict with our instincts that either the code is wrong or our sexual instincts are wrong. He thinks our instincts have gone wrong. And he illustrates this point with several examples: "You can get a large audience together for a strip tease act — that is, to watch a girl undress on the stage. Now suppose you came to a country where you could fill a theatre by simply bringing a covered plate on to the stage and then slowly lifting the cover so as to let every one see, just before the lights went out, that it contained a mutton chop or a bit of bacon, would you not think that in that country something had gone wrong with the appetite for food? And would not anyone who had grown up in a different world think there was something equally queer about the state of the sex instinct among us?"[21]

Lewis also points to the many sexual perversions as evidence that something has gone wrong. I mentioned these earlier along with the hundreds of sexual clinics that have cropped up and the increased incidence of rape, sexual abuse of children, and other pathology. Lewis presents a convincing argument. Something has definitely gone wrong with our sexual instincts. They appear to be different now than when first created — different than they were before the fall. The first chapter of Genesis relates human sexuality to our creation in the image of God: "So God created man in his own image, in the image of God he created him; male and female he created them" (Gen. 1:27). We find here that our maleness and femaleness, our sexuality, relates in some way to our creation in the image of God. Karl Barth pointed out that our sexuality is grounded in the *imago Dei*. The biblical view therefore makes unmistakably clear a definite spiritual dimension to sexuality. In Genesis 2:24 we read, "Therefore a man leaves his father and his mother and cleaves to his wife, and they become *one flesh*" (RSV, emphasis added). Jesus emphasized the "one flesh" principle. We also read of the fall in Genesis — how the man and the woman rejected God's way so that not only the relationship between God and human beings but also the relationship between man and woman was ruptured. Part of the curse involved man's ruling over woman, and thus began the long history of evil domination of women by men. In Genesis 3:16 we read that God said to the woman, the man "shall rule over you." This domination, as Genesis makes clear and as theologians continually point out, is not part of God's creation but rather is a result of the fall. In the Song of Solomon, we find a joyous celebration of sexuality, and in

20. Lewis, *Mere Christianity* (New York: Macmillan, 1952), p. 89.
21. Lewis, *Mere Christianity*, pp. 89-90.

Proverbs we have another ringing endorsement of sexuality within marriage: "Rejoice with the wife of thy youth. . . . Let her be as the loving hind and pleasant roe; let her breasts satisfy thee at all times; and be thou ravished always with her love" (Prov. 5:18-19, KJV). In the New Testament, Christ affirms sex and marriage. He denounces lust, saying, "I tell you that anyone who looks at a woman lustfully has already committed adultery with her in his heart" (Matt. 5:28). This does not mean that we need to feel guilty if we find ourselves attracted to another person or have fantasies that involve that person. Lust involves a calculating attempt to exploit another person, to use that person as a sexual object. It separates the physical, genital union of two individuals from the deeply emotional and spiritual union, which the biblical view emphasizes must never be done. When he was asked by the Pharisees about grounds for divorce, Christ responded by referring to the creation story, which states that a husband and wife become one flesh. "So they are no longer two, but one. Therefore what God has joined together, let man not separate" (Matt. 19:6).

Paul also honored marriage, comparing it to the covenant relationship between Christ and the church. He also encouraged sexual fulfillment: "The husband should fulfill his marital duty to his wife, and likewise the wife to her husband" (1 Cor. 7:3). The Christian faith is almost the only faith that approves of the body and considers it the temple of the Holy Spirit. God himself took on a human body, and the Scriptures tell us that we will be given a new body in heaven. The New Testament glorifies marriage, and both the Old and the New Testaments celebrate sexuality as an intimate part of our spirituality. Our spirituality and sexuality enhance one another.

What about sexuality for the unmarried person? In our era, chastity is not only grossly unpopular but also extremely difficult. It conflicts with all that we see around us. Nevertheless, the biblical perspective prohibits sexual intercourse for the single person. According to the Old and New Testaments, sexual intercourse creates a mysterious "one-flesh" bond that has spiritual overtones. Christ refers to this bond when he speaks of divorce, and so does Paul when he urges husbands to love their wives because "He who loves his wife loves himself" (Eph. 5:28). Paul also states, "Do you not know that he who joins himself to a prostitute becomes one body with her? For, as it is written, 'The two shall become one flesh'" (1 Cor. 6:16, RSV). The Bible keeps referring to some mysterious union that takes place that makes sexual intercourse far more than just physical. It touches the spirit and unites two lives in ways we don't fully understand, ways that have lasting consequences. To become involved in it outside of the permanent commitment to marriage does violence to this deep bonding and unchanging nature of intercourse. Outside of this commitment, the sexual act becomes hollow, empty, and ultimately frustrating. Recall the earlier mention of college students who complained of using others and being used as sexual objects. A great many young people who attempt to follow Christ today succeed in having close, warm, gratifying relationships with the opposite sex, while still maintaining the biblical sexual ethic.

One question that is often raised today about those who try to follow this ethic is this: Does not this rather strict standard create all sorts of severe emotional disorders? The answer, very simply, is no. Absolutely no evidence exists that conscious control of sexual impulses is psychologically harmful. If anything, control of one's impulses is indicative of and fosters ego strength. The New Testament standard, carried to even a lustful look, is extremely difficult — but as with all of God's standards, it helps us to realize that we cannot come close to attaining it without his help.

What about the biblical view of homosexuality? As with adultery and fornication, the Old and New Testaments clearly prohibit homosexuality.[22] The Scriptures make clear that the Creator intended the sexual union to be between male and female. The overall context of these passages make unmistakably clear that homosexuality conflicts with the purpose of sexuality as stated in Genesis. There sexuality is mentioned along with the command to reproduce. In addition to this overall meaning of sexuality, the Bible gives specific prohibitions against homosexual practice. For example, we read in Leviticus 18:22, "You shall not lie with a male as with a woman; it is an abomination" (RSV). We read further in Leviticus 20:13, "If a man lies with a male as with a woman, both of them have committed an abomination; they shall be put to death, their blood is upon them" (RSV). In the New Testament we have further evidence of homosexuality being a transgression of God's will. In Romans 1:26-27 we read, "For this reason [their idolatry] God gave them up to dishonorable passions. Their women exchanged natural relations for unnatural, and the men likewise gave up natural relations with women and were consumed with passion for one another, men committing shameless acts with men and receiving in their own persons the due penalty for their error" (RSV). In 1 Corinthians 6:9-10 we read, "Or do you not know that the unrighteous shall not inherit the kingdom of God? Do not be deceived; neither fornicators nor idolators nor adulterers nor effeminates nor homosexuals nor thieves nor the covetous nor drunkards nor revilers nor swindlers shall inherit the kingdom of God" (NASV). In 1 Timothy 1:9-10, we see homosexuals included with kidnappers, murderers, fornicators, liars, and perjurers. Most theologians consider

22. See *Issues in Human Sexuality,* a statement of the House of Bishops of the General Synod of the Church of England (London: Church House Publishing, 1991).

the *condition* of homosexuality as illness, and this, as I mentioned earlier, conforms with the preponderance of medical opinion. This opinion classifies homosexuality as a form of psychopathology that warrants medical intervention. If homosexuality is illness, how can it therefore be considered sinful? Most theologians consider the homosexual *condition* — that is, the presence of homosexual feelings — as a transgression of God's law. This is not unlike the condition of kleptomania — that is, the compulsion to steal. The compulsion itself would be considered sickness and would warrant medical attention. The acting out of that compulsion would be a transgression of God's law. So it is not unusual for an aspect of human behavior to be considered both sickness and sin.

The view of Scripture on sexuality can perhaps be best summed up by a recent statement of the Church of England: "There is, therefore, an evolving convergence on the ideal of lifelong, monogamous, heterosexual unions as the setting intended by God for the proper development of men and women as sexual beings. Sexual activity of any kind outside of marriage comes to be seen as sinful, and homosexual practice as especially dishonorable."[23]

Though we have more knowledge about sexuality today than at any previous time in our history, we also have more confusion and appear to be more ignorant. We have more illegitimate pregnancies, more pornography, more rape, more perversion, more intractable venereal disease, and more overall pathology than ever before. Something has gone deadly wrong. We have attempted to separate the physical aspects of sexuality from the emotional and spiritual dimensions of it, and the result has been catastrophic. Our minds and our bodies appear to have protested the direction we have taken. The hollowness, emptiness, and despair — the feelings of using and being used as sexual objects — appear to be symptoms of a psychological protest. The many new frightening venereal diseases such as AIDS, as well as other diseases such as the increase in cervical cancer among women who begin sexual intercourse at an early age or who have multiple partners — all appear to be a biological protest. Some evidence suggests that society is beginning to realize that the new sexual permissiveness begun in the sixties and seventies is not in our best interest.

Everything we know about human behavior points to a universal need for close, enduring, warm, and gratifying relationships with other human beings. The time and effort needed to establish these relationships cannot be short-circuited through a quick and casual sexual relationship. Our society has repudiated the Judeo-Christian standards of morality, and with

23. *Issues in Human Sexuality.*

this repudiation everything has become relative. One person's opinion is as right as any other's. Clearly defined moral precepts no longer exist. As a society, we have gradually come to acknowledge infidelity, homosexuality, fornication, pornography (with the increasing exploitation of small children), sadism, and violence as normal, acceptable behavior. The lines between right and wrong behavior have become blurred, and the result is confusion.

The biblical view of sexual morality is clear-cut: either marriage with complete fidelity or abstinence. This perspective emphasizes that sexuality is created by God, and that, like all of creation, it is considered good. The Old and New Testaments give us broad, clear, specific guidelines on how we are to live our lives sexually. Adultery and fornication and homosexuality are prohibited; sex within marriage is encouraged and honored. We are given no detailed instructions concerning other aspects of sexuality, such as petting, and we are left to determine how to work out these details within the broad guidelines we are given.

The Old and New Testaments make clear that the center of morality is not sexuality. As C. S. Lewis puts it, "The sins of the flesh are bad, but they are the least bad of all sins. All the worst pleasures are purely spiritual: the pleasure of putting other people in the wrong, of bossing and patronising and spoiling sport, and back-biting; the pleasures of power, of hatred. For there are two things inside me, competing with the human self which I must try to become. They are the Animal self, and the Diabolical self. The Diabolical self is the worse of the two."[24] The Scriptures make clear that the overriding concern of the Creator is our relationships. The two great commandments have to do with our relationships: first, our relationship to God, and second, our relationship to others. The Old and New Testaments indicate clearly that through a transforming faith in Christ we can establish a personal relationship with our Creator. Once established, we then have the necessary resources to carry out the difficult second commandment of loving our neighbors as ourselves. From these resources we gain the motivation and the strength to live the difficult sexual ethic spelled out in the biblical perspective. Though we may fail often, God knows and understands the difficulties imposed by the environment in which we live, and with God's forgiveness we have the opportunity to start again.

24. Lewis, *Mere Christianity,* pp. 94-95.

Leisure and Life-Style:
Leisure, Pleasure, and Treasure

J. I. PACKER

CARL HENRY has won his spurs many times over as dogmatician, apologist, and ethicist, but I am not aware that he has ever dealt in print with my present theme. If he has, I have missed it and must apologize to him, for in a book such as this my oversight must appear both incompetent and discourteous. If, however, I am right in thinking he has not, I can appeal to that fact as symptomatic of the situation that I now attempt to address. Since the Second World War the West has grown affluent. Society practices and promotes spending rather than saving, self-indulgence rather than self-improvement, and amusement at all costs. (*Amusing Ourselves to Death* is the telling title of Neil Postman's assessment of television;[1] the same phrase might be used to describe the behavior that has led to the AIDS epidemic.) Evangelical Christians have responded by emphasizing work rather than leisure,[2] activity rather than rest, and life commitments rather than life-style choices. Thus they have sought to tool themselves up to be salt and light in our dying culture. But on leisure and life-style they have had little to say.

To note this comparative silence is to state a fact, not to offer a criticism. Indeed, criticism would be out of place here. For Christians to be preoccupied with living and working for God is healthy, just as a

---

1. Postman, *Amusing Ourselves to Death: Public Discourse in the Age of Show Business* (New York: Viking Press, 1985).
2. On the Christian view of work, see Carl F. H. Henry, *Aspects of Christian Social Ethics* (Grand Rapids: Eerdmans, 1964), pp. 37-71; and Leland Ryken, *Work and Leisure in Christian Perspective* (Portland: Multnomah, 1987).

preoccupation with leisure and luxury is unhealthy. If, as it appears, leisure and luxury are becoming the main interests of the Western world, a deadly decadence has already set in, against which Christians ought to be standing with all their might, advocating and modeling something entirely different. Christians must see this kind of decadence as a form of worldliness and invoke against it such Scripture passages as 1 John 2:15-16: "Do not love the world or the things in the world. The love of the Father is not in those who love the world; for all that is in the world — the desire of the flesh, the desire of the eyes, the pride in riches — comes not from the Father but from the world" (NRSV).[3] God forbid that paying any attention to questions about leisure and life-style should have the effect of promoting in the church a worldliness like that of the modern West.

Yet if these questions are not discussed, evangelicals will be in trouble another way. All around the world, as capitalist consumerism and the market economy grind on, carrying all before them, leisure and life-style are becoming areas of entrapment for Christian people. Failure to see this as a fact, to perceive it as a problem, to think about it in biblical antithesis to the ruling secular notions, and to plan to operate as God's counterculture in these areas would indicate that we were already falling into the traps, or (to change the metaphor) being blown up in the minefield. My best hope for this essay is that it might offer the makings of a mine-detecting survival kit. Carl Henry himself has worked prodigiously for half a century as one of the leading mine detectors of our time, and these pages will not be much of a tribute to him if they fall down at this point.

We begin with definitions, to make sure that we know what we are talking about. My copy of Webster's defines *leisure* thus: "freedom from occupation or business; vacant time; time free from employment; time which may be appropriated to any specific object." *Life-style* is too recent a coinage for my Webster's to take note of, but the contents of a junk mail envelope that arrived recently, with the words "Valuable Coupons Inside — Save on All Your Life-style Needs" printed on its front, gives the idea. Inside were coupons offering great deals on ornamental painted plates; the world's greatest perfumes (that is what was claimed, anyway); scenic address labels; items of personal hygiene; carpet shampooing; a course in piano playing that focuses on leading singing at parties; wigs; baseball cards; a doll built for lifetime companionship; family photos; furnace cleaning; a machine for streamlining the female figure; videos featuring Victor Borge; the *Encyclopedia Britannica;* skin cream; book club mem-

3. See "Hot Tub Religion: Towards a Theology of Pleasure," chapter 4 in my book *Hot Tub Religion* (Wheaton, IL: Tyndale House, 1987).

bership; and deodorant. All one's life-style needs? Hardly, but the selection points to the definition. *Life-style* is evidently an umbrella-word used to describe the way of living that we achieve by our choices among the various options that our affluent consumerist society makes available to us — choices of clothes, food, hobbies, vacations, places of residence, cars, clubs, careers, associates, amusements, and (of course) a church of our choice, as well as choices of luxury items such as those listed above. "Life-style" is the label for both the ideal existence that our choices aim at and the actual existence that our choices produce. Our concept of our life-style hovers between being directional, stating how we want to live, and being descriptive, showing how we do live. In a day of multiple choices with regard to almost everything, we may well say: By their life-style you will know them; by my life-style you will know me. Where society sets us free to choose, our choices will show who and what we are, where we want to be, and where we are actually going.

Not all life-style choices are leisure choices, as we can see; but, as we can also see, all leisure choices are life-style choices, and they will say something about our view of life as a whole.

What sort of problems do we face in connection with leisure and life-style? There are three obvious ones, all with far-reaching theological, moral, and devotional implications.

The first problem is *idolatry*, the worship of false gods. The basic biblical insights here are that whatever controls and shapes one's life is in effect the god one worships, and that human nature is so constituted that no one can avoid a personal subservience to some god or other. As Bob Dylan sang some years ago, "You've got to serve somebody," and those who do not live to exalt the God of the Bible will inevitably be enslaved to some modern counterpart of the Baals and Molechs of the nature- and nation-worshiping cults that Scripture denounces. Then one's god may be some human individual or group — one's employer, perhaps, whose interests one devotes oneself to advancing; or one will worship and serve oneself directly, treating the gratifying of one's desires as all that matters and seeing everything as a means to that end — a life-style in which one constantly falls victim to "greed, which is idolatry" (Col. 3:5). Greed, the mind-set that reaches out to grab things for oneself, becomes the liturgy of self-worship. In idolizing objects of desire, we idolize ourselves, the desirers; and so idolatry in this twofold sense becomes our life.

Regarding the matter in hand, we see that some people idolize work while others idolize play; some make a god of leisure activities (vacations, sports, hobbies, music, books, gardening, and so on) while others make a god of their bank balance and social position or of power; and others again make a god of their addictions (drink, drugs, sex, or whatever). Motivations and self-perceptions get very tangled here and need a lot of sorting out in particular cases, yet the bottom line is always the same. To the extent that we are not actively living to God, for God, and in the presence of God, seeking to glorify and enjoy him in and through all we do, we have lapsed into some form of idolatry whereby we worship and serve created things rather than the Creator (cf. Rom. 1:25). But idolatry must be avoided.

The second problem is *hedonism,* with which we may join, as its opposite, *anti-hedonism.* What is in question here is the place of pleasure in Christian living. Hedonism means the enthroning of pleasure as life's supreme value and therefore as a goal that everyone should pursue directly. Hedonism says, in effect, that pleasure-seeking is the height of wisdom and virtue and that maximizing pleasure is the highest service we can render them. Popular Western culture is largely hedonist, and modern Christians are constantly exposed to its brainwashing influences through the media and the relationships of life that draw them along the hedonist path. That God wants us all to be happy, right now; that total satisfaction is what Jesus offers, right now; that it is a good and godly thing to dismiss a spouse with whom one is not perfectly happy and marry someone else; that it is a good and godly thing to engage in genital homosexual behavior, if that gives you positive pleasure — all of these notions have become very familiar in the church in recent years. That leisure is entirely for pleasure and that improving one's life-style means simply increasing one's pleasures are unchallenged axioms in today's advertising industry and unquestioned assumptions among many professed Christians. There is clearly a major problem here.

Recently, the phrase "Christian hedonism" has gained prominence as a tag for the truth that the God who promises his people joy and delight in their relationship with him, both here and hereafter, does in fact fulfill his promise here and now.[4] As a corrective of what we may call "Christian anti-hedonism" (the view that pleasure has no place in godly living, that God will always want us to do what we least want to do, and that the real Christian life on earth will always be, in Churchillian phrase, blood, toil, tears, and sweat — in short, sustained heroic misery), Christian hedonism speaks a word in season. In itself, however, "Christian hedonism" is not a good phrase for its purpose; for it seems to say that rating pleasure as life's supreme value is something that Christianity itself teaches us to do, and that is not so. Biblical Christianity does not teach that any pleasure or good

---

4. See John Piper, *Desiring God: Meditations of a Christian Hedonist* (Portland: Multnomah, 1986); Ryken, *Work and Leisure,* pp. 191ff.

feelings, or any form of present ease and contentment, should be sought as life's highest good. What it teaches, rather, is that glorifying God by our worship and service is the true human goal, that rejoicing and delighting in God is central to worship, and that the firstfruits of our heritage of pleasures forevermore will be given us as we set ourselves to do this; but should we start to seek pleasure rather than God, we would be in danger of losing both. It is apparent that this is what the exponents of Christian hedonism do themselves think, so my difficulty is limited to their choice of words. But hedonism — real hedonism — must be avoided.

The third problem is *utilitarianism,* the view that the value of anything is to be found in the extent to which it is useful and productive as a means to an end beyond itself. Utilitarian thinking is very widely applied today in the realm of technology and business, but it has a radical built-in shortcoming: it overlooks the fact that what it values as a means to an end may have an intrinsic value too, for the sake of which it should be promoted and preserved irrespective of how it rates in the means-to-end calculus. Leisure is a case in point. Utilitarianism says that the whole rationale of leisure and recreation is to "re-create" people for more productive work. Christianly speaking, this is part of the rationale of leisure, no doubt; after the sabbath rest one goes back to work. But where utilitarianism urges that leisure and rest be kept to a minimum so that productive work may be maximized (hence the fearfully long working hours of the early days of industrialization), Christian thinkers find intrinsic value in leisure activity that is, as Leland Ryken puts it, "nonproductive in the sense in which we ordinarily use that term. Leisure does not meet our needs of physical or economic survival. It does not put bread on the table or clothes in the closet. Leisure is a self-enclosed world that carries its own reward. . . . [As Lee W. Gibbs puts it,] 'the purpose of play is in the play itself.' "[5] The Christian work ethic has sometimes been misrepresented as a sanctified workaholism, but this ignores the biblical celebration of God as the one who "richly provides us with everything for our enjoyment" (1 Tim. 6:17) — a divine generosity that requires leisure for its appreciation, as the exponents of the authentic Christian work ethic well knew. So Christians should value leisure as more than a periodic pit stop before further work, and they should resist

5. Ryken, *Work and Leisure,* p. 187, citing Gibbs, "Ritual, Play and Transcendent Mystery," paper presented to the American Academy of Religion, Midwestern Sectional Meeting, Chicago, Illinois, 17 February 1973, p. 4. Ryken's book, along with R. K. Johnston's *The Christian at Play* (Grand Rapids: Eerdmans, 1983), Johan Huizinga's *Homo Ludens: A Study of the Play-element in Culture* (1950; repr. Boston: Beacon Press, 1955), and Josef Pieper's *Leisure the Basis of Culture,* trans. Alexander Dru (New York: Pantheon Books, 1952), are basic for the Christian study of leisure.

the narrowing impact of the money- and manufacture-mesmerized mind-set that marks utilitarian social thinking. High though it rides as a public philosophy today, utilitarianism too must be avoided.

This identification of the three main problem areas in relation to leisure and life-style gives parameters for the rest of our study. We should not lapse into idolizing either work or leisure; it is not Christian to be either a workaholic or a drone. Nor should we lapse into hedonism, letting the pursuit of pleasure shape our lives, any more than we should lapse into anti-hedonism, censuring pleasure in Manichean style as a worthless and unhelpful distraction and treating pleasurelessness as an index of virtue. Nor should we lapse into utilitarianism, valuing work or leisure or any aspect of life-style purely as a means to an end beyond itself and not at all as a field of creativity, a means of expression, or a form of enjoyment. So far, however, all of this has been negative; we have merely noted what we should not do. Now we have to ask, What positive principles of action should be guiding us in the area of life we are studying? To answer this question is our next task.

Let us then stand back for a moment and look at the overall ideal of a redeemed sinner's life in Christ, which is the frame into which biblical teaching on leisure and life-style fits. The redeemed life is commonly spoken of these days in terms of *wholeness;* fifty years ago, it was thought of in terms of *balance;* Thomas Aquinas saw it as life in *proportion;* and John Calvin spoke of it as a life of *moderation* — and indeed, it has all of these qualities. It is the life for which Jesus, himself the perfect man, is the model. Thomas's four cardinal virtues — prudence (wisdom), temperance (self-possession), justice (fairness), and fortitude (stick-to-itiveness, or guts) — are basic to it. His three theological virtues — faith, hope, and love — are central to it. And the ninefold fruit of the Spirit that Paul lists — love, joy, peace, patience, kindness, goodness, faithfulness, gentleness, and self-control (Gal. 5:22-23) — constitute a character profile of it, just as they do of the Lord Jesus himself. It is a superhuman version of human life; it is our natural life supernaturalized by grace.

On what principles is this redeemed life lived? Four may be briefly mentioned.

First, it is lived as a life of *duty to God,* glorifying him by our obedience out of gratitude for his grace. The phrase derives from the Catechism in Cranmer's Prayer Book (1549): "My duty towards God, is to believe in him, to fear him, and to love him . . . to worship him, to give him thanks, to put my whole trust in him, to call upon him, to honour his holy Name and his Word, and to serve him truly all the days of my life."

Second, this redeemed life is lived as a life of *neighbor-love.* "My duty towards my Neighbour," Cranmer's Catechism continues, "is to love him as myself, and to do to all men, as I would they should do unto me."[6] Love seeks the well-being and advancement of the loved one in every way that it can; it is a matter of the mind and will more than of the feelings, and of sustained commitment rather than momentary intensities. The duty of love, to one's neighbor as to one's God, calls for discipline of life.

Third, the redeemed life is lived as a life of *freedom* (cf. Gal. 5:1), in four senses: freedom from the need to work for salvation; freedom from the restrictions imposed by the typical enactments of God's Old Testament law; freedom for the use and enjoyment of all created things (1 Tim. 4:4-5; 6:17); and freedom in the sense of fulfillment and contentment in working for God ("whose service is perfect freedom," as Cranmer's Prayer Book declares).[7]

Finally, the redeemed life is lived as a life of *openness to God,* to receive both his word and his gifts — including the providential gifts of leisure and pleasure, which are our special concern at present.

Within this framework I now offer brief ethical reflections on our theme to indicate the specific positives that should guide us through leisure and life-style perplexities. Giving myself the pleasure of tidy titling, I shall arrange my matter under three headings: the role of leisure, the place of pleasure, and the use of treasure.

THE ROLE OF LEISURE

What is leisure? We have already cited a dictionary definition, but more needs to be said.

Leisure is one of a pair of words, the other of which is *work.* Work means not just one's wage-earning employment but everything that one sees oneself as having to do as a matter of obligation, whether one enjoys it or not. Jobs and commitments out of the house, jobs that need to be done in the house, necessary studying, fulfilling promises one has made — all of these count as work because of the sense of "having to" that attaches to them. By contrast, leisure means time that is ours to use for our own pleasure on a discretionary basis. Some leisure time we fill with things we choose to do for their own sake, just because we want to do them; these are the activities of absolute leisure. Some leisure time we spend doing things we both want and ought to do, from joining in public worship and fulfilling volunteer roles at church or in a club to looking after pets and

---

6. Cranmer's wording is retained in the catechism in the statutory *Book of Common Prayer* of the Church of England; I am quoting here from the 1962 Canadian revision, *Book of Common Prayer* (Toronto: Anglican Book Centre, 1962), p. 548.

7. "Morning Prayer," in the *Book of Common Prayer,* p. 11.

reading to keep informed; these are better called activities of "semi-leisure." All leisure, including semi-leisure, is a gift from God that, when used wisely, "provides rest, relaxation, enjoyment, and physical and psychic health. It allows people to recover the distinctly human values, to build relationships, to strengthen family ties, and to put themselves in touch with the world and nature. Leisure can lead to wholeness, gratitude, self-expression, self-fulfillment, creativity, personal growth, and a sense of achievement."[8] So leisure should be valued and not despised.

What Bible truths bear on our use of our leisure? At least the following:

(1) *The duty of rest.* In the quasi-liturgical, quasi-poetical, highly stylized narrative of Genesis 1:1–2:3, God the Creator presents himself as setting the world in order in six days, after which he rested on the seventh. Whether the six days should be understood as 144 of our hours, or as six vast geological epochs, or as a pictorial projection of the fact (the *what*) of creation that gives no information about the time (the *when*) or the method (the *how*) of creation is an interpretive question that need not concern us now.[9] What matters for us here is that on the basis of this presentation God directs that each seventh day be kept as a day of rest from the labors of the previous six (Exod. 20:8-11; 31:12-17). The day is to be kept "holy" — that is, it is to be used for honoring God the Creator by worship, as well as for refreshing human creatures by the break from their otherwise unending toil.

This prescribed rhythm of work and rest is part of the order of creation. Human beings are so made that they need this six-plus-one rhythm, and we suffer in one way or another if we do not get it. The leisure, or at least semi-leisure, of a weekly day for worship and rest is a divine ordinance that our work-oriented world ignores to the peril of its health. In today's community as Christian faith fades, society's standards fall, and economic competition becomes more cutthroat, the historic function of the Christian day of rest as a bulwark against employers' demands for a seven-day week is being increasingly circumvented, and the outlook is somewhat bleak.

(2) *The goodness of pleasure.* This has already been confirmed and will be fully discussed in the next section, so here I merely quote the pregnant words of Ecclesiastes 8:15, "I commend the enjoyment of life," and move on.

(3) *The rightness of festivity.* The Bible is full of feasts. In Leviticus 23, six "holy convocations," at which work was prohibited, were prescribed for Israel each year; they are all called "appointed feasts." In John 2, Jesus

8. Ryken, *Work and Leisure,* p. 38.

9. See Henri Blocher, *In the Beginning,* trans. David G. Preston (Downers Grove, IL: InterVarsity, 1984), for an orientation to this question.

is found at a wedding feast, miraculously creating extra wine; the fact that his critics were able to dismiss him as "a glutton and a drunkard" (Matt. 11:19) shows that such festal celebrations were a recurring part of his life. All through the Bible the feast table is the place and the emblem of refreshing, celebratory fellowship — a very proper leisure activity, and certainly one to encourage.

(4) *The reality of stewardship.* We are stewards of the time God gives us, of the abilities and skills that are ours, and of the opportunities that we find ourselves offered. We are also stewards of our own bodies and of this earth. Stewardship means responsibility for managing, caring for, and making the most of the resources God commits to our trust, and doing it in a way that squares with his known wishes. That does not in any way diminish our freedom to make use of created things for our enjoyment, but it does mean that in doing so we shall take care not to seem to approve what is immoral and demoralizing, nor to expose others to unhelpful influences, nor to play with fire ourselves. The Puritans closed theaters not because they did not enjoy drama but because the theaters of their day were immoral and demoralizing places. In a positive sense, recognition of our stewardship — both its privileges and its responsibilities — should incline us to choose among the leisure activities that we enjoy those that bring us closest to God, to people, to beauty, and to all that ennobles. "Whatever is true, whatever is noble, whatever is right, whatever is pure, whatever is lovely, whatever is admirable — if anything is excellent or praiseworthy — think about such things" (Phil. 4:8). We should not let the mediocre become the enemy of the good in leisure activity, nor should we let the good become the enemy of the best.

THE PLACE OF PLEASURE

What is pleasure? Webster defines it as "the gratification of the senses or of the mind; agreeable sensations or emotions; the feeling produced by enjoyment or the expectation of good." Like joy, it is a gift of God, but whereas joy is basically active (one rejoices), pleasure is basically passive (one is pleased). Pleasures are feelings — feelings of stimulation or of tensions relaxed in the body, or realizations of something good in the mind, or conscious mastery in some performance or exercise of skill.

Pleasure belongs to God's plan for humankind. As God himself takes pleasure in being God and in doing what he does,[10] so he means human

10. See John Piper, *The Pleasures of God: Meditations on God's Delight in Being God* (Portland: Multnomah, 1991).

beings to find pleasure in being his. Adam and Eve's state was all pleasure before they sinned (Eden, God's pleasure-garden, pictures that), and when the redemption of Christians is complete, pleasure — total, constant, and entire — will have become their permanent condition.

> Never again will they hunger;
> never again will they thirst.
> The sun will not beat upon them,
> nor any scorching heat.
> For the Lamb . . . will be their shepherd;
> he will lead them to springs of living water.
> And God will wipe away every tear from their eyes.
>
> (Rev. 7:16-17)

Thus the words of Psalm 16:11, "You will fill me with joy in your presence, with eternal pleasures at your right hand," and Psalm 36:8, "You give them drink from your river of delights," will find fulfillment. God values pleasure, both his and ours, and it is his pleasure to give us pleasure as a fruit of his saving love.

Pleasure is Janus-faced: as a human reality it may be good and holy, or it may be sinful and vile. This is not because of the nature of the pleased feeling itself, for that in itself is morally neutral; it is because of what goes with it. If pleasure comes unsought, and if we receive it gratefully as a providential gift, and if it does no damage to ourselves or to others, and if the delight of it prompts fresh thanksgiving to God, then it is holy. But if the pursuit of one's pleasure is a gesture of egoism and self-indulgence whereby one pleases oneself without a thought as to whether one pleases God, then, however harmless in itself the pleasure pursued may be, one has been entrapped by what the Bible sees as the pleasures of the world and of sin (see Luke 8:14; 1 Tim. 5:6; 2 Tim. 3:4; Titus 3:3; Heb. 11:25; James 4:3; 5:5; 2 Pet. 2:13; cf. Isa. 58:13). The same pleasant experience — eating, drinking, making love, listening to music, painting, playing games, or whatever — will be good or bad, holy or unholy, depending on how it is handled.

In the order of creation, pleasures as such are meant to serve as pointers to God. Pleasure-seeking in itself sooner or later brings boredom and disgust, as the wise man testifies (Eccles. 2:1-11). Appreciating pleasures as they come our way, however, is one mark of a reverent, God-centered heart. A Jewish rabbi is credited with affirming that on the day of judgment God will hold us accountable for any neglect we have shown of pleasures he provided. Christian teachers have insisted that contempt for pleasure, far from demonstrating superior spirituality, is actually an expression of the Manichean heresy (the view that the material world and

everything that it yields have no value and are indeed evil) and a manifestation of spiritual pride. Pleasure is divinely designed to raise our sense
of God's goodness, deepen our gratitude to him, and strengthen our hope
as Christians looking forward to richer pleasures in the world to come.

This truth about pleasure was not fully grasped in the first Christian
centuries. The Greco-Roman world that the early church confronted was
in the grip of a frenzied pleasure-seeking mentality, so it is no wonder that
patristic writers spent more time attacking sinful pleasures than celebrating
godly ones, nor that this perspective was carried into the Middle Ages, in
which the world-renouncing asceticism of the monastery was thought of
as the highest form of Christianity. But through the Reformers' and the
Puritans' appreciation of God's grace and insistence on the sanctity of
secular life, the biblical theology of pleasure finally broke surface. John
Calvin states it best, in a chapter of his *Institutes* entitled "How We Should
Use This Present Life and Its Helps," where he warns against the extremes
of both overdone austerity and overdone indulgence. He affirms that not
to use for pleasure those created realities that afford pleasure is ingratitude
to their Creator. At the same time, however, he enforces Paul's admonition
not to cling to sources of pleasure since we may one day lose them (1 Cor.
7:29-31); and he recommends moderation — that is, deliberate restraint —
in availing ourselves of pleasures, lest our hearts be enslaved to them and
we become unable cheerfully to do without them.[11] Here as elsewhere,
Calvin's Christian wisdom is of classic quality.

It is ironic that Calvin, who is so often considered the embodiment
of gloomy austerity, should actually be a masterful theologian of pleasure.
It is no less ironic that the Puritans, whose public image is of professional
kill-joys (H. L. Mencken defined Puritanism as the haunting fear that
somewhere, somehow, somebody may be happy), should have been the
ones who have insisted again and again that, in the words of Isaac Watts,
their leading songster, "Religion never was designed / To make our pleasures less." And it is supremely ironic that, after two millennia of Christian
culture, the West should now be plunging back into a self-defeating hedonism that is horribly similar to the barbaric pagan life-style of the first
century, and that it should be doing so in the belief that the Christian religion
is basically anti-human because it does not set up pleasing oneself as life's
highest value. But Calvin's wisdom about pleasure remains basic to authentic Christian living, in this or any age.

---

11. Calvin, *Institutes of the Christian Religion*, 3.10.

THE USE OF TREASURE

Should I apologize for dignifying our money with the label "treasure," when the word suggests something of enormous value, even though I know firsthand that I — and I suspect most of my readers — do not rate among the world's wealthy? Not necessarily. One does not have to have a lot of money for it to become "my precious," as Gollum constantly calls the fateful ring in J. R. R. Tolkien's epic, and for it to affect one as Jelly-Roll Morton sang that jazz affected him — "The more I have, the more I want, it seems; I page old Doctor Jazz in my dreams."[12] Small sums of money are almost more effective than large ones in grabbing the heart and setting one dreaming and scheming about ways of getting more.

In his wise and searching book *Money, Possessions and Eternity,* Randy Alcorn quotes Cyprian's description of the affluent of his day: "Their property held them in chains . . . chains which shackled their courage and choked their faith and hampered their judgement and throttled their souls. . . . They think of themselves as owners, whereas it is they rather who are owned; enslaved as they are to their own property, they are not the masters of their money but its slaves." Alongside this Alcorn sets the testimony of John Wesley, whose word to his preachers and society members was: "Gain all you can, save all you can, give all you can. . . . Money never stays with me. It would burn me if it did. I throw it out of my hands as soon as possible, lest it find its way into my heart."[13] From these quotations the impossibility that Jesus announced — that of serving both God and mammon (money) — becomes plain (Matt. 6:24). A conscious refusal to serve money is therefore a necessary part of the Christian life-style, as the following quotations show:

> Do not store up for yourselves treasures on earth, where moth and rust destroy, and where thieves break in and steal. But store up for yourselves treasures in heaven, where moth and rust do not destroy, and where thieves do not break in and steal. For where your treasure is, there your heart will be also. (Matt. 6:19-21)
>
> Command those who are rich in this present world not to be arrogant nor to put their hope in wealth, which is so uncertain, but to put their hope in God, who richly provides us with everything for our enjoyment. Command them to do good, to be rich in good deeds, and to be generous

12. "Doctor Jazz," by Jelly-Roll Morton and his Red Hot Peppers (Victor Records, 1926; various reissues).

13. Alcorn, *Money, Possessions and Eternity* (Wheaton, IL: Tyndale House, 1989), pp. 402-3.

and willing to share. In this way they will lay up treasure for themselves as a firm foundation for the coming age, so that they may take hold of the life that is truly life. (1 Tim. 6:17-19)

The point is plain. Money is for giving, and it is to be used to do good. It is not to be loved and hoarded; rather, it is to be stewarded for the service of God and one's neighbor. Frugality, rather than conspicuous consumption, must mark the Christian, and if that means that he or she cannot keep up with the world's wealthiest Joneses, well, so be it. There are in any case more important things to do.

In a post-Christian era such as ours in the West, an authentic Christian life-style — with its built-in balance of work and leisure, worship and witness, self-denial and self-giving for the glory of God and the good of others — is bound to seem countercultural and implicitly censorious, just as it did in the pre-Christian world of first-century Greco-Roman paganism and in the pre-evangelical world of Elizabethan and Jacobean England, where the Puritans sought the conversion of their country and became highly unpopular for doing so. Some unpopularity is inseparable from the practice of consistent Christianity, and we had better brace ourselves to meet it; for as things stand now in the West, it can only increase. But as Jesus has told us, "wisdom is proved right by her actions" (Matt. 11:19). The motto of the first institution at which I taught was "Be right and persist"; that is a word in season for all who would honor their Lord by their lives today.

Carl Ferdinand Howard Henry:
An Appreciation

KENNETH S. KANTZER

I HAVE BEEN an admirer of Carl Henry for nearly half a century. In earlier years, I was proud to consider myself his acquaintance, though I scarcely dared to reckon myself his friend. I admired him from a distance. Yet from his heights, he never seemed to act condescendingly toward me. He accepted me an an equal — though it was quite obvious that he was quite a bit "more equal" than I.

I first met Carl in Boston. We were all part of a group of budding evangelical scholars centering around our various graduate programs. Most of us were working on Ph.D.s in history and philosophy of religion at Harvard University. The group included John Gerstner from Westminster Seminary, who later went on to teach church history at Western (Presbyterian) Seminary in Pittsburgh; Roger Nicole, a graduate of Gordon, who remained in the Boston area teaching systematic theology at Gordon-Conwell; Samuel Schultz from Faith Seminary, later professor of Old Testament and chairman of the department of Bible and philosophy at Wheaton College; Harold Kuhn, Harold Greenlee, and George Turner, all from Asbury Seminary and all of whom later returned to teach at Asbury College and Theological Seminary; Paul Jewett and Edward Carnell from Westminster, who eventually became teachers of systematic theology at Fuller Seminary and, in the case of Ed Carnell, its president; George Ladd, a Gordon graduate, who became the distinguished New Testament professor at Fuller; Stanley Horton, who gave his life to teaching systematic theology at Evangel Bible College and Seminary; and Lemoyne Lewis, who returned to his denominational seminary at Texas Christian University. To these and many more names might be added the name of Joseph Bayly, who then served as head of InterVarsity Christian Fellowship in the New England area.

Carl Henry himself, when he first showed up in the Boston area, had already earned his Th.D. at Northern Baptist Seminary and was full professor at his alma mater, teaching primarily in the area of philosophy of religion and systematic theology. He was completing a Ph.D. at Boston University, studying under Edgar S. Brightman, the personal idealist noted for his defense of a finite God, Albert Knudson, professor of systematic theology, and Harold DeWolfe and Peter Bertocci, who together rounded out an illustrious faculty in philosophy at Boston University.

The climate at Harvard, for the most part, was humanist and radically anti-evangelical. Reinhold Niebuhr, who frequently came up to Boston to preach or lecture, was, with only a bit of tongue in cheek, reckoned as a sort of pseudo-fundamentalist. No doubt he was educated and intelligent (as Machen, too, had been); but at heart he was akin to the fundamentalists on the other side of the tracks. The professors at Harvard did not quite understand why there was this sudden invasion of fundamentalist students. There had not been very many of that kind around since Walter Maier, the Lutheran evangelist from Concordia Seminary, who had secured his doctorate in Old Testament at Harvard some time back. Merrill Tenney, at that time professor of New Testament at Wheaton College Graduate School of Theology, had preceded the group of which I was part and had been a lonely exception at Harvard while continuing his teaching at Gordon.

On the whole, however, the faculty under whom we were studying in those years were impressed with the caliber of this influx of evangelical students; and they were tolerant. My own mentor, Johann Abraham Christophel Faginger Auer of *Humanist Manifesto* fame, put it bluntly, yet kindly: "You may believe the earth is flat if you wish, but you will have to know why other people, including me, do not. And you will have to explain intelligibly why you do believe it to be flat. If you meet these standards, I will support you in your program towards the degree." I, for one, appreciated his honesty. Though we did not think the earth was flat, all of us gladly met the challenge to our evangelical commitment. In any case, most of us secured our degrees.

I have never been privileged to work so closely with quite such a dedicated group of evangelical scholars, sharing our thinking almost daily, and with minds made sharp by constant intellectual battle to survive in an environment that was utterly alien to our deepest convictions. The amazing thing about it was that we came through so unscathed from these constant attacks against the very fundamentals of our religious convictions. It was not because we walled ourselves off in a private ghetto. We were in constant interchange with our fellow students, who, generally speaking, were committed to the views of our teachers. And individually and as a group, we tried to digest what our teachers were saying and to interact with the voluminous readings and research through which they guided us.

It is not that we were uninfluenced by our liberal instructors and fellow students. That would be wholly false and unappreciative of the contribution our professors, as well as our peers among the students, had on us and our thinking. We went through many soul-searching and mind-stretching experiences. Yet none of us, so far as I know, departed basically from his evangelical convictions; and we all returned to our evangelical institutions. In many ways, we were more keenly committed to evangelical Christianity than ever because now we understood our own evangelicalism better, and we also had gained a keen realization of the ultimate religious bankruptcy of its liberal alternative. But we were also subtly changed. We had secured a deep appreciation for the disciplined life of a scholar, and the importance of scholarship if evangelicalism were to make its necessary impact upon our society. We believed we had in some measure mastered the skills to foster an intellectual rehabilitation of fundamentalist or evangelical scholarship that, with a few brilliant exceptions, had drifted into eddies of thinking isolated from the main currents of the day.

In spite of the fact that his relationship with the group was intermittent due to his regular teaching load at Northern Baptist, Carl Henry was in many ways the intellectual leader of the group. The club, if it can be called that, was thoroughly open and its meetings were always informal. Evangelical students usually met alongside non-evangelical students in the halls. Standing around in the intermission between classes, or on the way to the library, we would discuss the issues that had come up in class. Informal meetings took place in our homes where we honed our Christian world and life view. And naturally, as beginning students working toward our doctorates, we were convinced that we had the answers for which the world was waiting.

Carl did not know as much Old Testament as Sam Schultz, who was completing his work in Old Testament under Charles Pfeiffer. He did not know as much New Testament as Harold Greenlee and George Ladd, both studying under Henry Joel Cadbury. He did not know as much of the history of doctrine as did Paul Jewett and I. And he did not know as much philosophy as Harold Kuhn, who was assistant to Arthur Darby Nock, chairman of the department. But on all crucial points, he knew enough to argue intelligently toe to toe with any of us. In short, he already had the makings of a first-rate evangelical theologian leaning toward philosophy of religion. No evangelical theologian who bases his or her understanding of Christianity on the norm of Scripture and seeks to communicate that faith effectively to the world of scholarship around us can ignore any of these fields. Not least, Carl Henry knew what was going on in the world. Perhaps that was a part of his heritage from his newspaper days.

Carl, moreover, was never afraid of new ideas. He constantly searched for new ways of presenting the Christian message to the world of the mid-twentieth century. He rigorously sought to discard the extraneous chaff from what is central to a truly biblically grounded Christianity. He downplayed the nonessentials and concentrated on the heart issues. His emphasis was always on the big picture. Above all he sought to think clearly and effectively, consistently and comprehensively about the total Christian world and life view. From the very first he exhibited an impassioned desire to serve God with the mind.

This combination of concerns, in my judgment, is the key to Carl's life and ministry. They represent the centripetal force that held him on track amid the wild turbulences that again and again shook the theological structure of Western Christianity. And they explain in large part those factors that bore him to the top during the last two-thirds of the twentieth century, in which he has been acknowledged by almost all as the dean and outstanding theological representative of the conservative evangelical movement.

When I moved from Boston to my first full-time teaching position at Wheaton College, Dr. Henry, who was teaching there part-time, shared an office with me. We found common ground in our mutual concern to spell out a truly evangelical world and life view. The energies of conservative evangelicalism, so it seemed to us, were largely expended in haphazard and even aimless fashion — something still largely true today. More than anything else it needed and still needs direction to guide its exuberant, sometimes misdirected, often erratic endeavors to chart a course through an increasingly turbulent theological scene. After all, these years have been marked not only by worldwide depression, the Second World War, numerous lesser wars, the threat of nuclear extermination, the spread of Soviet-dominated communism around the world, the rise of unnumbered independent nations in Africa, Asia, and Oceania, economic domination by Japan, the complete collapse of the Soviet empire in eastern Europe, the rise of the United States as the sole world power, and the radical and rapid shift of America from the wealthiest nation on earth to the greatest debtor nation on earth.

But these have also been the years of the near obliteration of Christianity as a force in western Europe, the reconstruction and modernization of Roman Catholicism under Pope John XXIII, the resurgence of conservative evangelical Christianity in America, the unbelievable successes of evangelicalism (and especially of the charismatic movement as a new form of conservative evangelicalism) in Central and South America, the mass turning to Christianity in Africa south of the equator, the amazing rise to world significance of Christianity in Korea and mainland China, and the new openness and religious freedom for the gospel in much of eastern Europe. Since Christianity has appeared on the scene, no century has ever seen such devastating and earth-shaking changes, with the possible exception of the age of Constantine, the conquests of Islam under the crescent banner of Mohammed, and the Reformation.

Carl Henry and I also shared our dreams of a great evangelical university that could provide the basis for an evangelical impact on our increasingly materialistic and anti-Christian Western society. To this day, that has not come. But we agreed that it is too necessary not to be pursued. To abandon it is to encourage surrendering the brightest minds of our day to nonbiblical and anti-Christian forces — forces that will determine the direction taken by the intellectual and moral and spiritual leadership of the world of tomorrow.

But there was another way to bring Christian leadership into the marketplace — through graduate theological (seminary) education. And we both took this route. I can remember the day when Carl marched into our office bursting with news. A new seminary was in process of formation, dedicated to quality graduate-level theological education in order to prepare leaders for the evangelical Christian church. And so Carl moved off to Fuller. Later, he left Fuller to take on the editorship of *Christianity Today.* But in his mind, that wasn't a shift away from quality education. He was still educating ministers, preparing them in quality ways to penetrate their community effectively through the pulpit and through the use of the resources of the church. He was also seeking to penetrate the non-evangelical religious world by defining Christianity accurately and removing some of the false stereotypes that carried such wide acceptance in intellectual and prestigious circles of the day.

After Dr. Henry left for the West Coast, our pathways crossed less frequently. Intermittently, however, our contacts continued; and on my part, I developed a growing admiration for him and for what he was seeking to do. Gradually through the years, admiration developed into a firm friendship. He is one of those friends with whom you never feel a need to "catch up." You begin right where you left off the last time you met. We would dig into the basic issues of the moment and trade insights as to the path to take for the future. Such a relationship can only exist and be maintained through common interests and, indeed, common goals. His first question to me was always, "What have you written?" and my apologetic reply would invariably be, "Not much." I did not need to ask what he had written because I had read it.

Yet it would be wrong to see Carl Henry as first of all a scholar or a theological strategist. There were things infinitely more important to him than his scholarship or his humanly devised strategy for the advance of evangelical faith — his love for Christ and desire to serve Christ and his church, for example. "What do you treasure most?" someone asked him after he had reached his full threescore years and ten. His answer: "Jesus Christ as personal Savior and Lord. . . . [I]nto the darkness of my young life he put bright stars that still shine and sparkle." Scholarship, at best, was but one way, however crucial it might be, in which to serve his Lord. And I admired him the more for that basic and fundamental commitment.

Accordingly Carl was also a man of prayer. John Wesley once said that he didn't have much use for any man who spent less than three hours a day in prayer and personal devotions. I don't know whether Carl Henry spent that much time each day in prayer or not. But in all my relationships with him, I knew him as a man of prayer. Across the years, he lived each day, and he still continues to live today, in constant dependence upon and in unbroken communion with his Lord. Prayer was neither a public pose nor simply a private duty. It was a way of life, the normal Christian life. I remember on one occasion my wife and I invited Carl and Helga, his wife, to dinner with another friend, a widow whose husband had recently died. At the table, our conversation turned, among many other things, to the adjustment that the bereaved woman was having to make. She shared her grief, her struggles, and her triumphs. And we shared with her our common concern. Then in the midst of the meal, Carl said, "Why don't we pray for our dear sister?" He stood up, walked over behind the chair of the woman, laid his hand on her shoulder; and then we prayed. That was the most natural thing for him to do because it was a part of his daily life. Christian piety — as opposed to pietism or trust in one's own piety, which he abhorred — represented a crucial part of the warp and woof of Carl's inner soul. "I [have] walked with God as my friend," he once wrote. And then he added, "I have enjoyed God's incomparable companionship."

But allied to his piety and equally integral to his being was his personal integrity. Carl is honest. He met his obligations carefully (a dean gets to know those things about his faculty). He was honest in his scholarship. He strove, above all, to interpret his theological opponents fairly. There are few situations in which the temptation to twist an opponent's thought or to shade it a bit becomes more luring. There is no law against the practice. Few of your readers will ever detect it, and it sets the stage for a powerful and convincing counterargument that will destroy the opponent's position. But it would be, at best, a cheap victory. Carl knew that such shoddy treatment and loose handling of truth to set up an opponent is in the long run self-defeating. It only convinces the already convinced, and it rarely convinces those committed to another view. "It does not lead to change; and all evangelical theologians — and, in fact, every Christian —should be an agent of change. Yet for Carl, fairness was not a preferred strategy; it was the right and the only way to go. I have always admired Carl immensely for that quality of intellectual integrity and honesty.

Carl's integrity carried over into his marriage. He was an affectionate person. He was a man of warm and deep emotions (usually quite out of sight as he stood on the podium of a lecture hall or in the pulpit of a church). But his students and his friends knew the real Carl Henry. His love for his wife was evident. He cared for her. He always spoke of her with respect and deep appreciation. He supported her in her own ministries.

Despite the important tasks to which he was always committed and on which the church so much depended in the worldwide cause of Christ, he insisted that she be Helga. Of course, she also cared for him and supported him in equal love and encouragement. Often she did so at great personal sacrifice. She researched his papers for him, and she checked his work for clarity, for style, and for accuracy. She insisted on clarity so that Carl would not assume that everyone would understand because he could. But Carl also supported her in her work. It was a mutual service, a mutual making of sacrifices, and a mutually loving husband and wife team, working in harmony together daily.

Surprising as it might seem to those who did not know him well, Carl is also a family man. He and Helga had a son and a daughter. Carl loves both. When the children were young, the Henrys grew together into a very tightly bound and loyal family. They are still that way today. To the degree that he could with the heavy demands laid upon him, Carl shared in the rearing of the children. He took time for them, and he communicated to them his love for Christ, his love for the church, and his daily dependence upon prayer and the sustaining presence of God in his life. He is extraordinarily proud of his son's career as congressman from central Michigan. To this day his face lights up when he is mentioned, and he displays his obvious pride in his son's achievements.

Carl's home meant a great deal to him. To those who did not know him personally, the center of his life seemed to be his teaching career at Northern Baptist, Fuller, and later at several other schools, or in *Christianity Today* or his theological writings. This was true, but it was only one side of his life. He also had another center — it was his home. He loved his home.

Carl never spoke to me of any hobbies — his home was his hobby. He enjoyed puttering around the yard encouraging some new plant struggling for life. Though this might be surprising to those who think of him primarily as a theologian, he was something of a handyman around the house. He loved to tinker (or was it his wife's tinkering?) with the household furniture. Especially in the early years of his family life, he often functioned as a plumber, wallpaper hanger, electrician, or whatever was needed to get things in order. The idea of Carl Henry doing such things with his hands might not seem quite like him to those who knew him only as leading a discussion of Plato or Aristotle or Augustine, or who saw him only in the pulpit of a church or by the lecture podium. Yet this, too, was Carl Henry. In his college days he became quite proficient as an amateur magician, and he developed a considerable repertoire of tricks with which he entertained other students and outside groups (sawing young ladies in two, ghost writing, and so forth). He still makes coins disappear and then reappear in strange places when he entertains small children in homes he visits.

Both he and Helga enjoy visitors, and they frequently invite guests to dinner. In addition to delicious food elegantly served by Helga, there is always conversation that seldom descends to trivia or gossip of the day. They modeled their home after that of Martin Luther and Catherine Bora, where theological problems and the great issues of the day were regular fare. The world was Carl Henry's place of work. His home was his hobby and his retreat, and he loved it.

Of course in the deepest sense these two centers — his public life and his home — found their inner unity in his life as bipolar centers under God. In the truest sense each was an overflow of his love and devotion to his sovereign Lord.

Needless to say, Carl Henry was also a churchman of highest order. Throughout his life he was extraordinarily loyal to the church he adopted after his conversion as a young man. The local church loomed very large in his life. The church, in fact, was a third center for his life and fellowship. He was faithful in his attendance and support of his local church.

Once while Carl's son was in college I happened to discover him on a cold wintry day trudging faithfully a long distance to church on the far north side of town. It was not a church particularly popular among his fellow college students. But it was *his* church. I thought to myself: "There goes a true son of Carl." Sunday morning is the time to be in church. He was following in his father's footsteps. That says something about Carl as a father as well as about Carl Henry, the churchman.

As a teacher, Dr. Henry was not known as a popular pedagogue. The reason for this lay deep in his own philosophy of education. Immanuel

Kant's teaching strategy was to concentrate on the middle third of students because the bottom third would never learn no matter how much time he spent with them and the top third would learn well no matter what or how he taught them. In contrast to Kant's strategy, Carl told me early in his teaching career that he focused on the top ten percent in his classes. When I gently remonstrated that the other students paid their tuition too, he made it clear that he felt a responsibility for them; but his primary concern was for the top ten percent. It was not a case of insensitivity or of preferential elitism, but rather a matter of kingdom strategy. This was the group from which the leaders come who will guide the church and society of the future.

In summary, Carl Henry is truly a man of God. He has many talents and gifts, but he has truly understood that all of his talents and gifts are to be used for the glory of God and the advancement of the church and in service of his fellow human beings. His primary calling has been to scholarship broadly interpreted, but he has never been a pedantic scholar or monk in a cell. Carl Henry is preeminently a man of God out in the bustling, wicked, confused world, seeking to build the edifice of a Christian world and life view and trading blows with all who would attack it, seeking to weaken or destroy it. This has been his passion.

Carl Henry has had many admirers whom he has influenced. We all owe much to him. In the good providence of God, through his speaking, teaching, witnessing, and personal encounters, he has woven his life into the warp and woof of the lives of millions. The entire evangelical church looks up to him, and I share richly in this heritage.

No wonder, when I read through his autobiography, it becomes for me like a motion picture of the world scene in which I moved and have lived out my life. It is a better world because of Carl Henry. And because of him, I am a better man.

Carl F. H. Henry:
Spokesperson for American Evangelicalism

JOHN D. WOODBRIDGE

THE TELEVISION LIGHTS swept across the platform. There he was, a tall figure with a kindly face, slowly ambling up to the microphone. The unblinking lenses of the television cameras began to capture his every gesture for the taping session.[1] Dr. Carl F. H. Henry had just been introduced to a crowd of some five hundred seminary students and professors as one of the principal spokespersons for American evangelicalism since World War II. A sense of anticipation rippled through the audience.

With his inimitable voice wavering here and there, Dr. Henry began to pull back the curtain on his perception of key turning points in the history of American evangelicalism. His perspective was worth hearing, for he had participated in many of the events he was describing.

There he was in 1991, edging toward his eightieth birthday, still charting cultural trends and probing the strengths and deficiencies of theological positions. There he was, still defending the great truths of the Christian faith; and this more than forty years after his work *The Uneasy Conscience of Modern Fundamentalism* had caused a stir, after having delivered literally hundreds of addresses and having granted scores of interviews in the United States and in distant lands, and after having penned literally hundreds of thousands of words about topics ranging from politics and society to the authority of the Bible. The students in the audience understood very well that they, too, had the

---

1. The videotape is entitled "Know Your Roots: Evangelicalism, Today and Tomorrow, Featuring Dr. Kenneth S. Kantzer and Dr. Carl F. H. Henry" (Produced by 2100 Productions; Trinity Evangelical Divinity School, 1991).

opportunity to benefit from the sage counsel of this indefatigable defender of evangelical faith.

Decades earlier, members of the media had already recognized Carl F. H. Henry as a major player in the resurgence of American evangelicalism, dubbing him "the thinking man's Billy Graham." More recently, Clark Pinnock, in reviewing Henry's *Confessions of a Theologian: An Autobiography,* had described him as "the decisive charismatic leader (in Max Weber's, not Jimmy Bakker's sense) of post-war evangelicalism in North America, the man who was uniquely able to lead a movement of people and command their admiration and respect."[2]

Indeed, what contours would the evangelical movement have assumed if Henry had not lent the considerable force of his mind and personality to its shaping and advocacy? Understandably, no hypothetical "what if" query can be answered in a satisfactory fashion. And yet, without Henry's vision for addressing North American culture with the gospel of Jesus Christ, the evangelical movement could conceivably have lost much of its will to engage secularism and unbelief. To recount the story of the creation of *Christianity Today* (1956) without rehearsing the pivotal role Carl F. H. Henry played as the founding editor is difficult to imagine. To suppose that a number of world congresses on evangelism would have been held without the impetus he gave to them is likewise difficult to contemplate. To believe that the hundreds of evangelical leaders who attended the Evangelical Affirmations conference in 1989 would have done so if chairpersons other than Dr. Henry and Dr. Kenneth Kantzer had extended the invitation seems fanciful. Indeed, to review the history of the evangelical movement during the last half-century almost ineluctably draws one to assess Dr. Henry's place in that history.

CONVERSION

What makes Henry the man that he is? The seriousness of his commitment to Christ explains much about his values and aspirations, his general approach to life. Those who know Carl Henry, the man behind the public persona, understand very well that he prizes more than anything else his walk with the Lord. Any heralded achievement and any garnered accolade has the worth of a mere tawdry trinket compared to the resplendent riches he finds in Christ Jesus.

2. Pinnock, "Carl F. H. Henry, *Confessions of a Theologian,*" *Christian Scholar's Review* 17 (1987-88): 211.

Born in New York City on January 22, 1913, the son of Johanna
Vaethroeder and Karl F. Heinrich, Carl F. H. Henry does not remember a
Bible in his home, or grace offered at table, or hearing more than one prayer
by his mother. To avoid a debate over differences of religion, his Lutheran
father and Roman Catholic mother sent him to an Episcopal mission church.
But few Christian values were emphasized at home. Henry's father
struggled with a drinking problem and during Prohibition ran a small
distillery out of the family kitchen.

By his own admission young Carl Henry (the family name was changed
from Heinrich to Henry in the wake of anti-German prejudice during World
War I) was a worldling before he was converted in June 1933, at age twenty,
to Jesus Christ. He wrote: "When Paul the Apostle spoke of our being 'dead
in . . . sins and wickedness' and following 'the evil ways of this present age'
and obeying 'the spiritual powers of the air, the spirit now at work among
God's rebel subjects,' he described not only the ancient Ephesians and my
New York contemporaries, but me as well. I, like the rest, lived my life in
sensuality and obeyed the prompting of my own instincts and notions. Yet by
God's grace I chose the road less traveled. I became a biblical theist, a
follower of Jesus of Nazareth."[3] Henry has never regretted that decision or
doubted his faith. In a 1987 interview, he declared of his conversion: "Christ
has been real to me in a vital way ever since June 1933. It was a blinding
experience. I know he is real. He's alive. He is the Risen One. I've never, even
in the most serious crises of life, doubted that."[4]

Moreover, Henry wants others to share a vital knowledge of Christ.
In his own way he has been an evangelist tirelessly looking for appropriate
occasions to say or write a word for his Savior. Henry's belief that Christian
conversion supernaturally changes lives has served as a working premise
of his ministry. In fact, transformed lives provide the theme for an early
book, *The Pacific Garden Mission: A Doorway to Heaven*. Hitting his
journalistic stride in the first lines of the piece, he described what it was
like when he went undercover as a "bum" to gain insights about street life
in Chicago: "Chicago's Loop, like the heart of any huge city, is three steps
from heaven and two steps from hell. It was a bristling evening in May.
Rough and ready, clad in old clothes like any man of the streets, I wandered
aimlessly through the Loop. Into the shifting eyes of down-and-outers who
sauntered by, I looked with conscious effort to feel the emotions of men

3. Henry, "If I Had It to Do Again" (Remarks addressed to the West Suburban
Evangelical Fellowship, Wheaton, Illinois, 7 May 1991), p. 1.
4. Diana Hochstedt Butler, "An Interview with Carl F. H. Henry," *TSF Bulletin* 4
(March-April 1987): 19.

whose feelings are jaded, and to think the thoughts of men too tired to think. It was no easy job, this business of a preacher being a bum, even for a night or two."[5] He then wandered into the Pacific Garden Mission to experience firsthand a service from the point of view of a street person. As it turned out, his cover was blown when he stood and mumbled a testimony, only to have the young songleader recognize him as his professor at Northern Baptist Theological Seminary. Undaunted by this minor setback, Henry, with his wife Helga, who has been his great Christian encourager and intellectual and spiritual partner in life, continued researching the Mission's history. In the volume, he recounted remarkable conversion stories of people like Billy Sunday, who had come to Christ at the Mission. Their lives had been changed just as Henry's life had been by the power of the gospel of Christ.

THE ROADS NOT TAKEN

Henry's personal interests could have taken him down paths far distant from the one that led to his leadership role in the evangelical movement. As a young man, he had dabbled in magic. At Wheaton College, however, a budding career as a magician — illusionism being his specialty — crashed mightily. During a literary society performance the day before an athletic contest, Henry correctly predicted that the Wheaton football team would defeat arch rival North Central College by a score of seven to six. As Henry later explained, one of his teachers, stunned by the precision of his forecast, "insisted it was all the work of demons. This brought my magical gifts — about which I have always enjoyed considerable skepticism — to a sudden fortuitous end."[6] He admitted later that his prediction of the game's exact score had been a fluke.

Journalism's siren call beckoned strongly as a potential career option. As a newspaperman he had written for a number of the great dailies, including *The New York Herald-Tribune*, *The New York Times*, and the tabloid *New York Daily News*. During college days at Wheaton he worked as a "stringer" for the *Chicago Tribune* and the *Wheaton Daily Journal*. "I still recall," he observes, "dragging into Latin class at eight in the morning from all night coverage of a double murder and suicide, to be greeted — when I hadn't prepared the lesson — by the professor's dispassionate re-

5. Henry, *The Pacific Garden Mission: A Doorway to Heaven* (Grand Rapids: Zondervan, 1942), p. 13.

6. Henry, "If I Had It to Do Again," pp. 2-3.

cital of the principal parts of the verb *flunko* (her creation): *flunko, flunkere,* faculty *flunktus.*"[7]

Henry was a wordsmith who could inundate his editor with a torrent of words or turn out a finely chiseled single phrase with almost embarrassing ease. He studied, among other writers, under Thomas Uzzell, a fiction editor of *Colliers.* He observes: "I learned the craft under gifted editors, and taught journalism without having taken a course in it."[8] But journalism did not become his ultimate field of endeavor, although he did later serve with great energy and distinction as the founding editor of *Christianity Today.*

Another possible option was to throw himself into the hurly-burly world of politics. Early on, he was heavily caught up in the excitement of editing Republican newspapers. He liked the hard-nosed nature of party politicking. But he turned his back on politics as a career too. His son Paul, however, has pursued a successful career as a member of the United States House of Representatives.

In brief, Henry declined to pursue a career in journalism and in politics. What then did he become? A theologian who has written thirty-five books. Moreover, as he says, he "can claim some credit for the reinvolvement of the evangelicals in the culture war for better or worse, and for having taught at almost all the best evangelical seminaries and colleges."[9] Henry sees himself, then, as a theologian who has helped to spark a renewed interest among evangelicals to engage their neighbors — whether professor, politician, or plumber — with the claims of Christ upon their minds, souls, and bodies. Rather than retreating from the field of battle, Henry called Christians to join him in the ongoing "culture war," which if anything, he believes, has intensified within recent years.

CHRIST AND CULTURE

Perhaps Henry's most famous book of cultural analysis is *The Uneasy Conscience of Modern Fundamentalism.* He wanted it understood that the "uneasy conscience" of which he wrote was not "one troubled about the great Biblical verities, which I consider the only outlook capable of resolving our problems, but rather one distressed by the frequent failure to apply them effectively to crucial problems confronting the modern

---

7. Henry, *Conversations with Carl Henry: Christianity for Today* (Lewiston: Edwin Mellen, 1986), p. 116.

8. Henry, "If I Had It to Do Again," p. 5.

9. Henry, "If I Had It to Do Again," p. 4.

mind."[10] Henry was concerned that "non-evangelicals" had criticized American fundamentalism for having "no social program calling for a practical attack on acknowledged world evils."[11] Indeed, Reinhold Niebuhr had earlier complained that, whereas Protestant liberals had accommodated themselves too much to the scientific spirit of the age, conservative Protestants had become too "quietistic" and silent about the social ills of the day. Prohibition's defeat had crushed the spirit of social reform among many Baptists and Methodists. The government's assumption of numerous social responsibilities during Roosevelt's two "New Deals" had bred a spirit of questioning regarding the parameters of the churches' own responsibilities for social reform. Fundamentalists' distrust of the liberal presuppositions of the "Social Gospel" movement spawned suspicions of talk about the social implications of the gospel. Fundamentalists were wary of programs of reform that seemed to ignore the spiritual condition of lost men and women.

According to Henry, many fundamentalist pastors during the thirties and forties had become "increasingly less vocal about social evils."[12] He went on to say: "Whereas once the redemptive Gospel was a world-changing message, now it was narrowed to a world resisting message."[13] Henry called upon conservative Christians to forsake what could become a deafening silence. But they need not abandon the great truths of Christian faith to do so. Rather, they should exploit the genius of those very truths as they addressed the social problems of the day. Unless they did so, he was "unsure" that they would gain "another world hearing for the Gospel": "That we can continue for a generation or two, even as a vital missionary force, here and there snatching brands from the burning, I do not question. But if we would press redemptive Christianity as the obvious solution of world problems, we had better busy ourselves with explicating the solution."[14]

FUNDAMENTALISM AND EVANGELICALISM

That Henry could criticize fundamentalism while upholding its central doctrines reflects his discomfort with aspects of the movement. In the 1940s the word *evangelical* was "in the air," but it was not especially associated

---

10. Henry, *The Uneasy Conscience of Modern Fundamentalism* (Grand Rapids: Eerdmans, 1947), preface.
11. Henry, *Uneasy Conscience*, p. 16.
12. Henry, *Uneasy Conscience*, p. 18.
13. Henry, *Uneasy Conscience*, p. 30.
14. Henry, *Uneasy Conscience*, preface.

with any specific movement. Nonetheless "evangelical Christians," Protestants who shared conservative beliefs but did not see themselves as fundamentalists, remained within the mainline denominations. Many Southern Baptists, Missouri Synod Lutherans, Black Bible believers, and others shared similar doctrinal convictions. But with the advent of the National Association of Evangelicals in 1942, formed to rival the political ambitions of aggressive Catholicism and to give a voice to the "millions" of unheard Christians not represented by the Federal Council of Churches, a specifically "evangelical" movement began to break away from fundamentalism. Led by Harold John Ockenga and others, these "new evangelicals" shared with fundamentalists a commitment to the central tenets of the faith (the "fundamentals") but believed that the "isolationist" or "Christ against culture" motif of fundamentalism cut conservative Christians off from opportunities for spiritual witness and social service.

Henry's own emergence as a spokesperson for the "new evangelical" movement did not become especially evident until after the publication of *The Uneasy Conscience of Modern Fundamentalism.* In the book Henry seemed to provide the biblical warrant for a socially involved evangelical Christianity. Harold Ockenga was especially appreciative of Henry's call for the application of biblically based ethics. He wrote in his introduction to Henry's book: "May this brief thesis be the harbinger of a new articulation of the growing revolt in evangelical circles on ethical indifferentism. . . . Here then is a healthy antidote to Fundamentalist aloofness in a distraught world. Dr. Henry may well call for an evangelical (Fundamentalist) ecumenicalism and for unity to face social needs."[15]

The next year (1948) Henry himself described the "new evangelicalism" in several articles in *Christian Life and Times:* "The new evangelicalism voices its plea for a vital presentation of redemptive Christianity which does not obscure its philosophical implications, its social imperatives, its eschatological challenge, its ecumenical opportunity and its revelational base."[16] A number of fundamentalists were highly critical of Henry's assessment of the weaknesses of their own movement.

15. Ockenga, introduction to Henry, *Uneasy Conscience.*
16. Cited in Henry's *Confessions of a Theologian: An Autobiography* (Waco, TX: Word Books, 1986), p. 117.

EVANGELIST-THEOLOGIAN AT FULLER THEOLOGICAL SEMINARY

In the first months of 1947, Wilbur Smith, then of Moody Bible Institute, happened upon Carl Henry, who was still teaching at Northern Baptist, and asked, "Has Harold Ockenga been in touch with you about a new seminary on the West Coast?" Henry replied, "No." Then Smith made this cryptic remark of the lightning bolt variety: "Well, he will."[17] Henry had already received a doctorate (Th.D.) from Northern Baptist in 1942 and was working during the summers on a doctorate in philosophy from Boston University. (See Kenneth Kantzer's appreciative comments about Henry's days at Boston.) With several important books to his credit, including *Remaking the Modern Mind*,[18] and teaching experience acquired at Northern Baptist, Wheaton (part-time instruction in journalism and typing), and Gordon College (summer school), it was not surprising that in May 1947 Ockenga invited him to meet at the Palmer House in Chicago with evangelist Charles E. Fuller and others to discuss and pray about the creation of the "new seminary" to which Wilbur Smith had briefly alluded.[19] Indeed, not only did Ockenga invite him to join the faculty of the fledgling school, but in its very first year Henry became acting dean of Fuller Theological Seminary in Pasadena, California.

Henry genuinely enjoyed his bustling days at Fuller Theological Seminary. The quality of the students especially impressed him: "No seminary faculty ever faced a student body more eager and dedicated than that group of pioneer seminarians."[20] They came from diverse educational and theological backgrounds and were evangelistically committed. Many later served as leaders in evangelical mission agencies, seminaries, colleges, and pastorates.

A workaholic, Henry threw himself into varied activities ranging from teaching duties and writing to organizing large public meetings such as the annual Rose Bowl East Sunrise Service (1949) and the Mid-Century Rose Bowl Rally (June 1950) — the largest evangelical gathering in southern California of the era — at which Billy Graham spoke to a crowd of fifty thousand.

Henry continued to hone his skills as a theologian and Christian apologist. He became, like his college mentor Gordon Clark, what might be called a rational presuppositionalist. In 1949 Henry played a pivotal role

---

17. Henry, *Confessions of a Theologian,* p. 113.
18. Henry, *Remaking the Modern Mind* (Grand Rapids: Eerdmans, 1946).
19. Henry, *Confessions of a Theologian,* p. 114.
20. Henry, *Confessions of a Theologian,* p. 118.

in the founding of the Evangelical Theological Society, suggesting the name for the society. His study *The Protestant Dilemma: An Analysis of the Current Impasse in Theology* appeared the same year. In it, he described the difficulties that proponents of Protestant liberalism and neo-orthodoxy were experiencing owing to their defective views of biblical authority, humankind, and the church. He concluded his study in this fashion: "The dilemma of Protestantism, no less than any other dilemma of human history, cannot hope for an abiding solution, unless it comes to terms with the word which, while couched in the words of men, has been for prophets and apostles, and for the Church, the *word of God.*"[21] In 1951 his doctoral dissertation was published under the title *Personal Idealism and Strong's Theology.* During the year 1955-1956, he devoted spare moments to crafting his *Christian Personal Ethics.*

But the pleasant and busy days at Fuller would soon end. By 1955, he was approached about assuming the editorship of a new magazine, *Christianity Today.* On August 18, 1955, he wrote to Billy Graham: "I have no personal reputation for bitterness; my friends have included men in all theological brackets. But in an evangelistic and missionary thrust, I have but one uncompromisable zeal — that Christ be known in his total claim upon life."[22]

CHRISTIANITY TODAY (1956-1968)

With the support of Billy Graham, L. Nelson Bell, Howard Pew, and others, *Christianity Today* was launched in 1956 to provide an evangelical alternative to *The Christian Century.* Early on, it was decided that not all contributors to the magazine would have to share fully the same doctrinal beliefs as the members of the staff or board of *Christianity Today.* This meant that writers who did not uphold the doctrine of biblical inerrancy, for example, could pen essays on other subjects in which they stood shoulder to shoulder with Henry and his colleagues. By this policy, the leadership of *Christianity Today* hoped that the magazine would rally Christians of diverse persuasions as a winsome and irenic voice for a broad-based evangelical ecumenism.

Billy Graham forewarned Henry that his task was a daunting one:

---

21. Henry, *The Protestant Dilemma: An Analysis of the Current Impasse in Theology* (Grand Rapids: Eerdmans, 1949), p. 225.

22. Letter from Carl F. H. Henry to Billy Graham/Dr. L. Nelson Bell, 18 August 1955, Trinity Evangelical Divinity School Archives, Billy Graham File, 1955-1956.

"You are going to need the wisdom of Solomon, the patience of Job, the courage of Elijah and the faith of Abraham."[23] Despite early struggles, the magazine met with spectacular success, its paid readership (150,000 in 1967) far surpassing that of *The Christian Century.* It became a powerful thought magazine recognized as a major voice for American evangelicalism. Moreover, by some accounts it was now the nation's most frequently quoted religious magazine.

As editor for *Christianity Today,* Henry interviewed theologians such as Emil Brunner, Karl Barth, Rudolf Bultmann, and Helmut Thielicke. He received numerous invitations to speak throughout the world. Henry's opinions were sought out by both the secular media and evangelical publications. On March 2, 1965, Billy Graham wrote to Henry: "I recently heard that *Time* magazine may do a cover story on you. This would be one of the greatest events that could help the evangelical cause that I could think of."[24] The cover story did not come to pass. The incident reveals, however, that more than ever Henry was now a spokesperson for American evangelicalism.

A high point in his ministry occurred when, as its tenth anniversary project, *Christianity Today* sponsored the World Congress on Evangelism (October 25–November 4, 1966) in West Berlin, with 1,200 evangelists and evangelism directors from more than one hundred countries in attendance. Billy Graham served as the honorary chairperson, Carl Henry as the chairperson.

The Congress represented a major breakthrough for world evangelism because it brought together Christians from diverse social, economic, and ethnic backgrounds to think through the task of the great commission in the context of theology and social concern. The members of the Congress defined evangelism only in terms of the proclamation of the gospel; they distanced themselves from "all theology and criticism that refuses to bring itself under the divine authority of Holy Scripture, and all traditionalism which weakens that authority by adding to the Word of God."[25] The Congress helped Christians work together more effectively, and it prepared the way for later Lausanne conferences.

But difficulties surfaced back at Henry's Washington base. In 1968 Henry was impelled to leave his position as editor of *Christianity Today* under less than pleasant circumstances. The byzantine motivations and

23. Henry, *Confessions of a Theologian,* p. 155.
24. Letter from Billy Graham to Carl F. H. Henry, 2 March 1965, Trinity Evangelical Divinity School Archives, Billy Graham File, 1957-1968.
25. Cited in Henry, *Confessions of a Theologian,* p. 261.

maneuvers that prompted this development are difficult for an outside observer to untangle, let alone understand. J. Howard Pew, who wanted more fiery criticism of the economic and political policies of the National Council of Churches, reportedly said to Billy Graham, "We've got to get rid of Carl."[26] When the full board reversed the hasty action by the executive committee and asked Henry for a lifelong commitment to the editorship, he declined on the grounds that it would be difficult to recover the prior relationship to the executive committee and that he should not be precluded from a vocational alternative in the future.

In later years Henry commented about his departure from the editorship of *Christianity Today* with sadness and with less than totally concealed pain. He was particularly perturbed that *Christianity Today* began to lose its non-evangelical readership and its commitment to scholarly theological reflection. In his view the magazine also began to shy away from a head-on tackling of social and political problems and adopted a more popular format in quest of a "mass market readership." The magazine, Henry believed, was no longer serving as an "indispensable theological guide" for clergy and laypeople.

To forget the reversal at *Christianity Today,* Henry and his wife Helga traveled to Cambridge, England, and enjoyed a productive "sabbatical" year in 1968-1969. There he concentrated on research and writing the first two of six volumes of *God, Revelation and Authority;*[27] these first two volumes appeared in 1976.

During the 1970s and 1980s, Henry's teaching stints at such schools as Eastern Baptist (1969-1974) and Trinity Evangelical Divinity School, his global role as lecturer-at-large for World Vision International (1974-1986), and more recently for Chuck Colson's Prison Fellowship, filled his days with innumerable opportunities for speaking and writing.

When the first two volumes of *God, Revelation, and Authority* appeared in 1976, *Time* magazine gave them a full-page review. The same year, in his *Evangelicals in Search of Identity,*[28] Henry raised questions about a crumbling unity within the evangelical movement. Like a theological seismologist, Henry registered before many in the general public knew of its existence the unsettling rumbling that "all was not well" among conservative Protestant Christians. They were dividing over a bevy of issues ranging from definitions of biblical authority to women's ordination, and this despite the fact that some "evangelicals" were basking in the

26. Henry, *Confessions of a Theologian,* p. 251.
27. Henry, *God, Revelation and Authority,* 6 vols. (Waco,TX: Word Books, 1976-83).
28. Henry, *Evangelicals in Search of Identity* (Waco, TX: Word Books, 1976).

national limelight and their future appeared bright. Jimmy Carter's candidacy for the presidency as a "born-again" politician had helped convert 1976 into the "year of the Evangelical."[29]

In the 1970s and 1980s, Henry struggled to find a way to bolster what appeared to him to be a faltering evangelical movement now possessing a wing known by the 1980s as the progressive or "open evangelicals." These "open evangelicals" defended a form of biblical infallibility limited to matters of "faith and practice" (not including history and science), claimed that their stance was the "central tradition of the church," and portrayed the doctrine of biblical inerrancy as a fundamentalist doctrinal innovation.

Henry roundly disagreed with the analysis of "open evangelicals" regarding the nature and history of biblical authority. He personally affirmed the doctrine of biblical inerrancy: "The doctrine of inerrancy is to me not a dispensable doctrine, and the Church has nothing to gain by evading the issue."[30] He nonetheless lamented the fact that a debate over the meaning and significance of inerrancy had turned acrid and divided the ranks of evangelicals. But he did not have at his disposal the editorship of a magazine like *Christianity Today* with which he could enjoin members of the evangelical community to desist from in-fighting and to close ranks around essentials.

Nor was Henry persuaded that the National Association of Evangelicals (N.A.E.) had the will or the capacity to act as an agent of reconciliation. To his mind it was not filling the huge gap in the religious landscape left by the failure of the National Council of Churches to meet the needs of Protestant Christians, nor had it fully mended evangelical fences. A teaching stint at Fuller in 1980 convinced him that the spirit of pluralism was wearing down even the evangelical consensus that had existed there when he taught at that school in the 1950s: "We were glad that many evangelical emphases survived, yet we noted considerable theological diversity among faculty. The policy of accepting a colleague's differences from the norm, one professor observed, was the price each teacher paid for the unchallenged acceptance of his own departures; few faculty dreamed, however, that the end result would be so far-reaching."[31] Significant studies by James Davison Hunter reinforced Henry's conviction that even at some Christian colleges faculty members were straying from the evangelical convictions he and his colleagues from Boston days had fought for and held so dearly

29. *Newsweek,* 25 Oct. 1976.
30. Henry, *Conversations with Carl Henry,* p. 27.
31. Henry, *Confessions of a Theologian,* pp. 371-72.

— leaders such as Edward Carnell, Kenneth Kantzer, Harold Kuhn, Roger Nicole, Samuel Schultz, and others.

Then again, a group of younger historians seemed to glory in the pluralistic motif that evangelicalism was one vast mosaic, with each group refracting its own colors in ways that made it quite distinct from other groups. These historians were doubtful that shared doctrine had bound the founders of the N.A.E. together; nor, they alleged, did it bind together the contemporary evangelical movement. Rather, they argued that evangelicalism essentially consisted of a movement of voluntary societies. Henry himself disliked the "ism" in the word *evangelicalism;* he often said that an "ism" becomes a "wasm." But his own ecclesiology and experience of working with countless evangelicals for half a century convinced him that these historians were patently mistaken when they claimed that shared doctrinal commitments had not created the common bond of the evangelical movement in earlier decades.

By the mid-1980s, Henry thought it propitious to take personal stock of his colorful life. He wrote a remarkably engaging piece entitled *Confessions of a Theologian: An Autobiography* in which, like Saint Augustine, he confessed the glory of God and also engaged in confession in the sense of personal disclosure. In the book he dazzled readers with detailed technicolor descriptions of incidents small and great as seen from the cockpit of the evangelical movement. But he also closed the volume with a section entitled "The Evangelical Prospect in America." There he set forth an agenda for the movement with which he was so intimately associated. He also recounted his view of its successes as well as its missed opportunities (the failure to create an evangelical university, for example). He was quite concerned that by the 1970s the expression "evangelical" had begun to lose its meaning: "The term evangelical during the past fifteen years has become ambiguous through deliberate distortion by critics and needless confusion invited by some of the movement's own leaders."[32]

Henry realized that the "new evangelical" appeal of the late 1940s for Christians to penetrate society had sadly been accompanied by an unfortunate development: an uncomfortable number of evangelicals had been impacted by the secular values of the culture they were trying to reach for Christ. Henry put it this way: "While evangelicals seek to penetrate the culture, the culture simultaneously makes disconcerting inroads into evangelical life. . . . A disturbing number of church members cling to the idols of money and material things, sex and status, that bewitch the Western world."[33]

32. Henry, *Confessions of a Theologian,* p. 387.
33. Henry, *Confessions of a Theologian,* p. 388.

Ironically, in the late 1950s and 1960s fundamentalist critics had predicted that the "new evangelicals" would be affected negatively by the culture with which they were to be involved. By the 1980s, studies of evangelical schools and life-styles seemed to provide at least a partial vindication of these fundamentalist predictions.

Henry understood very well the temptations of cultural accommodation facing evangelicals. An announced optimist in 1986, he still could not shake his worries about the undeniable signs of disunity among evangelical Christians. But he was by no means disposed to urge evangelicals to reassume the "Christ against culture" motif of fundamentalism (dramatically abandoned by Jerry Falwell) or to privatize piety. Rather, he renewed his appeal for evangelicals to mount a biblically based spiritual, social, and intellectual offensive in the "culture war." Was he merely tilting at illusory windmills? Not in his opinion. He wrote: "I remain profoundly convinced that evangelicals are now facing their biggest opportunity since the Reformation, and yet are forfeiting it; unless soon enlarged, the present opening, at least in the United States, may not long remain."[34]

Perhaps gripped by a baleful sense of evangelical fragmentation, Henry acceded to the request that he join Dr. Kenneth Kantzer as co-chair of the Evangelical Affirmations conference in 1989. To this conference came some four hundred evangelical teachers, pastors, and laypersons, as well as two hundred seminarians. At the conference charismatics mixed with staunch Lutherans, advocates of causes of the political left worked side by side with advocates of the political right. The participants helped to draw up and then approved a document entitled *Evangelical Affirmations 89* — affirmations that seemed to reflect the doctrines and social concerns that Henry and other evangelicals had been defending for years. Indeed, discerning readers of this document could decipher more than a touch of the thought of Dr. Henry and Dr. Kantzer. The conference was sponsored by the National Association of Evangelicals and Trinity Evangelical Divinity School.

The diversity of the conference's membership seemed to confirm the premise that the evangelical centrist positions with which Dr. Henry and Dr. Kantzer have so long been identified remain very attractive to large swaths of American Protestantism. For critics, however, the conference was a minuscule blip on the religious horizon, providing an illusory impression of unity among evangelicals — a unity that did not in fact exist.

Henry had other related concerns on his mind as the 1990s approached. In *Twilight of a Great Civilization: The Drift towards Neo-*

---

34. Henry, *Confessions of a Theologian,* p. 402.

Paganism, he claimed that a "Western culture nightfall may be close at hand."[35] In 1990 he observed: "the believing Church is the West's last and only real bastion against barbarism. If Christians do not lead the way people will turn to self-proclaimed gurus from the East, to private revelations, to chemical stimulants, or to other follies of our time; indeed, some of the young seem to be turning even to carbon monoxide."[36] Once again, he emphasized the need for evangelical unity: "We must build and network bridges and find ways of reinforcing a mutual witness to a bewildered world." He also warned Christians that they could not win the world by trying to accommodate themselves to the claims of the world: "The Church can hardly challenge the world's marginalization of the Church by ecclesial quasi-conversion to the secular world-life view. . . . The churches that are languishing are those that deliberately accommodate themselves to the modern mindset."[37]

Ever encouraging his evangelical brothers and sisters to hold true to the gospel of Jesus Christ in word and deed, Carl F. H. Henry in the early 1990s continued to do what he had been doing for more than a half-century: to be himself a disciple of the Lord who had saved him. In a 1991 piece entitled "If I Had It to Do Again," he wrote:

> I have in any event done what I was convinced to do in behalf of a cause that we believe matters more than all others, in the hope that this fallible effort has in our lifetime helped to hold high the flag of biblical faith. At the very least, I have helped to dispute the view that to be evangelical is to be theologically illiterate and have nurtured the view that what lies beyond the sunset is more rewarding than a pluralistic smorgasbord. From the outset of my Christian walk I have treasured the Book that speaks of the God of ultimate beginnings and endings, and illumines all that falls between. . . . An evangelical Christian believes incomparable good news: that Christ died in the stead of sinners and arose the third day as living head of the church of the twice-born, the people of God, whose mission is mandated by the scripturally given Word of God. The term evangelical — whose core is the "evangel" — therefore embraces the best of all good tidings, that on the ground of the substitutionary death of Christ Jesus, God forgives penitent sinners and that He shelters their eternal destiny by the Risen Lord who triumphed over death and

---

35. Henry, *Twilight of a Great Civilization* (Westchester, IL: Crossway, 1988).

36. Henry, "Christianity and Resurgent Paganism" (Address given at the dedication of the Kenneth S. Kantzer Faculty Center at Trinity Evangelical Divinity School in Deerfield, Illinois, 27 October 1990), p. 10.

37. Henry, "Christianity and Resurgent Paganism," pp. 11-12.

over all that would have destroyed him and his cause. That good news, as the Apostle Paul makes clear, is validated and verified by the sacred Scriptures. Those who contrast the authority of Christ with the authority of Scripture do so at high risk. Scripture gives us the authentic teaching of Jesus and Jesus exhorted his apostles to approach Scripture as divinely authoritative. There is no confident road into the future for any theological cause that provides a fragmented Scriptural authority and — in consequence — an unstable Christology. Founded by the true and living Lord, and armed with the truthfulness of Scripture, the church of God is invincible. Whatever I might want to change in this pilgrim life, it would surely not be any of these high and holy commitments.[38]

* * *

The unblinking television cameras continued to roll. There he was in 1991, still defending the great verities of the Christian faith, still probing and testing the validity of philosophies and theologies in light of biblical truths. The five hundred students and professors who had come to hear Carl F. H. Henry present his perceptions of turning points in the history of post–World War II evangelicalism began to sense even more fully that they were listening to one of evangelicalism's senior statesmen. Like countless others before them, they too were in Henry's great debt. For decades, he had provided the evangelical community with a model of Christian service as an evangelist-theologian, stalwart apologist, and wise strategist.

In 1991 Carl Henry still did not take any ultimate credit for his many accomplishments. If some of these accomplishments happened to have enduring value, they were in fact, he wanted people to remember, God's doing. In 1991 Carl Henry still was not wavering in his desire to serve Christ, whom he had come to love and confess as Savior and Lord in June 1933, nearly sixty years earlier.

In 1991 Carl F. H. Henry, a converted newspaperman, and Helga, his beloved wife, were still looking forward to what more they could do with the Holy Spirit's strength for Christ's church. The evangelical movement is deeply in debt to these very humane and winsome Christians.

38. Henry, "If I Had It to Do Again," pp. 8-9.

Brief *Curriculum Vitae* of Carl F. H. Henry

1913	Born in New York City, January 22
1933	Conversion to Christ
1938	B.A. from Wheaton College
1940	Marries Helga Bender
1941	Receives M.A. from Wheaton College; ordained; begins at Northern Baptist Theological Seminary as an instructor
1942	Receives Th.D. from Northern Baptist; *The Pacific Garden Mission: A Doorway to Heaven* appears
1946	*Remaking the Modern Mind*
1947	*The Uneasy Conscience of Modern Fundamentalism;* begins teaching at Fuller Theological Seminary (1947-1956)
1948	*The Protestant Dilemma: An Analysis of the Current Impasse in Theology*
1949	Receives Ph.D. in philosophy from Boston University
1951	*Personal Idealism and Strong's Theology*
1956	Assumes editorship of *Christianity Today*
1966	Serves as chairperson of the World Congress on Evangelism
1968	Leaves editorship of *Christianity Today*
1968-1969	Research and writing at Cambridge University
1969-1973	Teaches at Eastern Baptist Theological Seminary

1974	Becomes lecturer-at-large for World Vision
1976-1983	*God, Revelation and Authority*
1979	President of the American Theological Society
1986	*Confessions of a Theologian: An Autobiography*
1988	*Twilight of a Great Civilization: The Drift towards Neo-Paganism*
1989	Co-chairperson with Kenneth Kantzer of the Evangelical Affirmations conference

Chronological Selected Bibliography of the Works of Carl F. H. Henry

The Missionary and the Press. Chicago: Good News, 1941.

The Pacific Garden Mission: A Doorway to Heaven. Grand Rapids: Zondervan, 1942.

Successful Church Publicity. Grand Rapids: Zondervan, 1943.

The Uneasy Conscience of Modern Fundamentalism. Grand Rapids: Eerdmans, 1947.

The Protestant Dilemma: An Analysis of the Current Impasse in Theology. Grand Rapids: Eerdmans, 1948.

Remaking the Modern Mind. Grand Rapids: Eerdmans, 1948.

Bender in the Cameroons: The Story of Missionary Triumph in a Dark Region of the World's Darkest Continent. Cleveland: Roger Williams Press, 1949.

Fifty Years of Protestant Thought. Boston: Wilde, 1949.

Giving a Reason for Our Hope. Boston: Wilde, 1949.

Notes on the Doctrine of God. Boston: Wilde, 1949.

The Drift of Western Thought. Grand Rapids: Eerdmans, 1951.

Personal Idealism and Strong's Theology. Wheaton, IL: Van Kampen, 1951.

Glimpses of a Sacred Land. Boston: Wilde, 1953.

Christian Personal Ethics. Grand Rapids: Eerdmans, 1957.

(editor) *Contemporary Evangelical Thought.* Great Neck, NY: Channel, 1957.

Evangelical Responsibility in Contemporary Theology. Grand Rapids: Eerdmans, 1957.

(editor) *Revelation and the Bible.* Grand Rapids: Baker, 1958.

(consulting editor) *The Biblical Expositor.* 3 vols. Philadelphia: Holman, 1960.

(editor) *Basic Christian Doctrines.* New York: Holt, Rinehart, and Winston, 1962.

Aspects of Christian Social Ethics. Grand Rapids: Eerdmans, 1964.

(editor) *Christian Faith and Modern Theology.* New York: Channel, 1964.

(editor) *Frontiers in Modern Theology.* Chicago: Moody, 1966.

The God Who Shows Himself. Waco, TX: Word Books, 1966.

(editor) *Jesus of Nazareth: Saviour and Lord.* Grand Rapids: Eerdmans, 1966.

Evangelicals at the Brink of Crisis: Significance of the World Congress on Evangelism. Waco, TX: Word Books, 1967.

(editor) with W. S. Mooneyham. *One Race, One Gospel, One Task.* Minneapolis: Worldwide, 1967.

Faith at the Frontiers. Chicago: Moody, 1969.

(editor) *Fundamentals of the Faith.* Grand Rapids: Zondervan, 1969.

A Plea for Evangelical Demonstration. Grand Rapids: Baker, 1971.

New Strides of Faith. Chicago: Moody, 1972.

(editor) *Baker's Dictionary of Christian Ethics.* Grand Rapids: Baker, 1973.

(essays by Henry et al.) *Quest for Reality: Christianity and the Counter Culture.* Downers Grove, IL: InterVarsity, 1973.

Evangelicals in Search of Identity. Waco, TX: Word Books, 1976.

God, Revelation and Authority. 6 vols. Waco, TX: Word Books, 1976-1983.

Volume 1: *God Who Speaks and Shows: Preliminary Considerations,* 1976.

Volume 2: *God Who Speaks and Shows: Fifteen Theses, Part One,* 1976.

Volume 3: *God Who Speaks and Shows: Fifteen Theses, Part Two,* 1979.

Volume 4: *God Who Speaks and Shows: Fifteen Theses, Part Three,* 1979.

Volume 5: *God Who Stands and Stays, Part One,* 1982.

Volume 6: *God Who Stands and Stays, Part Two,* 1983.

(editor) *Horizons of Science: Christian Scholars Speak Out.* San Francisco: Harper & Row, 1978.

The Christian Mindset in a Secular Society. Portland: Multnomah, 1985.

Christian Countermoves in a Decadent Culture. Portland: Multnomah, 1986.

Confessions of a Theologian: An Autobiography. Waco, TX: Word Books, 1986.

Conversations with Carl Henry: Christianity for Today. Lewiston: Edwin Mellen, 1986.

Twilight of a Great Civilization: The Drift towards Neo-Paganism. Westchester, IL: Crossway, 1988.

Carl Henry at His Best. Portland: Multnomah, 1989.

(editor) with Kenneth S. Kantzer. *Evangelical Affirmations.* Grand Rapids: Zondervan, 1990.

Toward a Recovery of Christian Belief. Wheaton, IL: Crossway, 1990.